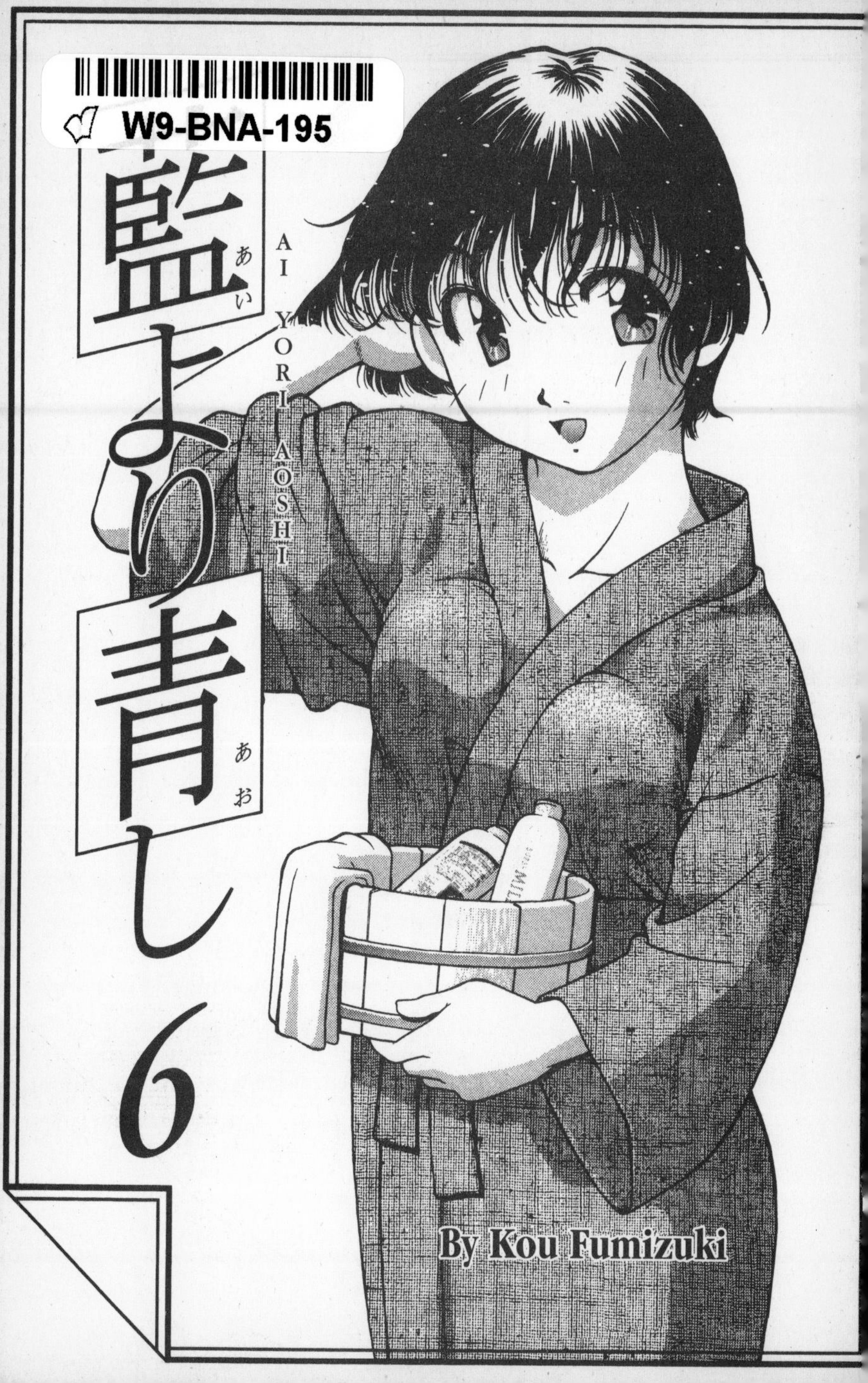
藍(あい)より青(あお)し
AI YORI AOSHI
6
By Kou Fumizuki

## *Ai Yori Aoshi Vol. 6*
### written by Kou Fumizuki
### illustrated by Kou Fumizuki

Translation - Alethea Nibley & Athena Nibley
Copy Editor - Kathy Schilling
English Adaptation - Jamie Rich
Retouch and Lettering - Patrick Tran
Graphic Designer - James Dashiell
Production Artist - Haruko Furukawa & Yoohae Yang
Cover Design - Gary Shum

Editor - Jake Forbes
Digital Imaging Manager - Chris Buford
Pre-Press Manager - Antonio DePietro
Production Managers - Jennifer Miller and Mutsumi Miyazaki
Art Director - Matt Alford
Managing Editor - Jill Freshney
VP of Production - Ron Klamert
President and C.O.O. - John Parker
Publisher and C.E.O. - Stuart Levy

A 🔵 **TOKYOPOP**® Manga

TOKYOPOP Inc.
5900 Wilshire Blvd. Suite 2000
Los Angeles, CA 90036

E-mail: info@TOKYOPOP.com
Come visit us online at www.TOKYOPOP.com

ISBN: 1-59182-650-0

First TOKYOPOP printing: November 2004
10 9 8 7 6 5 4 3 2 1
Printed in the USA

# 藍より青し

## AI YORI AOSHI™

## VOLUME 6
## STORY & ART
## BY
## KOU FUMIZUKI

HAMBURG // LONDON // LOS ANGELES // TOKYO

# 藍より青し

## Summary of the story so far...

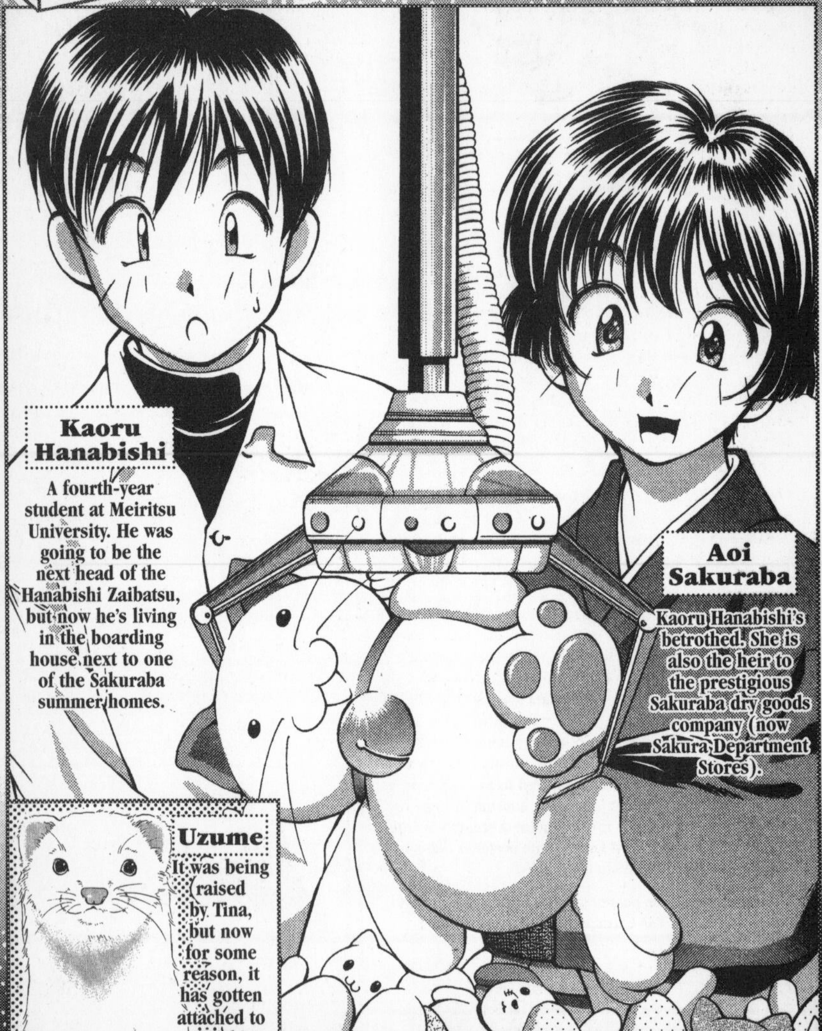
Aoi Sakuraba
Kaoru Hanabishi's betrothed. She is also the heir to the prestigious Sakuraba dry goods company (now Sakura Department Stores).
Kaoru Hanabishi
A fourth-year student at Meiritsu University. He was going to be the next head of the Hanabishi Zaibatsu, but now he's living in the boarding house next to one of the Sakuraba summer homes.
Uzume
It was being raised by Tina, but now for some reason, it has gotten attached to Miyabi.

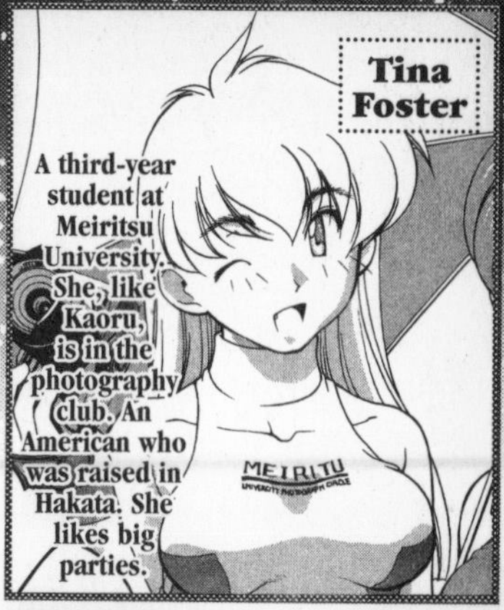
Tina Foster
A third-year student at Meiritsu University. She, like Kaoru, is in the photography club. An American who was raised in Hakata. She likes big parties.
MEIRITU

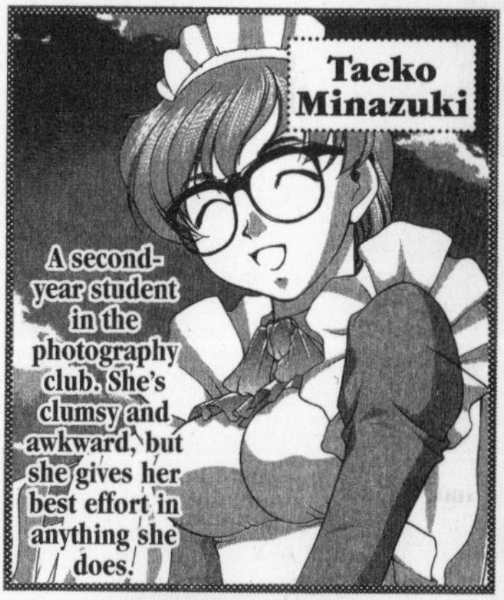
Taeko Minazuki
A second-year student in the photography club. She's clumsy and awkward, but she gives her best effort in anything she does.

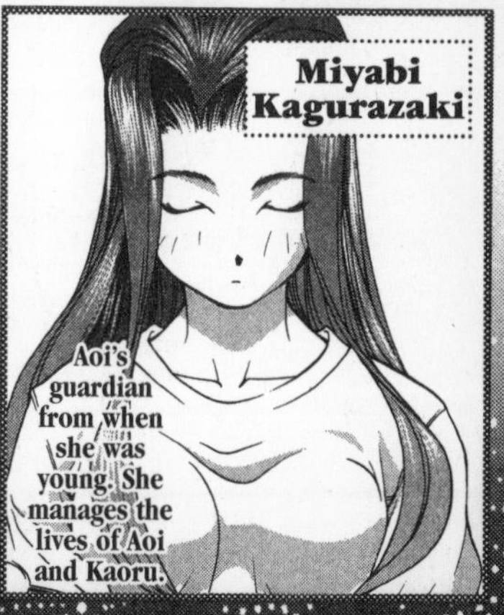
Miyabi Kagurazaki
Aoi's guardian from when she was young. She manages the lives of Aoi and Kaoru.

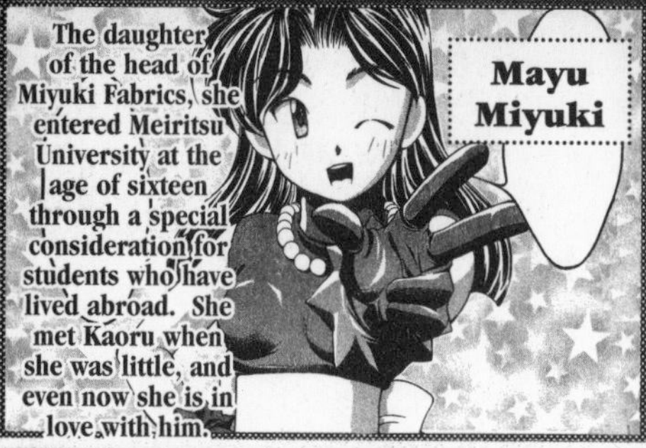
Mayu Miyuki
The daughter of the head of Miyuki Fabrics, she entered Meiritsu University at the age of sixteen through a special consideration for students who have lived abroad. She met Kaoru when she was little, and even now she is in love with him.

Kaoru Hanabishi was torn away from his mother when he was very young and raised as the heir of the Hanabishi Zaibatsu; however, he found he was unable to endure the harsh responsibilities placed on him, and he ran away from home to live by himself. He continued life in this fashion right up until the arrival of Aoi Sakuraba, who had been his betrothed and who had loved him for eighteen years. Kaoru was blown away by her devotion, but her request for him to go back to the Hanabishi was the one thing he could not do. Aoi recognized the pain this caused Kaoru, so she decided to leave her own family, the Sakuraba, instead. Rather than lose her daughter, Aoi's mother conceded to allow the two of them to live together.

The couple moved to a western-style house that had previously been one of the Sakuraba's summer homes, and they now share the estate with Aoi's guardian, Miyabi Kagurazaki. There is a catch, though--while Aoi and Miyabi live in the main house, Kaoru has to live in the boarding house adjacent to it.

Shortly after, Tina Foster and Taeko Minazuki, members of Kaoru's photography club, moved into the boarding house, as well. Tina, a native speaker of the Hakata dialect (having been raised in Hakata since she was five), moved in when she saw a fake flyer that Miyabi had posted to make people believe they were running a boarding house for real, as opposed to the two lovers living there illegitimately; Taeko, having been fired from her previous job as a housekeeper, joined the household to be its housekeeper. In order to avoid creating a scandal for the Sakuraba family, Aoi must keep up the pretense that she is Kaoru's landlady, and not his fiancée.

More than a year has passed since they moved onto that estate, and Kaoru has become a college senior. Also, Mayu Miyuki has returned to Japan from England. She had met Kaoru when she was young. He was a high school student at the time, and ever since, she secretly held a faint love for him in her heart. This fact is having more than a small effect on the relationship between Kaoru and Aoi.

AI YORI AOSHI

# CONTENTS

| | |
|---|---|
| Chapter 47: Kisei—Homecoming | 7 |
| Chapter 48: Jinchuu—Loyalty | 27 |
| Chapter 49: Enmusubi—Marriage | 47 |
| Chapter 50: On'you—Kindly Face | 69 |
| Chapter 51: Kasumi—Mist | 89 |
| Chapter 52: Ketsui—Determination | 111 |
| Chapter 53: Ieji—The Road Home | 131 |
| Special Chapter 1: Tsuredzure—Idleness | 151 |
| Special Chapter 2: Henge—Change | 167 |
| Chapter 54: Sesshoku—Diet | 183 |

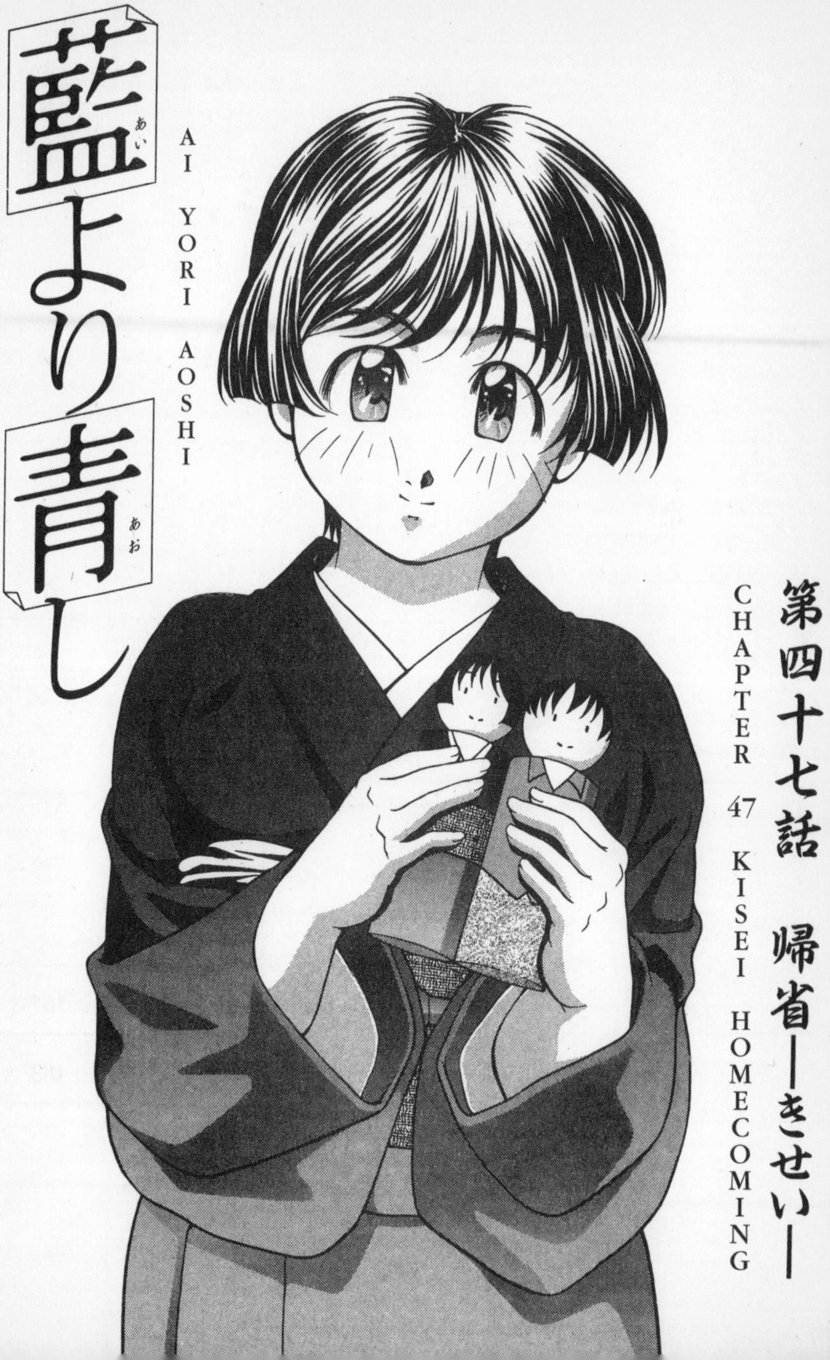
藍(あい)より青(あお)し
AI YORI AOSHI
第四十七話 帰省—きせい—
CHAPTER 47 KISEI HOMECOMING

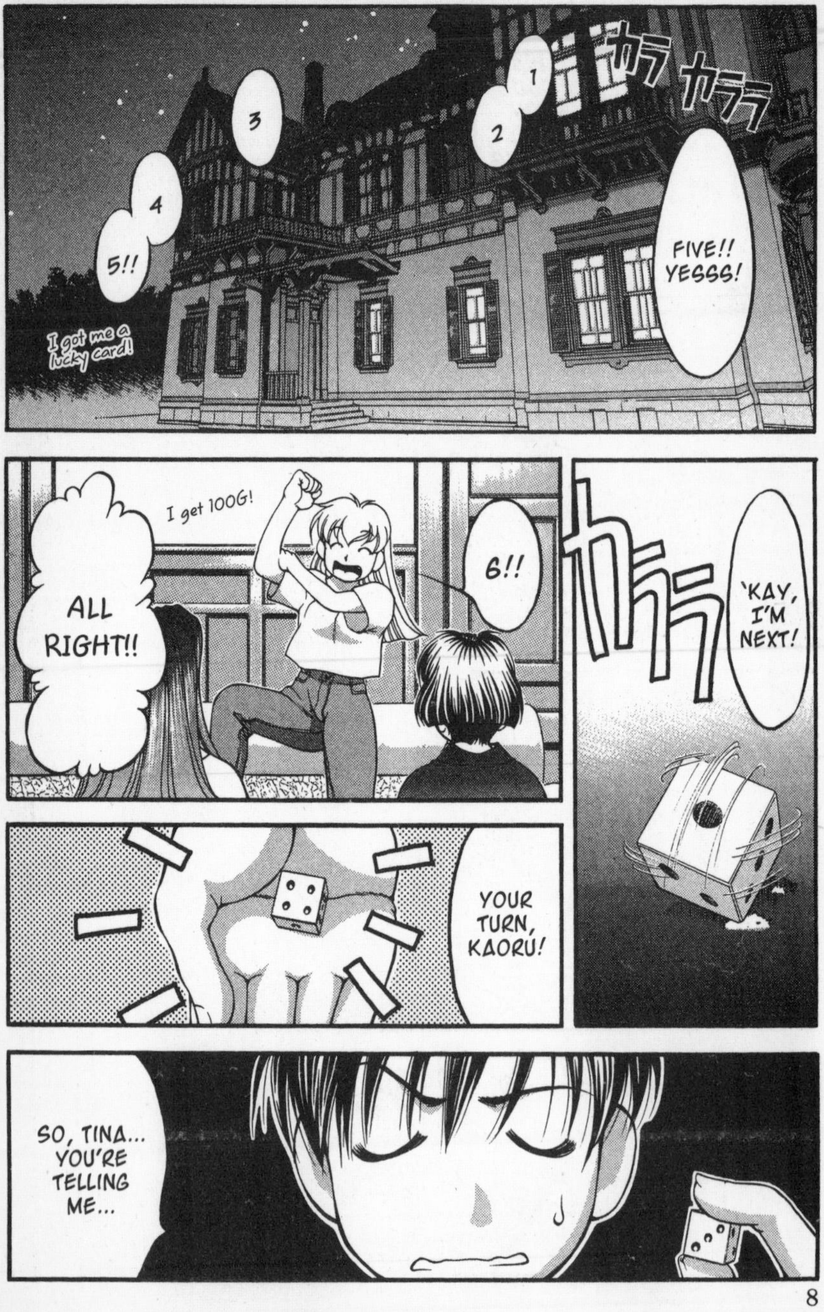

カラ カラララ
1
2
3
4
5!!
FIVE!! YESSS!
I got me a lucky card!
カラララ
`KAY, I'M NEXT!
6!!
I get 100G!
ALL RIGHT!!
YOUR TURN, KAORU!
SO, TINA... YOU'RE TELLING ME...

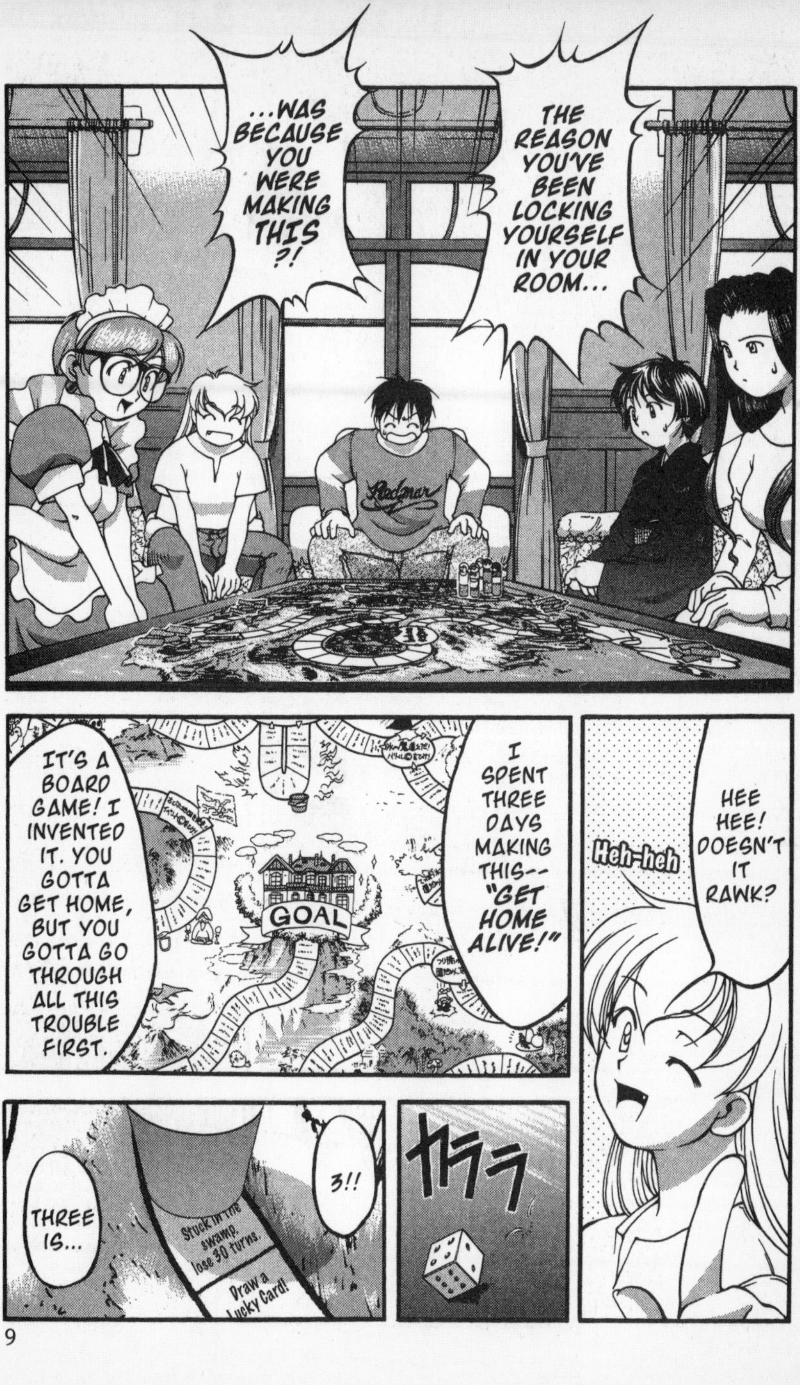
THE REASON YOU'VE BEEN LOCKING YOURSELF IN YOUR ROOM...
...WAS BECAUSE YOU WERE MAKING THIS?!
HEE HEE! DOESN'T IT RAWK?
Heh-heh
I SPENT THREE DAYS MAKING THIS-- "GET HOME ALIVE!"
IT'S A BOARD GAME! I INVENTED IT. YOU GOTTA GET HOME, BUT YOU GOTTA GO THROUGH ALL THIS TROUBLE FIRST.
GOAL
カララ
3!!
Stuck in the swamp, lose 30 turns.
Draw a Lucky Card!
THREE IS...

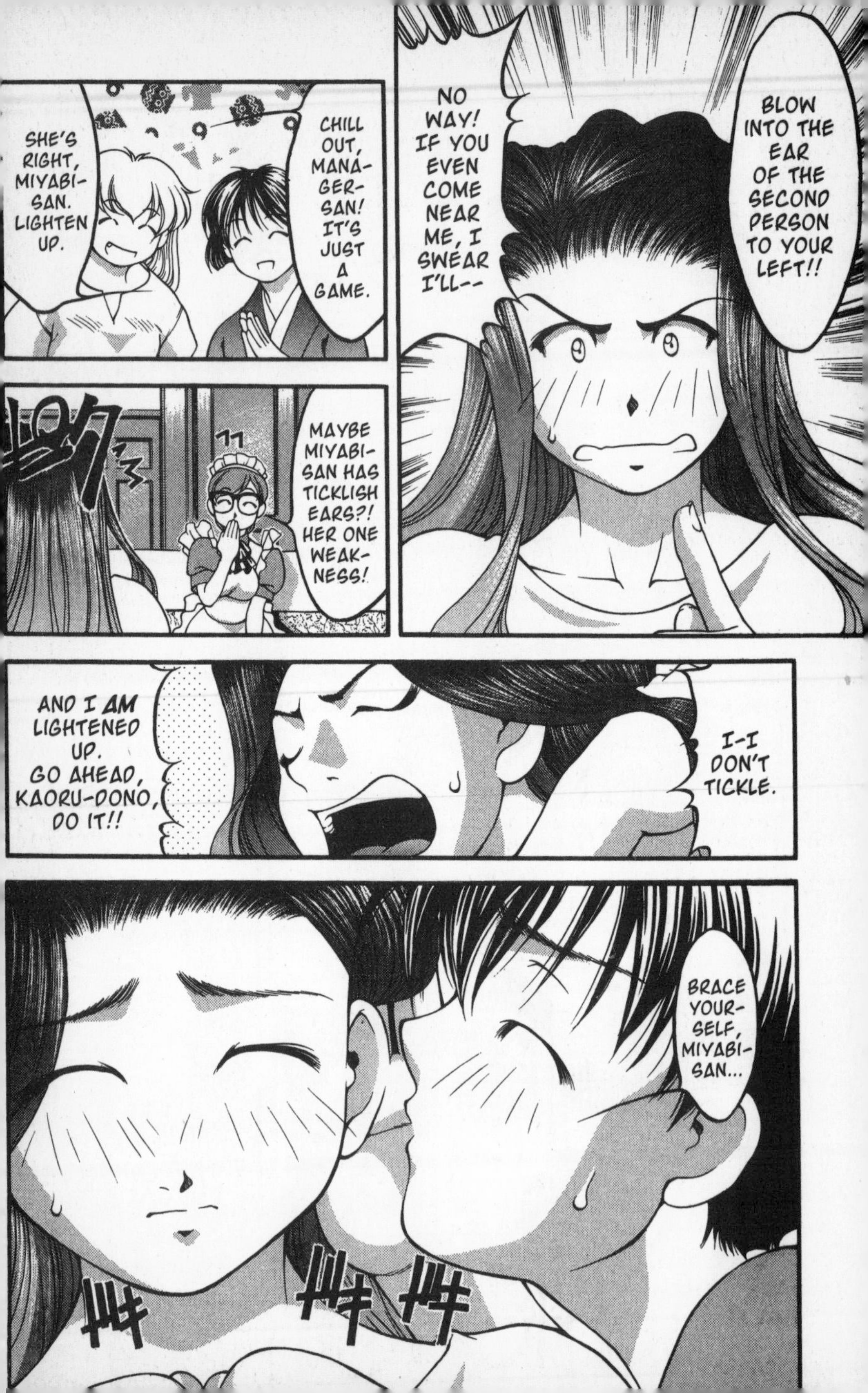
BLOW INTO THE EAR OF THE SECOND PERSON TO YOUR LEFT!!
NO WAY! IF YOU EVEN COME NEAR ME, I SWEAR I'LL--
CHILL OUT, MANA-GER-SAN! IT'S JUST A GAME.
SHE'S RIGHT, MIYABI-SAN. LIGHTEN UP.
MAYBE MIYABI-SAN HAS TICKLISH EARS?! HER ONE WEAK-NESS!
I-I DON'T TICKLE.
AND I AM LIGHTENED UP. GO AHEAD, KAORU-DONO, DO IT!!
BRACE YOUR-SELF, MIYABI-SAN...

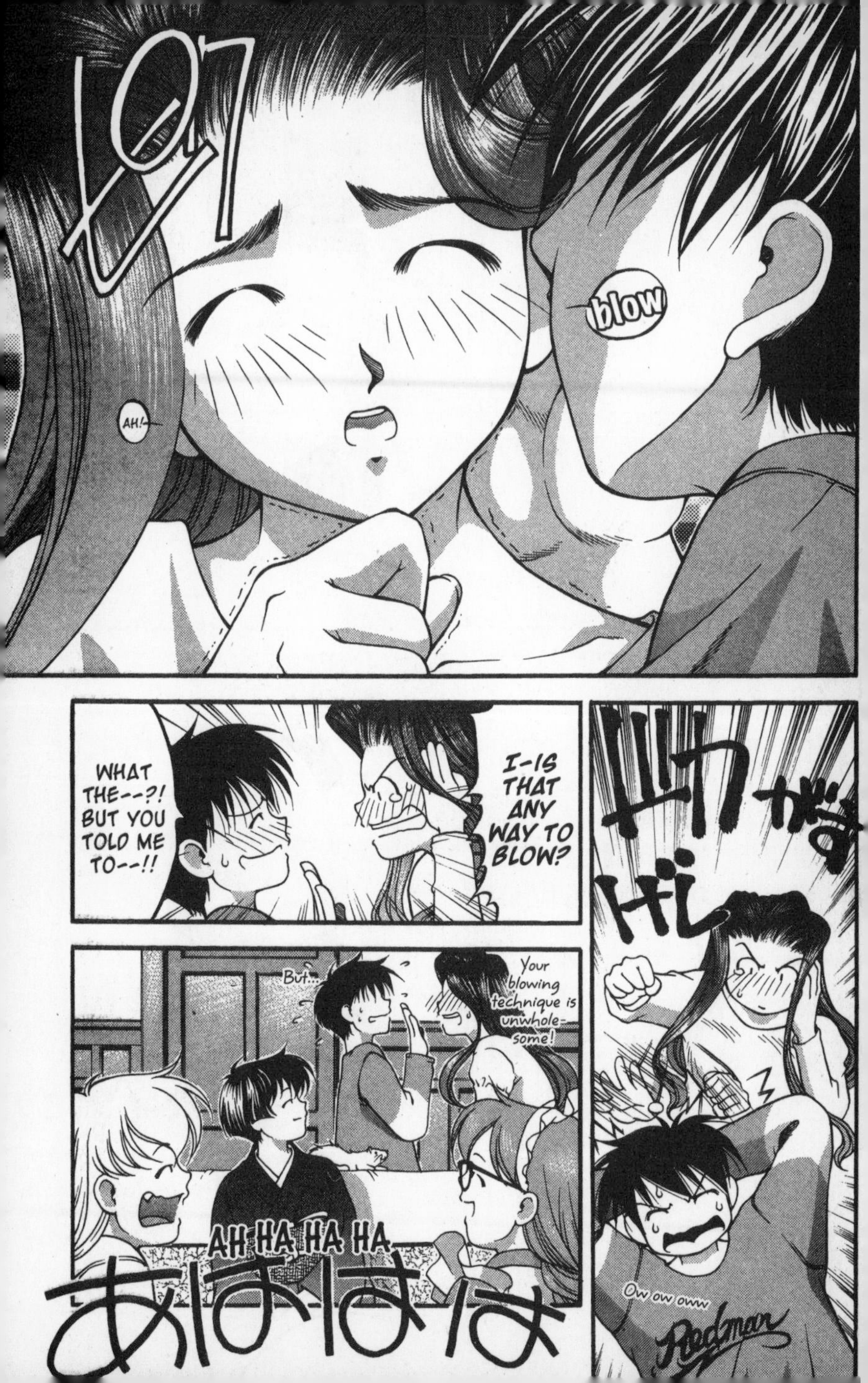
blow
AH!
Ow ow oww
I-IS THAT ANY WAY TO BLOW?
WHAT THE--?! BUT YOU TOLD ME TO--!!
Your blowing technique is unwhole-some!
But...
AH HA HA HA

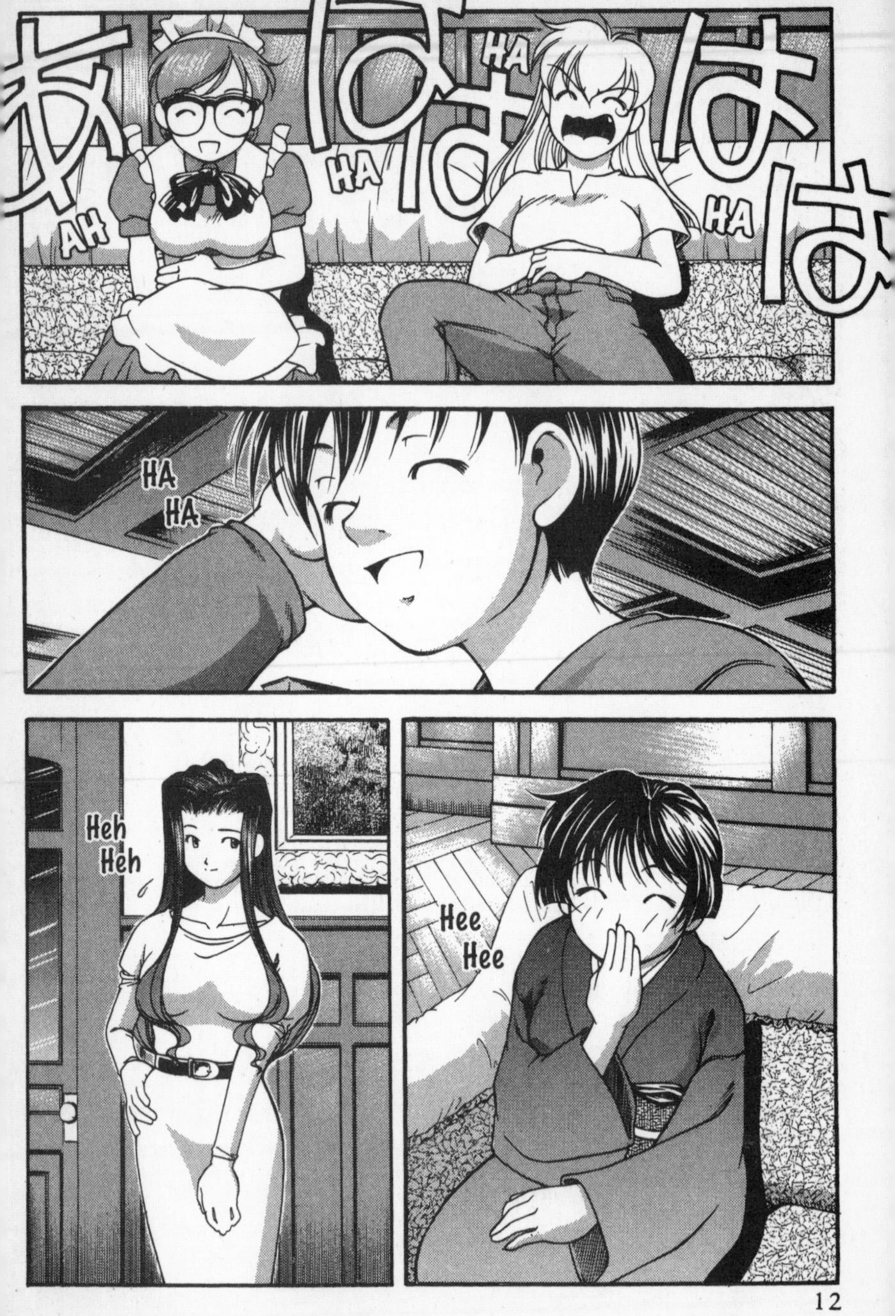
あはははは
HA
HA
HA
AH
HA
HA
Hee
Hee
Heh
Heh

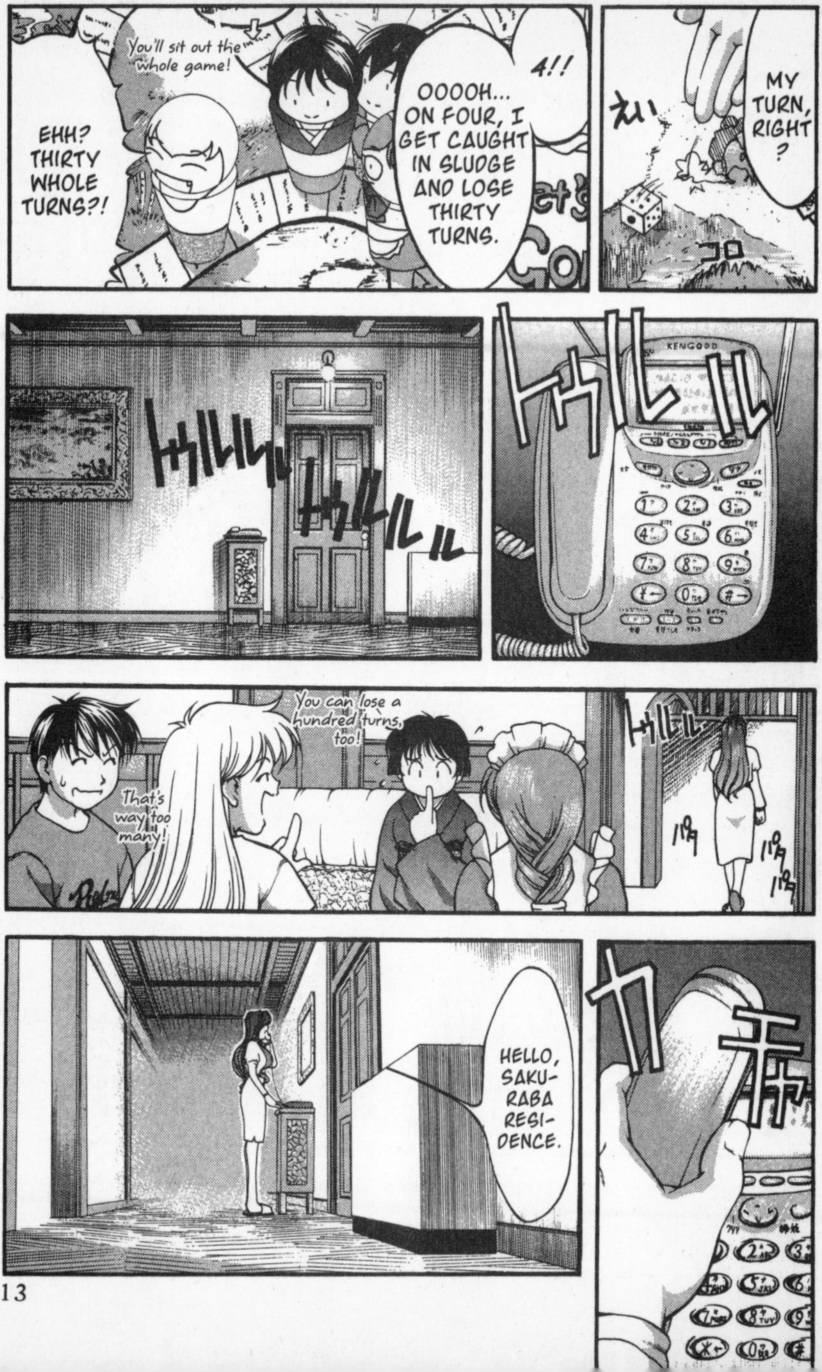
MY TURN, RIGHT?
えい
コロ
4!!
OOOOH... ON FOUR, I GET CAUGHT IN SLUDGE AND LOSE THIRTY TURNS.
You'll sit out the whole game!
EHH? THIRTY WHOLE TURNS?!
You can lose a hundred turns, too!
That's way too many!
HELLO, SAKURABA RESIDENCE.

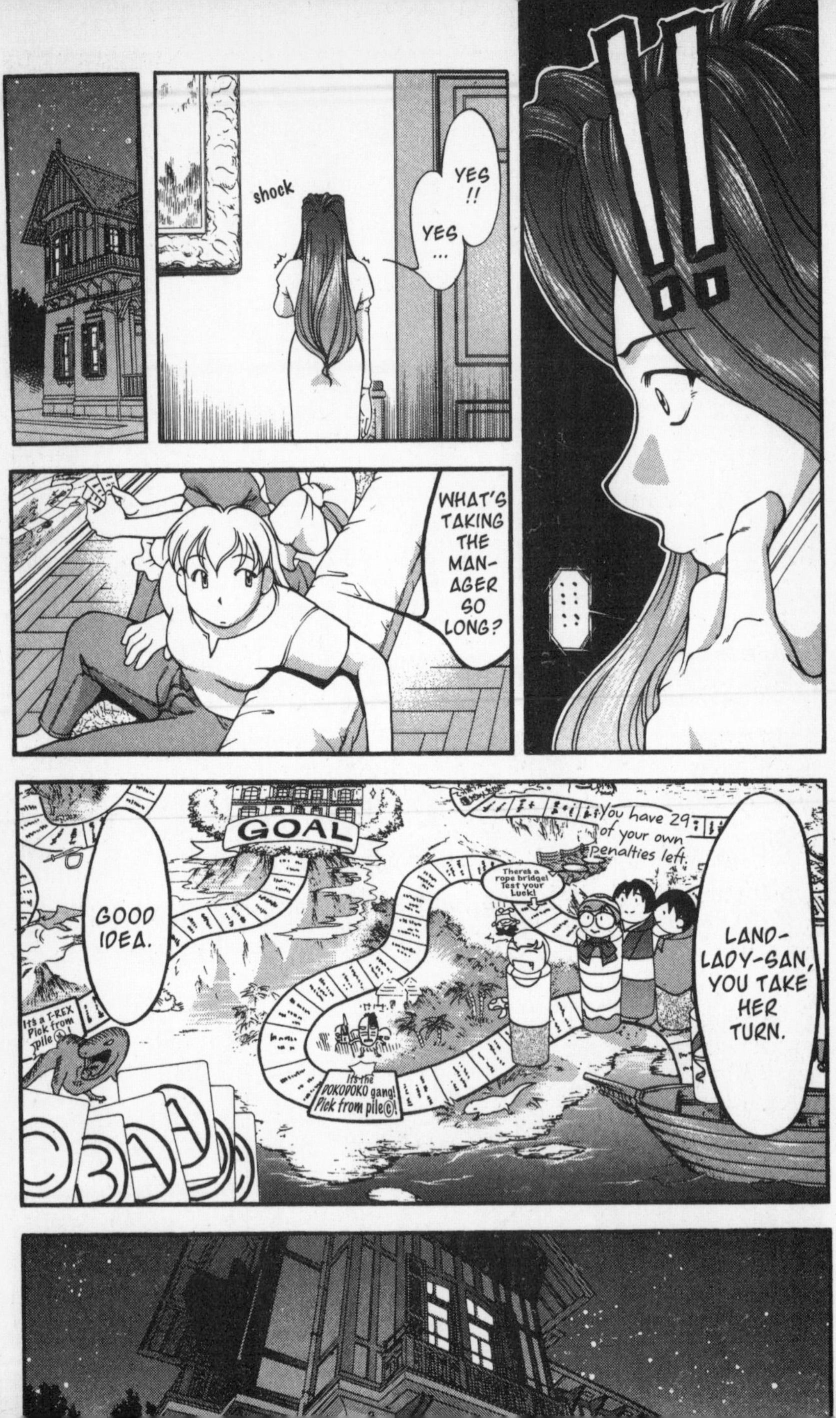
!!
......
YES !! YES ...
shock
WHAT'S TAKING THE MAN-AGER SO LONG?
LAND-LADY-SAN, YOU TAKE HER TURN.
You have 29 of your own penalties left.
There's a rope bridge! Test your Luck!
GOAL
It's the POKODOKO gang! Pick from pile Ⓒ!
It's a T-REX Pick from pile Ⓐ
GOOD IDEA.

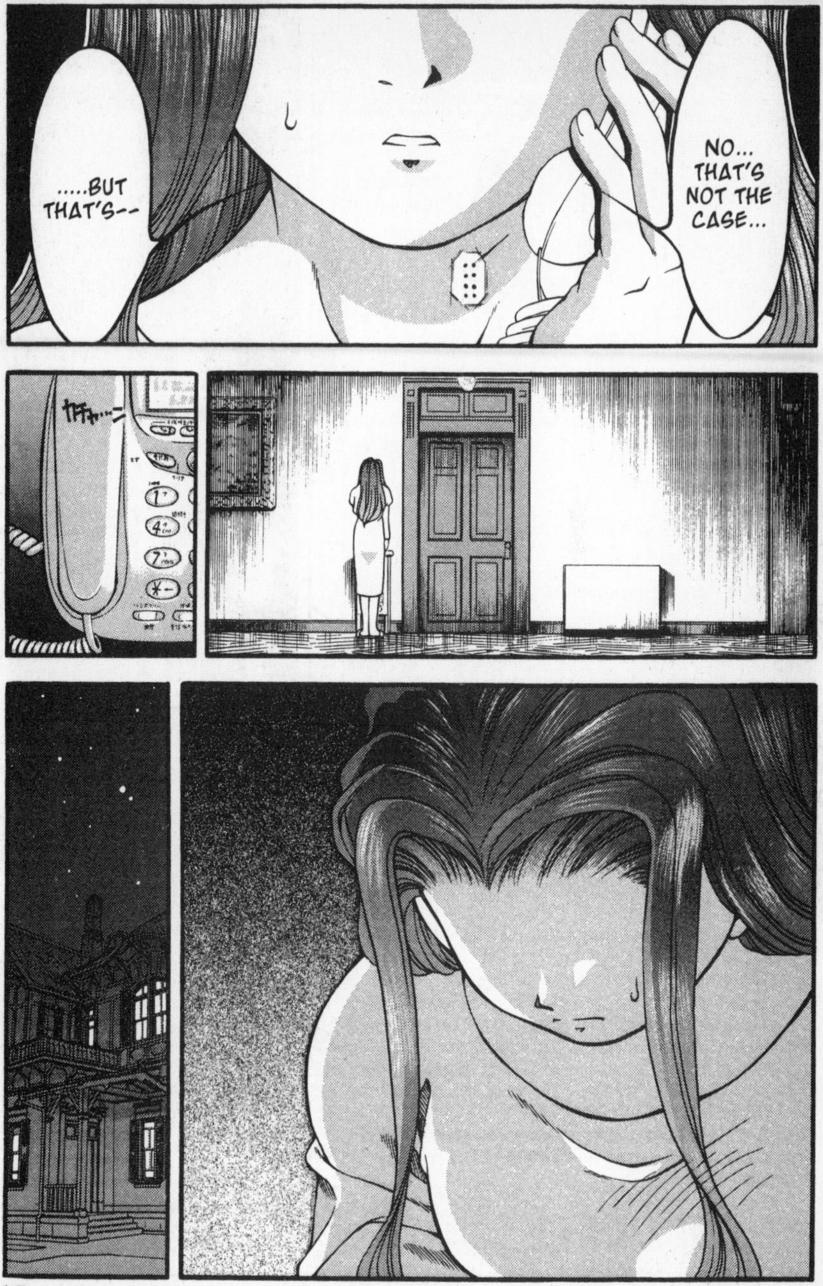
NO... THAT'S NOT THE CASE...
.....BUT THAT'S--

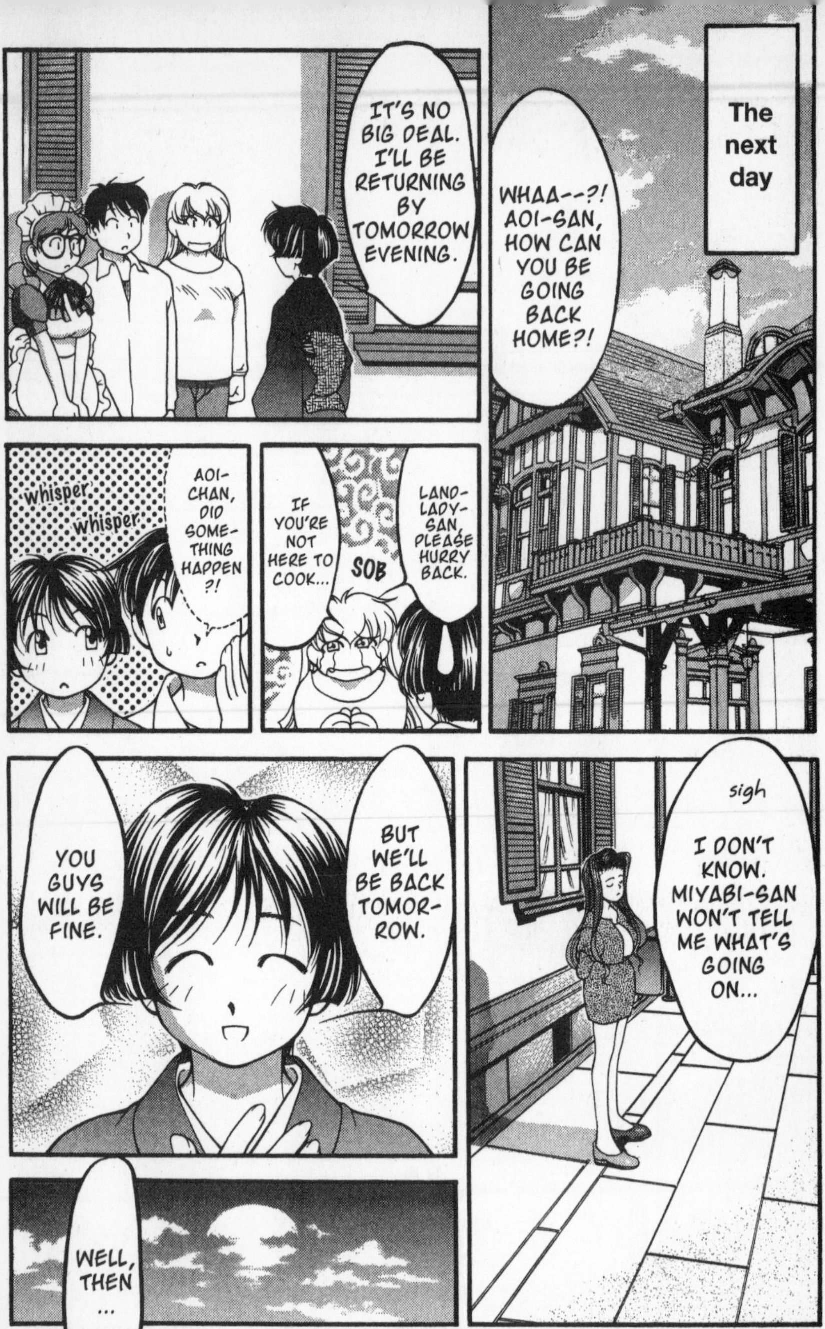
The next day
WHAA--?! AOI-SAN, HOW CAN YOU BE GOING BACK HOME?!
IT'S NO BIG DEAL. I'LL BE RETURNING BY TOMORROW EVENING.
LAND-LADY-SAN, PLEASE HURRY BACK.
IF YOU'RE NOT HERE TO COOK...
SOB
AOI-CHAN, DID SOME-THING HAPPEN?!
whisper
whisper
sigh
I DON'T KNOW. MIYABI-SAN WON'T TELL ME WHAT'S GOING ON...
BUT WE'LL BE BACK TOMOR-ROW.
YOU GUYS WILL BE FINE.
WELL, THEN ...

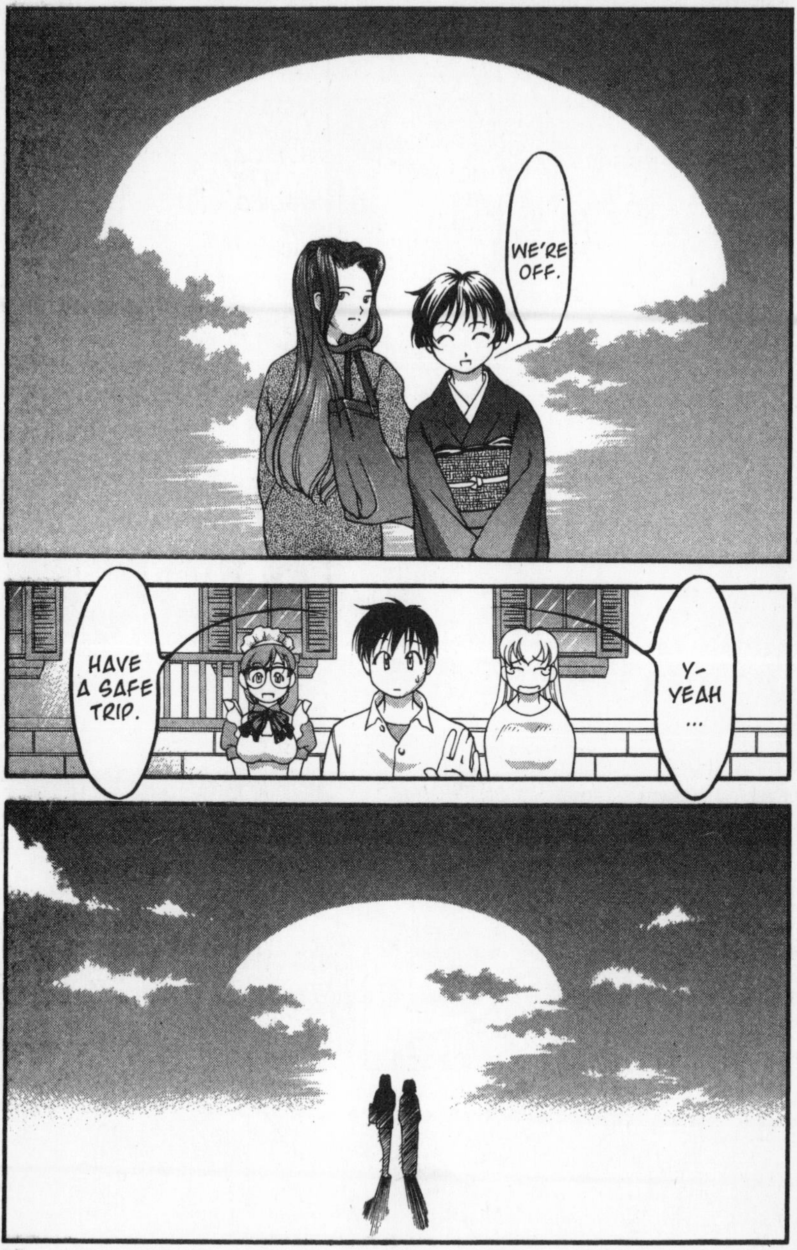
WE'RE OFF.
Y-YEAH ...
HAVE A SAFE TRIP.

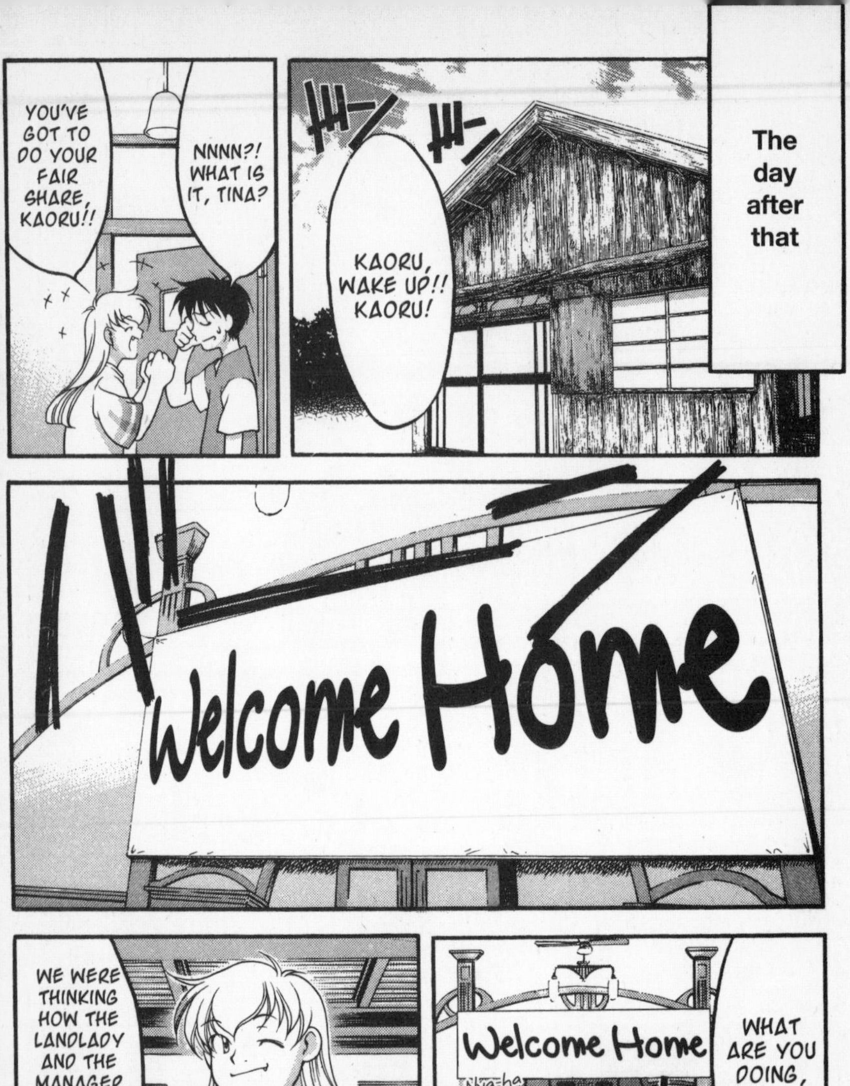
The day after that
KAORU, WAKE UP!! KAORU!
NNNN?! WHAT IS IT, TINA?
YOU'VE GOT TO DO YOUR FAIR SHARE, KAORU!!
Welcome Home
WHAT ARE YOU DOING, TINA...?
Welcome Home
Nya-ha
WE WERE THINKING HOW THE LANDLADY AND THE MANAGER ARE ALWAYS TAKING CARE OF US...
SAILING
CLUB

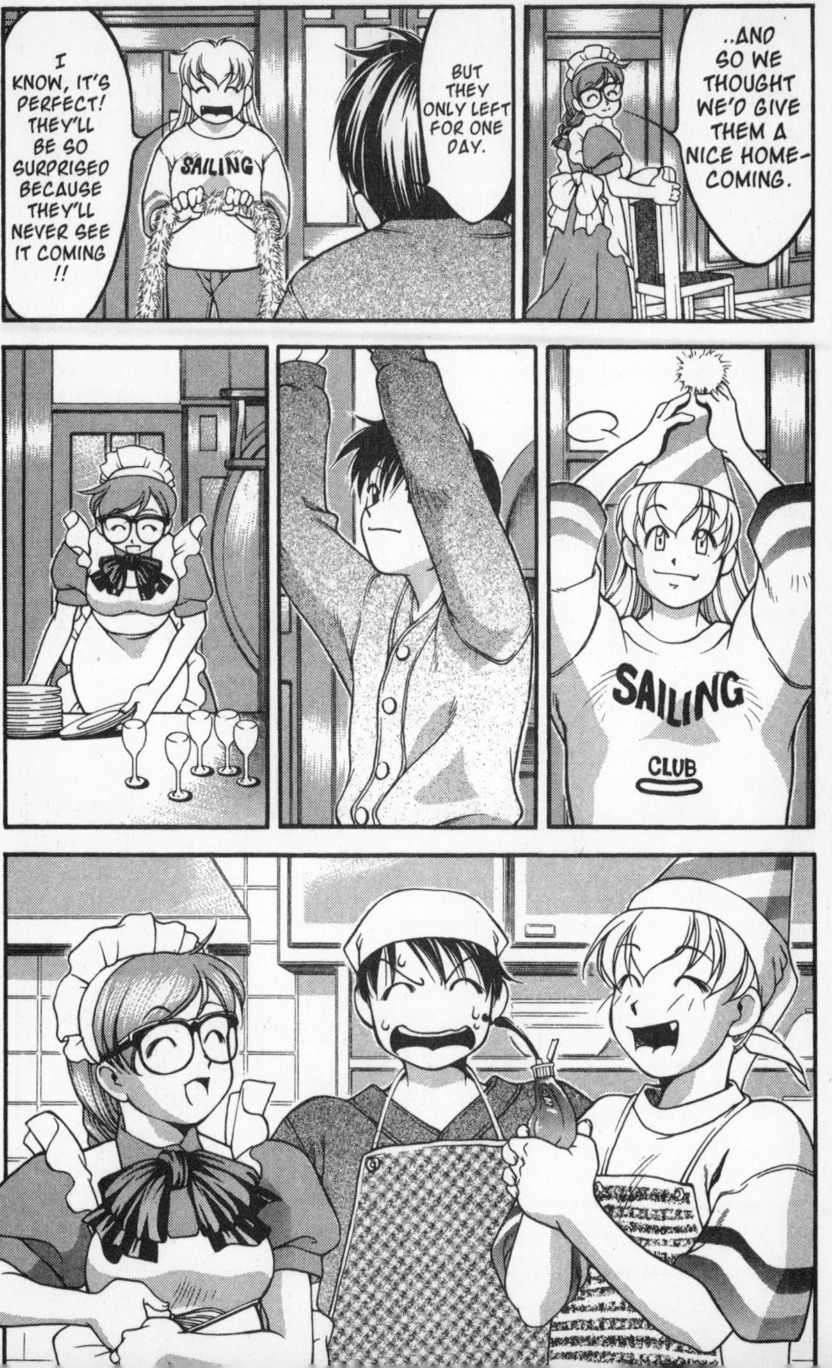
..AND SO WE THOUGHT WE'D GIVE THEM A NICE HOME-COMING.
BUT THEY ONLY LEFT FOR ONE DAY.
I KNOW, IT'S PERFECT! THEY'LL BE SO SURPRISED BECAUSE THEY'LL NEVER SEE IT COMING !!
SAILING
SAILING
CLUB

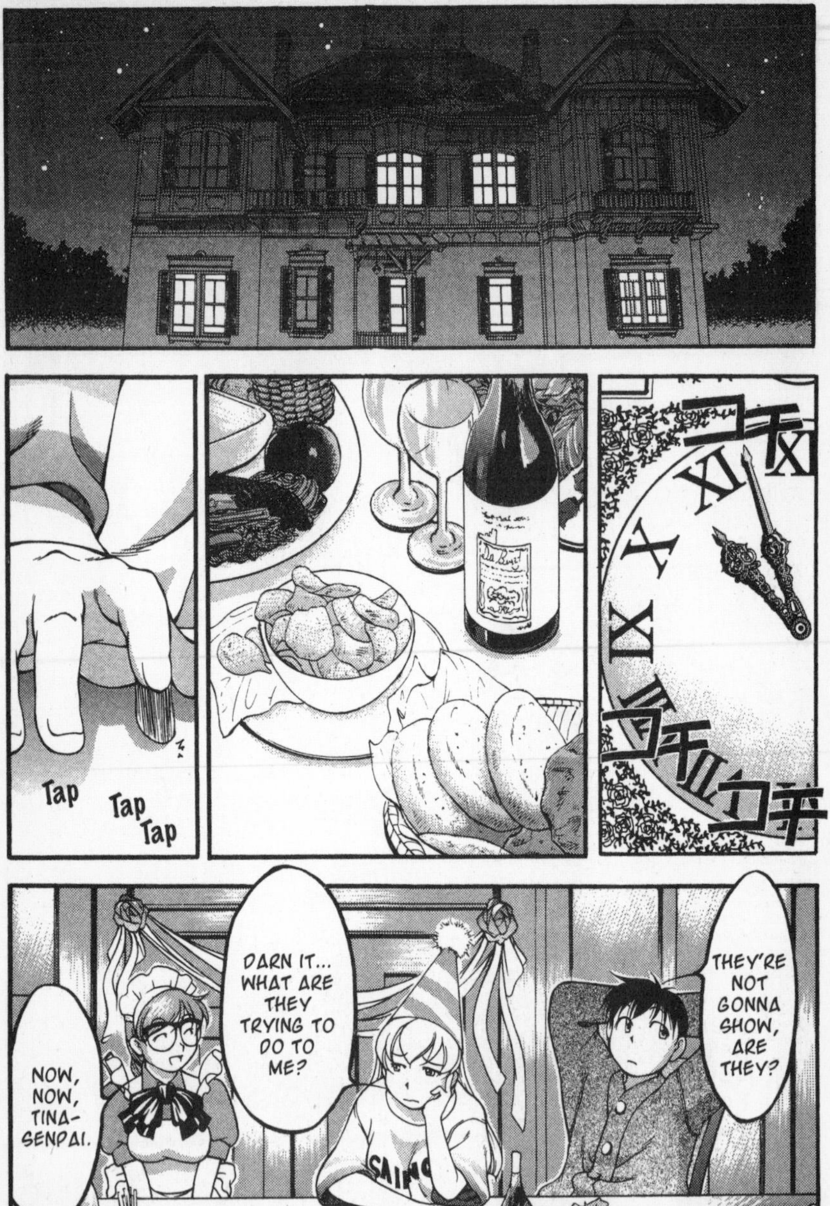
Tap
Tap
Tap
THEY'RE NOT GONNA SHOW, ARE THEY?
DARN IT... WHAT ARE THEY TRYING TO DO TO ME?
NOW, NOW, TINA-SENPAI.

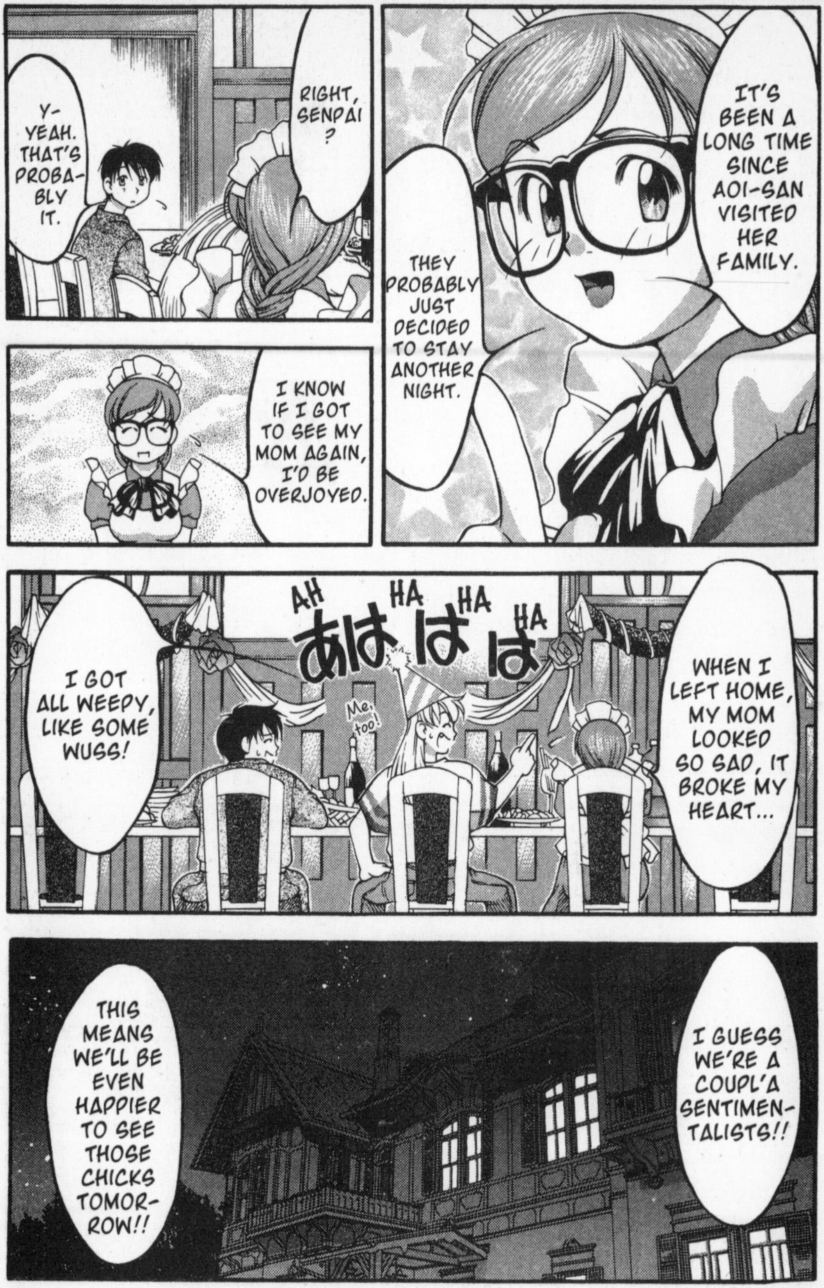
IT'S BEEN A LONG TIME SINCE AOI-SAN VISITED HER FAMILY.
THEY PROBABLY JUST DECIDED TO STAY ANOTHER NIGHT.
RIGHT, SENPAI?
Y-YEAH. THAT'S PROBABLY IT.
I KNOW IF I GOT TO SEE MY MOM AGAIN, I'D BE OVERJOYED.
WHEN I LEFT HOME, MY MOM LOOKED SO SAD, IT BROKE MY HEART...
AH HA HA HA
あははは
Me, too!
I GOT ALL WEEPY, LIKE SOME WUSS!
I GUESS WE'RE A COUPL'A SENTIMENTALISTS!!
THIS MEANS WE'LL BE EVEN HAPPIER TO SEE THOSE CHICKS TOMORROW!!

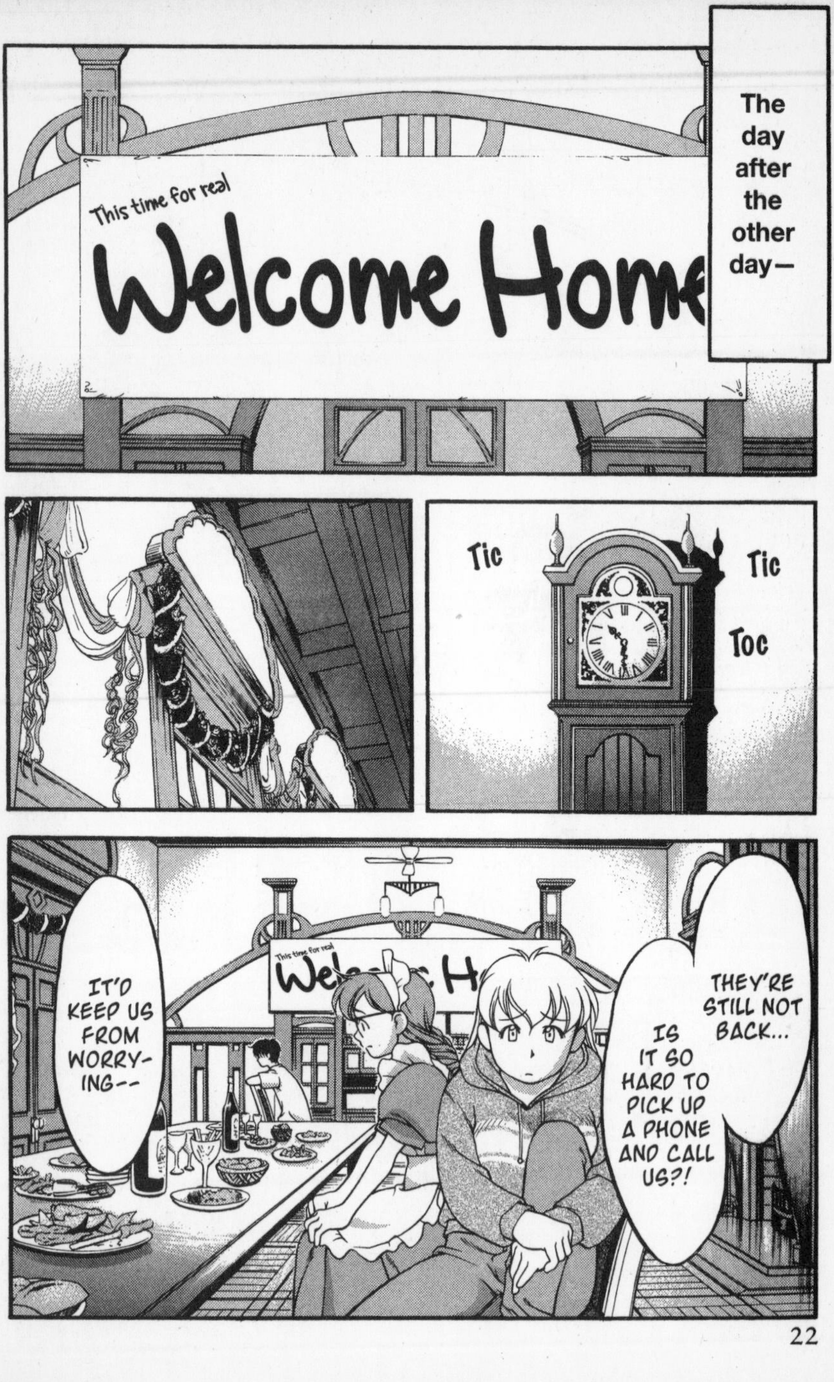
The day after the other day—
This time for real
Welcome Home
Tic
Tic
Toc
THEY'RE STILL NOT BACK...
IS IT SO HARD TO PICK UP A PHONE AND CALL US?!
IT'D KEEP US FROM WORRYING--

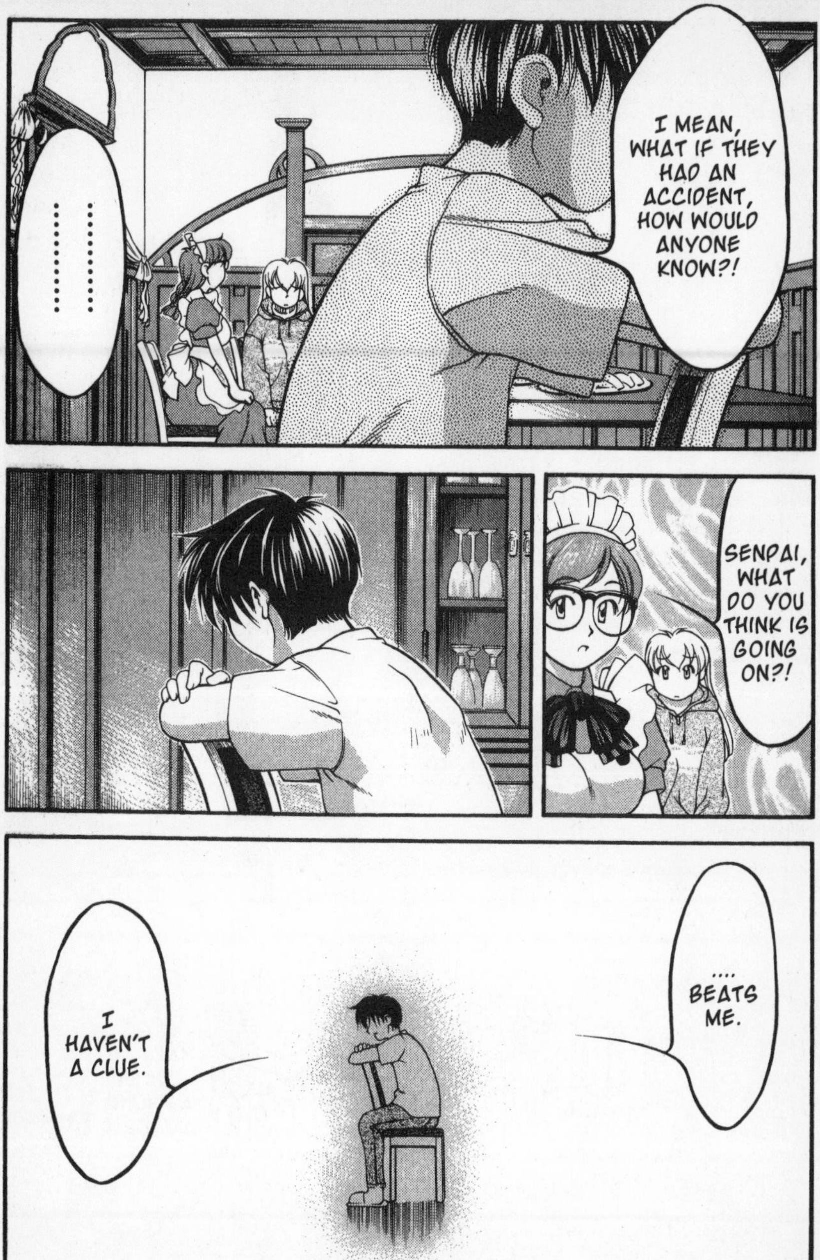
I MEAN, WHAT IF THEY HAD AN ACCIDENT, HOW WOULD ANYONE KNOW?!
......
SENPAI, WHAT DO YOU THINK IS GOING ON?!
.... BEATS ME.
I HAVEN'T A CLUE.

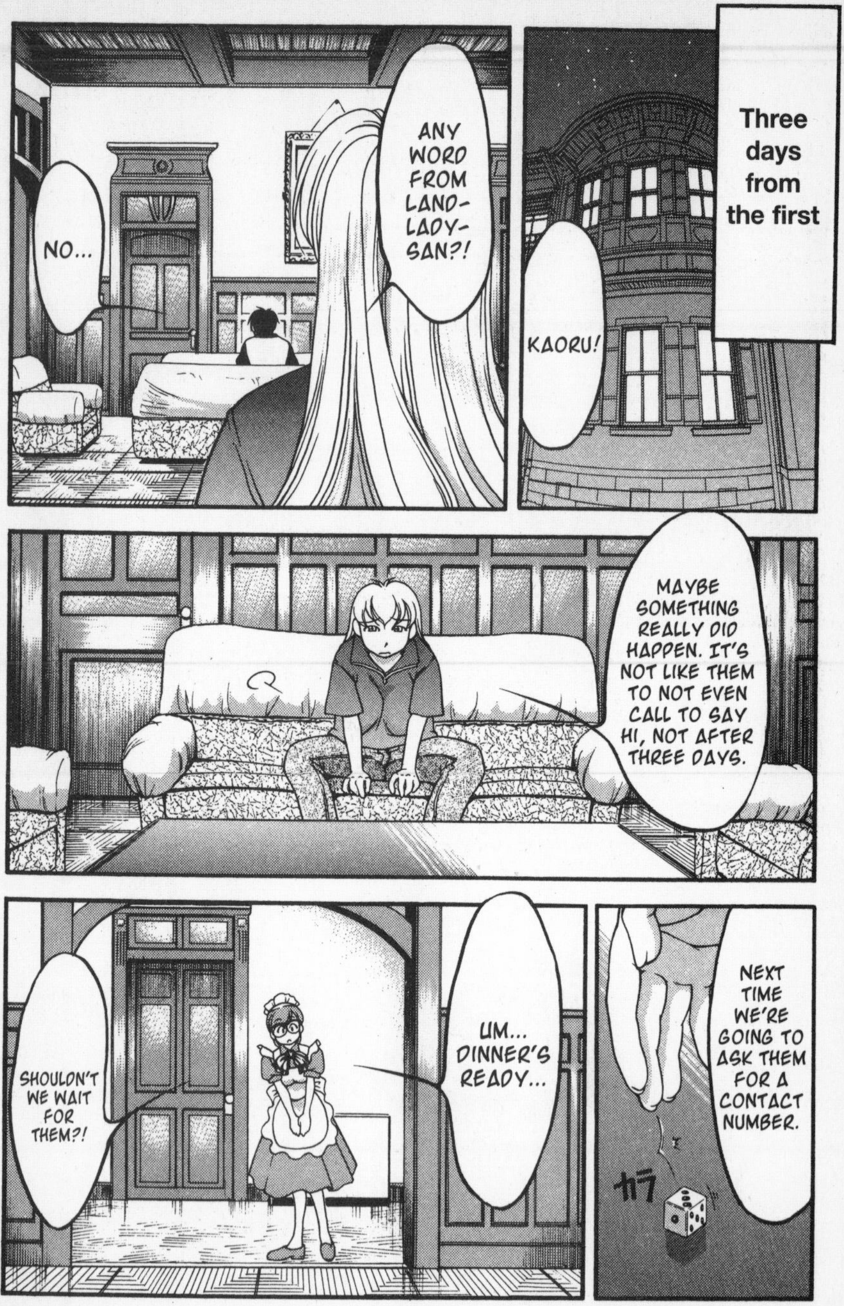
Three days from the first
KAORU!
ANY WORD FROM LAND-LADY-SAN?!
NO...
MAYBE SOMETHING REALLY DID HAPPEN. IT'S NOT LIKE THEM TO NOT EVEN CALL TO SAY HI, NOT AFTER THREE DAYS.
NEXT TIME WE'RE GOING TO ASK THEM FOR A CONTACT NUMBER.
カラ
UM... DINNER'S READY...
SHOULDN'T WE WAIT FOR THEM?!

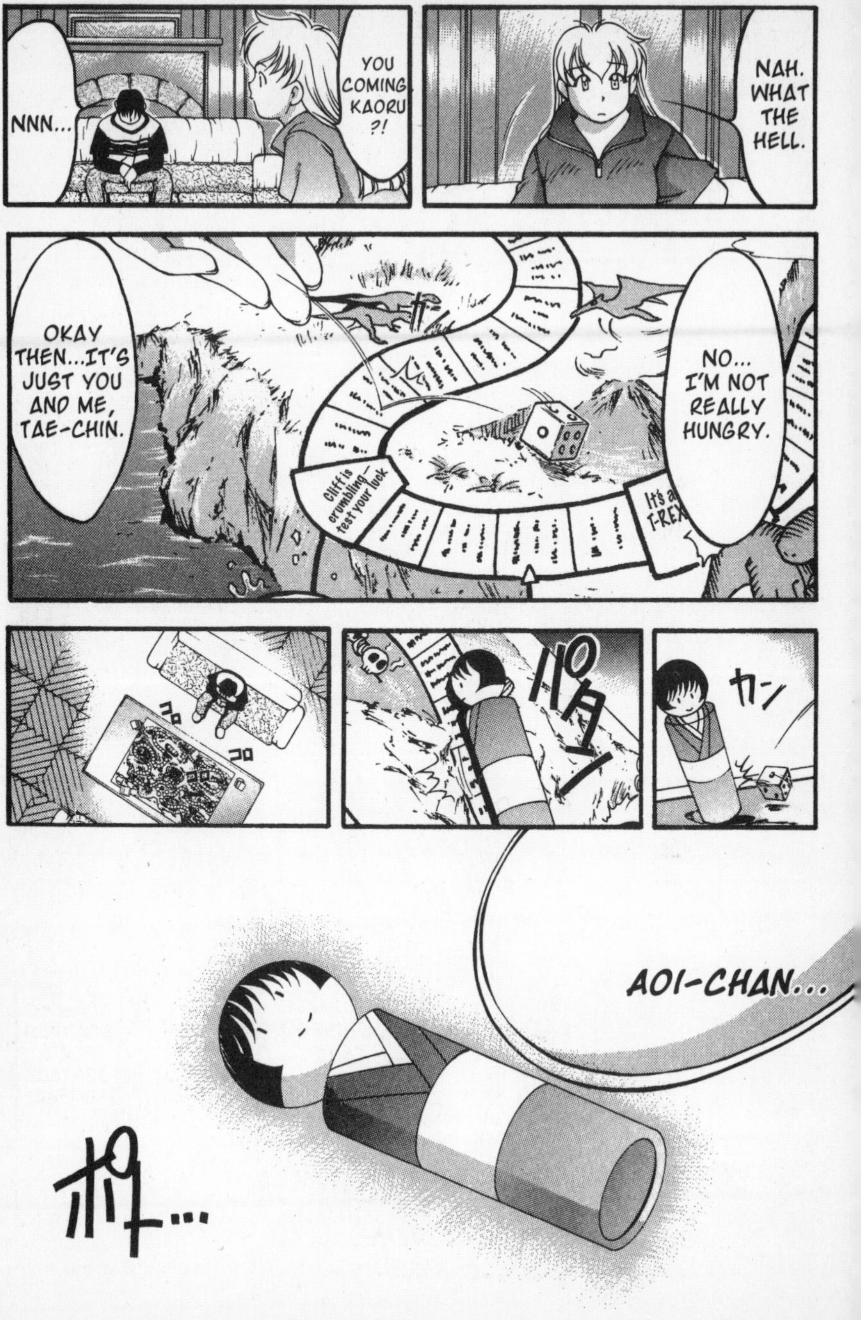
NAH. WHAT THE HELL.
YOU COMING, KAORU?!
NNN...
NO... I'M NOT REALLY HUNGRY.
It's a T-REX
Cliff is crumbling—test your luck
OKAY THEN...IT'S JUST YOU AND ME, TAE-CHIN.
カン
パタン
コロ
コロ
AOI-CHAN...
ポテ...

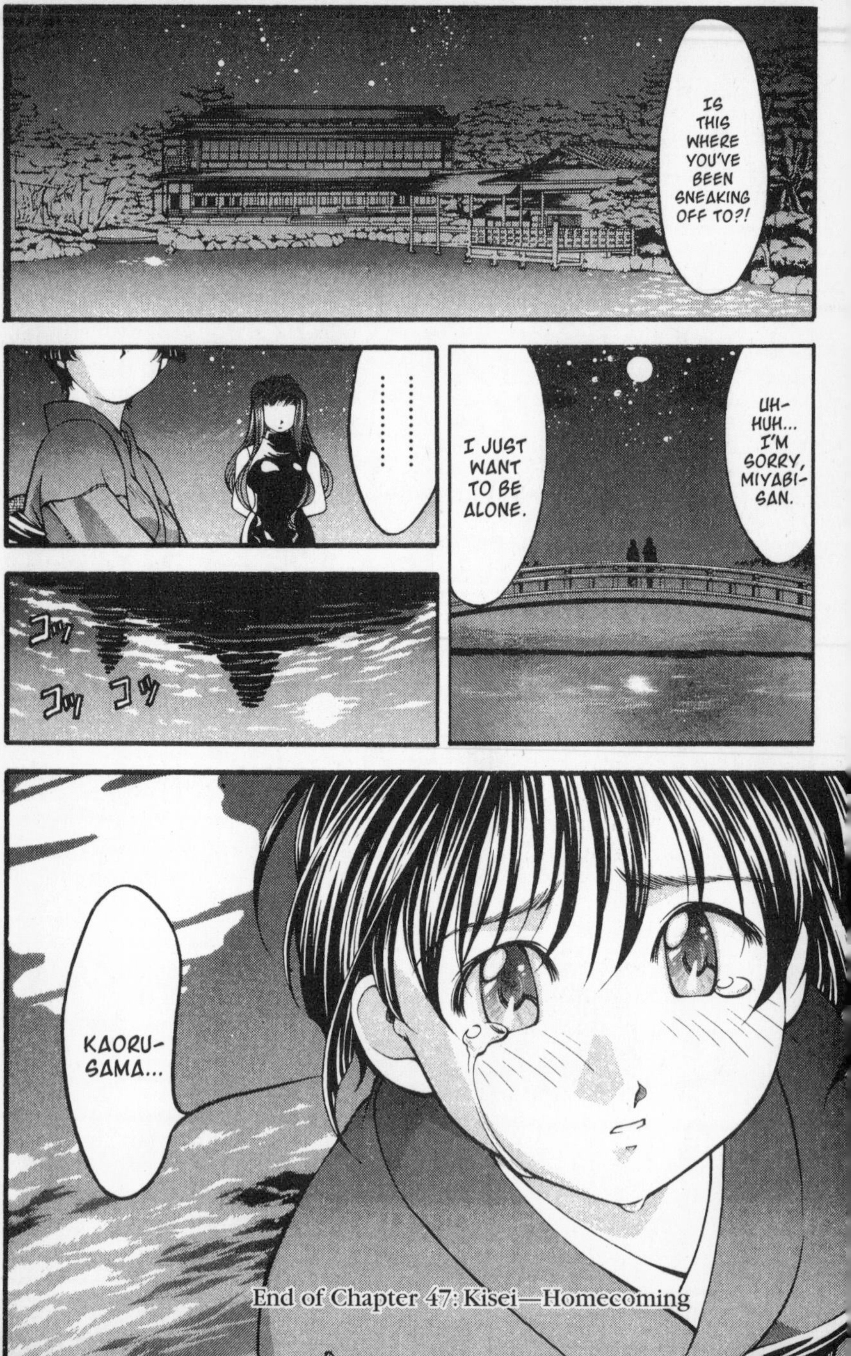
IS THIS WHERE YOU'VE BEEN SNEAKING OFF TO?!
UH-HUH... I'M SORRY, MIYABI-SAN.
I JUST WANT TO BE ALONE.
......
コッ
コッ
コッ
KAORU-SAMA...

End of Chapter 47: Kisei—Homecoming

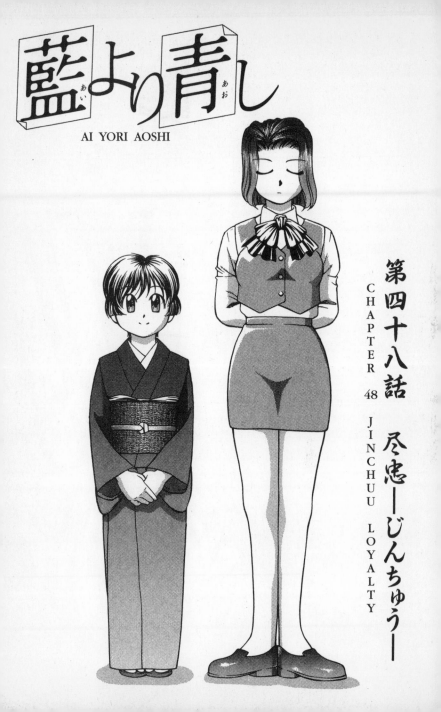

藍より青し

AI YORI AOSHI

第四十八話　尽忠―じんちゅう―

CHAPTER 48 JINCHUU LOYALTY

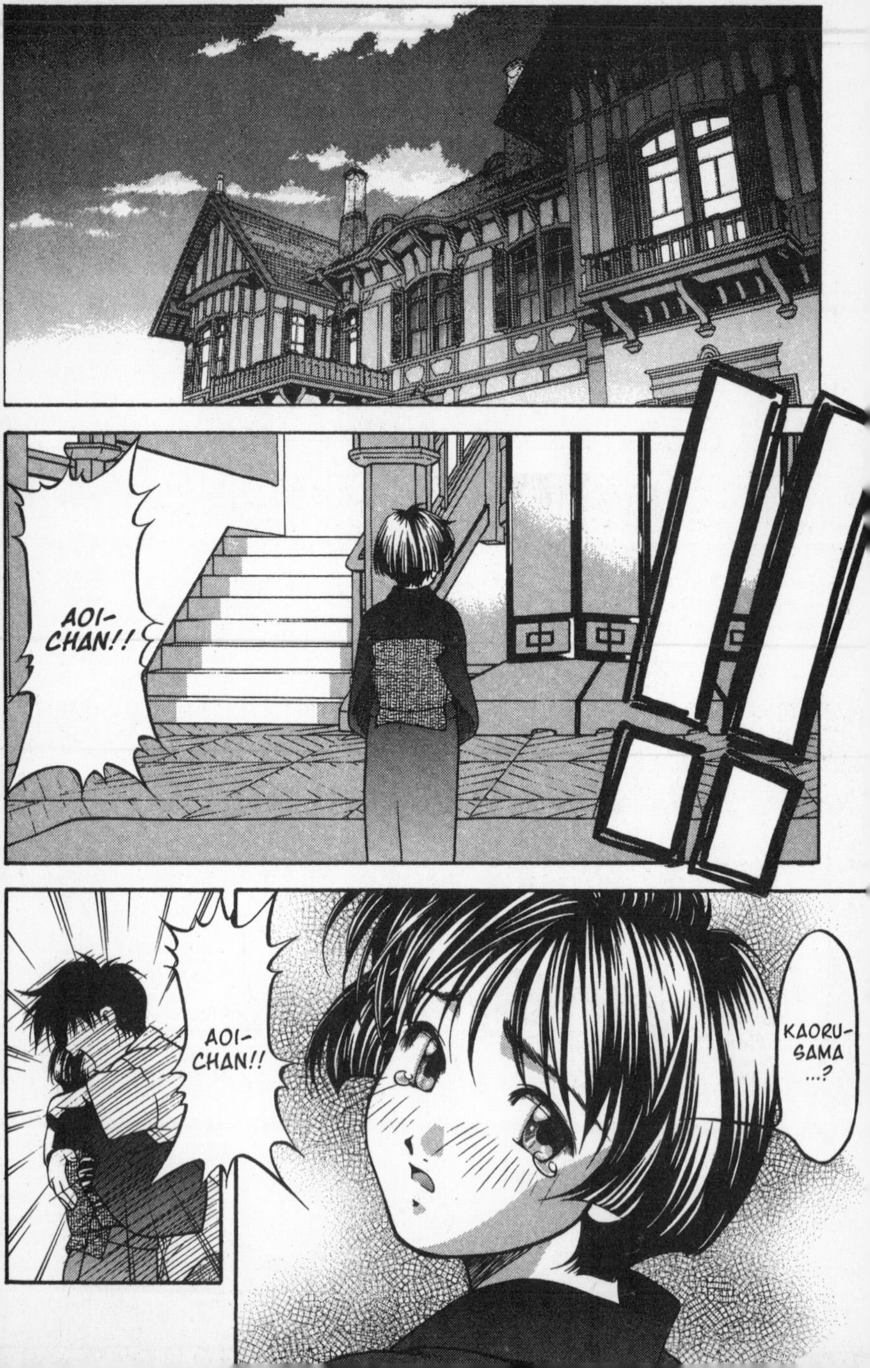
AOI-CHAN!!
KAORU-SAMA ...?
AOI-CHAN!!

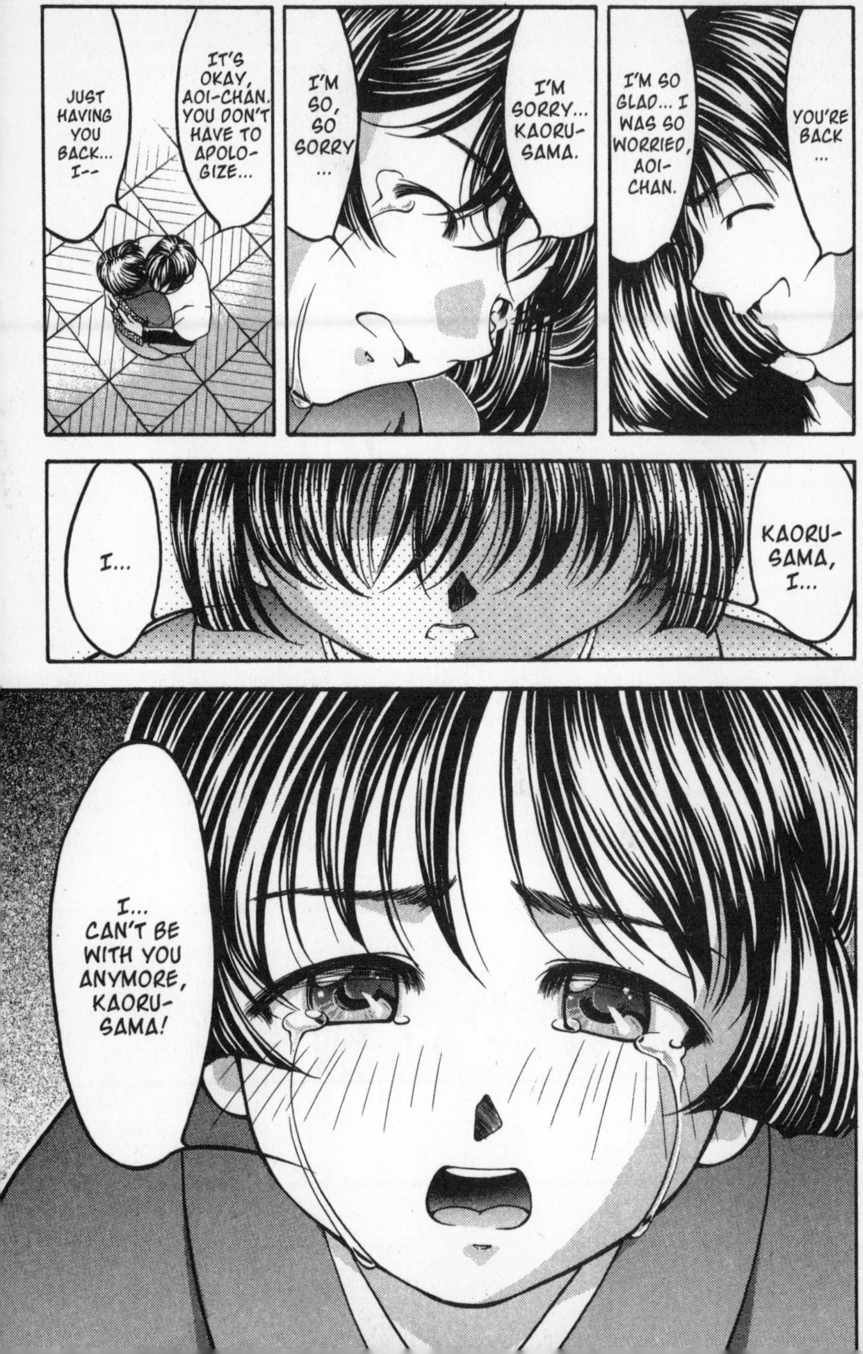
YOU'RE BACK ...
I'M SO GLAD... I WAS SO WORRIED, AOI-CHAN.
I'M SORRY... KAORU-SAMA.
I'M SO, SO SORRY ...
IT'S OKAY, AOI-CHAN. YOU DON'T HAVE TO APOLOGIZE...
JUST HAVING YOU BACK... I--
KAORU-SAMA, I...
I...
I... CAN'T BE WITH YOU ANYMORE, KAORU-SAMA!

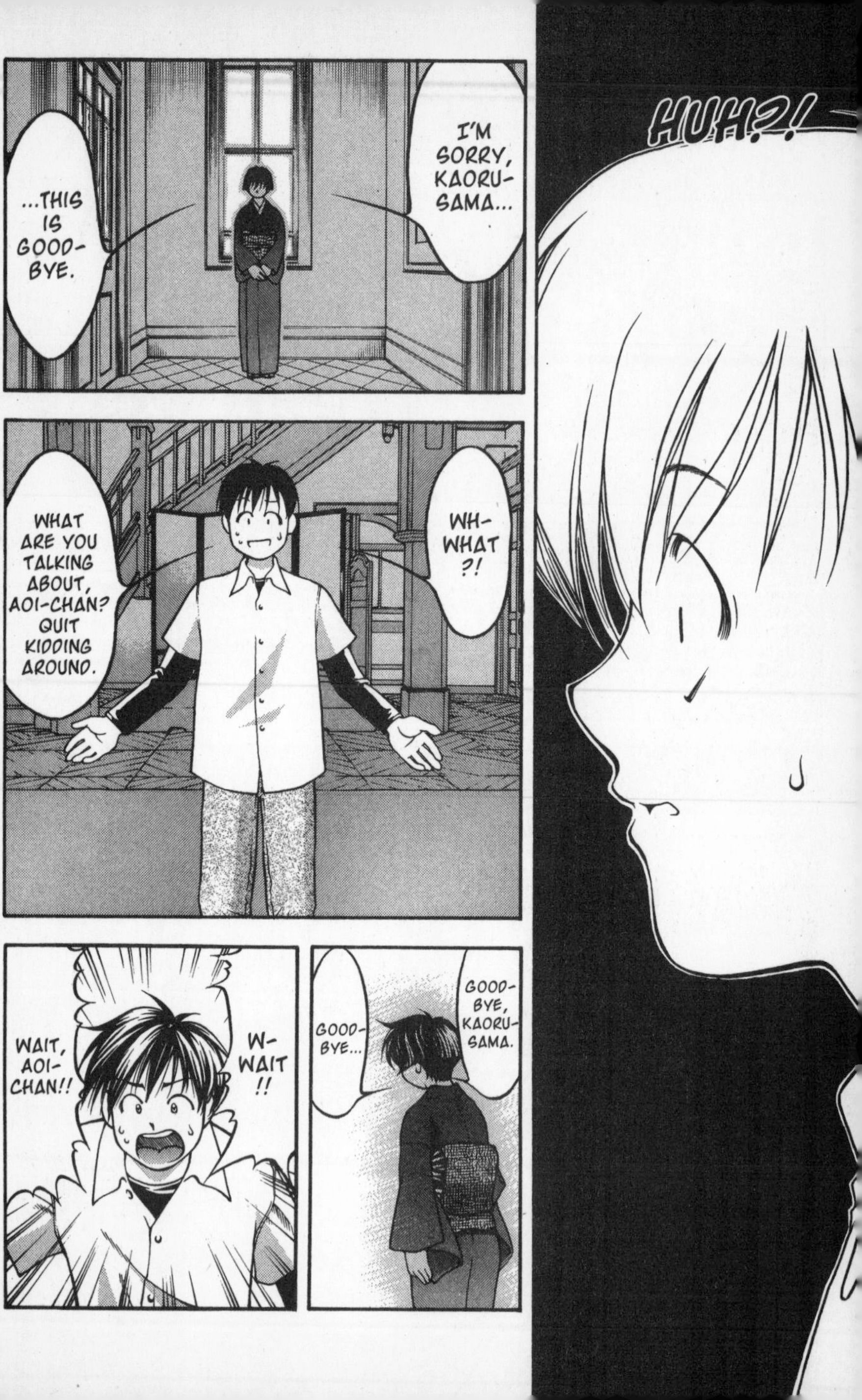
HUH?!
I'M SORRY, KAORU-SAMA...
...THIS IS GOOD-BYE.
WH-WHAT?!
WHAT ARE YOU TALKING ABOUT, AOI-CHAN? QUIT KIDDING AROUND.
GOOD-BYE, KAORU-SAMA.
GOOD-BYE...
W-WAIT!!
WAIT, AOI-CHAN!!

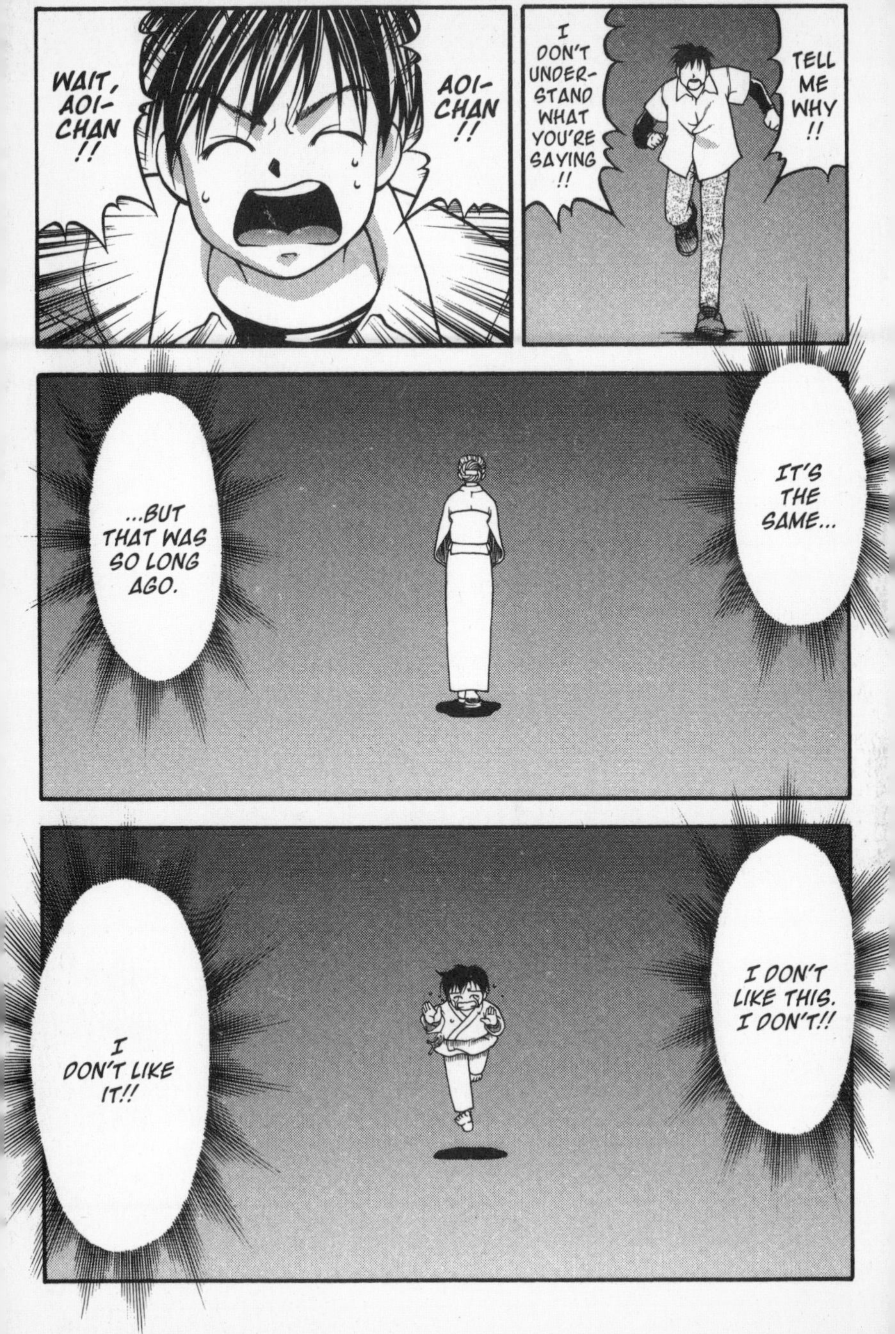
TELL ME WHY!!
I DON'T UNDER-STAND WHAT YOU'RE SAYING!!
AOI-CHAN!!
WAIT, AOI-CHAN!!
IT'S THE SAME...
...BUT THAT WAS SO LONG AGO.
I DON'T LIKE THIS. I DON'T!!
I DON'T LIKE IT!!

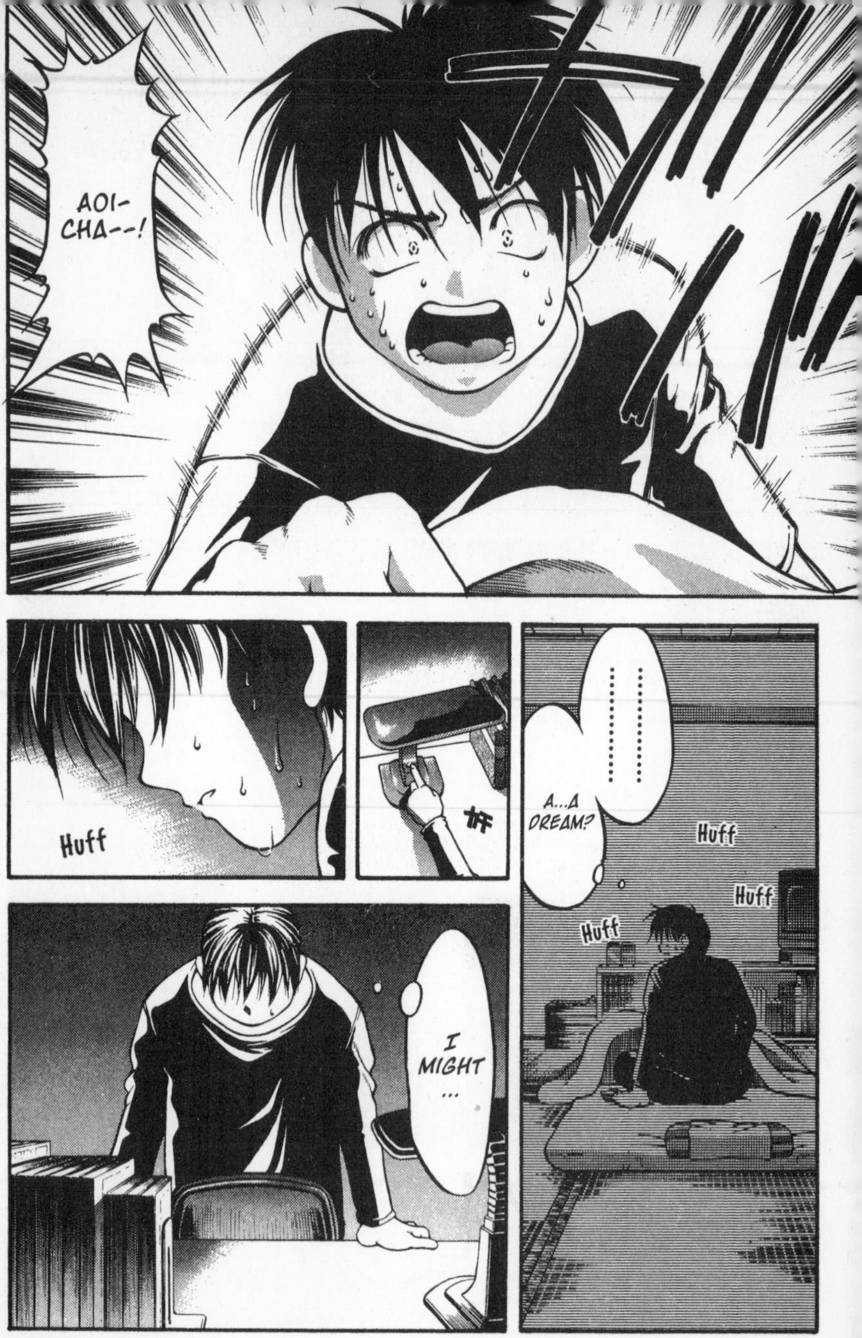
AOI-CHA--!
......
A...A DREAM?
Huff
Huff
Huff
Huff
I MIGHT ...

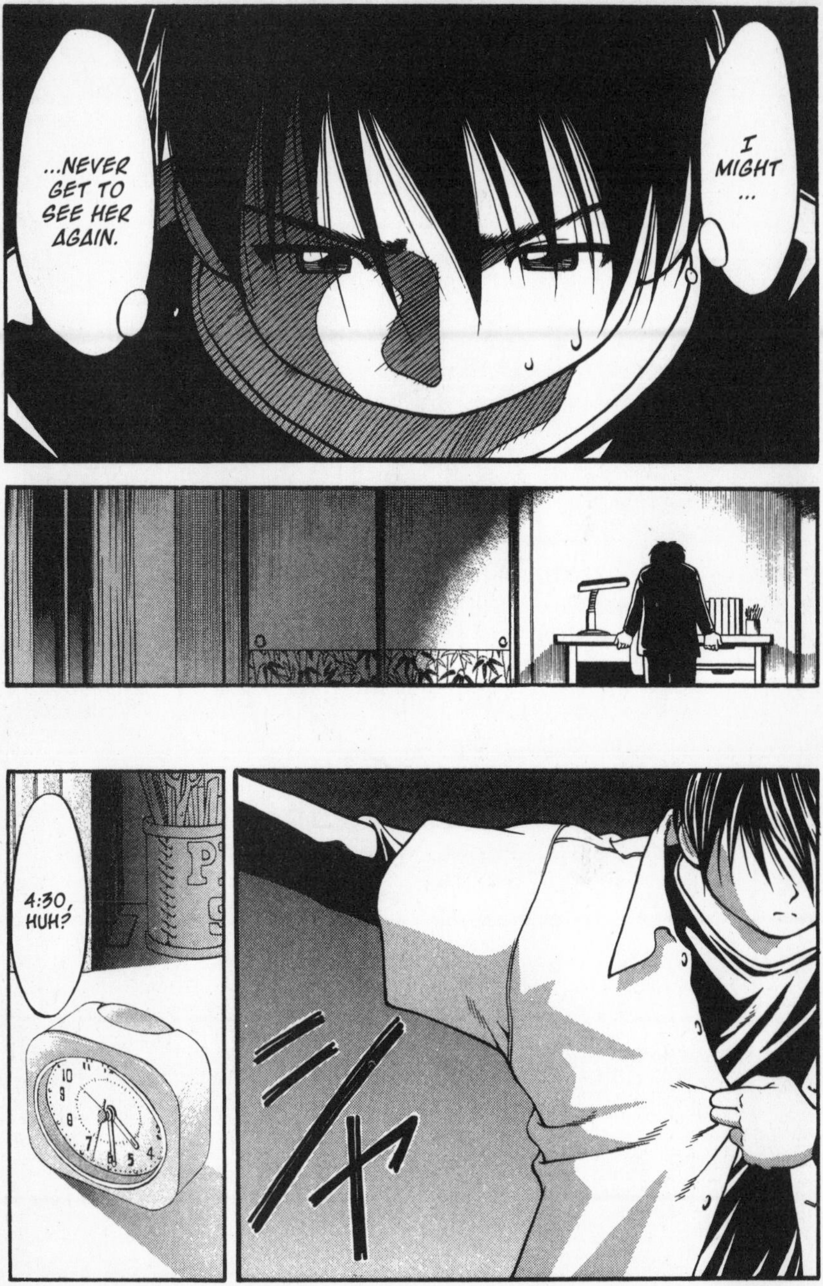
I MIGHT ...
...NEVER GET TO SEE HER AGAIN.
4:30, HUH?

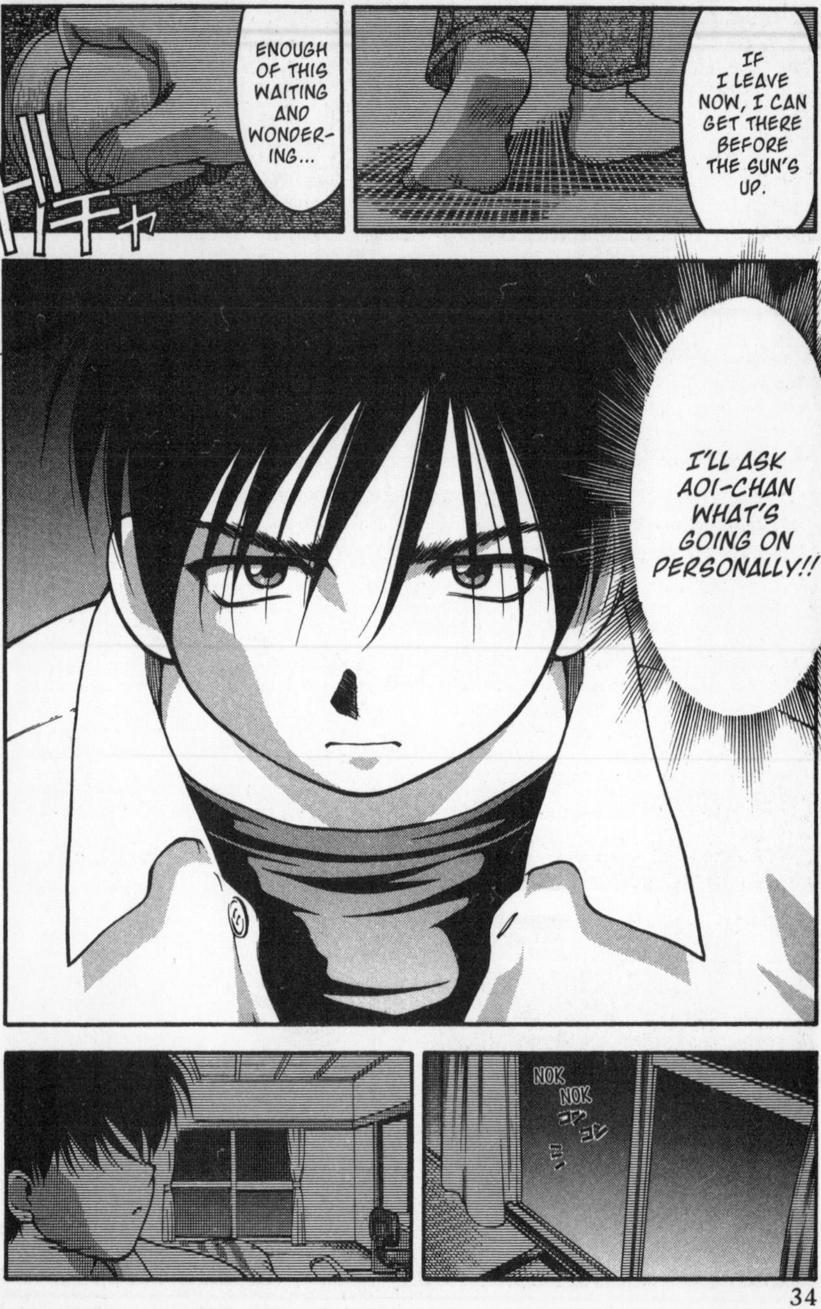
IF I LEAVE NOW, I CAN GET THERE BEFORE THE SUN'S UP.
ENOUGH OF THIS WAITING AND WONDER-ING...
ガチャ
I'LL ASK AOI-CHAN WHAT'S GOING ON PERSONALLY!!
NOK NOK

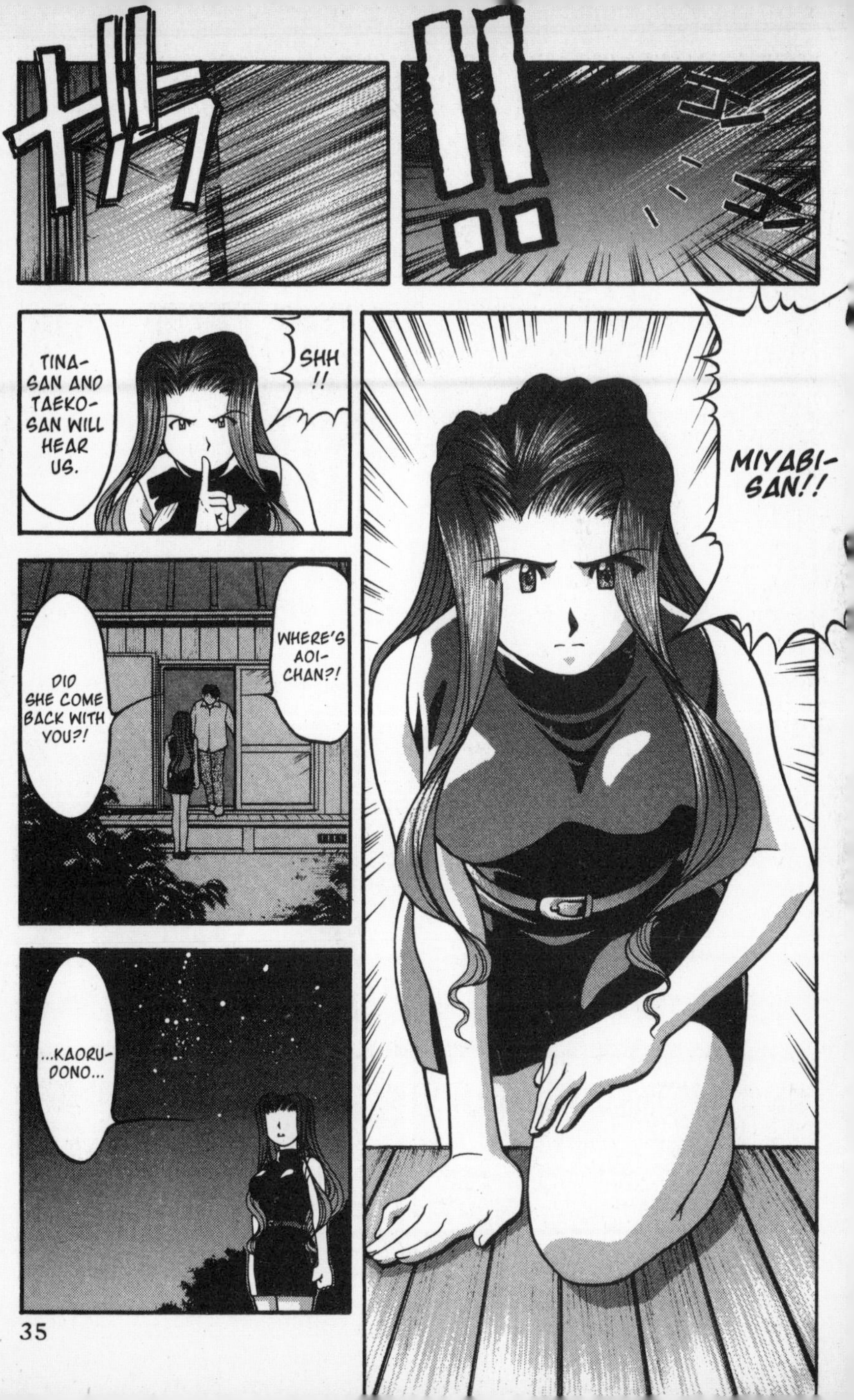
!!
ガラ
MIYABI-SAN!!
SHH!!
TINA-SAN AND TAEKO-SAN WILL HEAR US.
WHERE'S AOI-CHAN?!
DID SHE COME BACK WITH YOU?!
...KAORU-DONO...

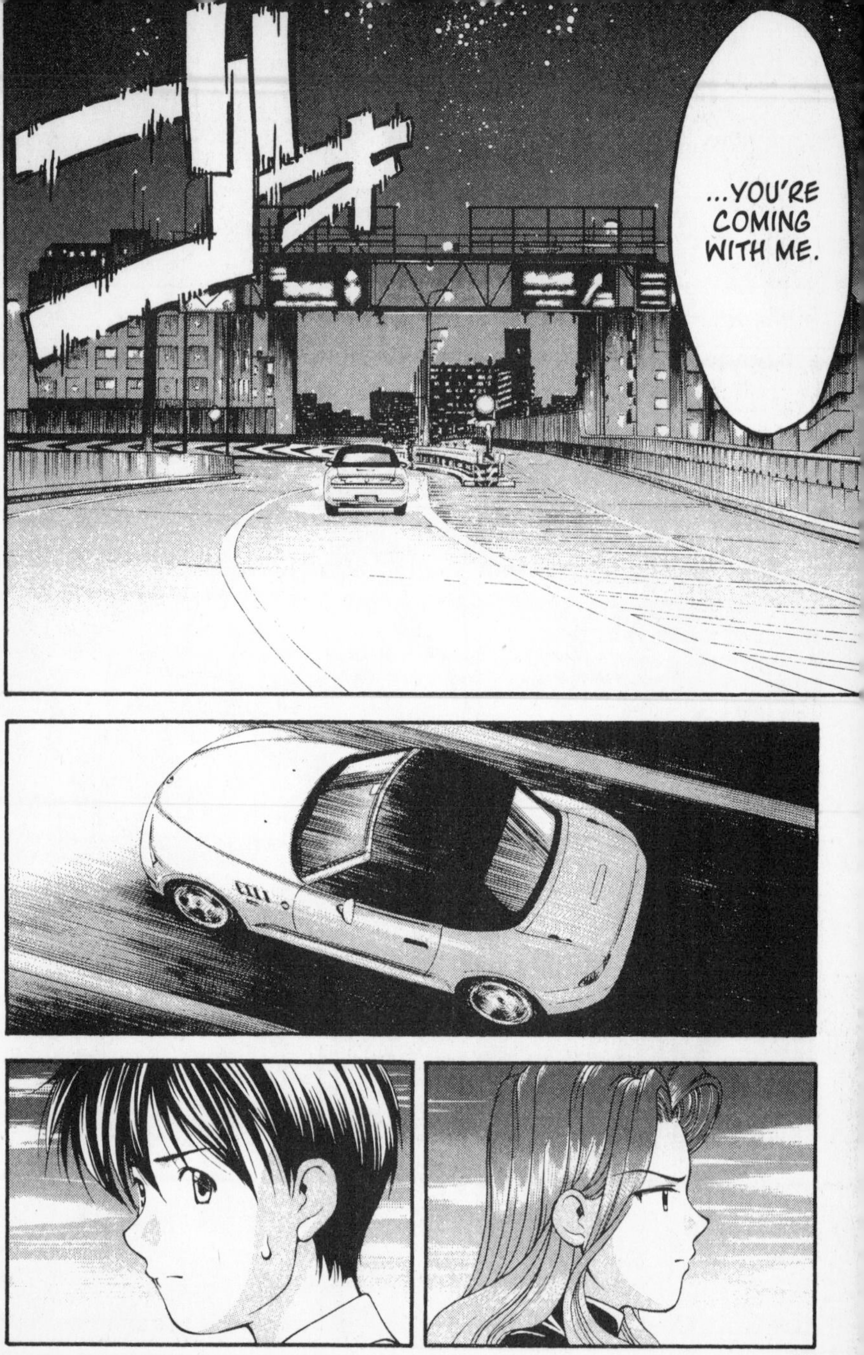
...YOU'RE COMING WITH ME.

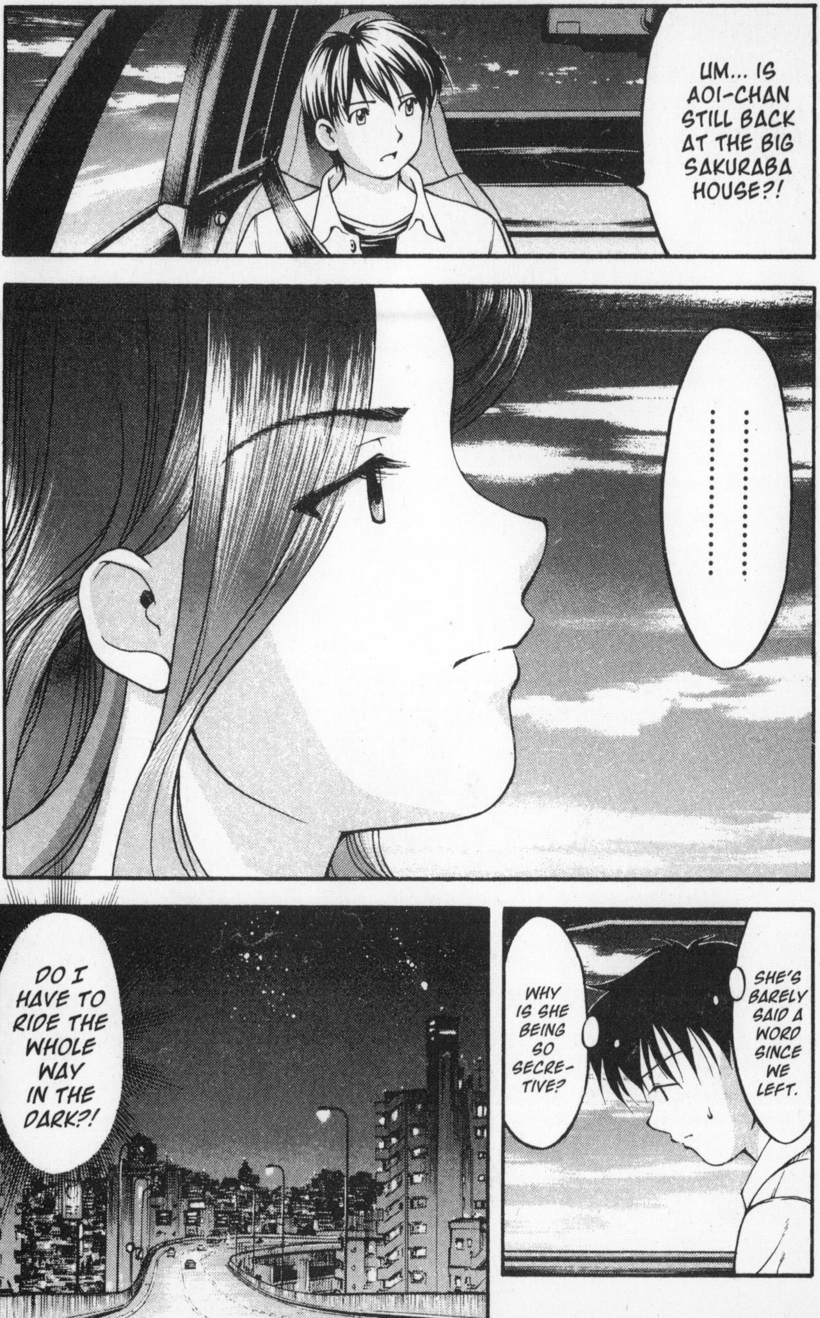
UM... IS AOI-CHAN STILL BACK AT THE BIG SAKURABA HOUSE?!
......
SHE'S BARELY SAID A WORD SINCE WE LEFT.
WHY IS SHE BEING SO SECRE-TIVE?
DO I HAVE TO RIDE THE WHOLE WAY IN THE DARK?!

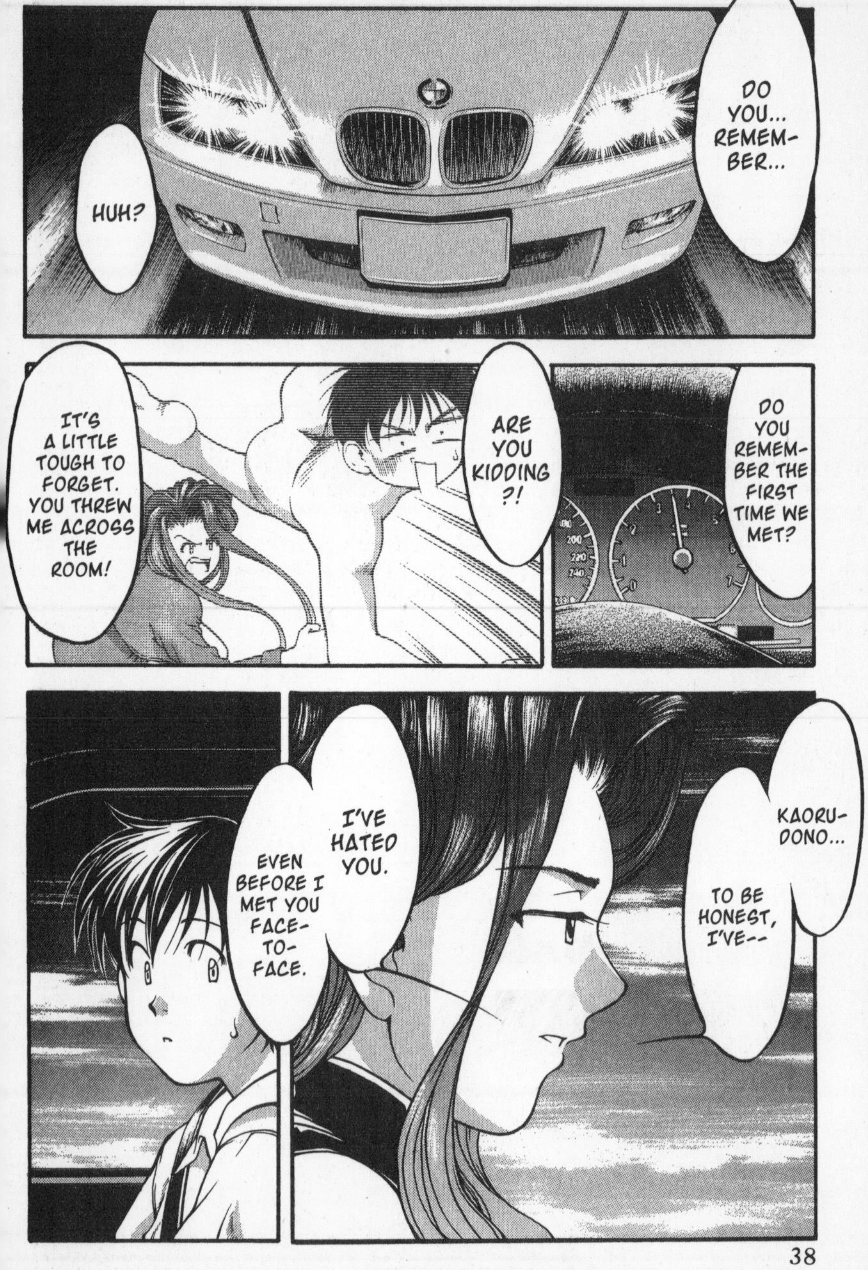
DO YOU... REMEMBER...
HUH?
DO YOU REMEMBER THE FIRST TIME WE MET?
ARE YOU KIDDING?!
IT'S A LITTLE TOUGH TO FORGET. YOU THREW ME ACROSS THE ROOM!
KAORU-DONO...
TO BE HONEST, I'VE--
I'VE HATED YOU.
EVEN BEFORE I MET YOU FACE-TO-FACE.

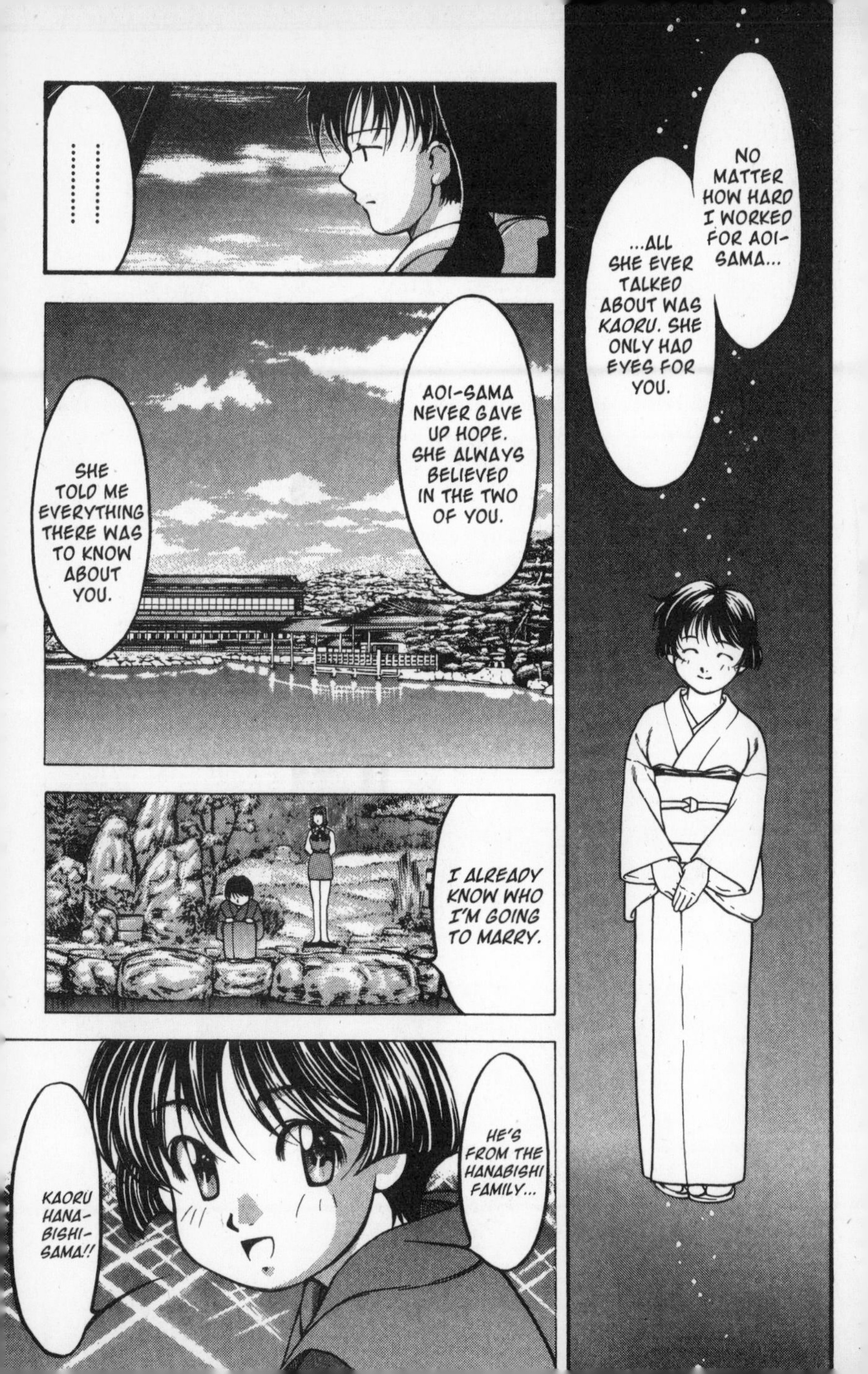
NO MATTER HOW HARD I WORKED FOR AOI-SAMA...
...ALL SHE EVER TALKED ABOUT WAS KAORU. SHE ONLY HAD EYES FOR YOU.
......
AOI-SAMA NEVER GAVE UP HOPE. SHE ALWAYS BELIEVED IN THE TWO OF YOU.
SHE TOLD ME EVERYTHING THERE WAS TO KNOW ABOUT YOU.
I ALREADY KNOW WHO I'M GOING TO MARRY.
HE'S FROM THE HANABISHI FAMILY...
KAORU HANA-BISHI-SAMA!!

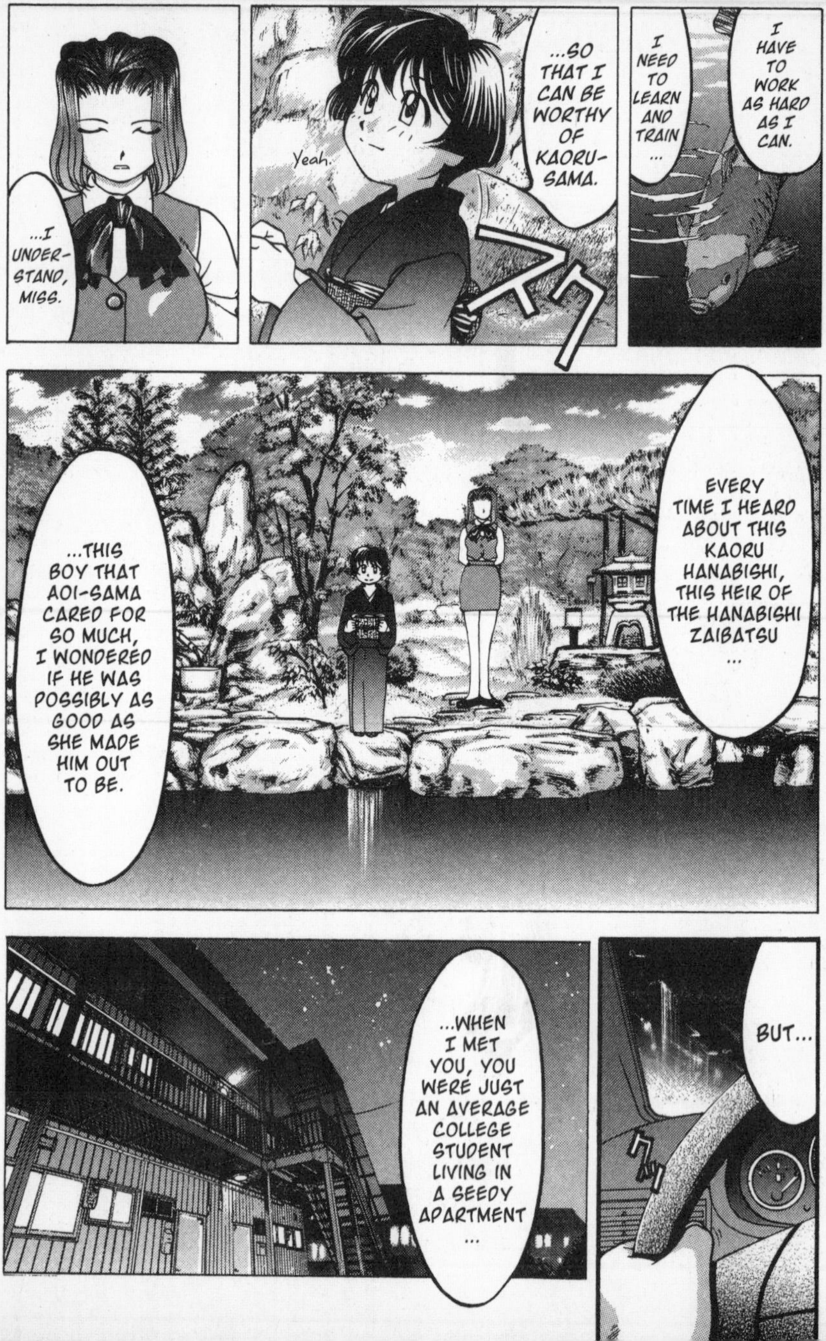
I HAVE TO WORK AS HARD AS I CAN.
I NEED TO LEARN AND TRAIN ...
...SO THAT I CAN BE WORTHY OF KAORU-SAMA.
Yeah.
...I UNDERSTAND, MISS.
EVERY TIME I HEARD ABOUT THIS KAORU HANABISHI, THIS HEIR OF THE HANABISHI ZAIBATSU ...
...THIS BOY THAT AOI-SAMA CARED FOR SO MUCH, I WONDERED IF HE WAS POSSIBLY AS GOOD AS SHE MADE HIM OUT TO BE.
BUT...
...WHEN I MET YOU, YOU WERE JUST AN AVERAGE COLLEGE STUDENT LIVING IN A SEEDY APARTMENT ...

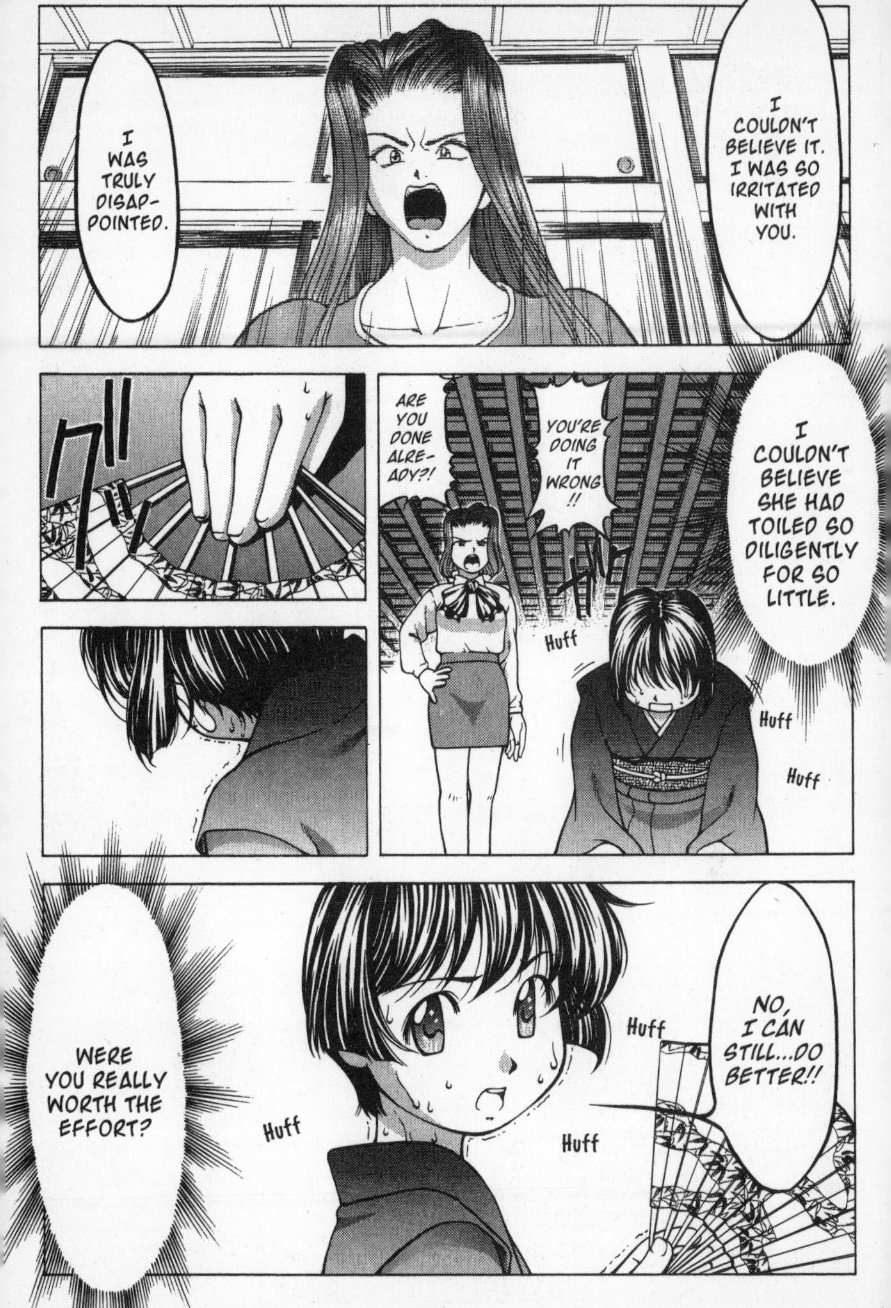
I COULDN'T BELIEVE IT. I WAS SO IRRITATED WITH YOU.
I WAS TRULY DISAP-POINTED.
I COULDN'T BELIEVE SHE HAD TOILED SO DILIGENTLY FOR SO LITTLE.
YOU'RE DOING IT WRONG!!
ARE YOU DONE ALREADY?!
Huff
Huff
Huff
NO, I CAN STILL...DO BETTER!!
Huff
Huff
Huff
WERE YOU REALLY WORTH THE EFFORT?

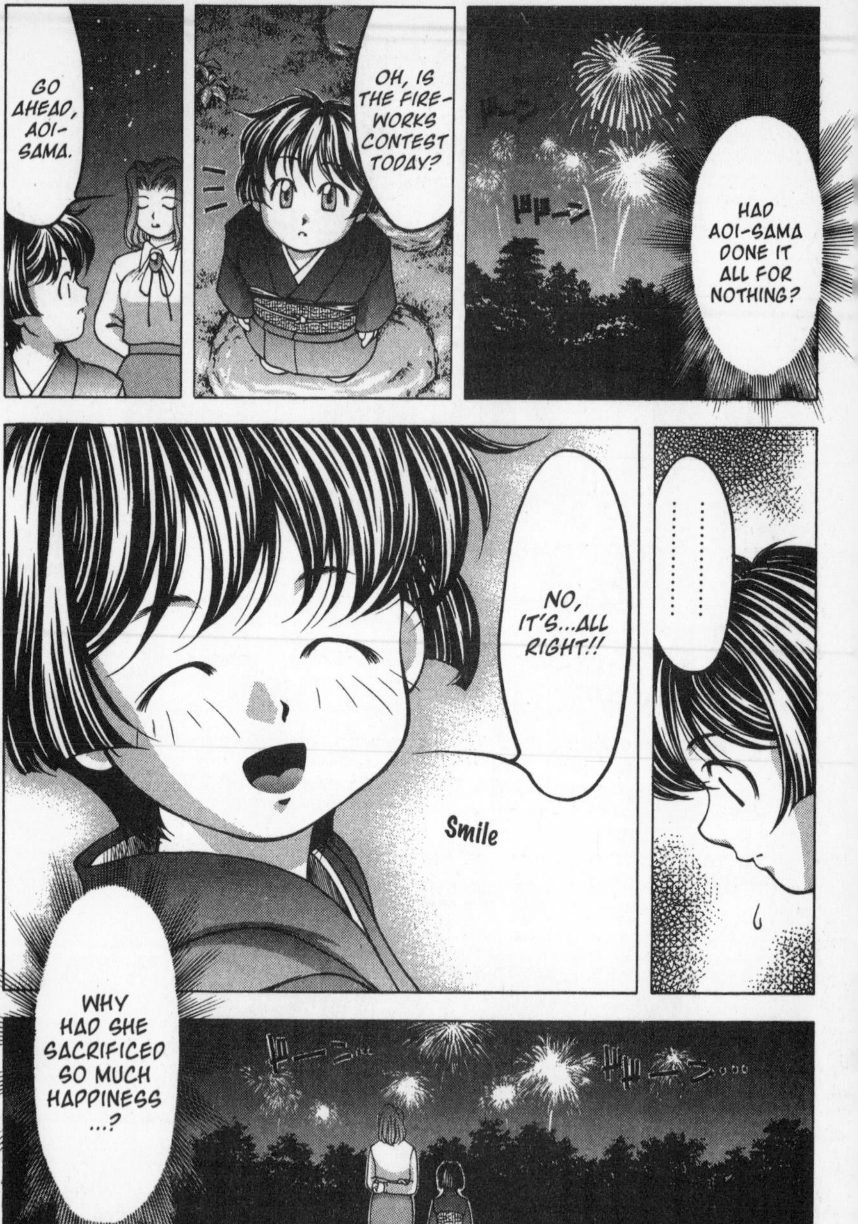
HAD AOI-SAMA DONE IT ALL FOR NOTHING?
OH, IS THE FIRE-WORKS CONTEST TODAY?
GO AHEAD, AOI-SAMA.
......
NO, IT'S...ALL RIGHT!!
Smile
WHY HAD SHE SACRIFICED SO MUCH HAPPINESS ...?

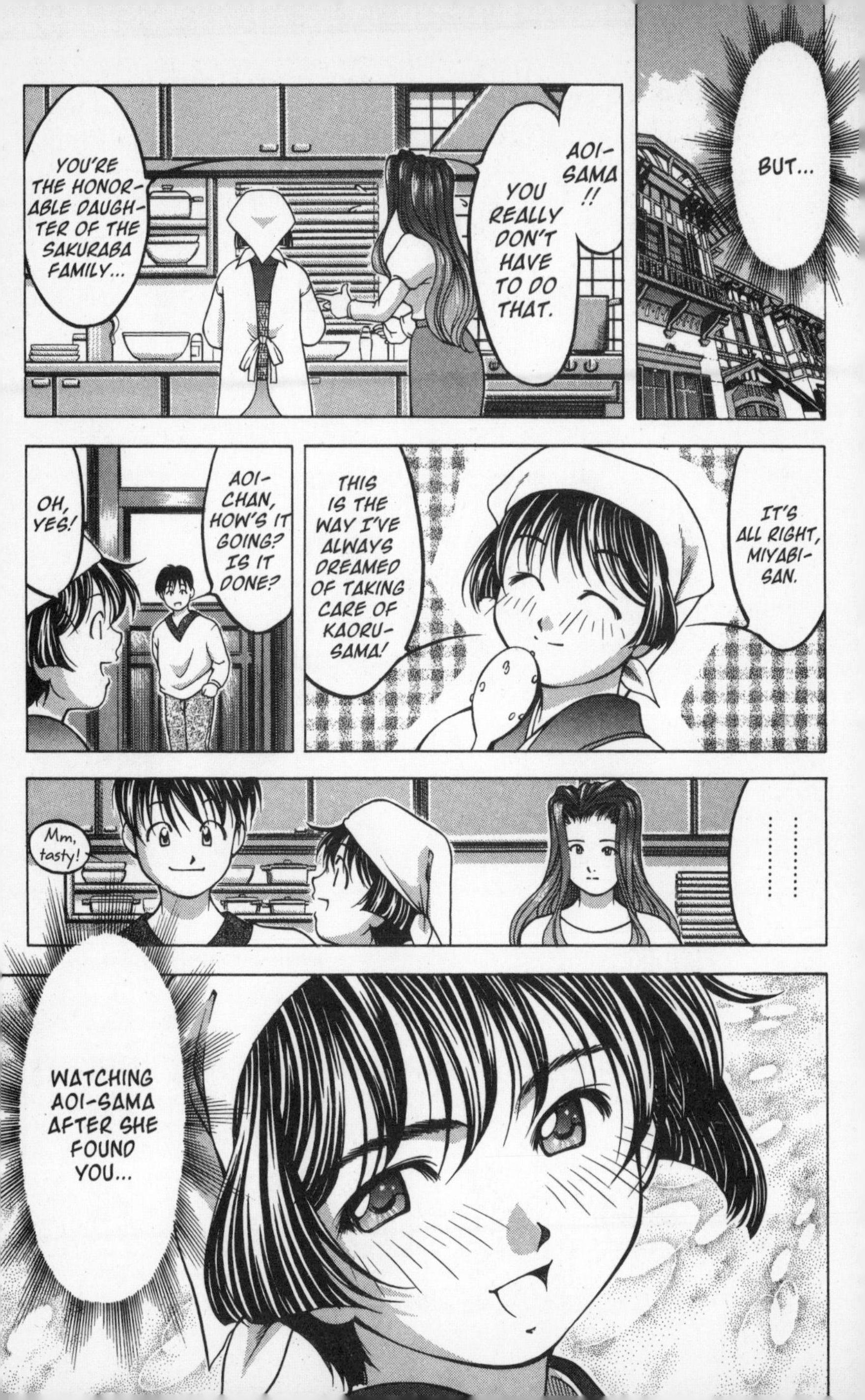
BUT...
AOI-SAMA!!
YOU REALLY DON'T HAVE TO DO THAT.
YOU'RE THE HONORABLE DAUGHTER OF THE SAKURABA FAMILY...
IT'S ALL RIGHT, MIYABI-SAN.
THIS IS THE WAY I'VE ALWAYS DREAMED OF TAKING CARE OF KAORU-SAMA!
AOI-CHAN, HOW'S IT GOING? IS IT DONE?
OH, YES!
......
Mm, tasty!
WATCHING AOI-SAMA AFTER SHE FOUND YOU...

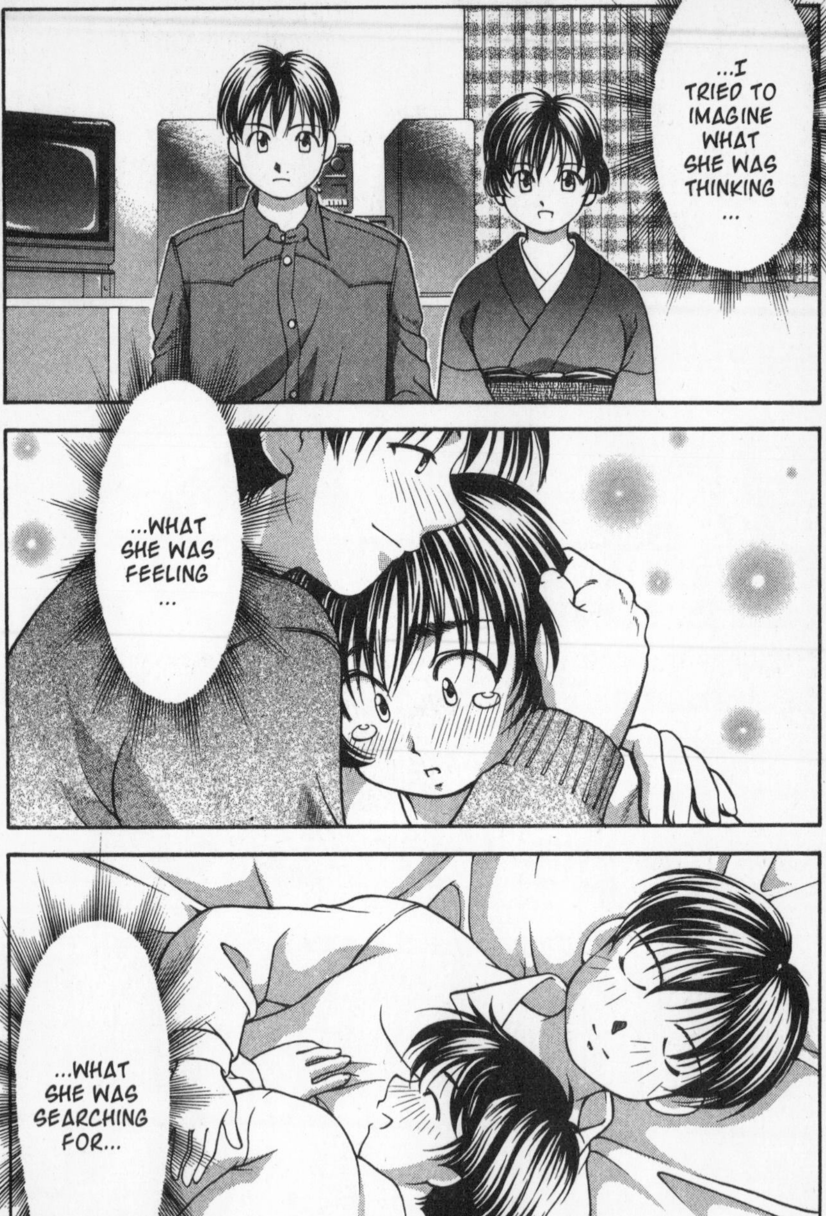
...I TRIED TO IMAGINE WHAT SHE WAS THINKING ...
...WHAT SHE WAS FEELING ...
...WHAT SHE WAS SEARCHING FOR...

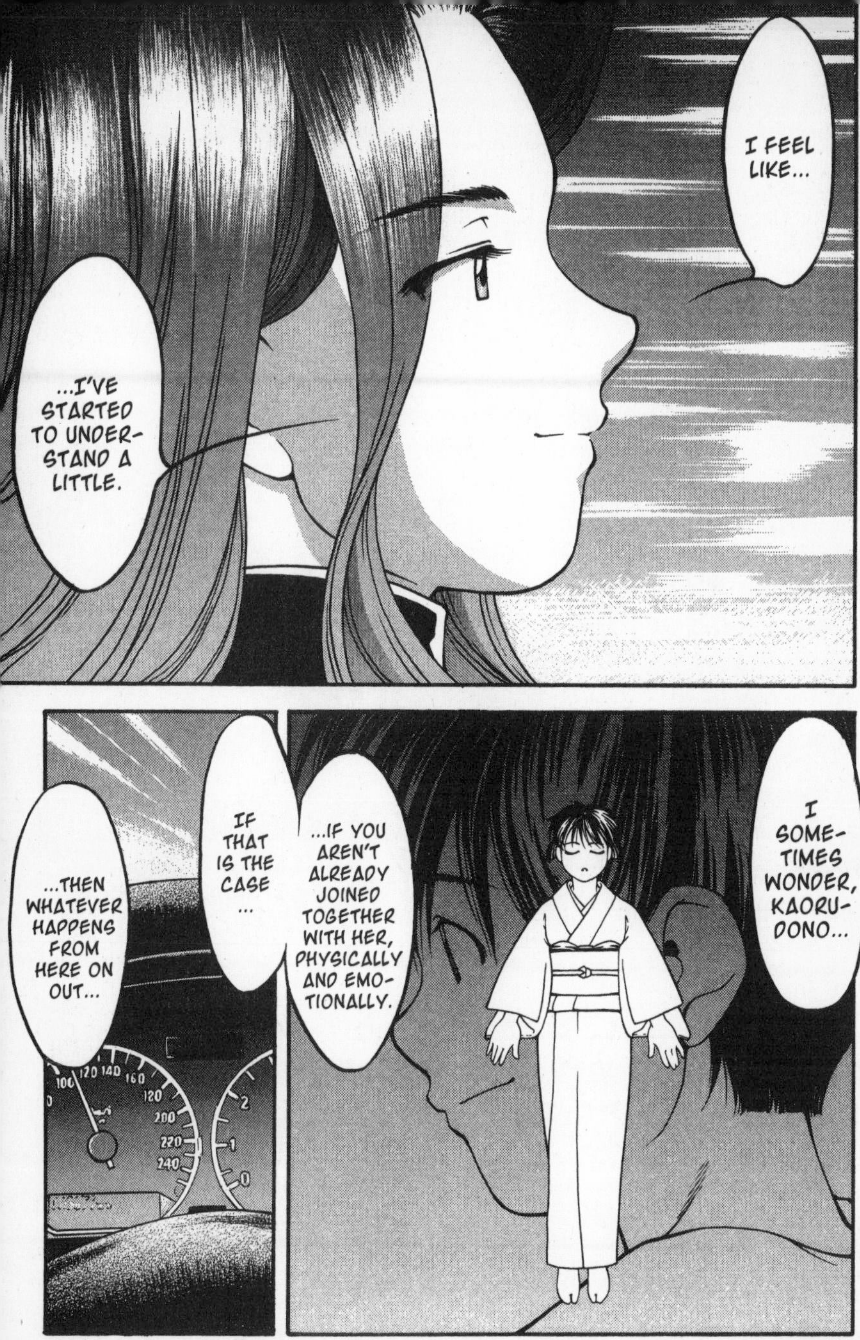
I FEEL LIKE...
...I'VE STARTED TO UNDER-STAND A LITTLE.
I SOME-TIMES WONDER, KAORU-DONO...
...IF YOU AREN'T ALREADY JOINED TOGETHER WITH HER, PHYSICALLY AND EMO-TIONALLY.
IF THAT IS THE CASE ...
...THEN WHATEVER HAPPENS FROM HERE ON OUT...

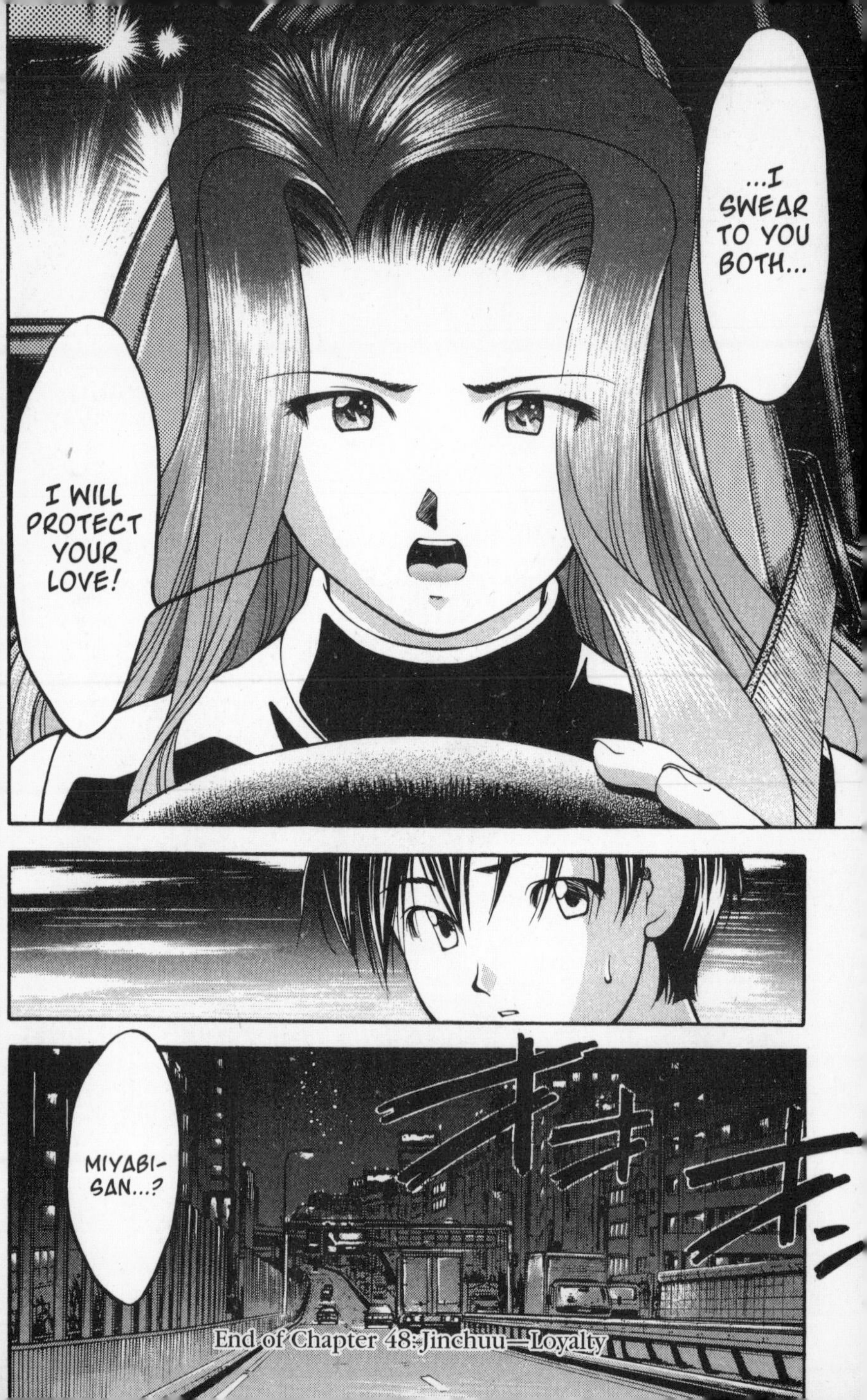
...I SWEAR TO YOU BOTH...
I WILL PROTECT YOUR LOVE!
MIYABI-SAN...?
End of Chapter 48: Jinchuu—Loyalty

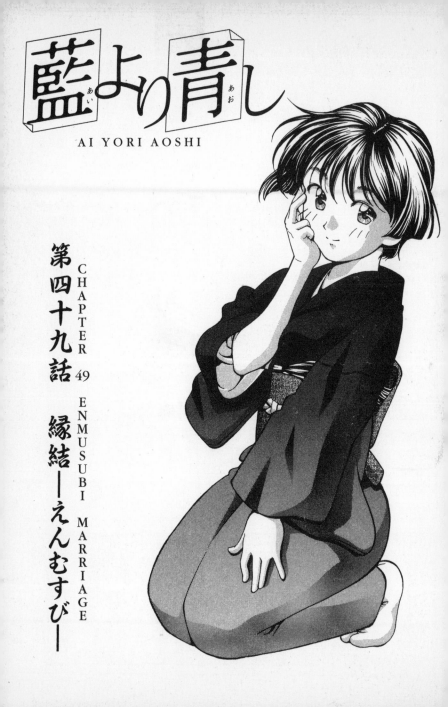

# 藍より青し

AI YORI AOSHI

## 第四十九話 縁結―えんむすび―

CHAPTER 49 ENMUSUBI MARRIAGE

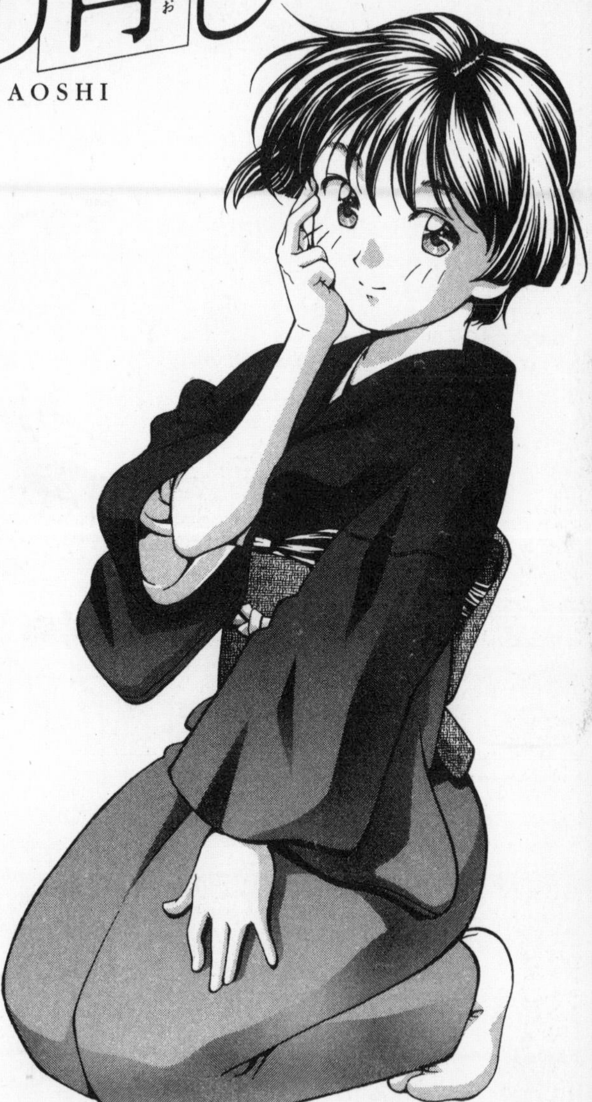

# Ai-Ao Theatre Part 12

## Beloved Car

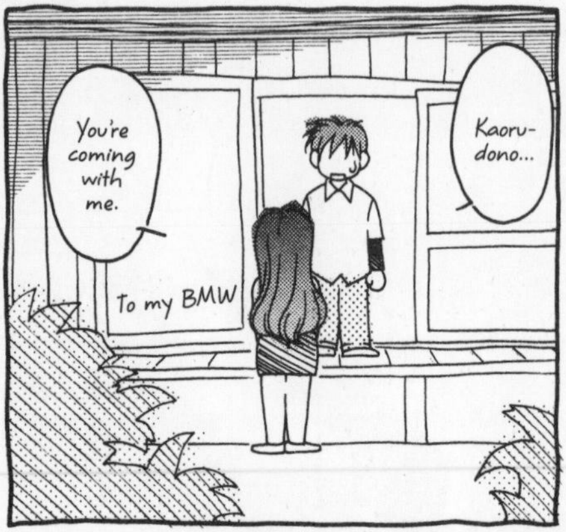
Kaoru-dono...
You're coming with me.
To my BMW

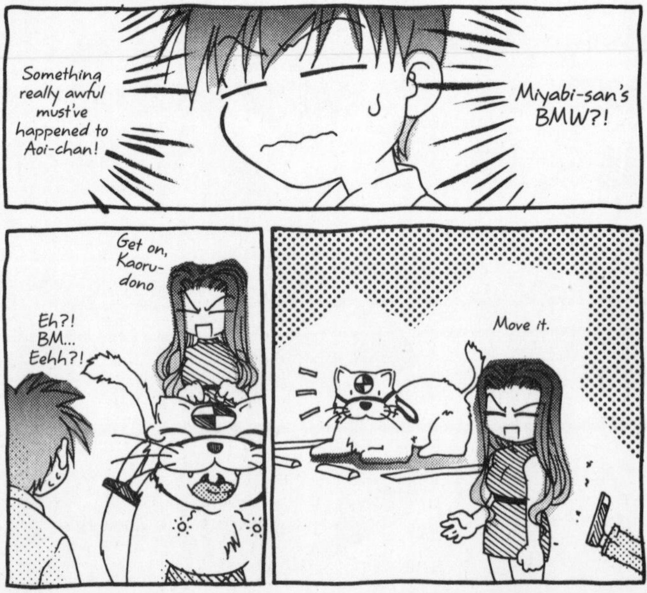
Miyabi-san's BMW?!
Something really awful must've happened to Aoi-chan!
Move it.
Get on, Kaoru-dono
Eh?! BM... Eehh?!

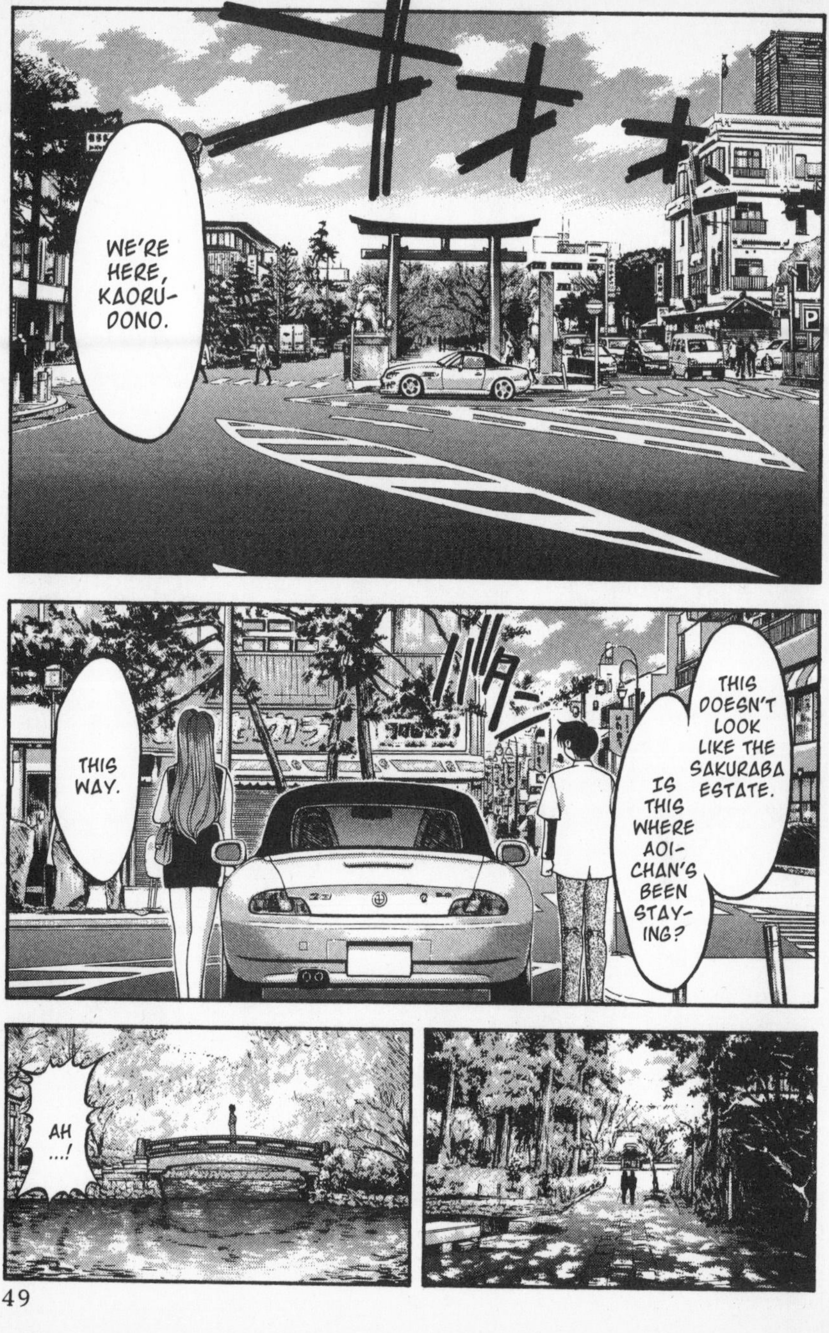
WE'RE HERE, KAORU-DONO.
THIS DOESN'T LOOK LIKE THE SAKURABA ESTATE.
IS THIS WHERE AOI-CHAN'S BEEN STAYING?
THIS WAY.
AH ...!

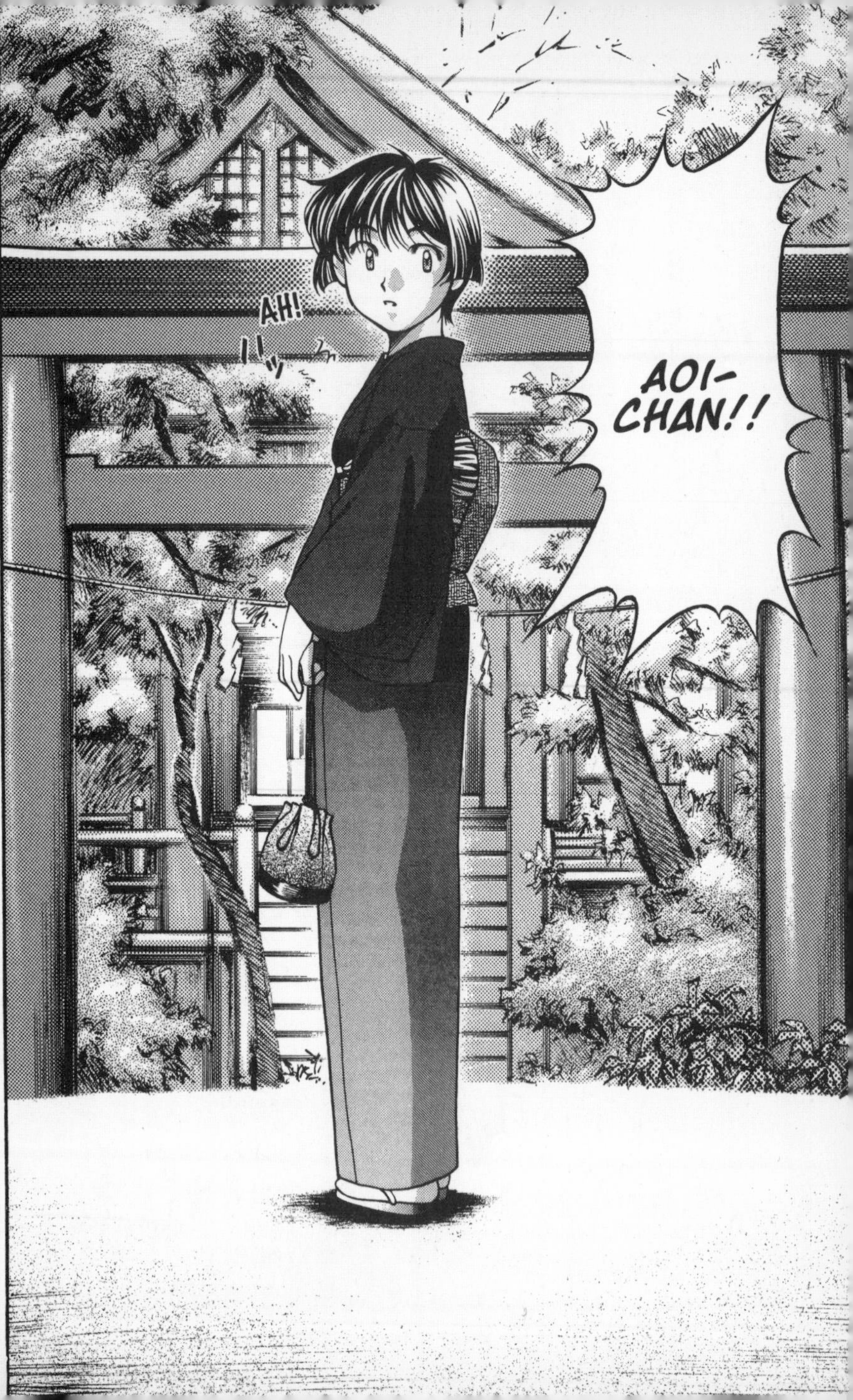
AOI-
CHAN!!
AH!

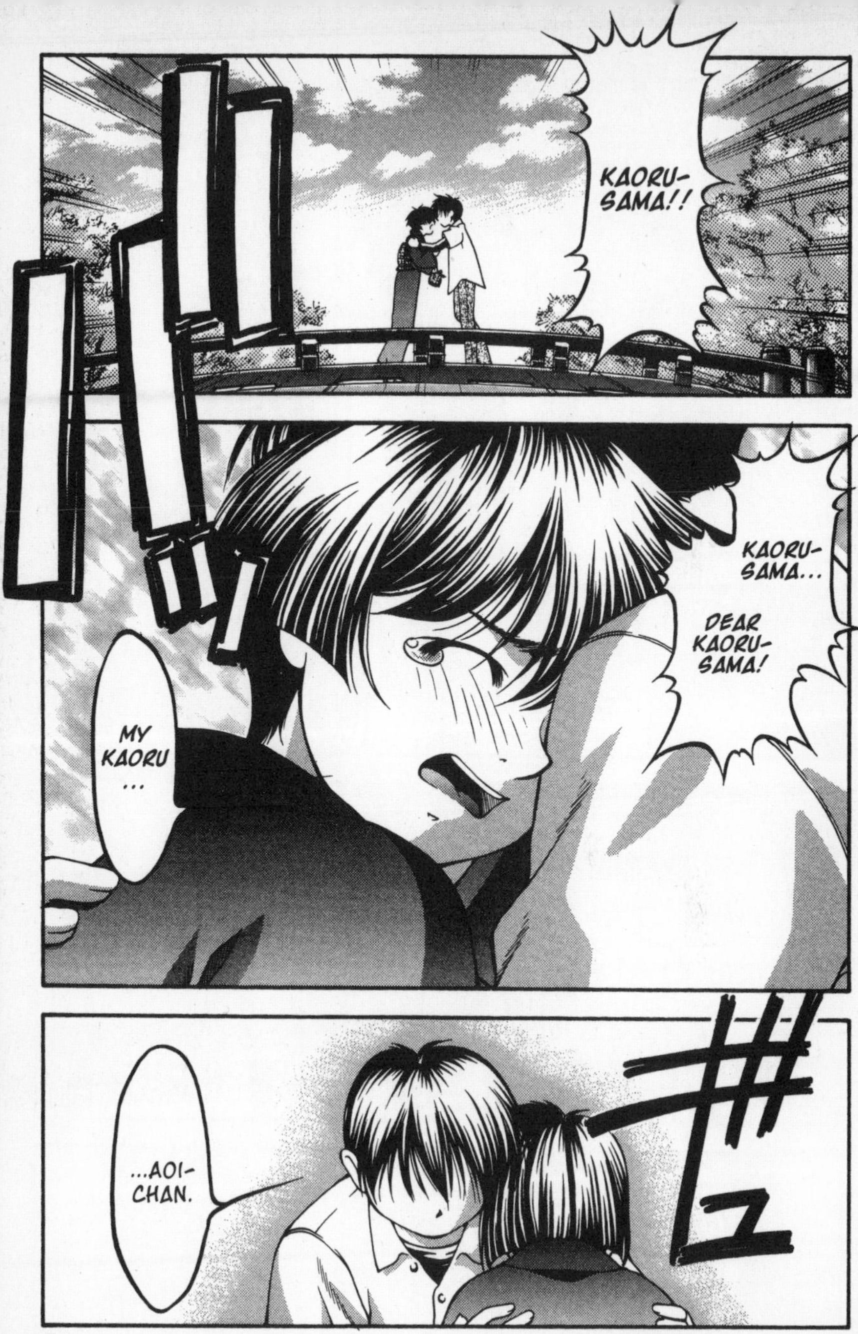
KAORU-SAMA!!
KAORU-SAMA...
DEAR KAORU-SAMA!
MY KAORU ...
...AOI-CHAN.

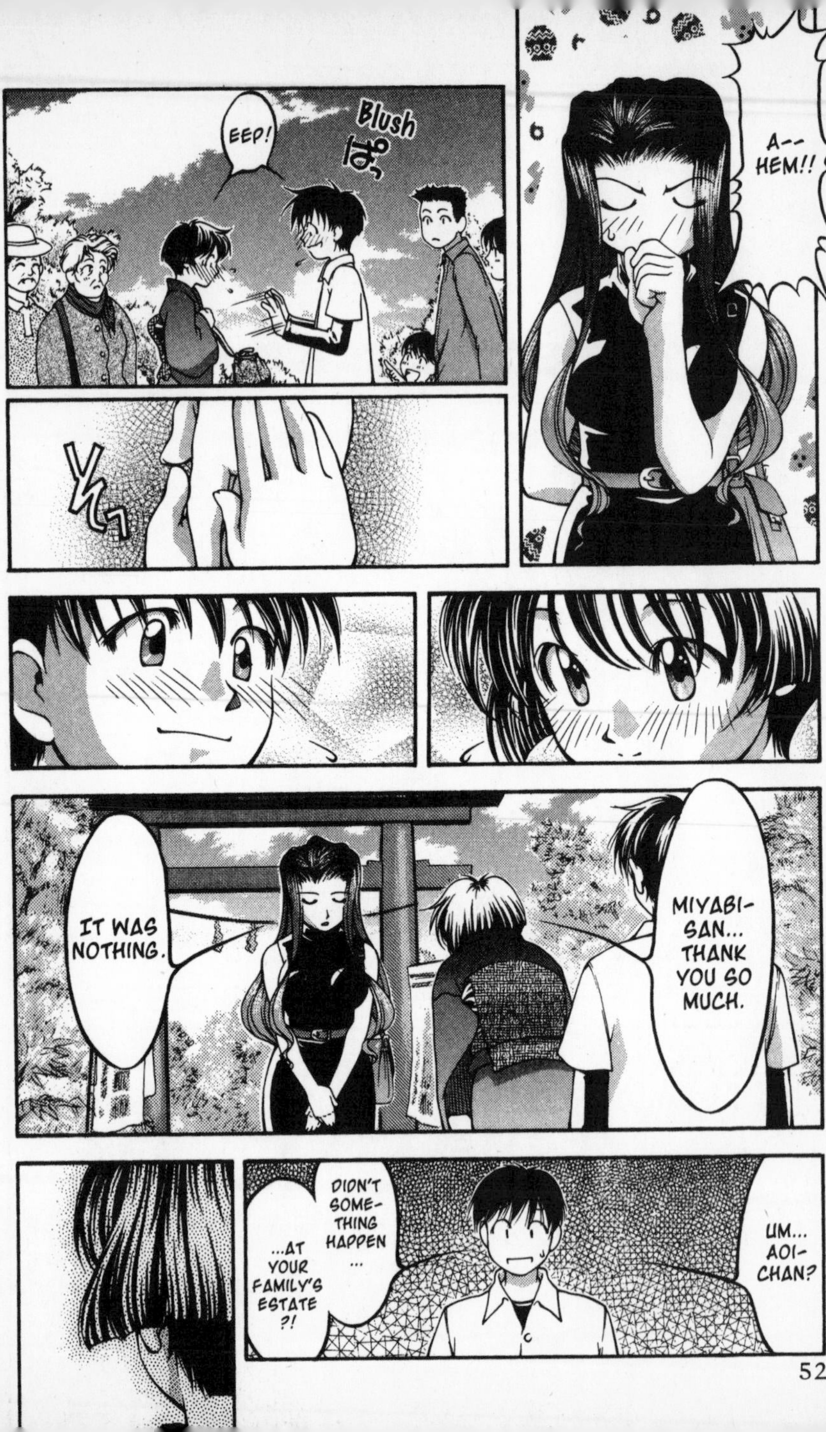
A-- HEM!!
EEP!
Blush
MIYABI-SAN... THANK YOU SO MUCH.
IT WAS NOTHING.
UM... AOI-CHAN?
DIDN'T SOME-THING HAPPEN ...
...AT YOUR FAMILY'S ESTATE ?!

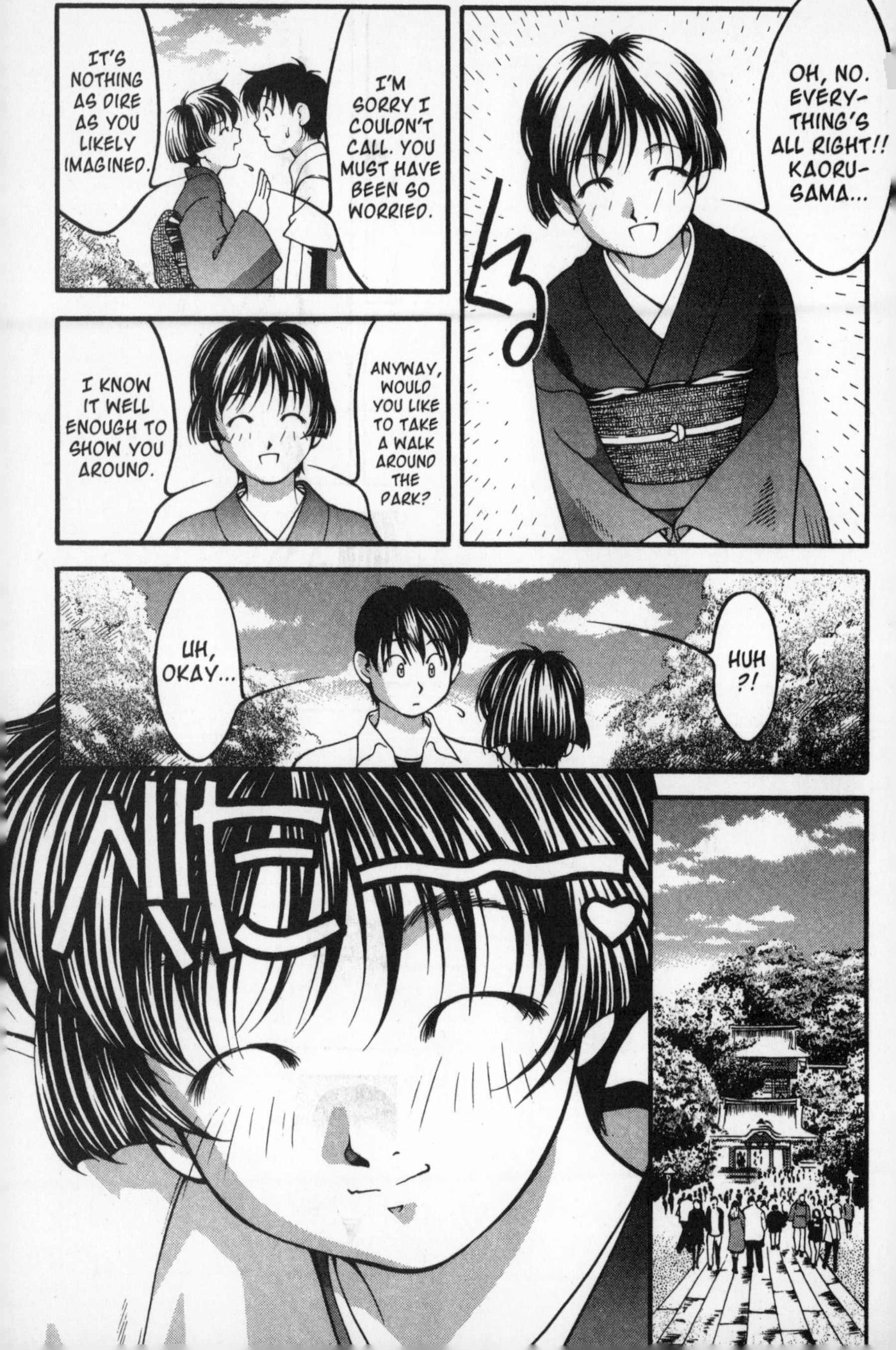
OH, NO. EVERYTHING'S ALL RIGHT!! KAORU-SAMA...
I'M SORRY I COULDN'T CALL. YOU MUST HAVE BEEN SO WORRIED.
IT'S NOTHING AS DIRE AS YOU LIKELY IMAGINED.
ANYWAY, WOULD YOU LIKE TO TAKE A WALK AROUND THE PARK?
I KNOW IT WELL ENOUGH TO SHOW YOU AROUND.
HUH?!
UH, OKAY...

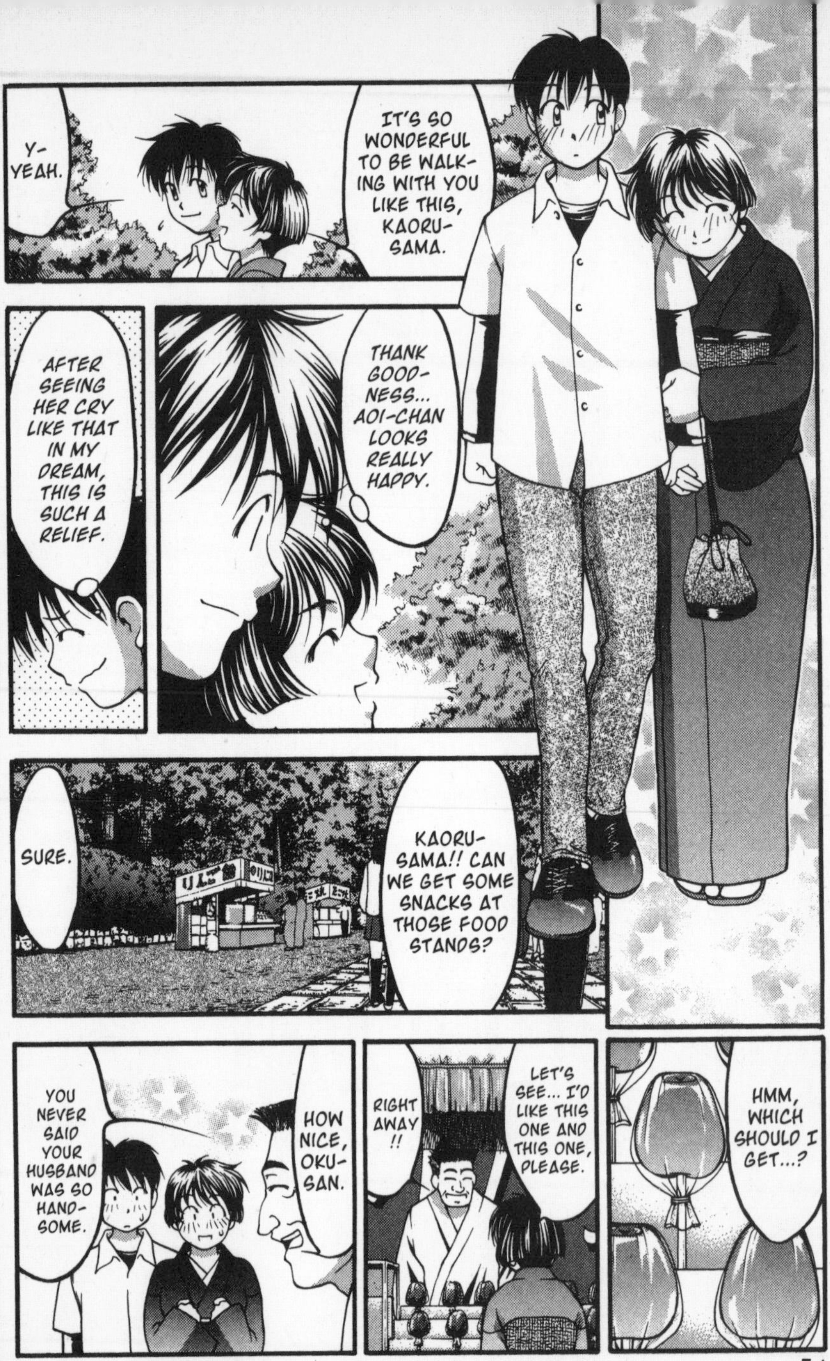
IT'S SO WONDERFUL TO BE WALKING WITH YOU LIKE THIS, KAORU-SAMA.
Y-YEAH.
THANK GOODNESS... AOI-CHAN LOOKS REALLY HAPPY.
AFTER SEEING HER CRY LIKE THAT IN MY DREAM, THIS IS SUCH A RELIEF.
KAORU-SAMA!! CAN WE GET SOME SNACKS AT THOSE FOOD STANDS?
SURE.
HMM, WHICH SHOULD I GET...?
LET'S SEE... I'D LIKE THIS ONE AND THIS ONE, PLEASE.
RIGHT AWAY!!
HOW NICE, OKU-SAN.
YOU NEVER SAID YOUR HUSBAND WAS SO HANDSOME.

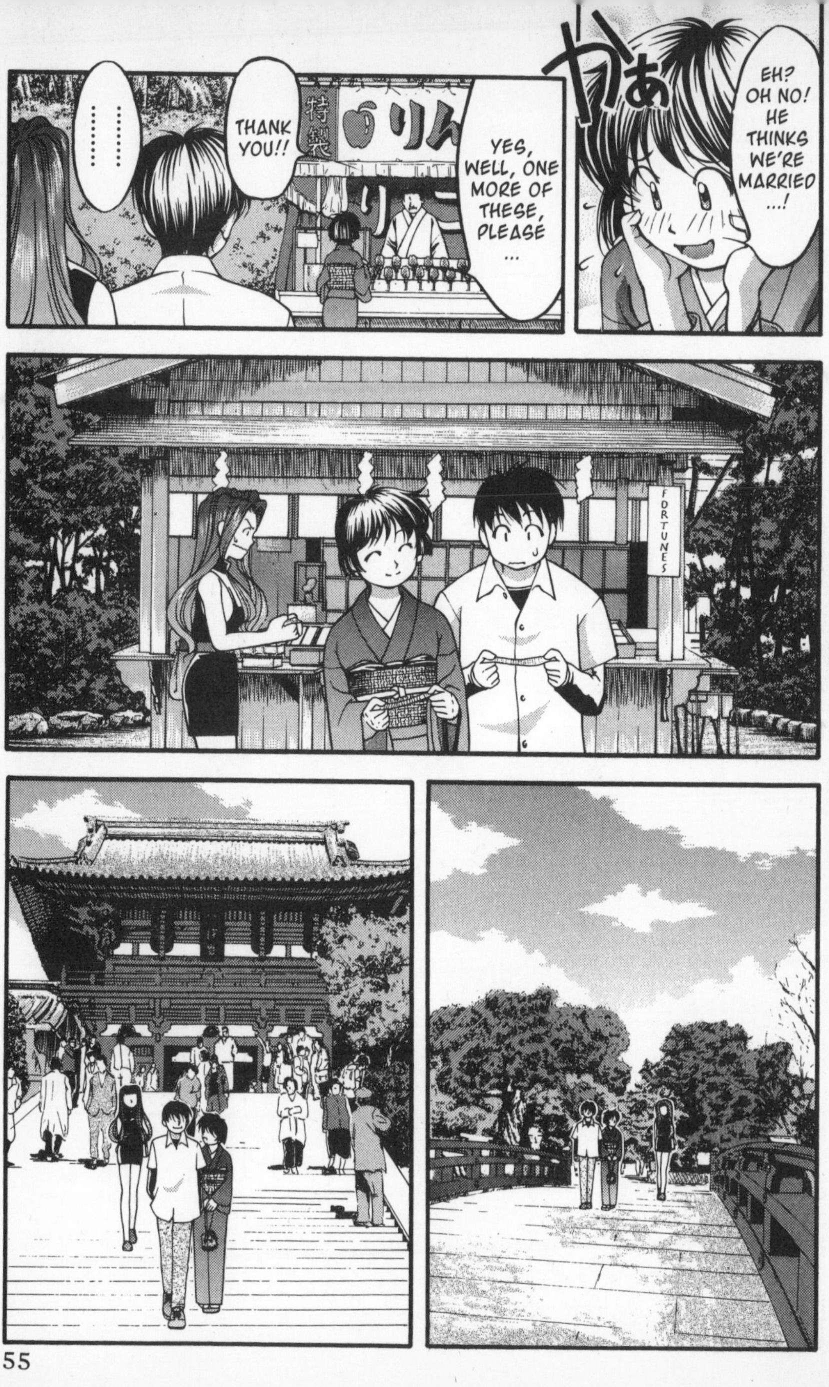
やぁ
EH? OH NO! HE THINKS WE'RE MARRIED ...!
YES, WELL, ONE MORE OF THESE, PLEASE ...
THANK YOU!!
特製
りん
......
FORTUNES

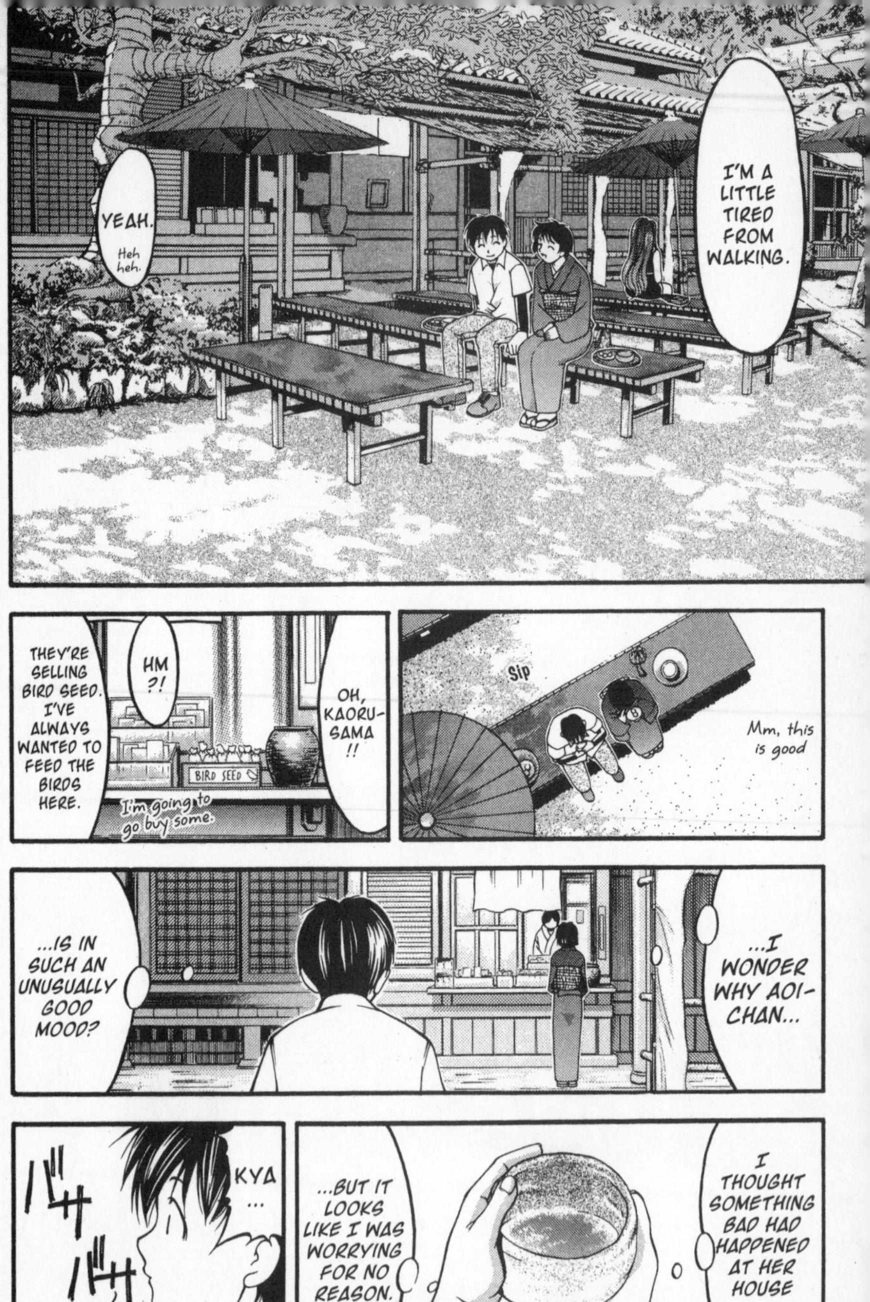

I'M A LITTLE TIRED FROM WALKING.
YEAH.
Heh heh.
Mm, this is good
Sip
OH, KAORU-SAMA!!
HM?!
THEY'RE SELLING BIRD SEED. I'VE ALWAYS WANTED TO FEED THE BIRDS HERE.
BIRD SEED
I'm going to go buy some.
...I WONDER WHY AOI-CHAN...
...IS IN SUCH AN UNUSUALLY GOOD MOOD?
I THOUGHT SOMETHING BAD HAD HAPPENED AT HER HOUSE...
...BUT IT LOOKS LIKE I WAS WORRYING FOR NO REASON.
KYA...
バサ
バサ

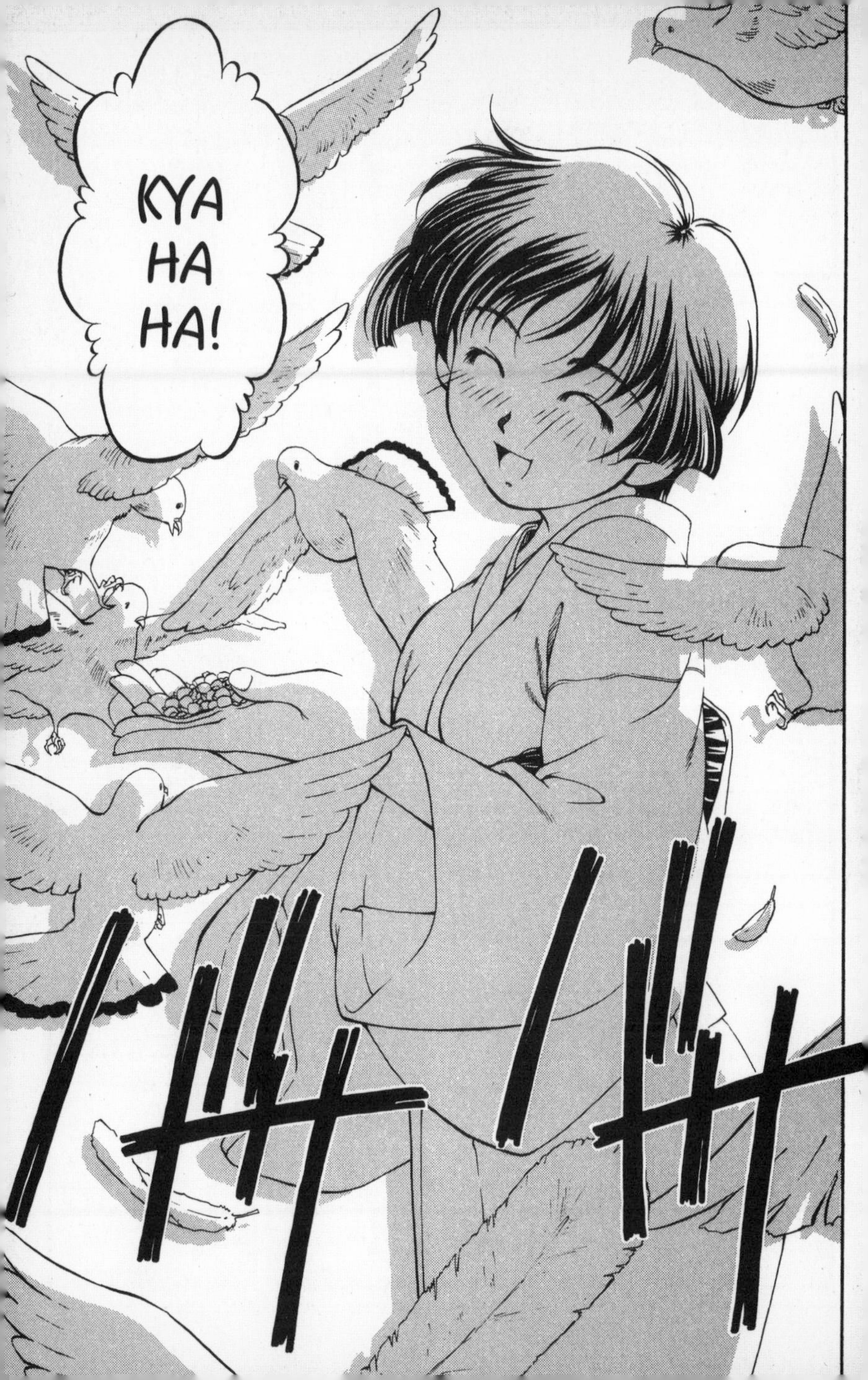
KYA HA HA!

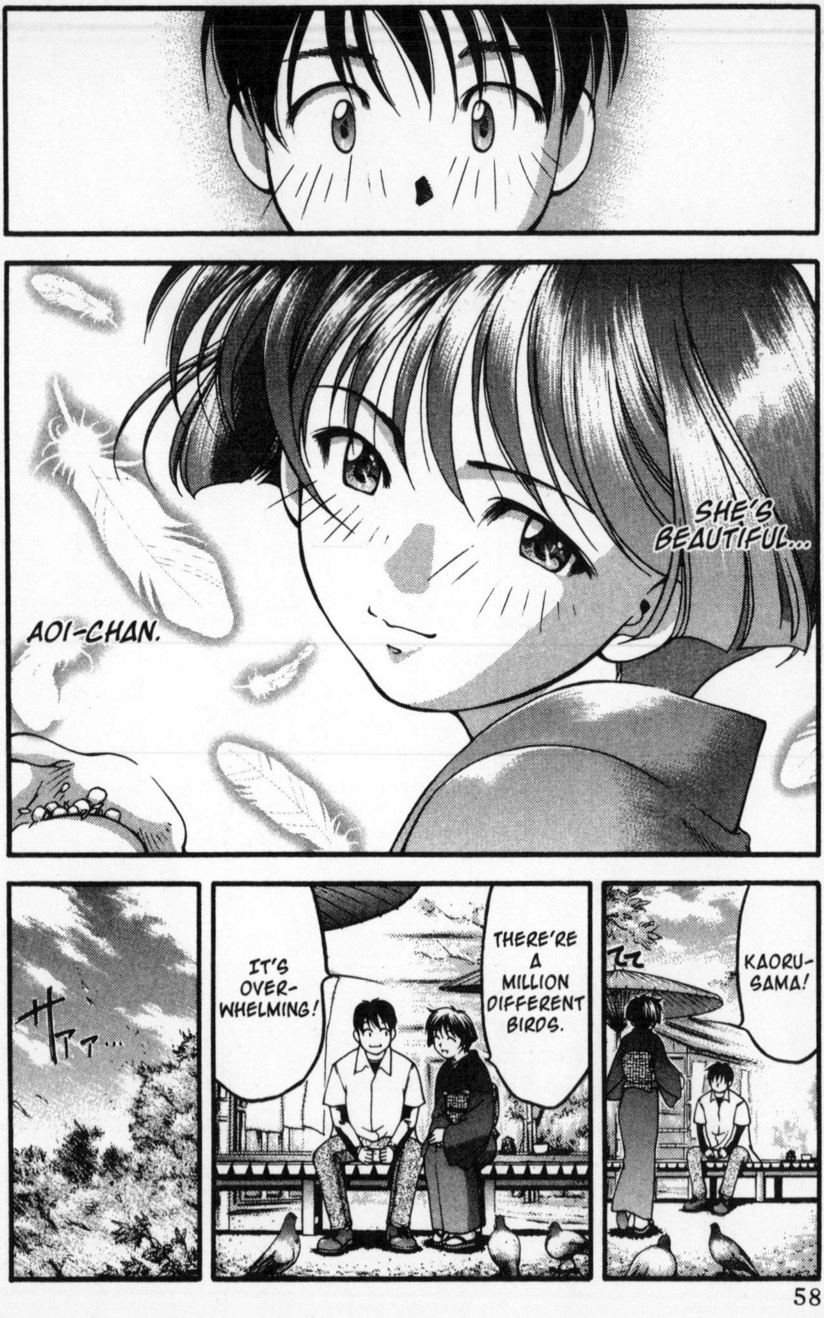
SHE'S BEAUTIFUL...
AOI-CHAN.
KAORU-SAMA!
THERE'RE A MILLION DIFFERENT BIRDS.
IT'S OVER-WHELMING!
サァァ...

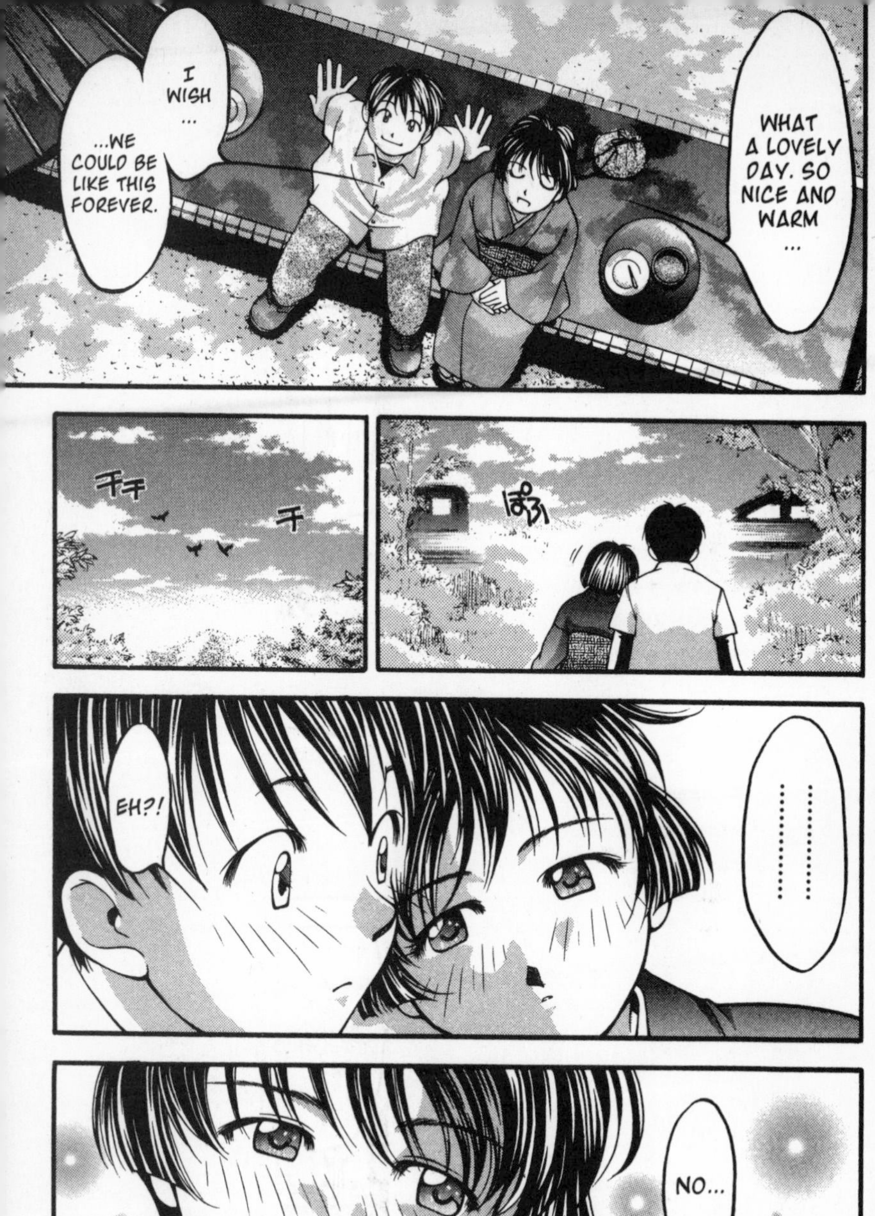
WHAT A LOVELY DAY. SO NICE AND WARM ...
I WISH ...
...WE COULD BE LIKE THIS FOREVER.
チチ
チ
......
......
EH?!
NO...

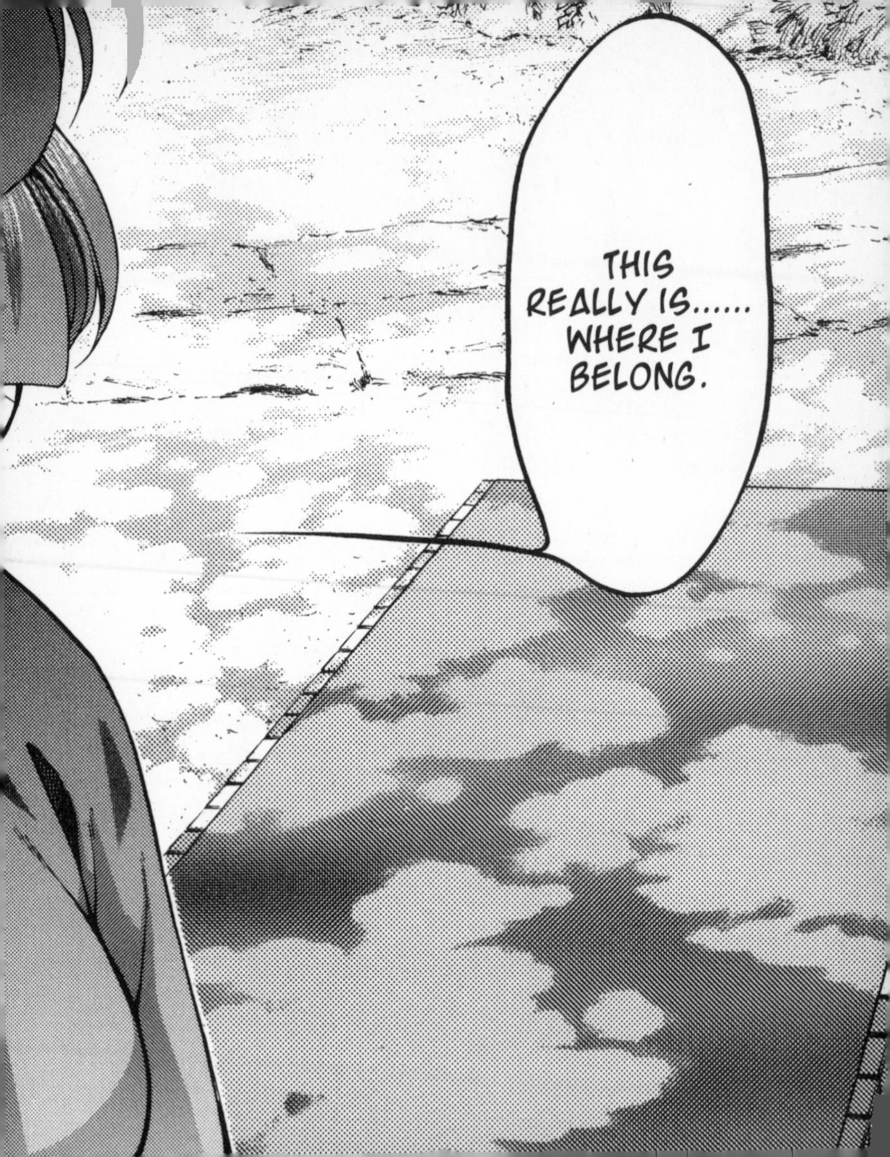
THIS REALLY IS...... WHERE I BELONG.

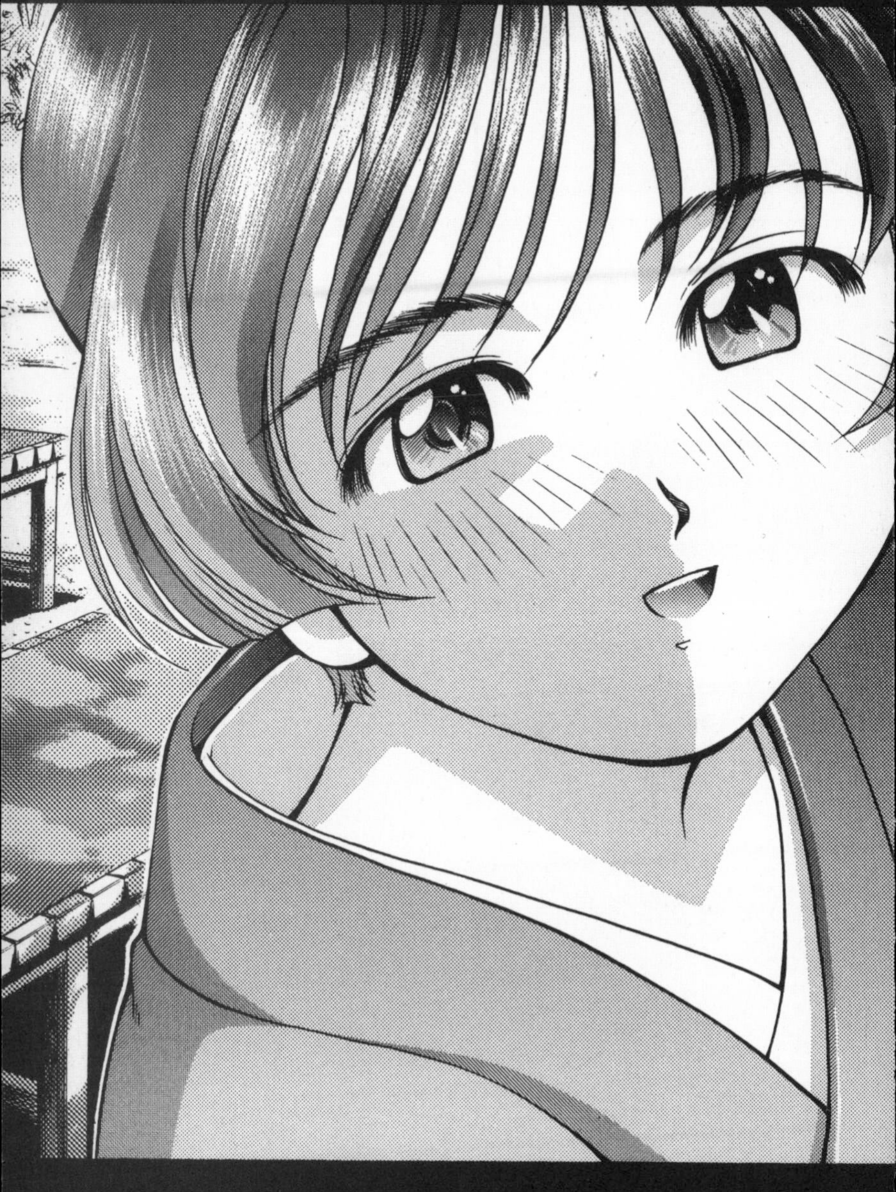

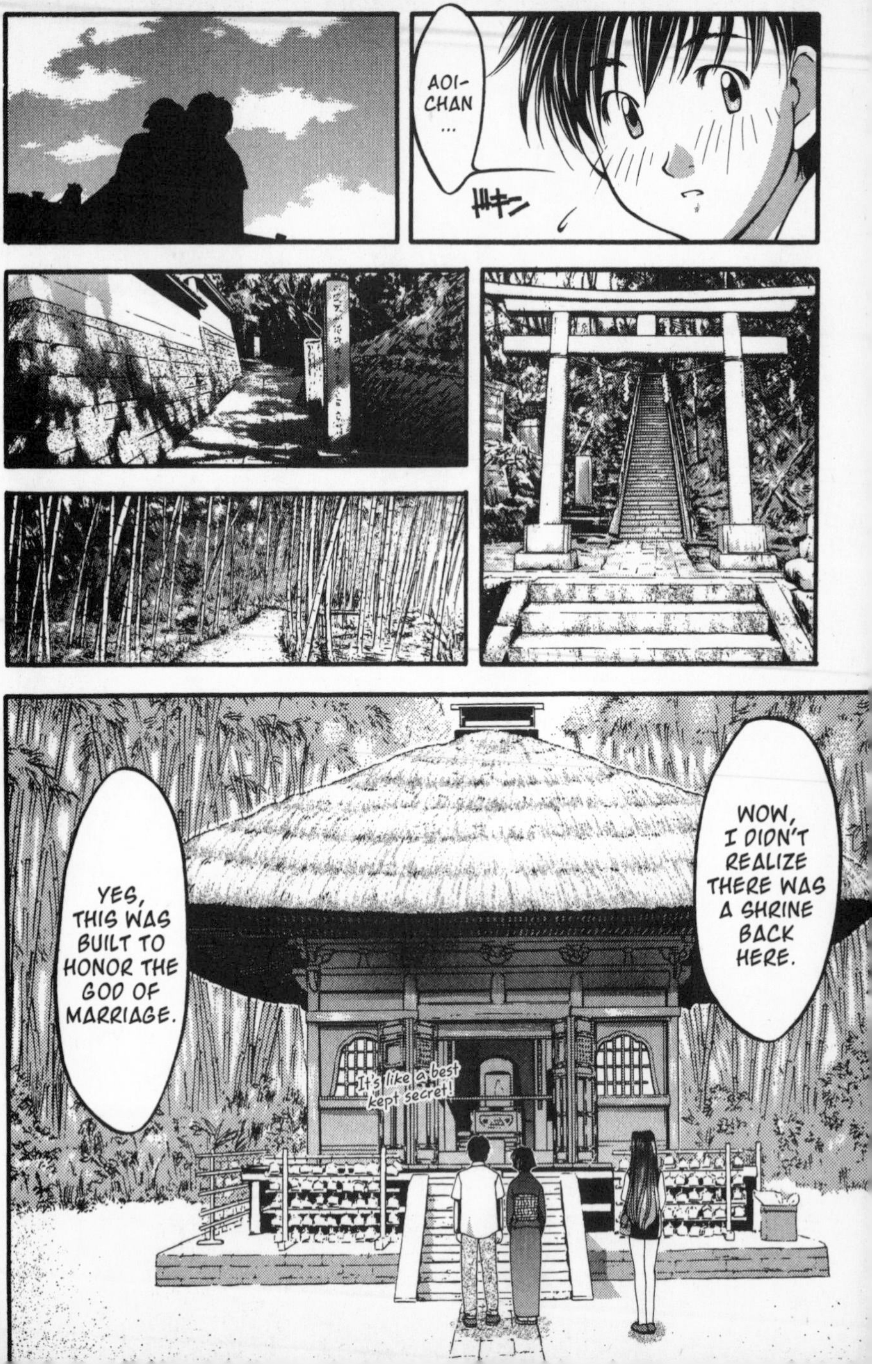
AOI-CHAN ...
WOW, I DIDN'T REALIZE THERE WAS A SHRINE BACK HERE.
It's like a best kept secret!
YES, THIS WAS BUILT TO HONOR THE GOD OF MARRIAGE.

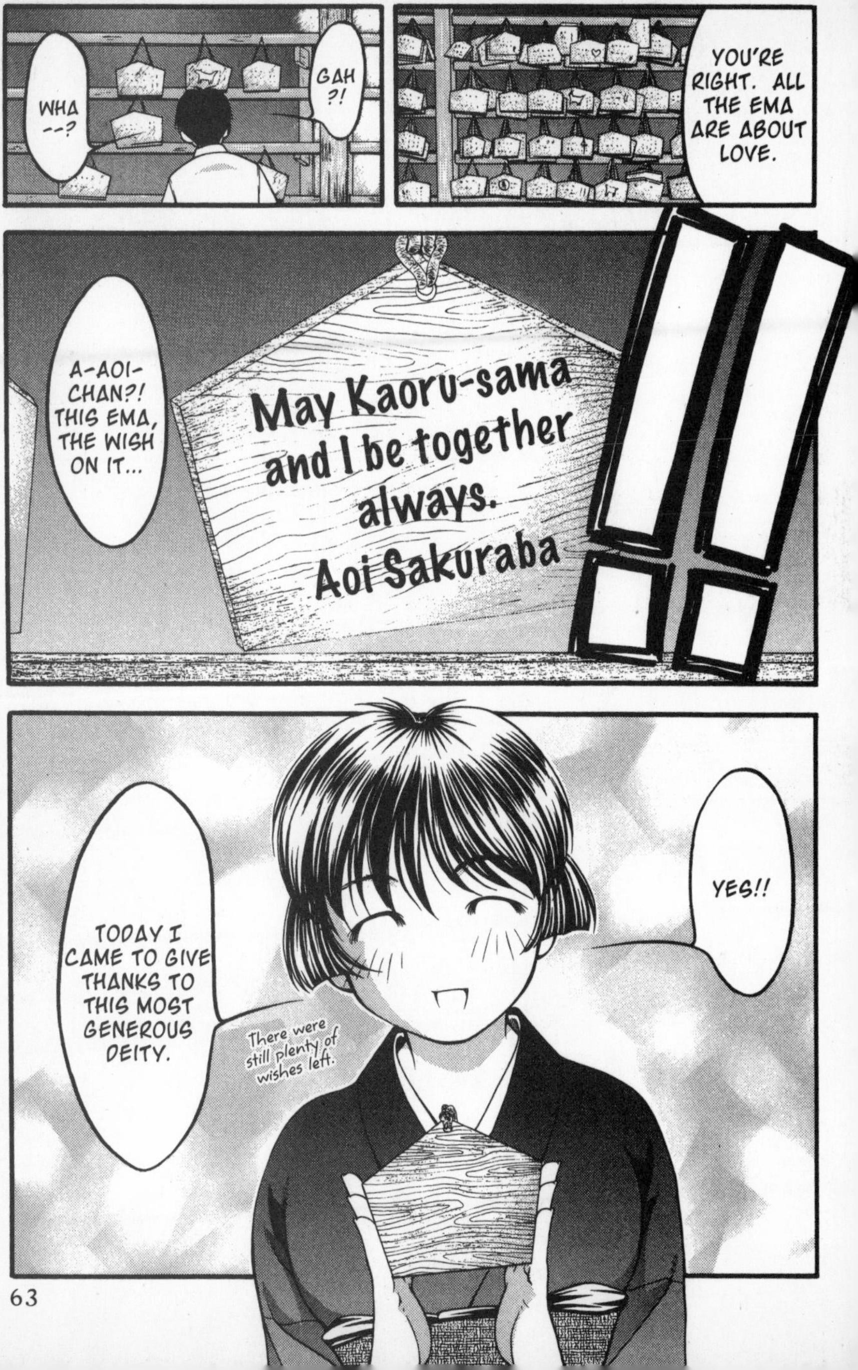
YOU'RE RIGHT. ALL THE EMA ARE ABOUT LOVE.
GAH ?!
WHA --?
May Kaoru-sama and I be together always. Aoi Sakuraba
A-AOI-CHAN?! THIS EMA, THE WISH ON IT...
YES!!
TODAY I CAME TO GIVE THANKS TO THIS MOST GENEROUS DEITY.
There were still plenty of wishes left.

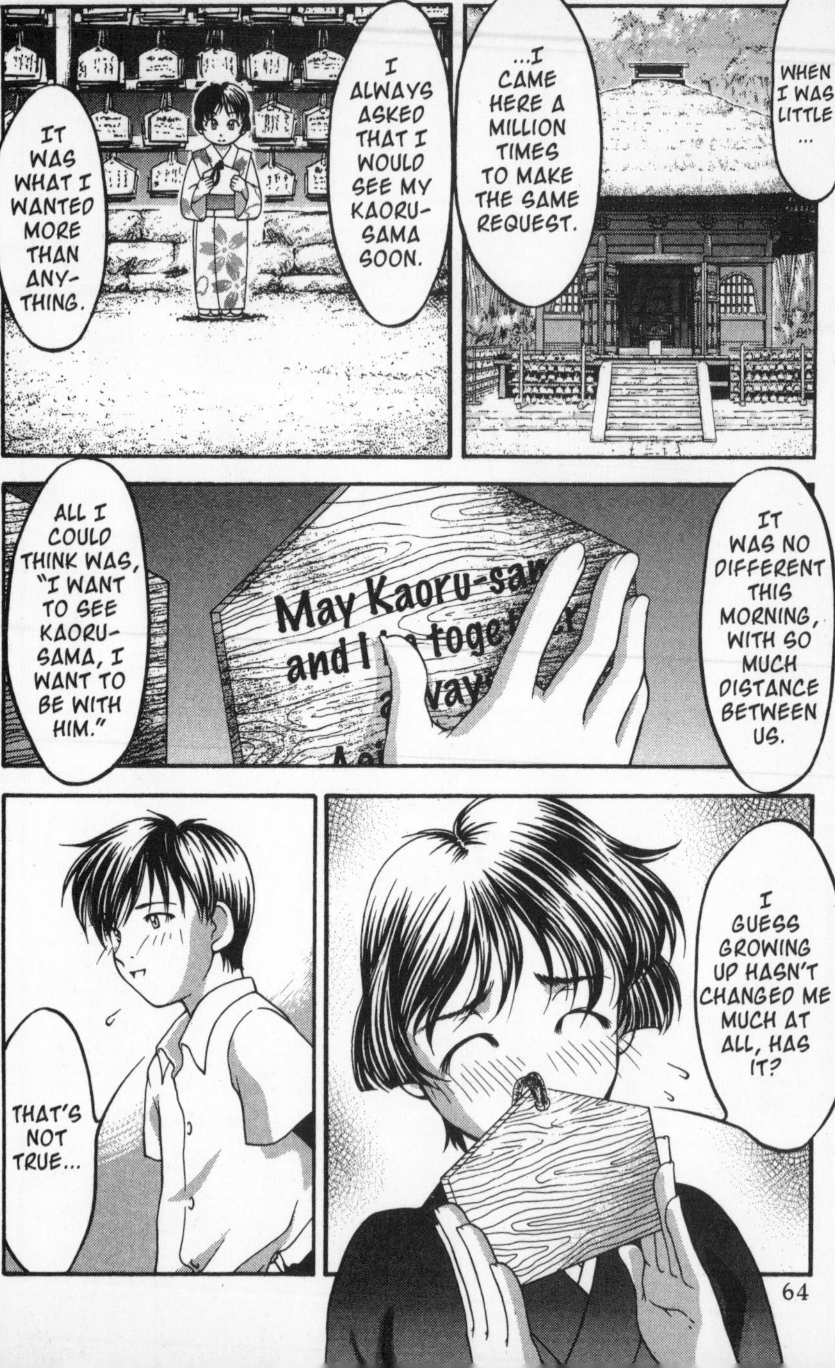
WHEN I WAS LITTLE ...
...I CAME HERE A MILLION TIMES TO MAKE THE SAME REQUEST.
I ALWAYS ASKED THAT I WOULD SEE MY KAORU-SAMA SOON.
IT WAS WHAT I WANTED MORE THAN ANY-THING.
IT WAS NO DIFFERENT THIS MORNING, WITH SO MUCH DISTANCE BETWEEN US.
ALL I COULD THINK WAS, "I WANT TO SEE KAORU-SAMA, I WANT TO BE WITH HIM."
I GUESS GROWING UP HASN'T CHANGED ME MUCH AT ALL, HAS IT?
THAT'S NOT TRUE...

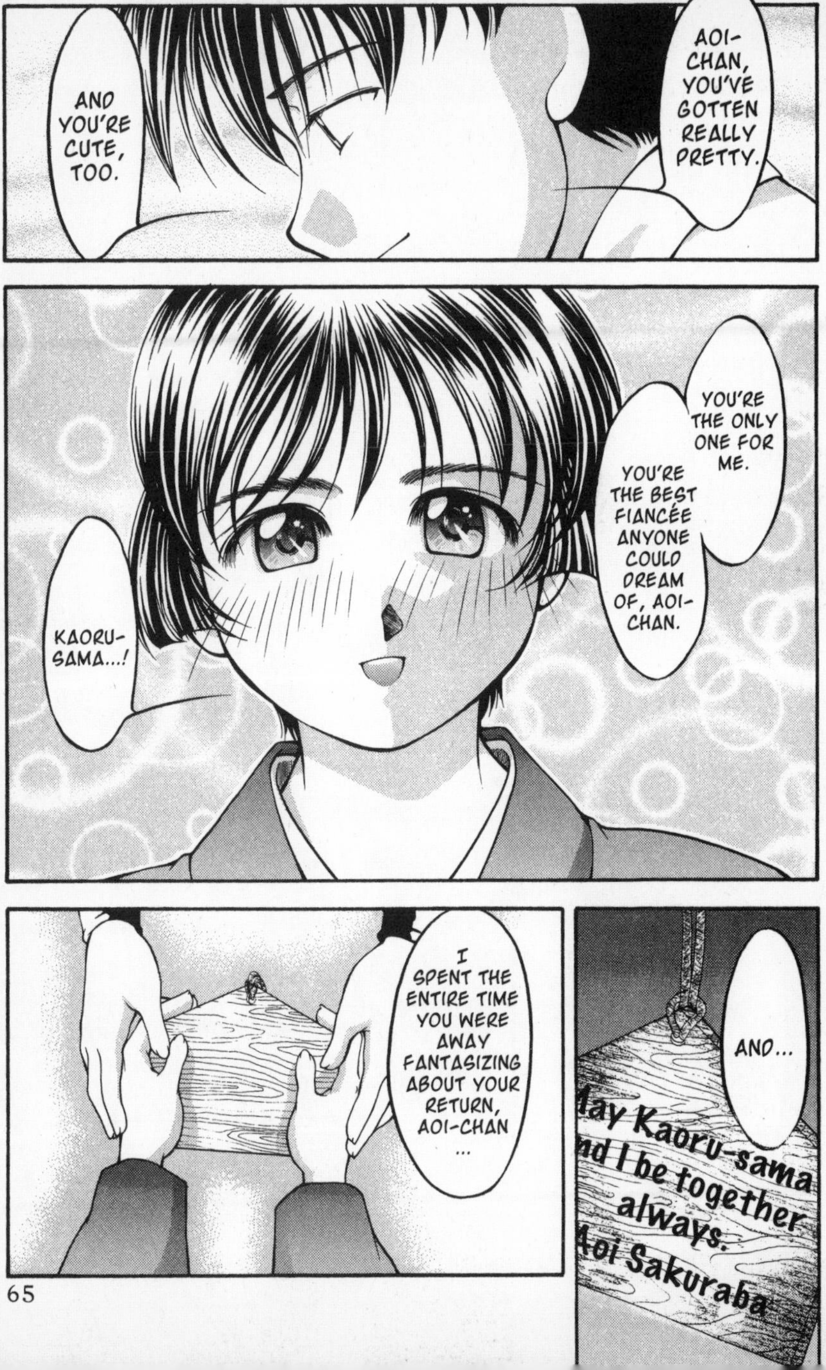
AOI-CHAN, YOU'VE GOTTEN REALLY PRETTY.
AND YOU'RE CUTE, TOO.
YOU'RE THE ONLY ONE FOR ME.
YOU'RE THE BEST FIANCÉE ANYONE COULD DREAM OF, AOI-CHAN.
KAORU-SAMA...!
AND...
May Kaoru-sama
nd I be together
always.
Aoi Sakuraba
I SPENT THE ENTIRE TIME YOU WERE AWAY FANTASIZING ABOUT YOUR RETURN, AOI-CHAN ...

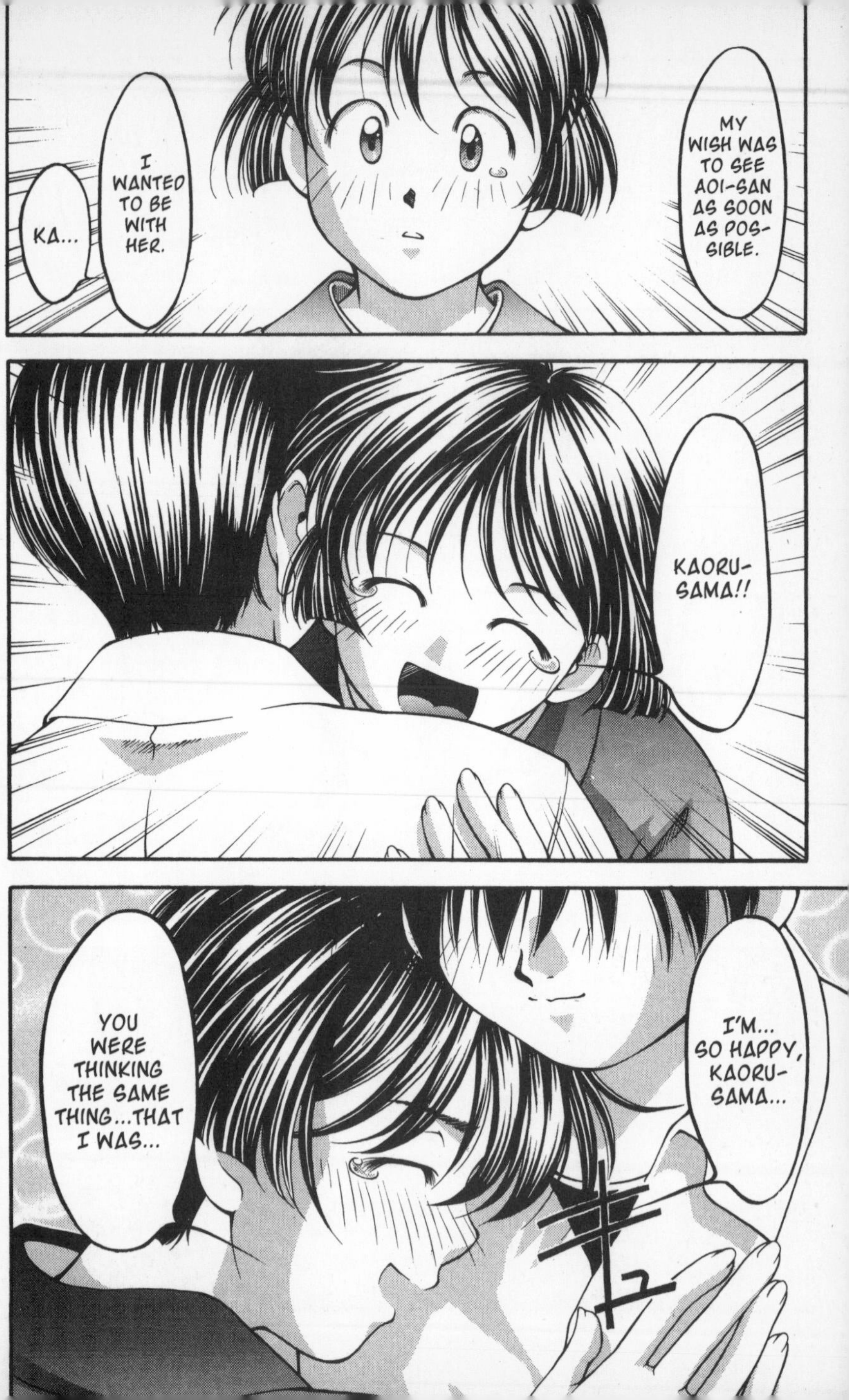
MY WISH WAS TO SEE AOI-SAN AS SOON AS POS-SIBLE.
I WANTED TO BE WITH HER.
KA...
KAORU-SAMA!!
I'M... SO HAPPY, KAORU-SAMA...
YOU WERE THINKING THE SAME THING...THAT I WAS...

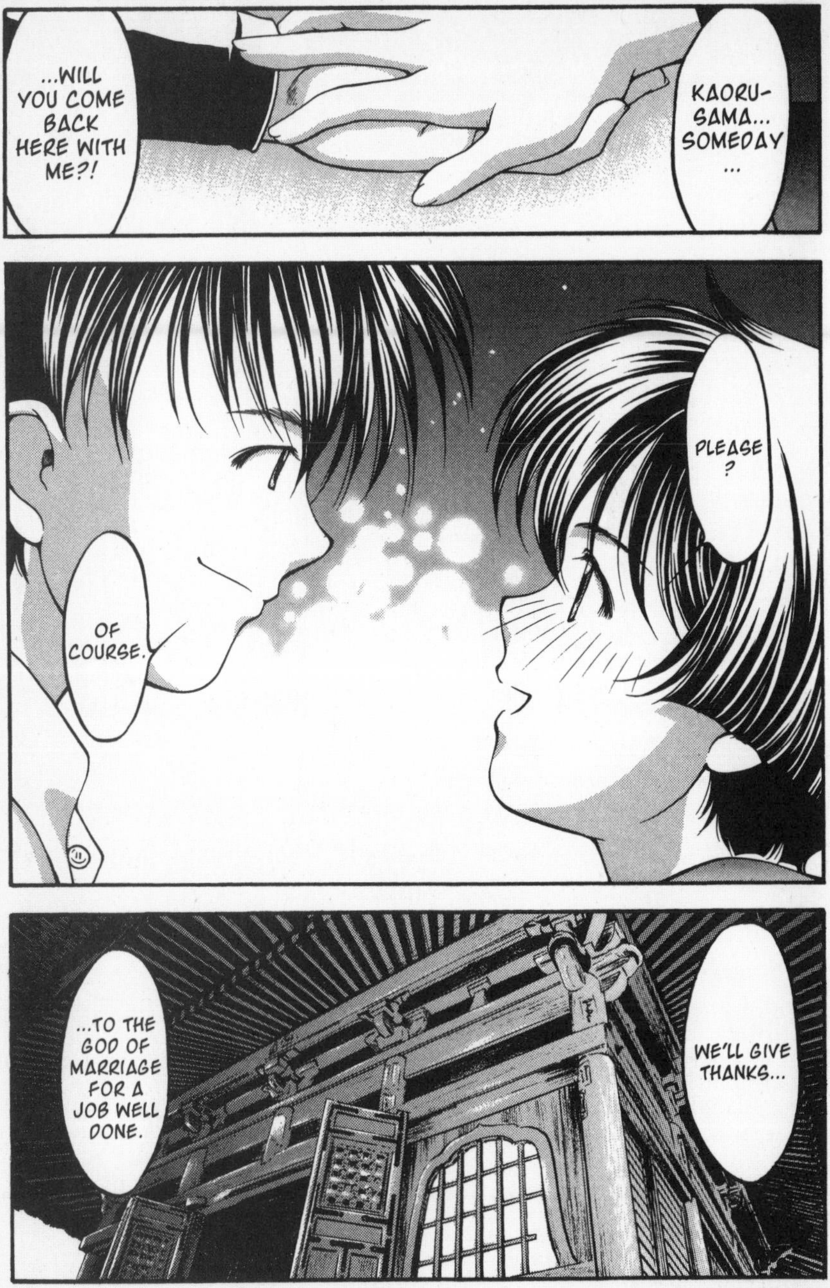
KAORU-SAMA... SOMEDAY ...
...WILL YOU COME BACK HERE WITH ME?!
PLEASE ?
OF COURSE.
WE'LL GIVE THANKS...
...TO THE GOD OF MARRIAGE FOR A JOB WELL DONE.

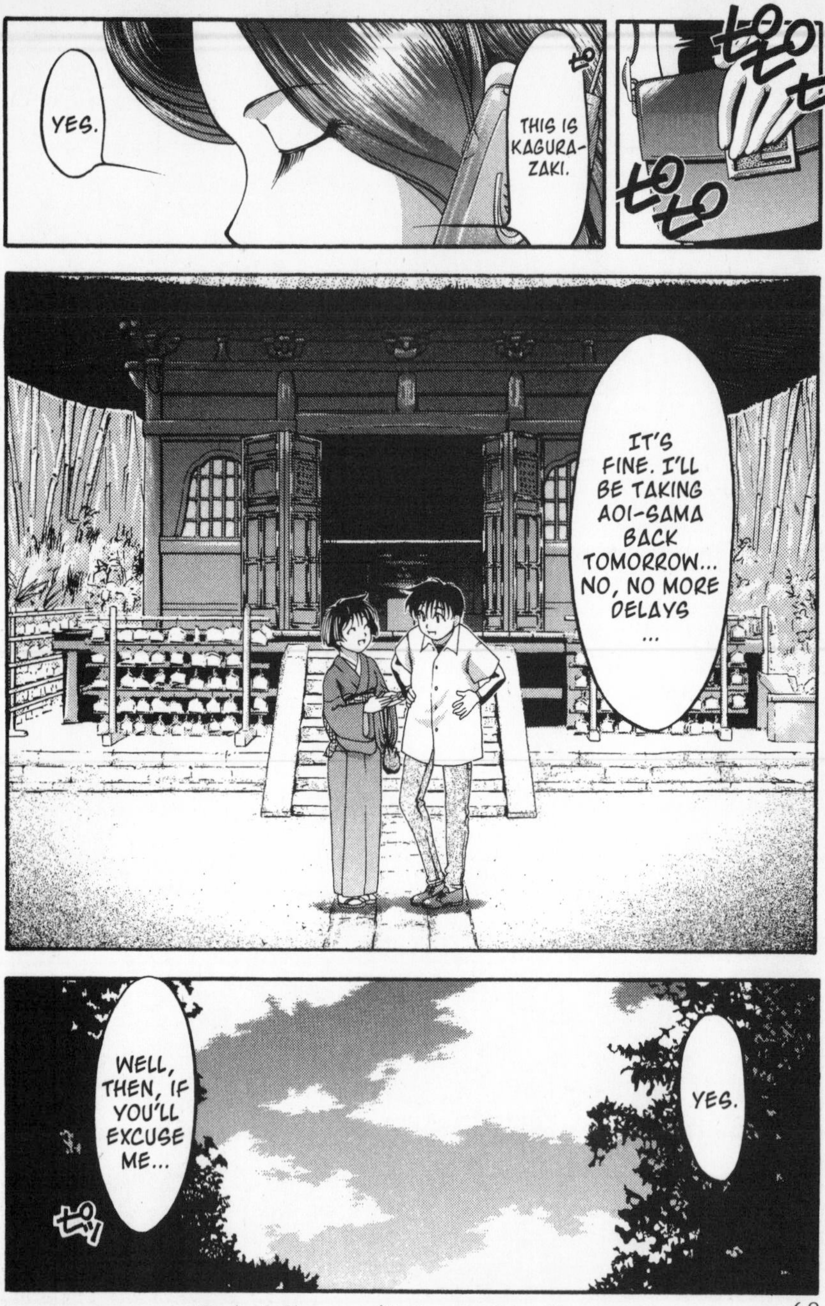
THIS IS KAGURA-ZAKI.
YES.
IT'S FINE. I'LL BE TAKING AOI-SAMA BACK TOMORROW... NO, NO MORE DELAYS ...
YES.
WELL, THEN, IF YOU'LL EXCUSE ME...

End of Chapter 49: Enmusubi—Marriage

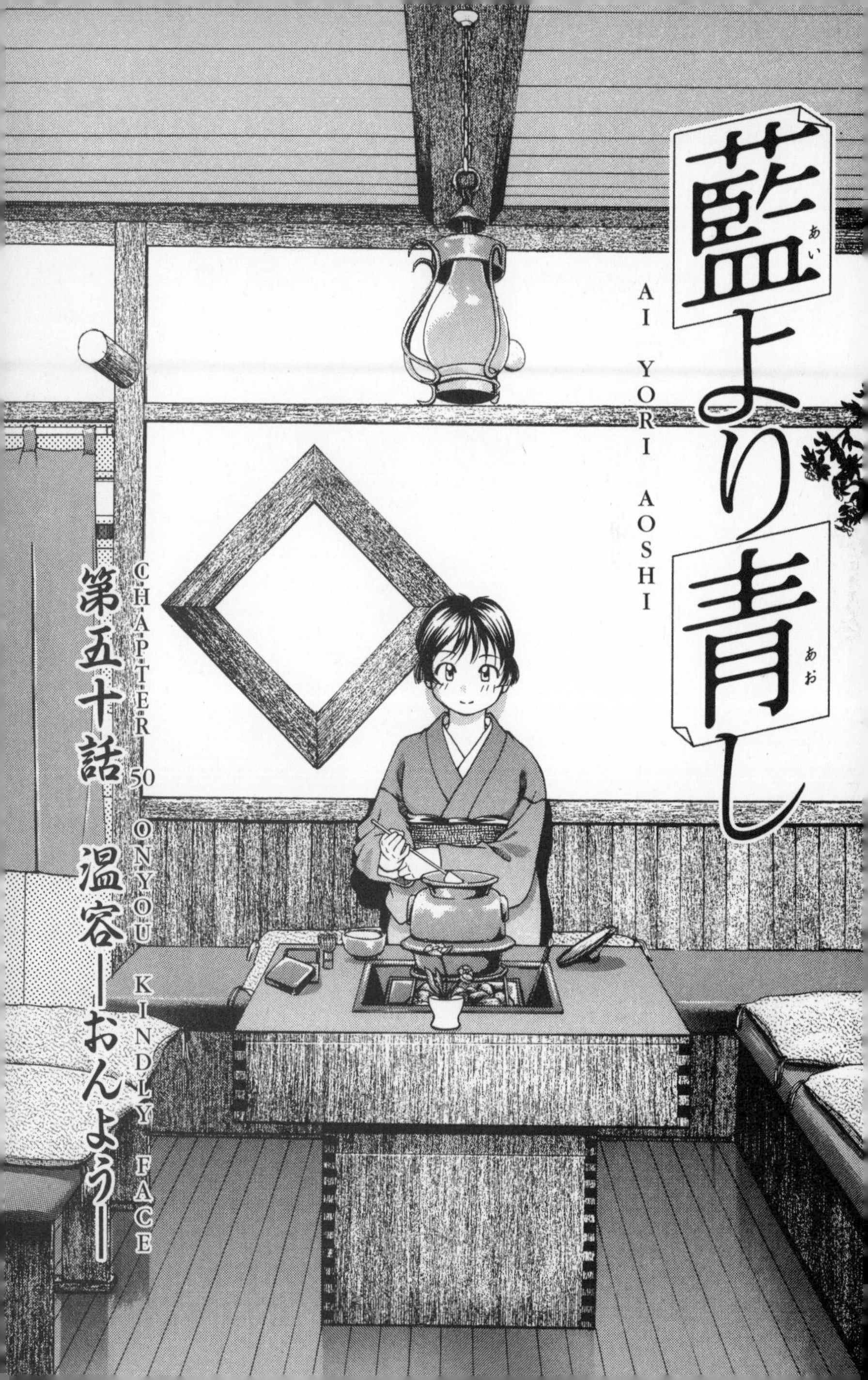
藍(あい)より青(あお)し
AI YORI AOSHI
第五十話
CHAPTER 50
温容—おんよう—
ONYOU KINDLY FACE

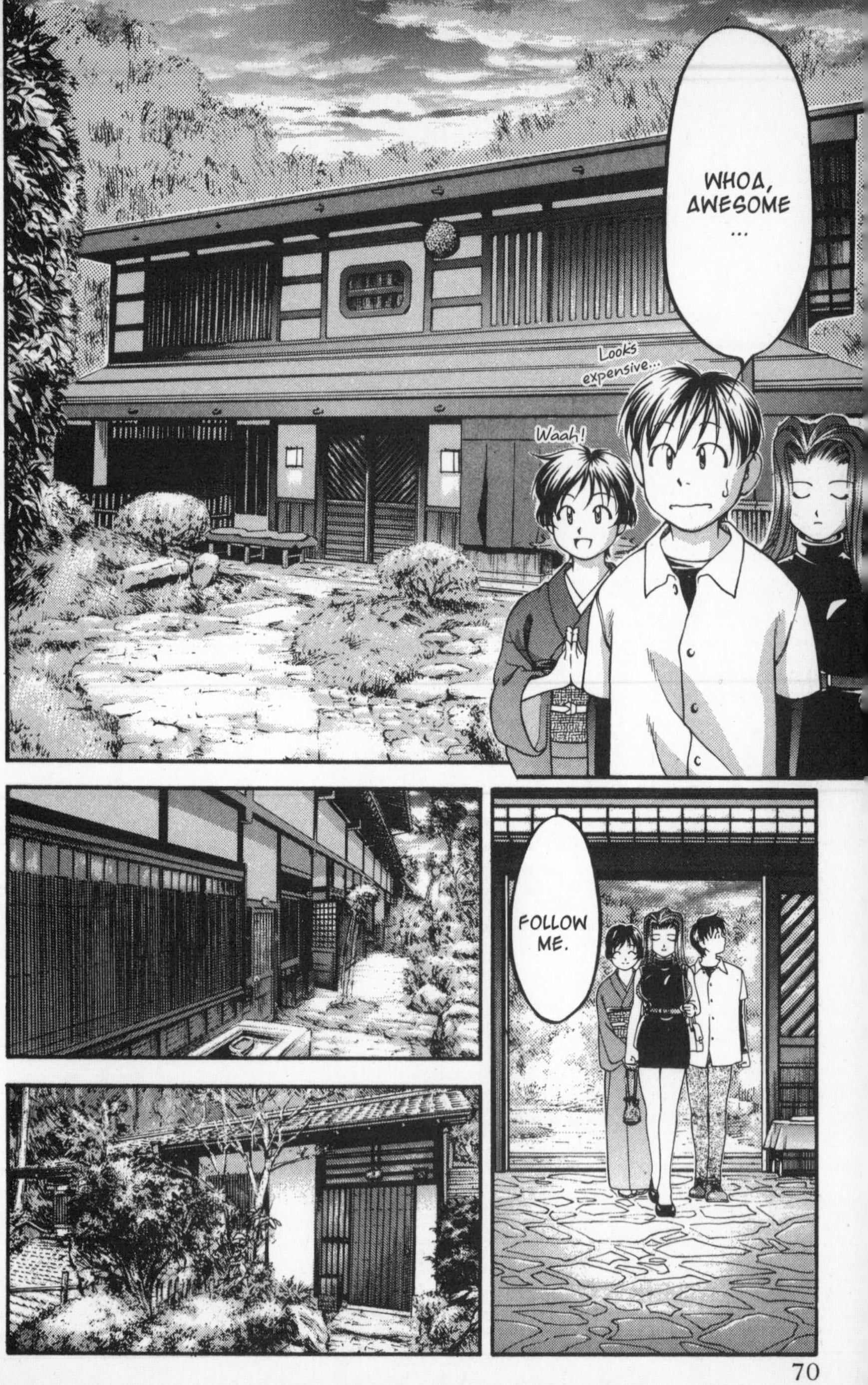
WHOA, AWESOME ...
Looks expensive...
Waah!
FOLLOW ME.

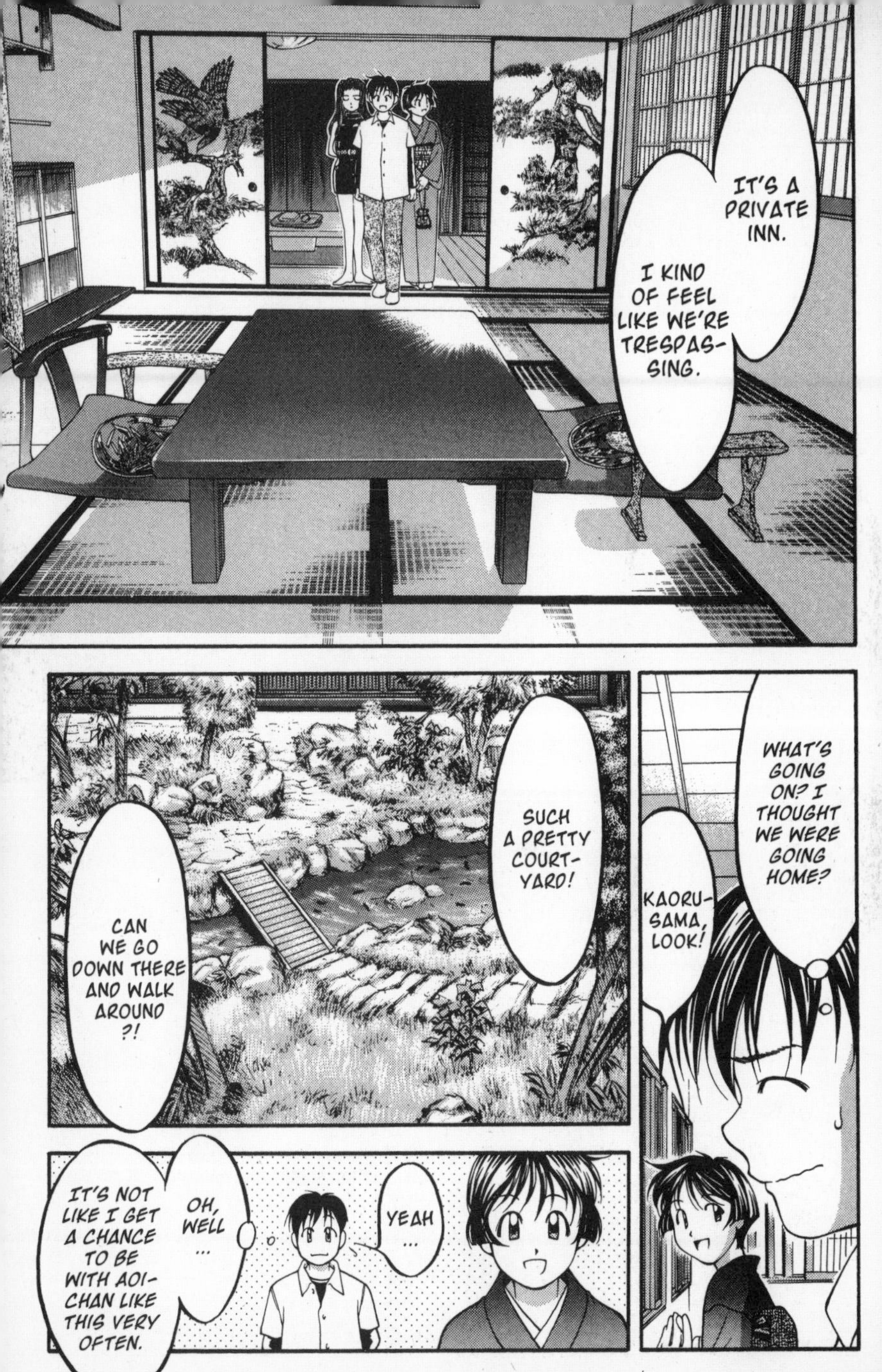
IT'S A PRIVATE INN.
I KIND OF FEEL LIKE WE'RE TRESPAS-SING.
WHAT'S GOING ON? I THOUGHT WE WERE GOING HOME?
KAORU-SAMA, LOOK!
SUCH A PRETTY COURT-YARD!
CAN WE GO DOWN THERE AND WALK AROUND ?!
YEAH ...
OH, WELL ...
IT'S NOT LIKE I GET A CHANCE TO BE WITH AOI-CHAN LIKE THIS VERY OFTEN.

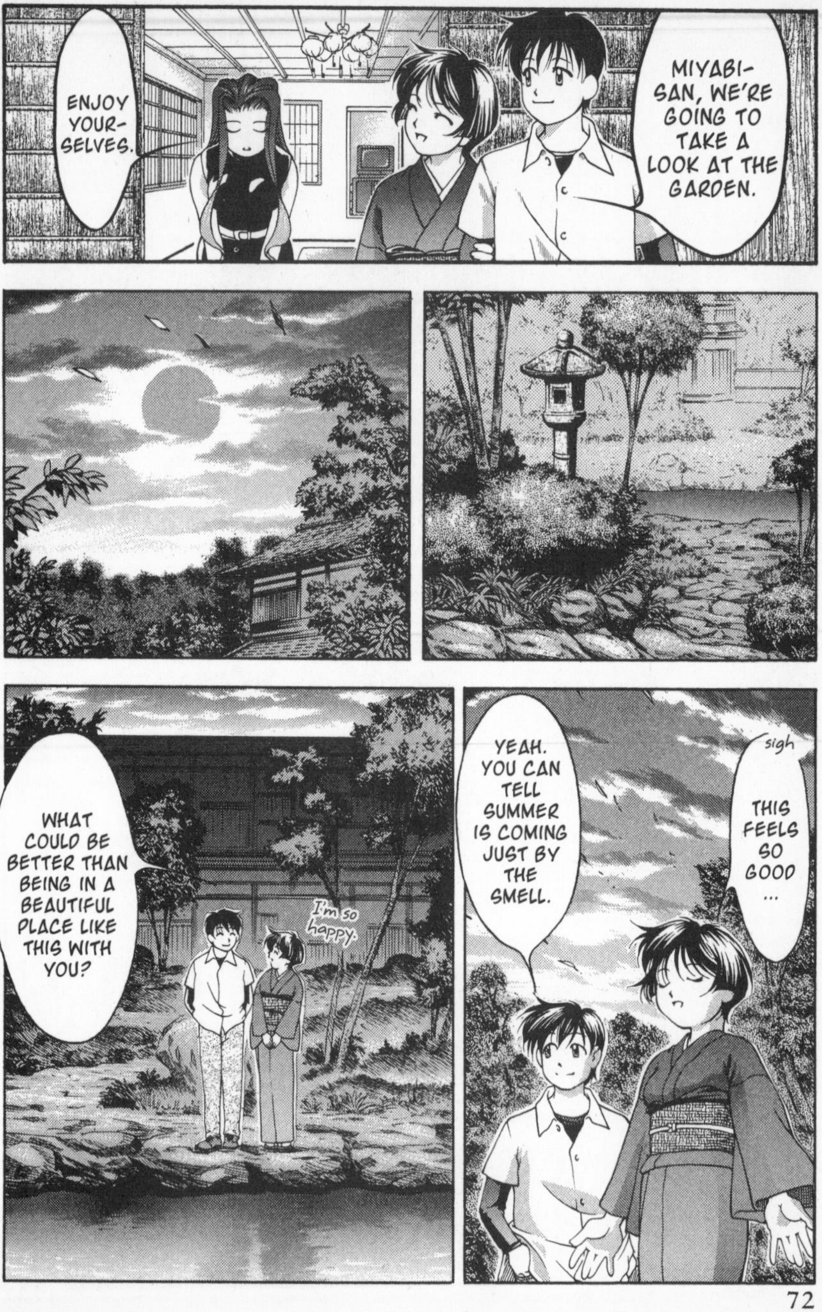
MIYABI-SAN, WE'RE GOING TO TAKE A LOOK AT THE GARDEN.
ENJOY YOURSELVES.
sigh
THIS FEELS SO GOOD ...
YEAH. YOU CAN TELL SUMMER IS COMING JUST BY THE SMELL.
WHAT COULD BE BETTER THAN BEING IN A BEAUTIFUL PLACE LIKE THIS WITH YOU?
I'm so happy.

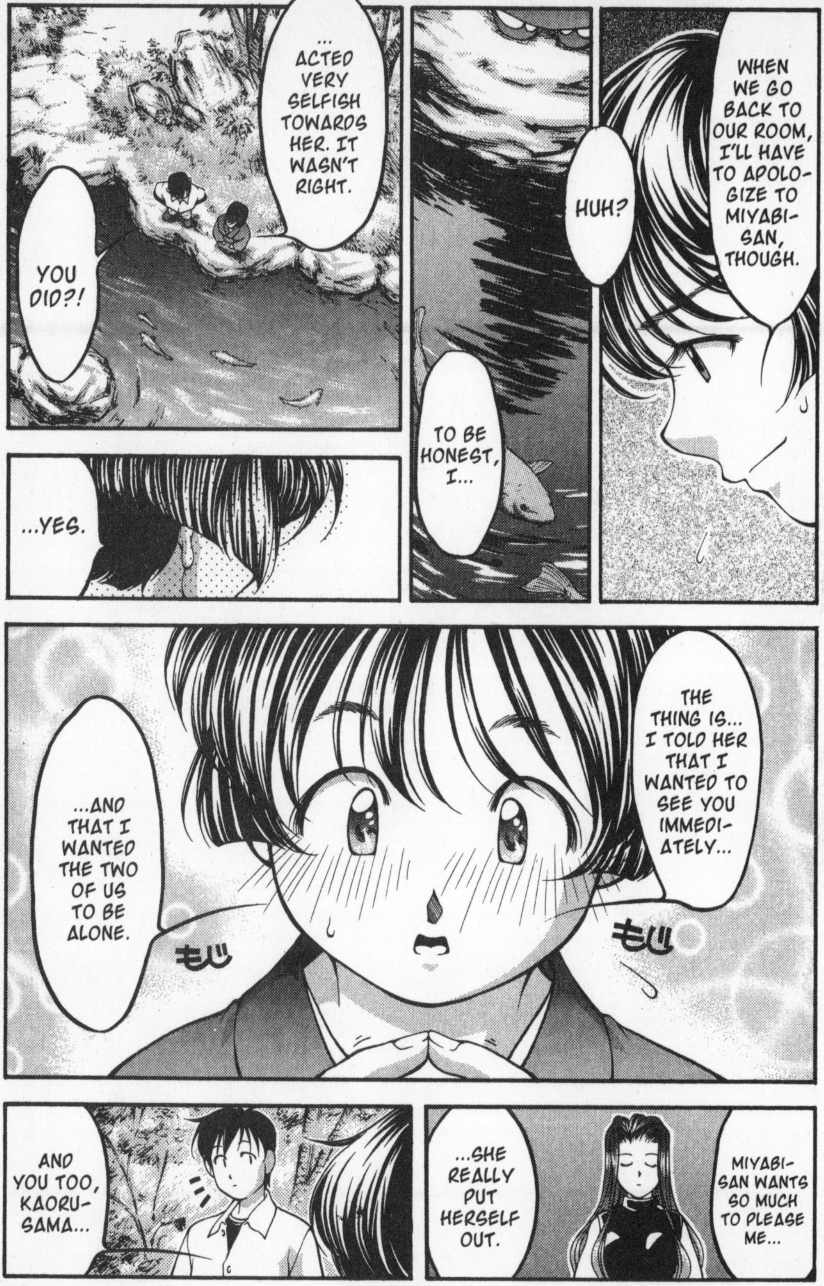
WHEN WE GO BACK TO OUR ROOM, I'LL HAVE TO APOLOGIZE TO MIYABI-SAN, THOUGH.
HUH?
TO BE HONEST, I...
... ACTED VERY SELFISH TOWARDS HER. IT WASN'T RIGHT.
YOU DID?!
...YES.
THE THING IS... I TOLD HER THAT I WANTED TO SEE YOU IMMEDIATELY...
...AND THAT I WANTED THE TWO OF US TO BE ALONE.
もじ
もじ
MIYABI-SAN WANTS SO MUCH TO PLEASE ME...
...SHE REALLY PUT HERSELF OUT.
AND YOU TOO, KAORU-SAMA...

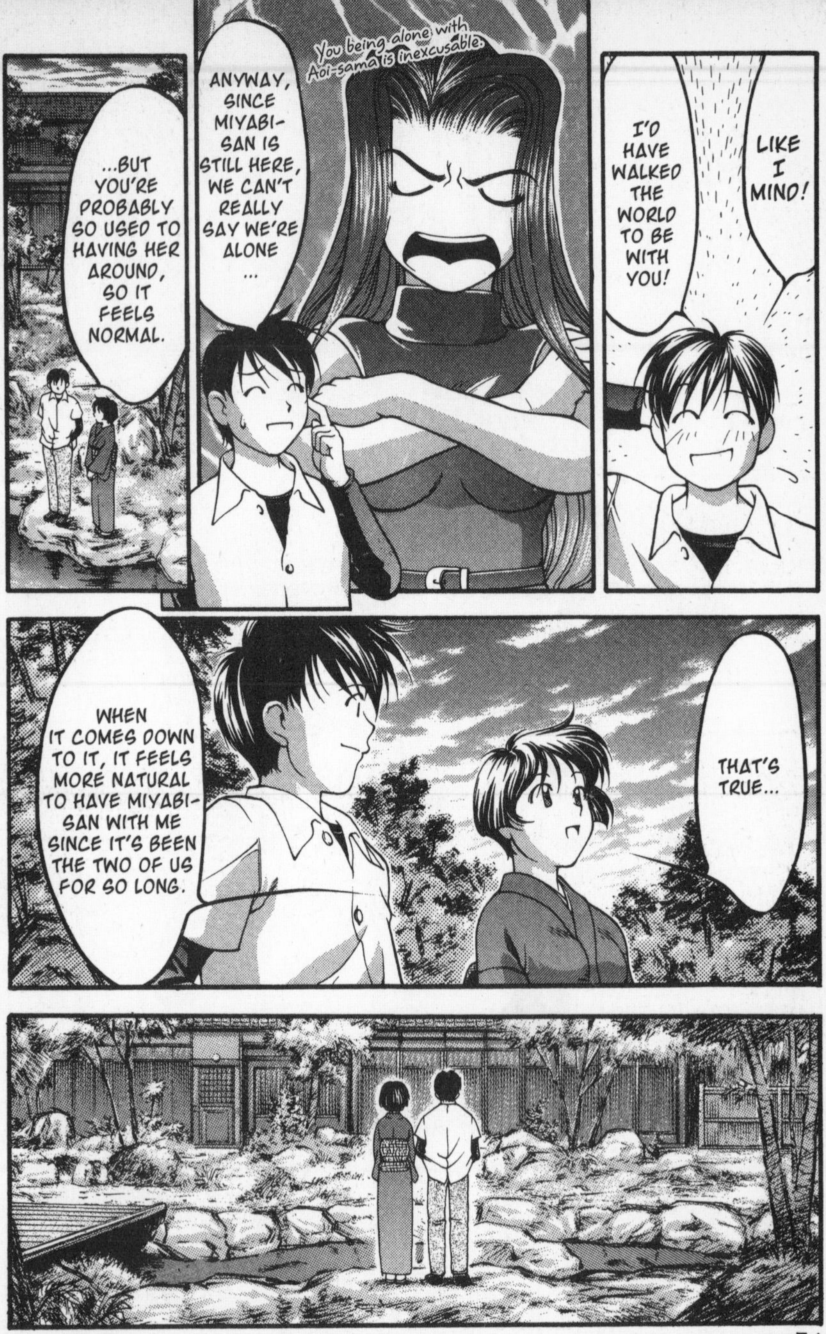
LIKE I MIND!
I'D HAVE WALKED THE WORLD TO BE WITH YOU!
You being alone with Aoi-sama is inexcusable.
ANYWAY, SINCE MIYABI-SAN IS STILL HERE, WE CAN'T REALLY SAY WE'RE ALONE ...
...BUT YOU'RE PROBABLY SO USED TO HAVING HER AROUND, SO IT FEELS NORMAL.
THAT'S TRUE...
WHEN IT COMES DOWN TO IT, IT FEELS MORE NATURAL TO HAVE MIYABI-SAN WITH ME SINCE IT'S BEEN THE TWO OF US FOR SO LONG.

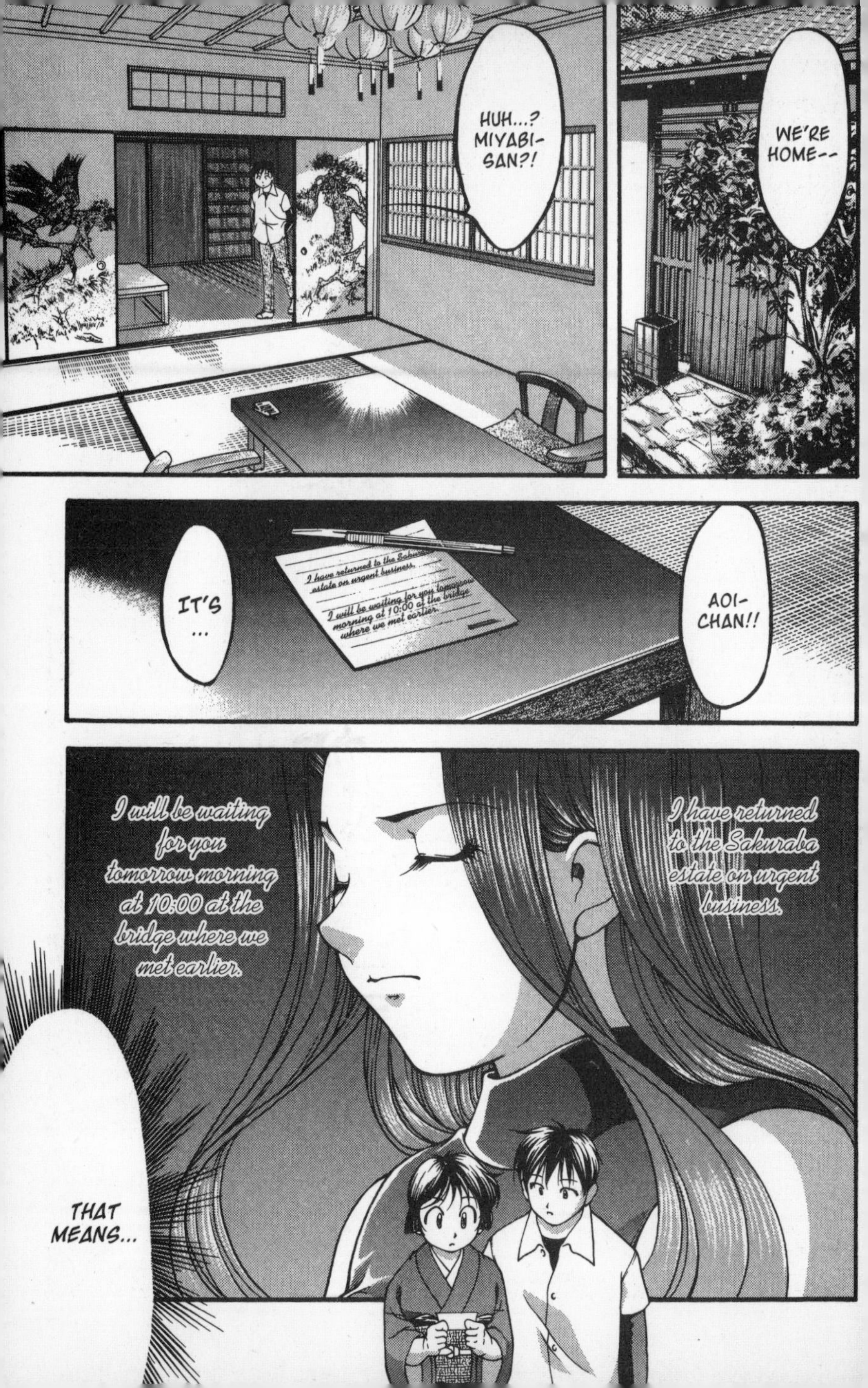
WE'RE HOME--
HUH...? MIYABI-SAN?!
AOI-CHAN!!
IT'S ...
I have returned to the Sakuraba estate on urgent business.
I will be waiting for you tomorrow morning at 10:00 at the bridge where we met earlier.
THAT MEANS...

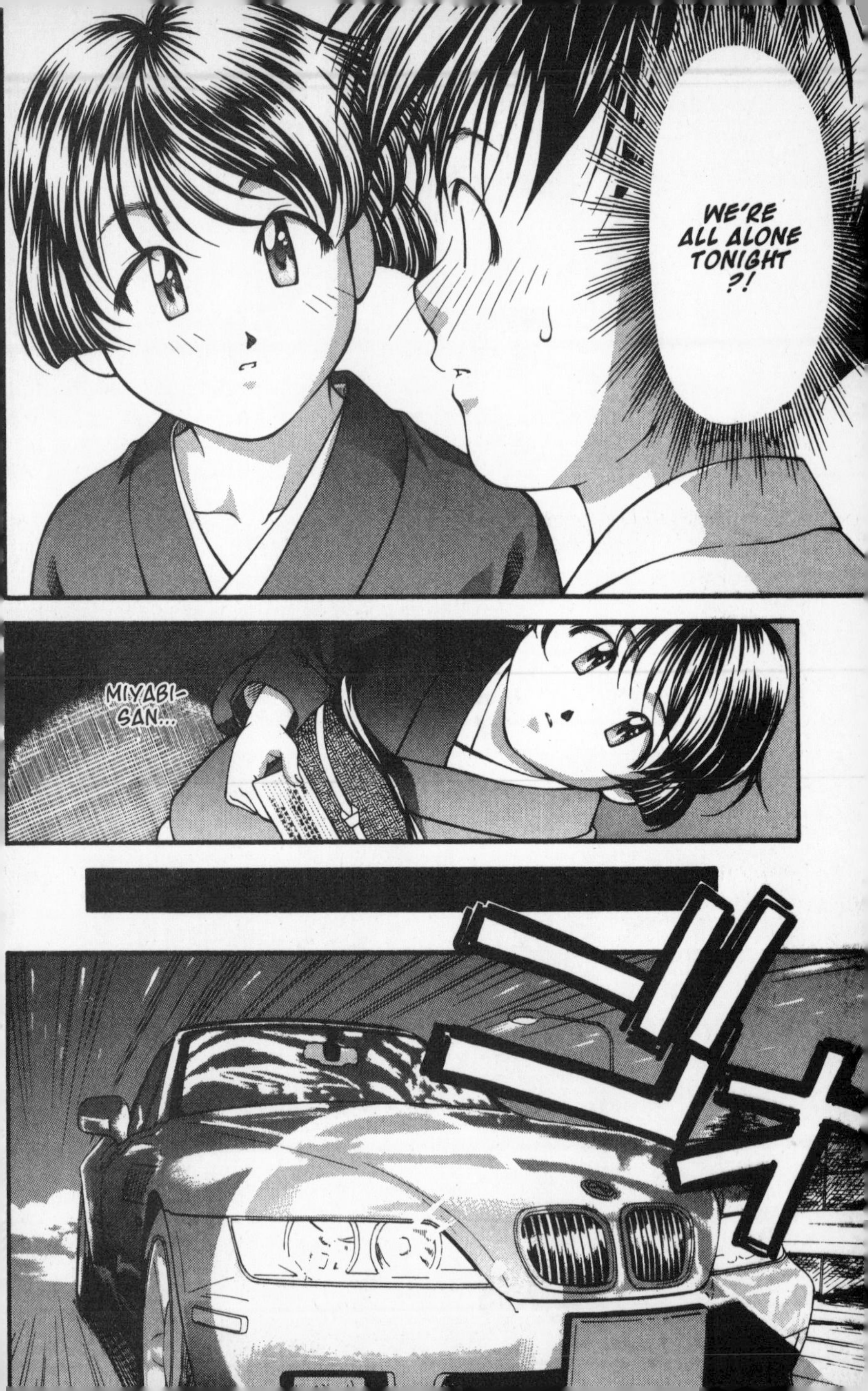
WE'RE ALL ALONE TONIGHT ?!
MIYABI-SAN...

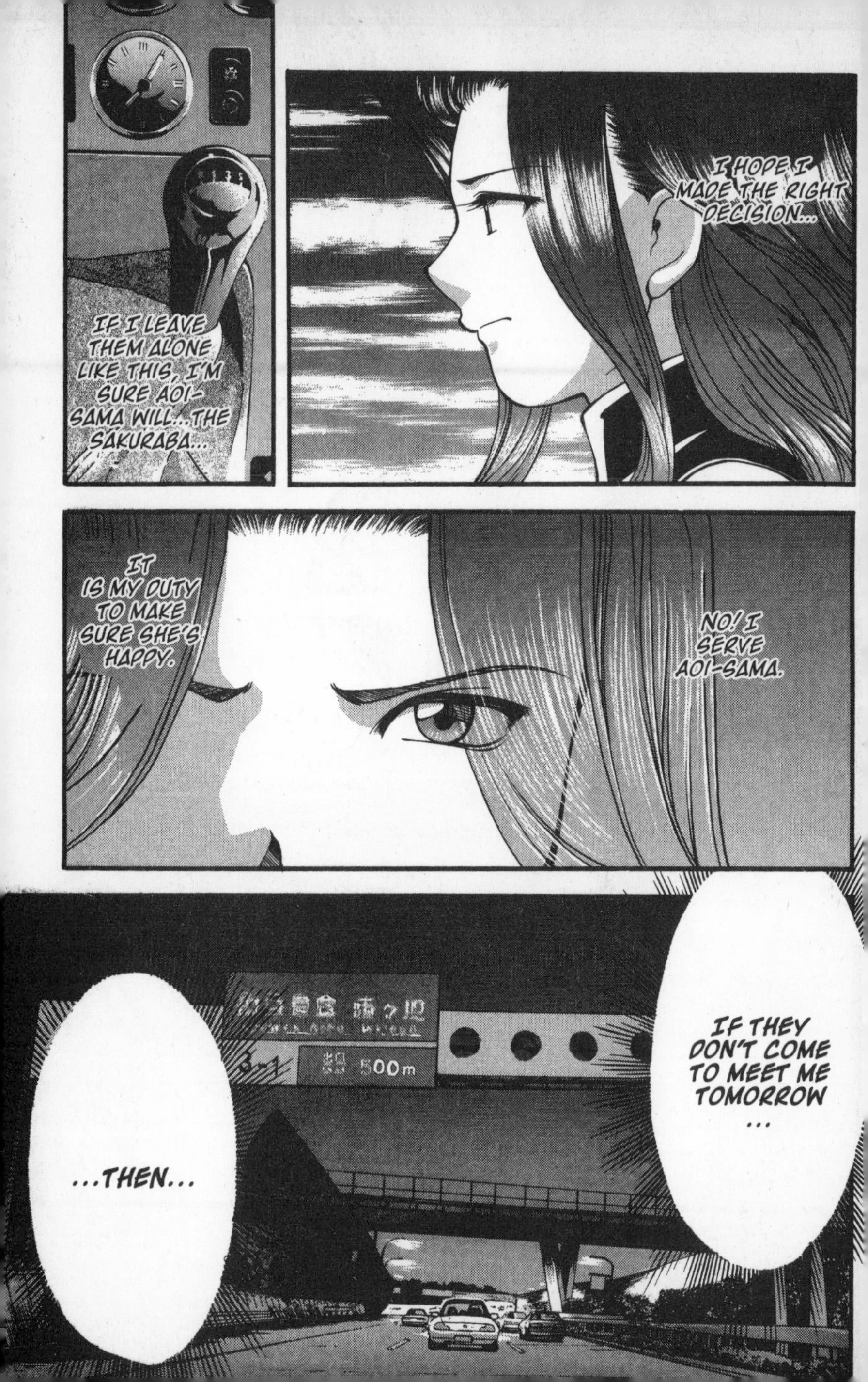
I HOPE I MADE THE RIGHT DECISION...
IF I LEAVE THEM ALONE LIKE THIS, I'M SURE AOI-SAMA WILL... THE SAKURABA...
NO! I SERVE AOI-SAMA.
IT IS MY DUTY TO MAKE SURE SHE'S HAPPY.
500m
IF THEY DON'T COME TO MEET ME TOMORROW ...
...THEN...

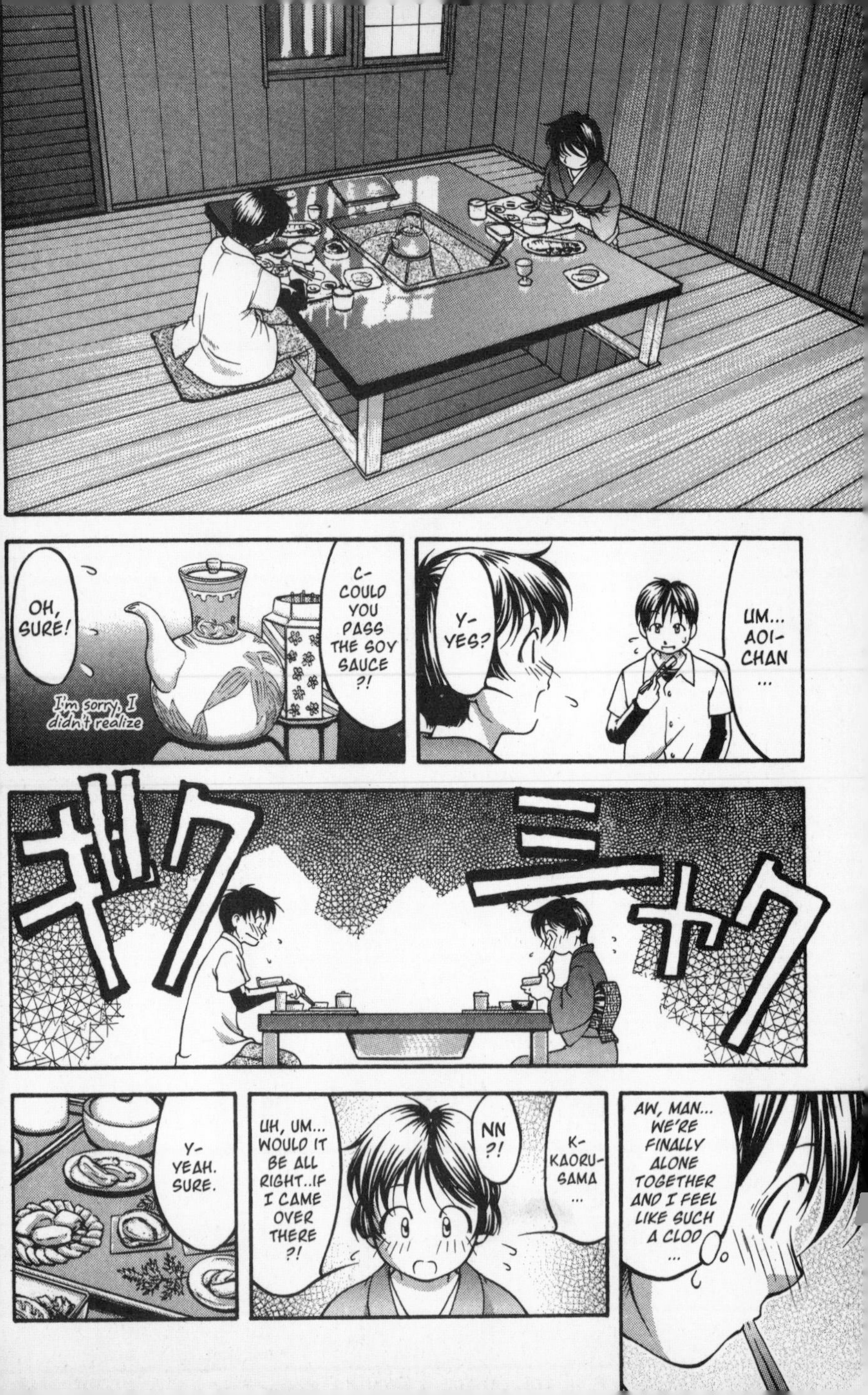
UM... AOI-CHAN ...
Y- YES?
C- COULD YOU PASS THE SOY SAUCE ?!
OH, SURE!
I'm sorry, I didn't realize
ギク
シャク
AW, MAN... WE'RE FINALLY ALONE TOGETHER AND I FEEL LIKE SUCH A CLOD ...
K- KAORU-SAMA ...
NN ?!
UH, UM... WOULD IT BE ALL RIGHT..IF I CAME OVER THERE ?!
Y- YEAH. SURE.

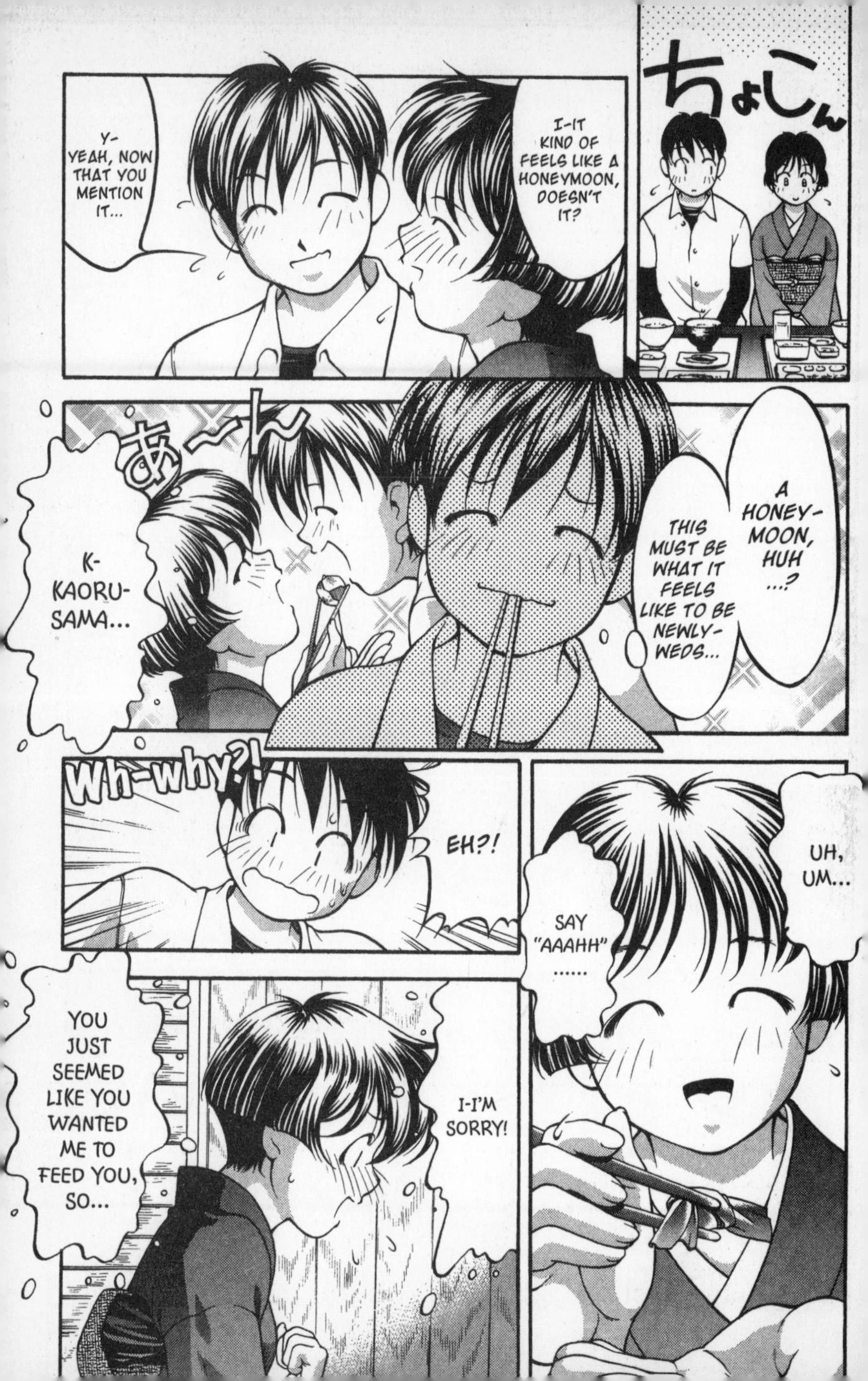
ちょこん
I-IT KIND OF FEELS LIKE A HONEYMOON, DOESN'T IT?
Y-YEAH, NOW THAT YOU MENTION IT...
A HONEY-MOON, HUH ...?
THIS MUST BE WHAT IT FEELS LIKE TO BE NEWLY-WEDS...
あ～ん
K-KAORU-SAMA...
UH, UM...
SAY "AAAHH" ......
Wh-why?!
EH?!
I-I'M SORRY!
YOU JUST SEEMED LIKE YOU WANTED ME TO FEED YOU, SO...

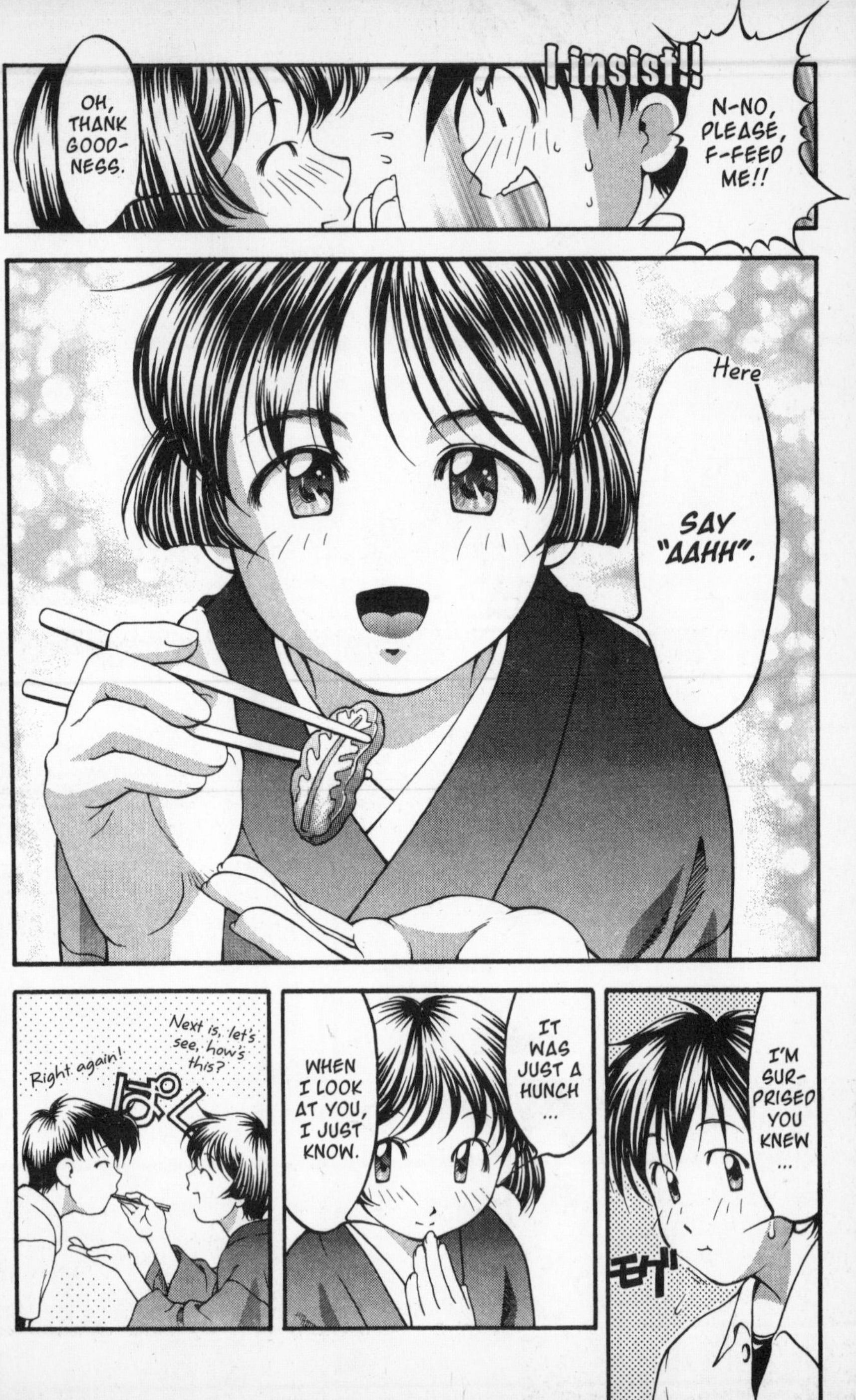
I insist!!
N-NO, PLEASE, F-FEED ME!!
OH, THANK GOOD-NESS.
Here
SAY "AAHH".
I'M SUR-PRISED YOU KNEW ...
モグ
IT WAS JUST A HUNCH ...
WHEN I LOOK AT YOU, I JUST KNOW.
Next is, let's see, how's this?
Right again!
ぱく

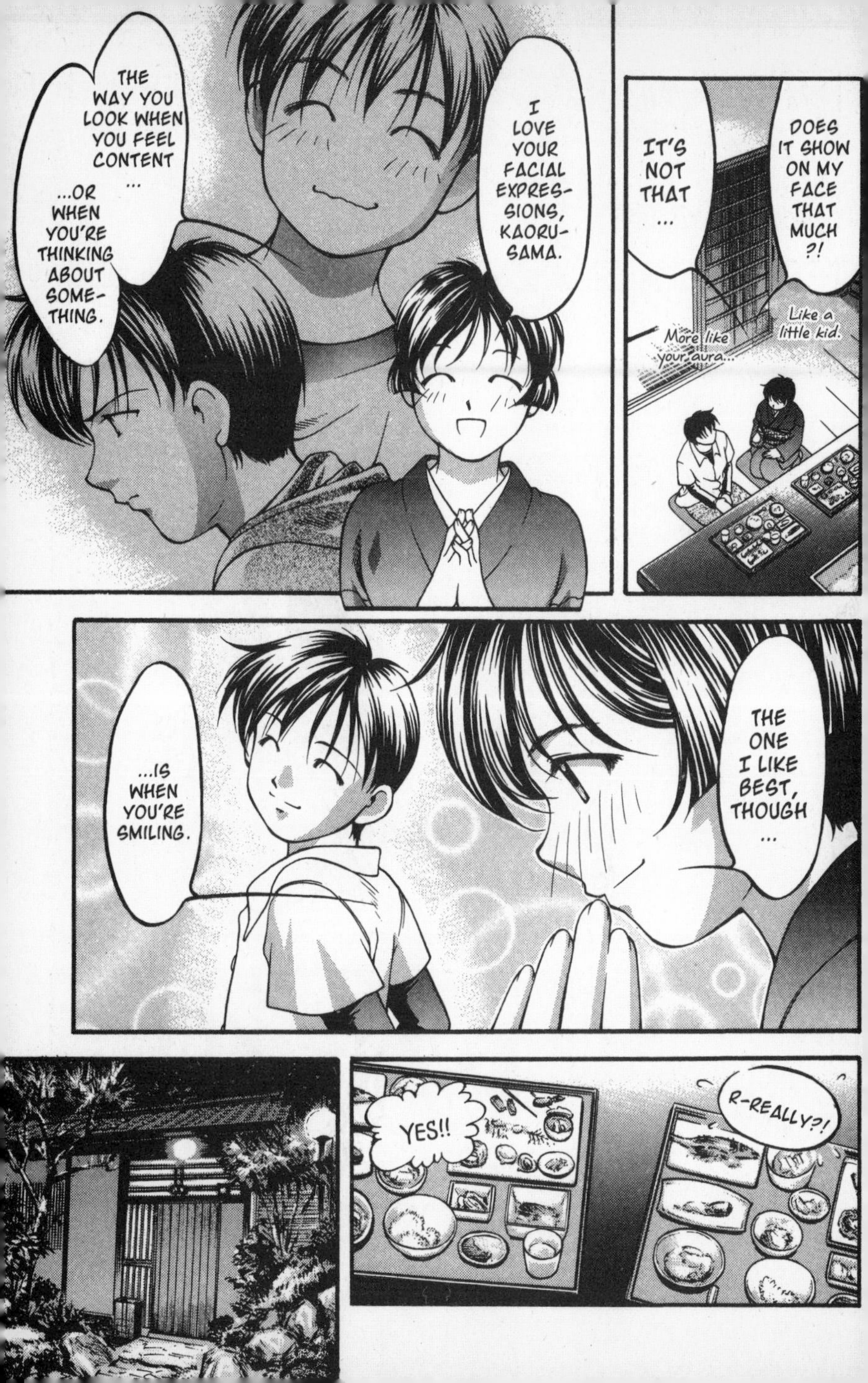
DOES IT SHOW ON MY FACE THAT MUCH?!
IT'S NOT THAT...
Like a little kid.
More like your aura...
I LOVE YOUR FACIAL EXPRES-SIONS, KAORU-SAMA.
THE WAY YOU LOOK WHEN YOU FEEL CONTENT...
...OR WHEN YOU'RE THINKING ABOUT SOME-THING.
THE ONE I LIKE BEST, THOUGH...
...IS WHEN YOU'RE SMILING.
R-REALLY?!
YES!!

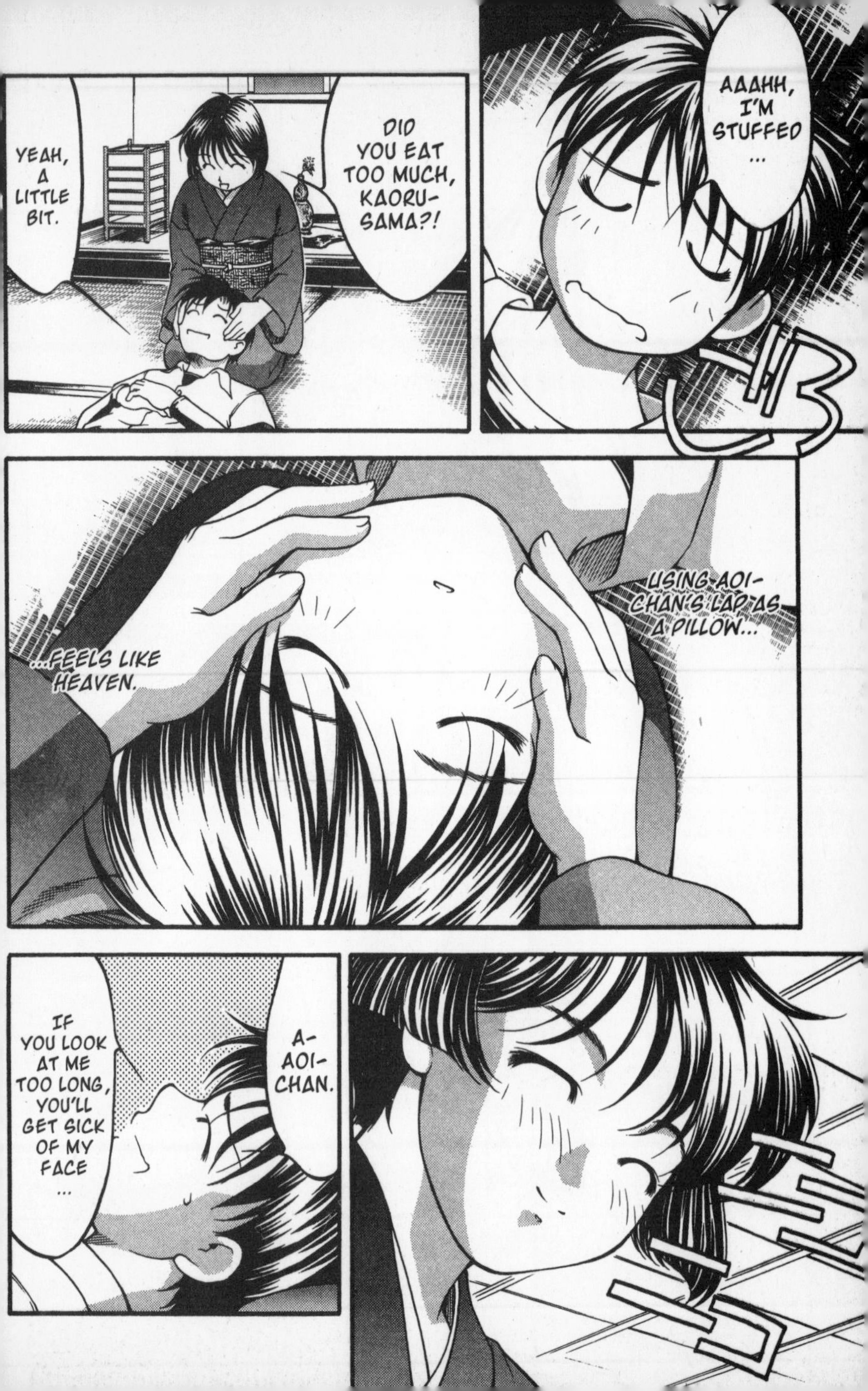
AAAHH, I'M STUFFED ...
DID YOU EAT TOO MUCH, KAORU-SAMA?!
YEAH, A LITTLE BIT.
USING AOI-CHAN'S LAP AS A PILLOW...
...FEELS LIKE HEAVEN.
A- AOI-CHAN.
IF YOU LOOK AT ME TOO LONG, YOU'LL GET SICK OF MY FACE ...

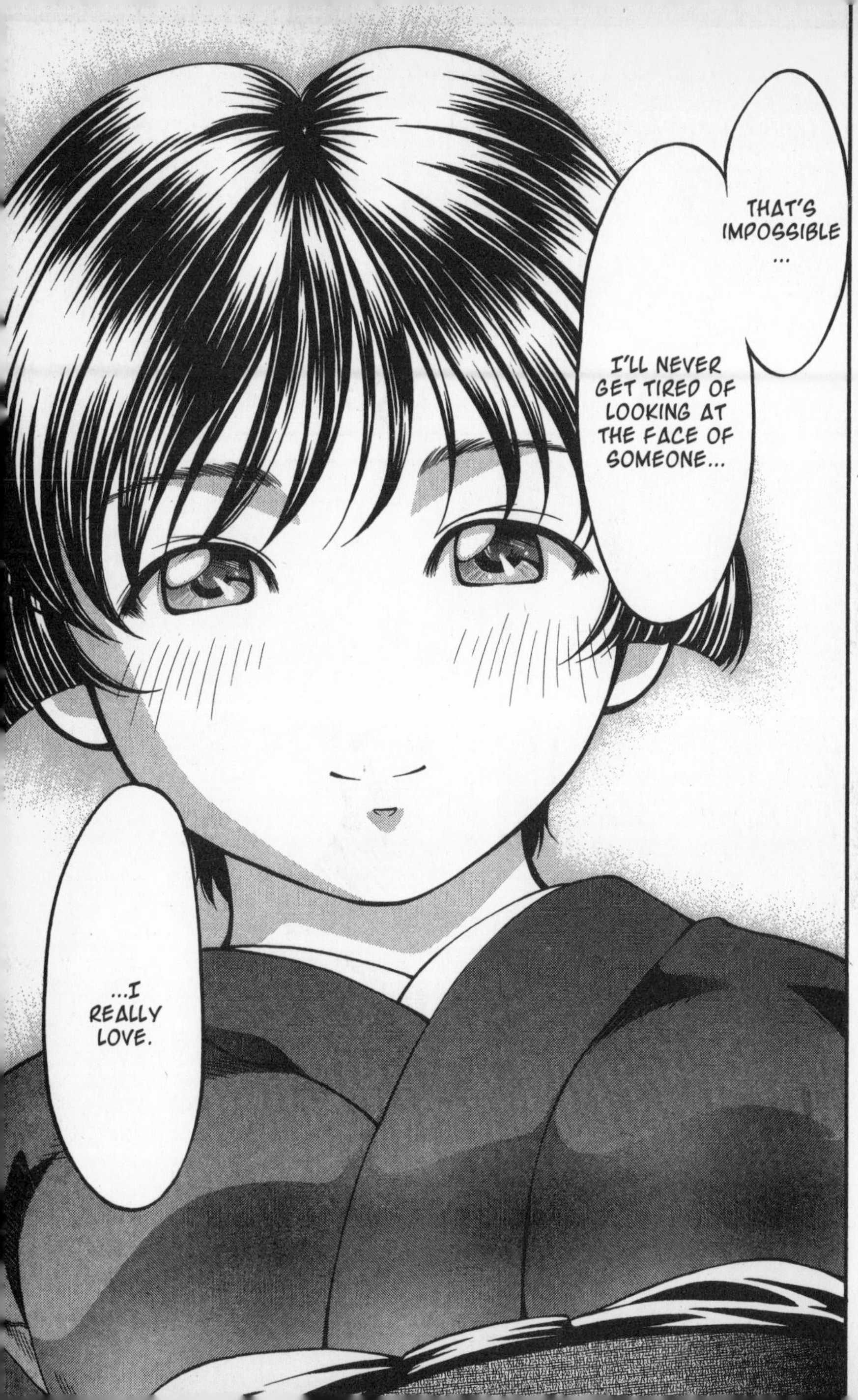
THAT'S IMPOSSIBLE ...
I'LL NEVER GET TIRED OF LOOKING AT THE FACE OF SOMEONE...
...I REALLY LOVE.

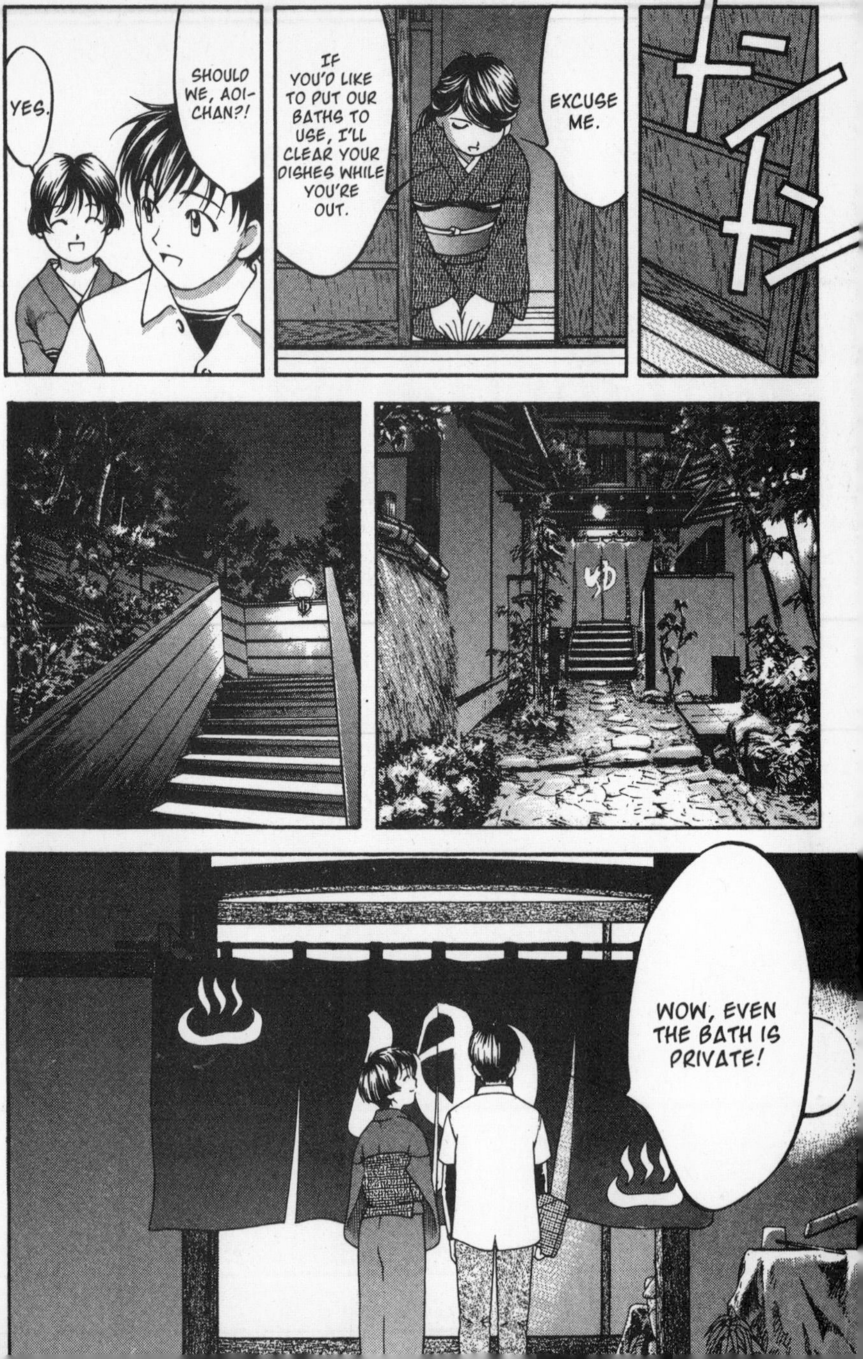
EXCUSE ME.
IF YOU'D LIKE TO PUT OUR BATHS TO USE, I'LL CLEAR YOUR DISHES WHILE YOU'RE OUT.
SHOULD WE, AOI-CHAN?!
YES.
WOW, EVEN THE BATH IS PRIVATE!

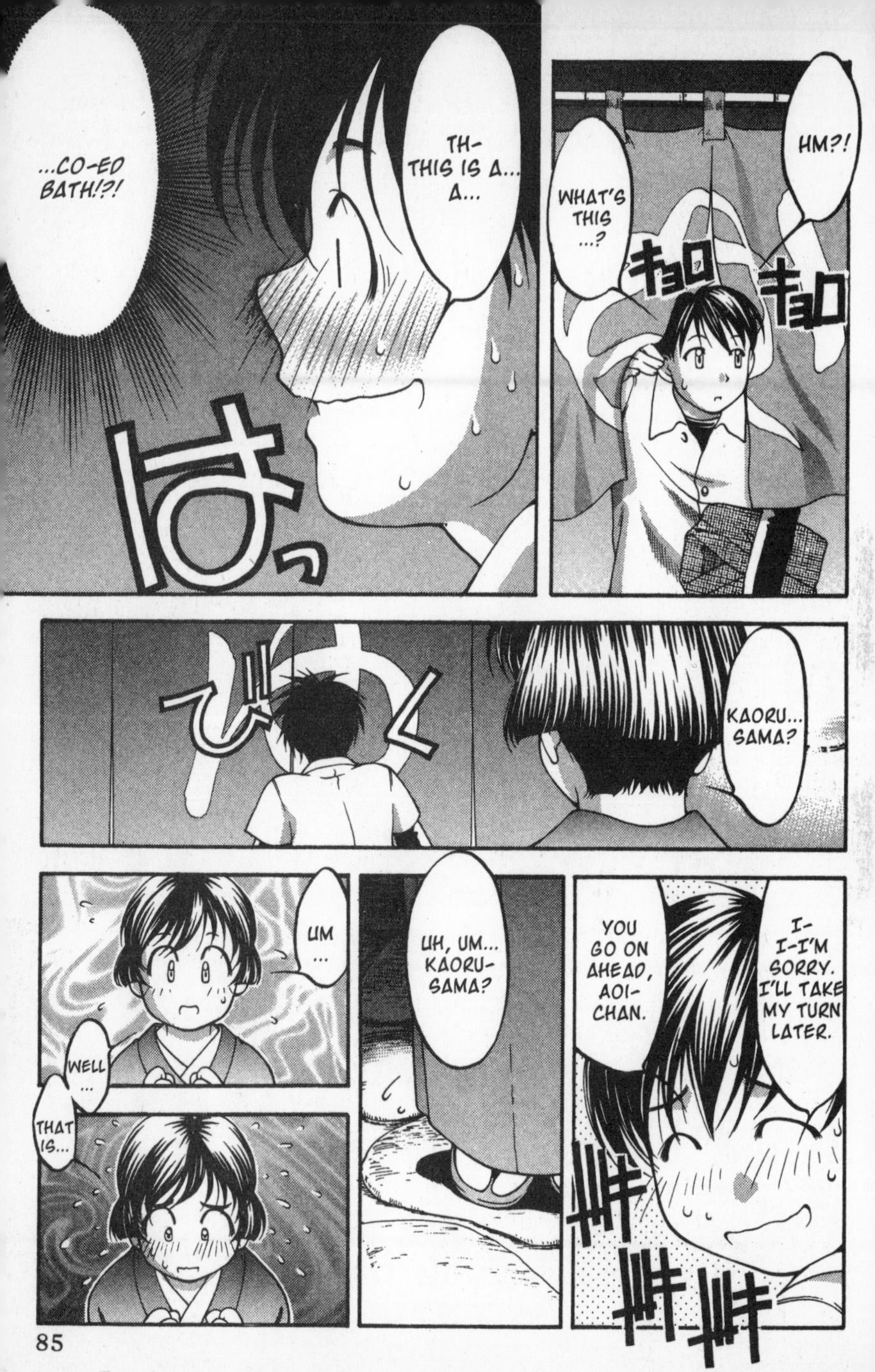
HM?!
WHAT'S THIS ...?
キョロ
キョロ
TH- THIS IS A... A...
...CO-ED BATH!?!
はっ
KAORU... SAMA?
びく
I- I-I'M SORRY. I'LL TAKE MY TURN LATER.
YOU GO ON AHEAD, AOI-CHAN.
UH, UM... KAORU-SAMA?
UM ...
WELL ...
THAT IS...

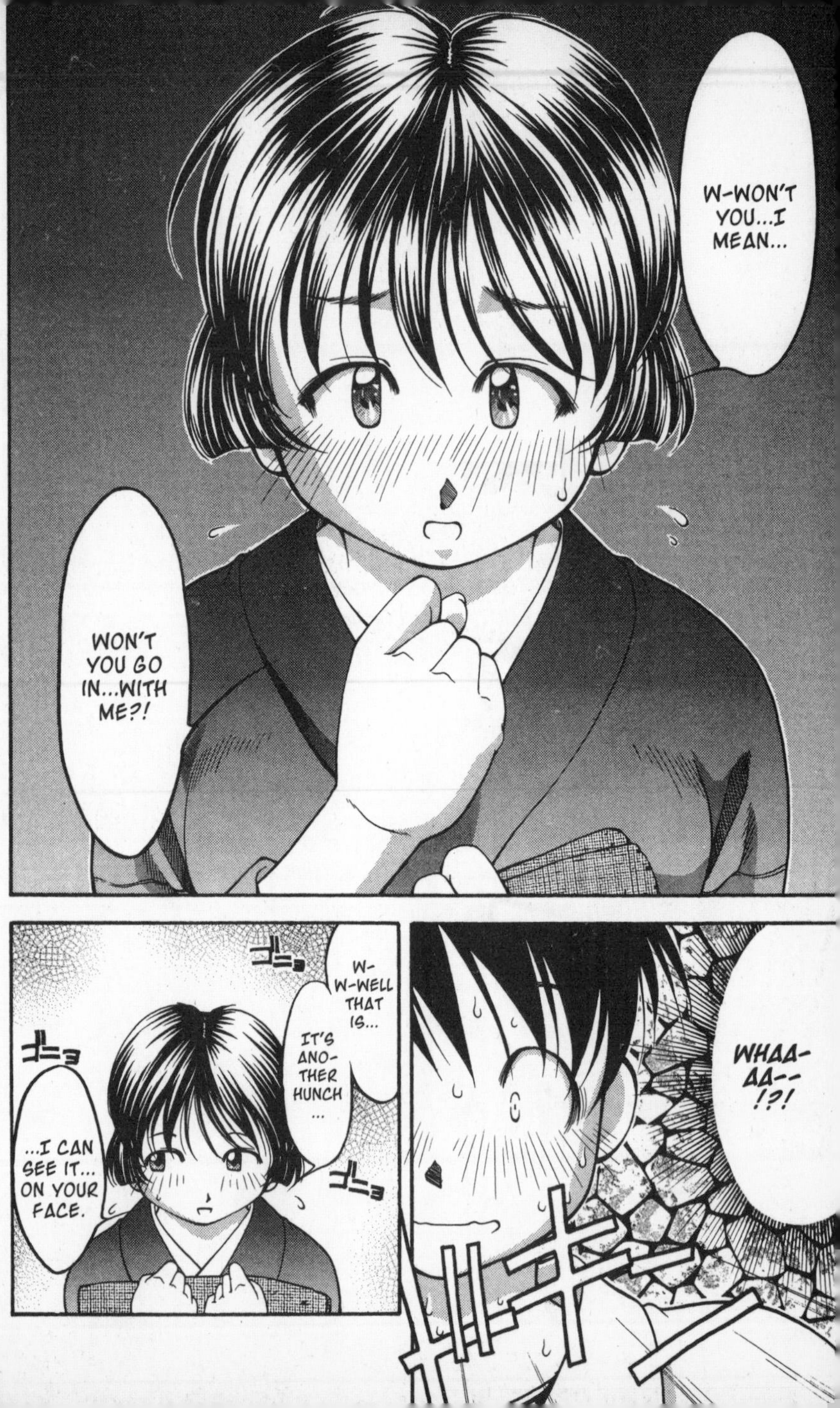
W-WON'T YOU...I MEAN...
WON'T YOU GO IN...WITH ME?!
WHAAA-AA--!?!
W-W-WELL THAT IS...
IT'S ANOTHER HUNCH...
...I CAN SEE IT... ON YOUR FACE.

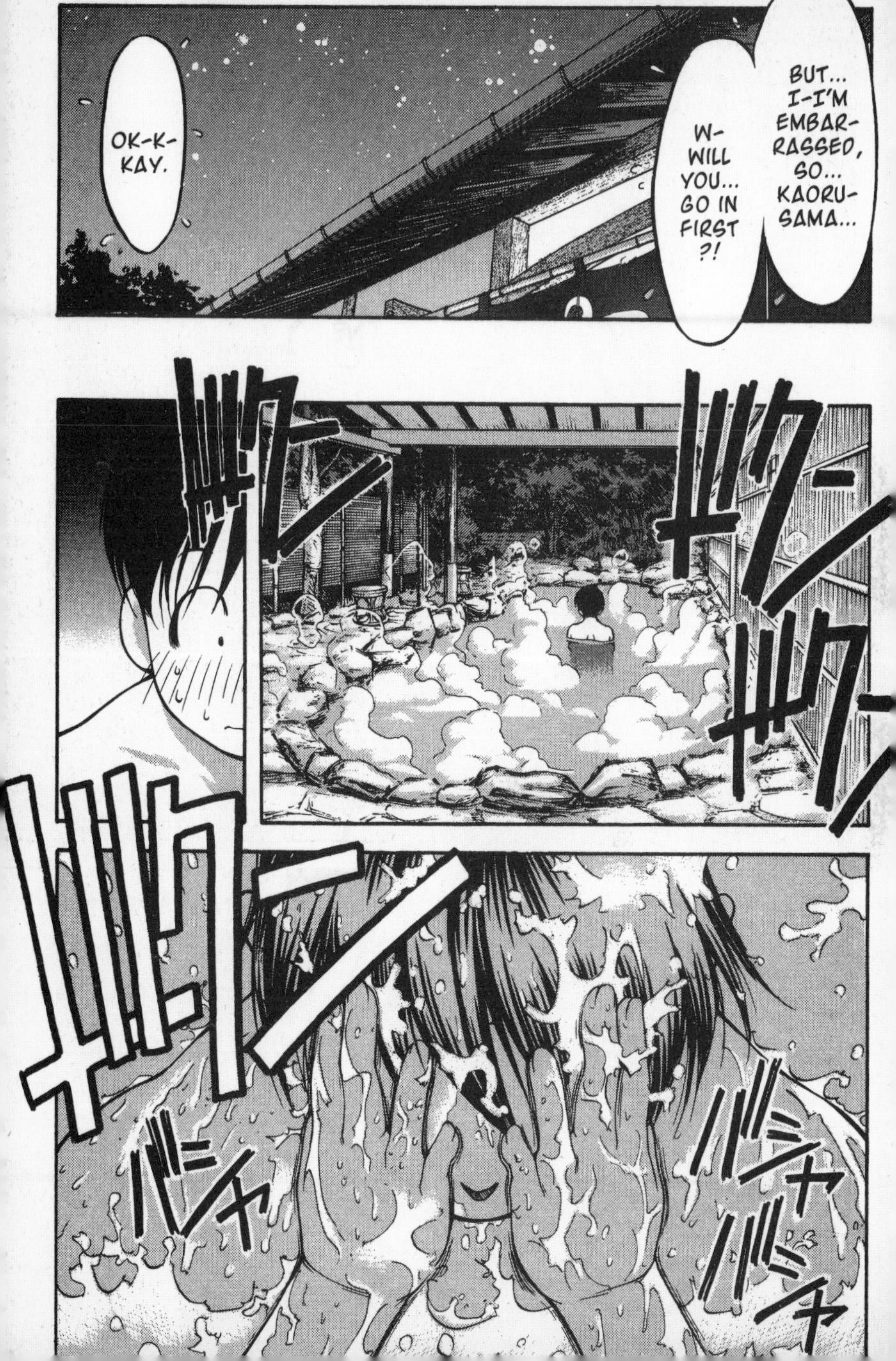
BUT... I-I'M EMBARRASSED, SO... KAORU-SAMA...
W-WILL YOU... GO IN FIRST?!
OK-K-KAY.

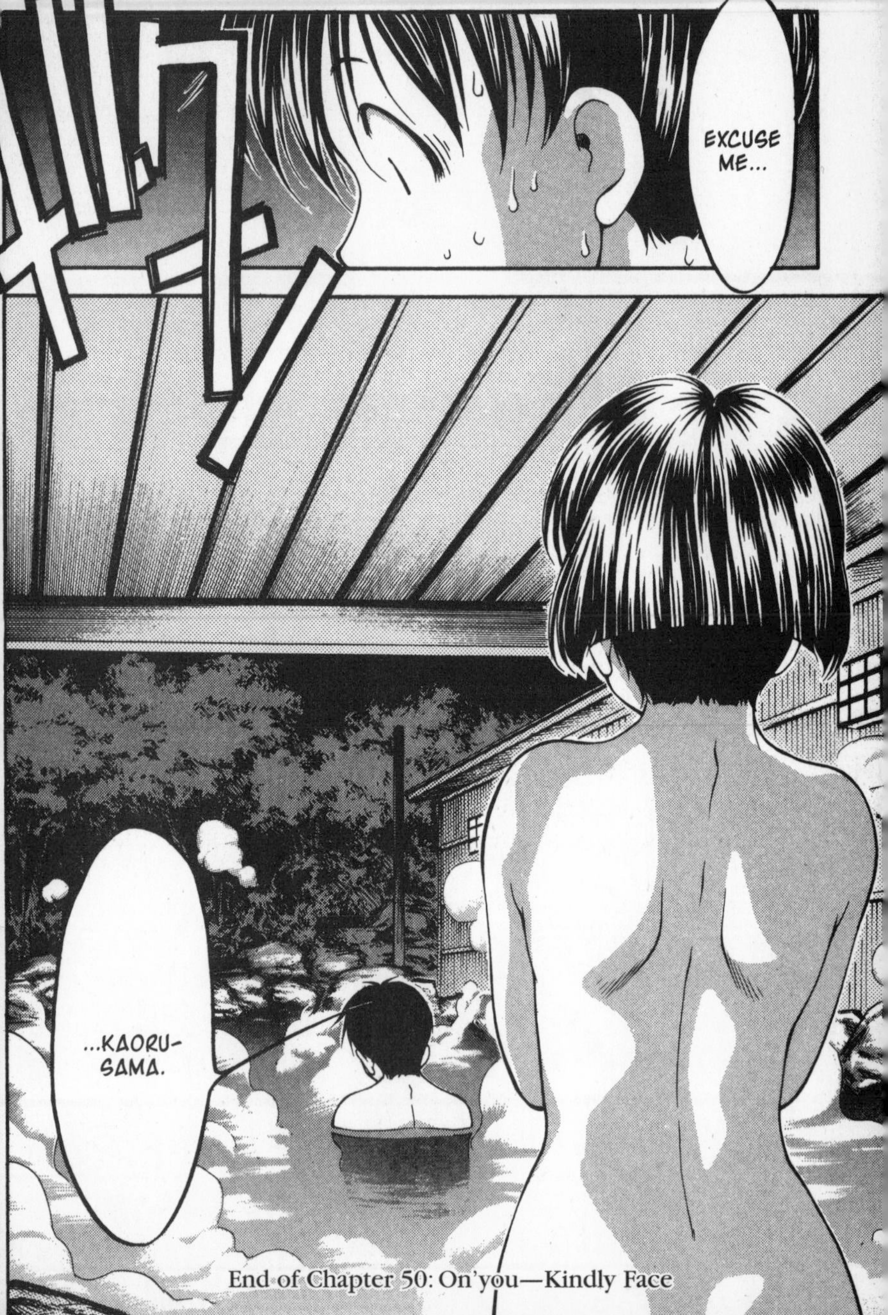
EXCUSE ME...
...KAORU-SAMA.
End of Chapter 50: On'you—Kindly Face

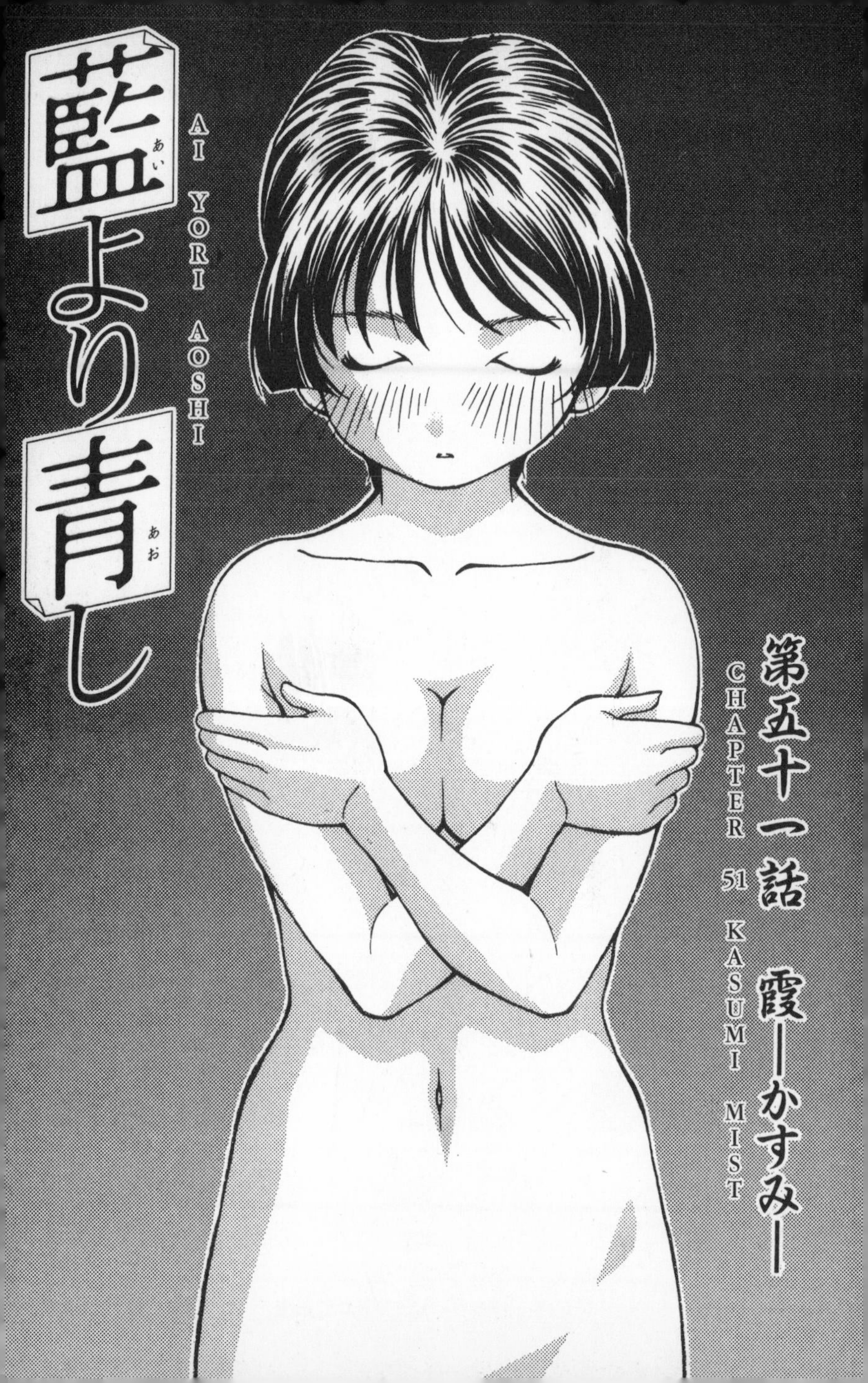
第五十一話 霞ーかすみー
CHAPTER 51 KASUMI MIST
AI YORI AOSHI
藍より青し

# Ai-Ao Theatre Part 13

Go, go! Our Waitress

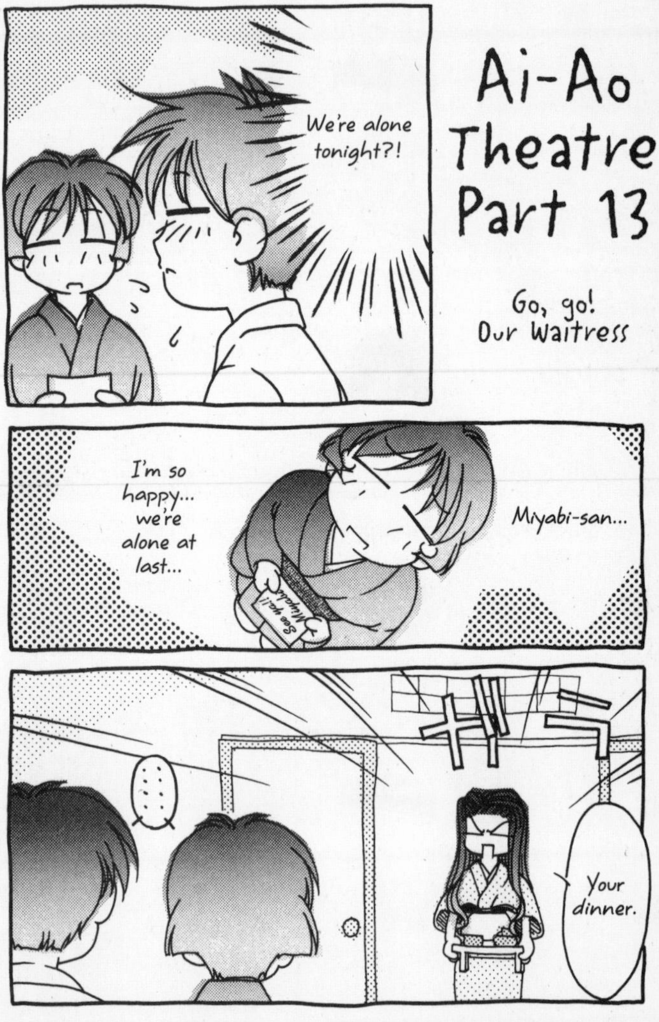
We're alone tonight?!
Miyabi-san...
I'm so happy... we're alone at last...
Your dinner.

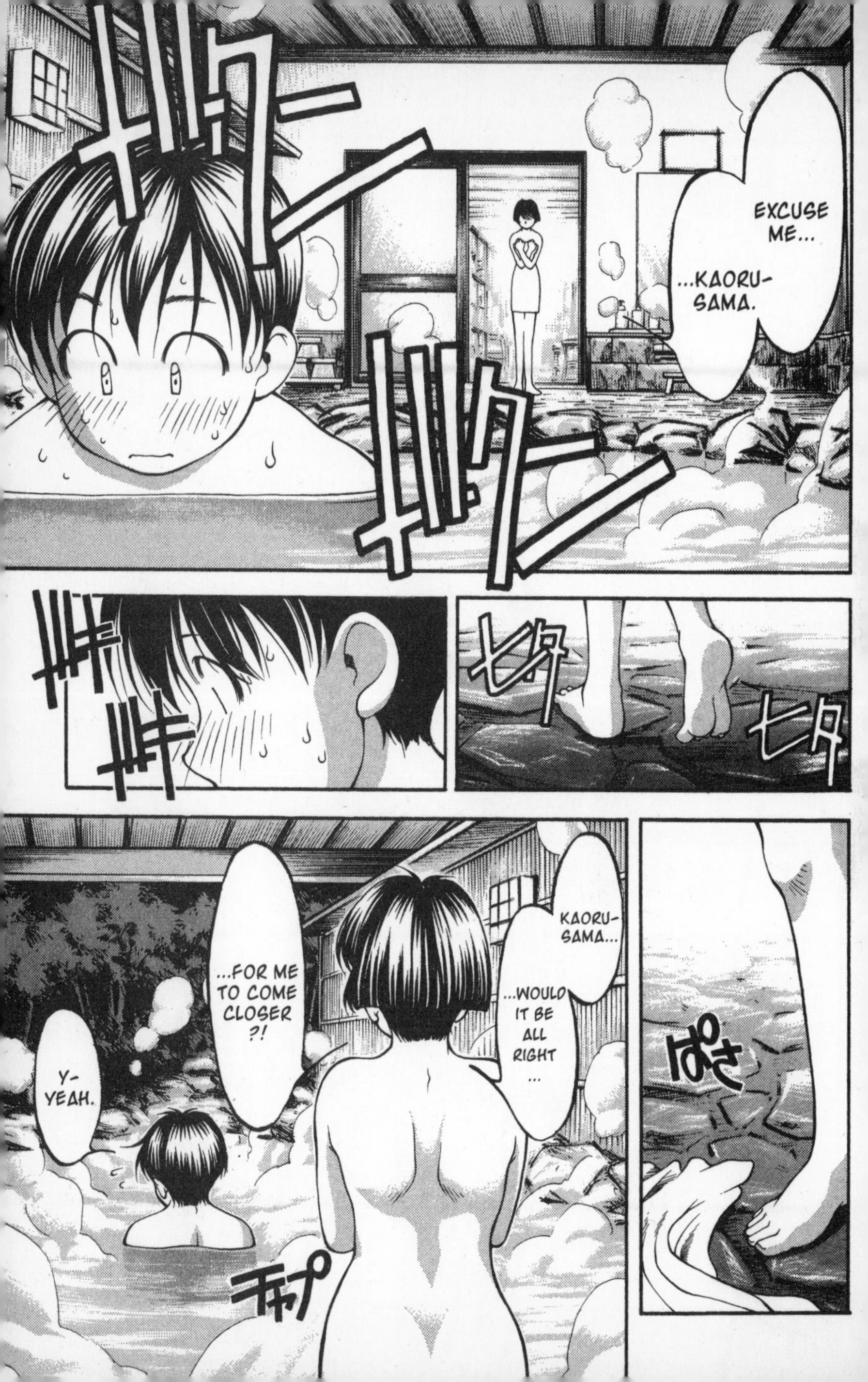
EXCUSE ME...
...KAORU-SAMA.
ヒタ
ヒタ
ドキ
ドキ
ぱさ
KAORU-SAMA...
...WOULD IT BE ALL RIGHT ...
...FOR ME TO COME CLOSER ?!
Y-YEAH.
チャプ

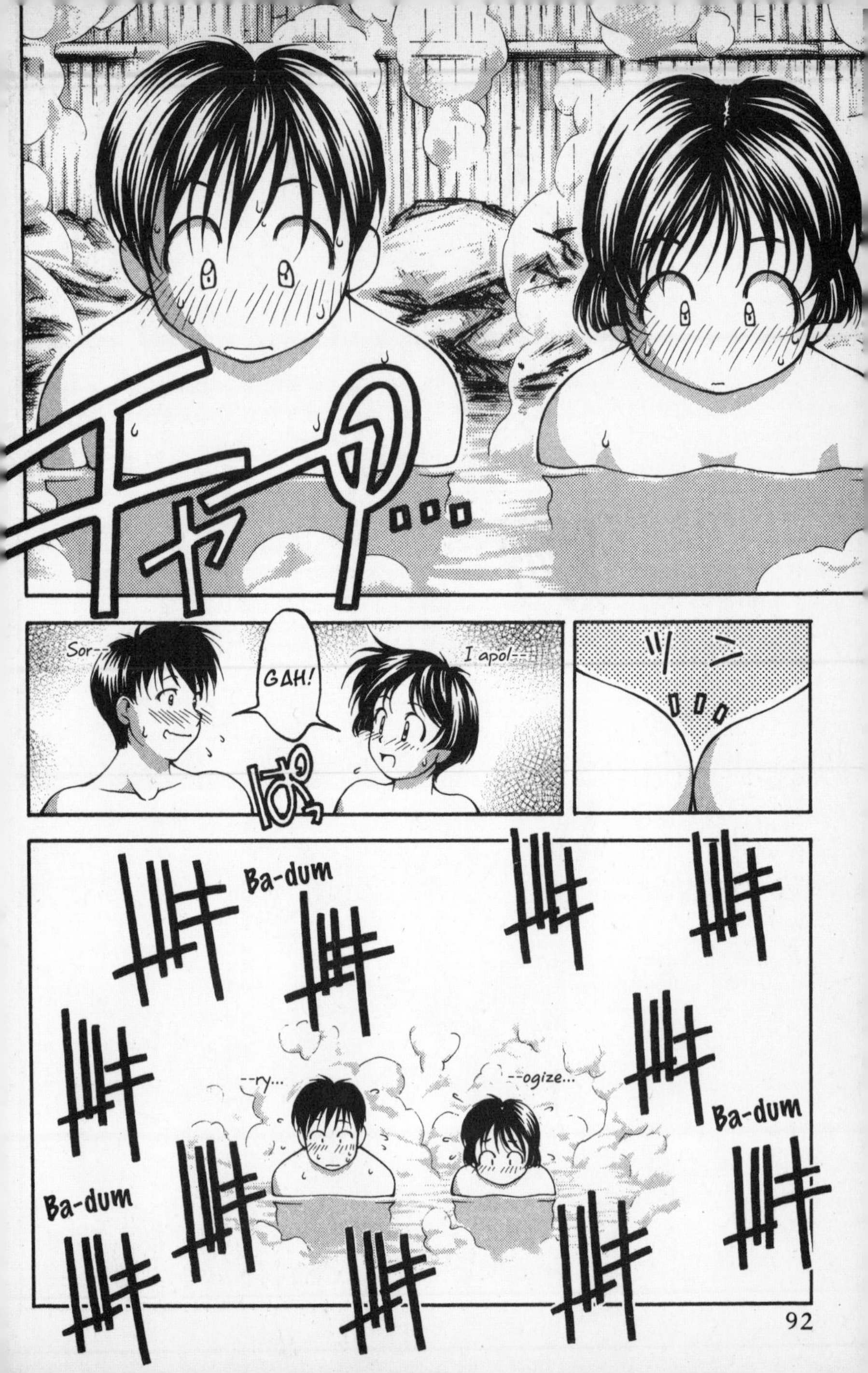
チャプ…
I apol--
GAH!
Sor--
Ba-dum
Ba-dum
--ogize...
--ry...
Ba-dum

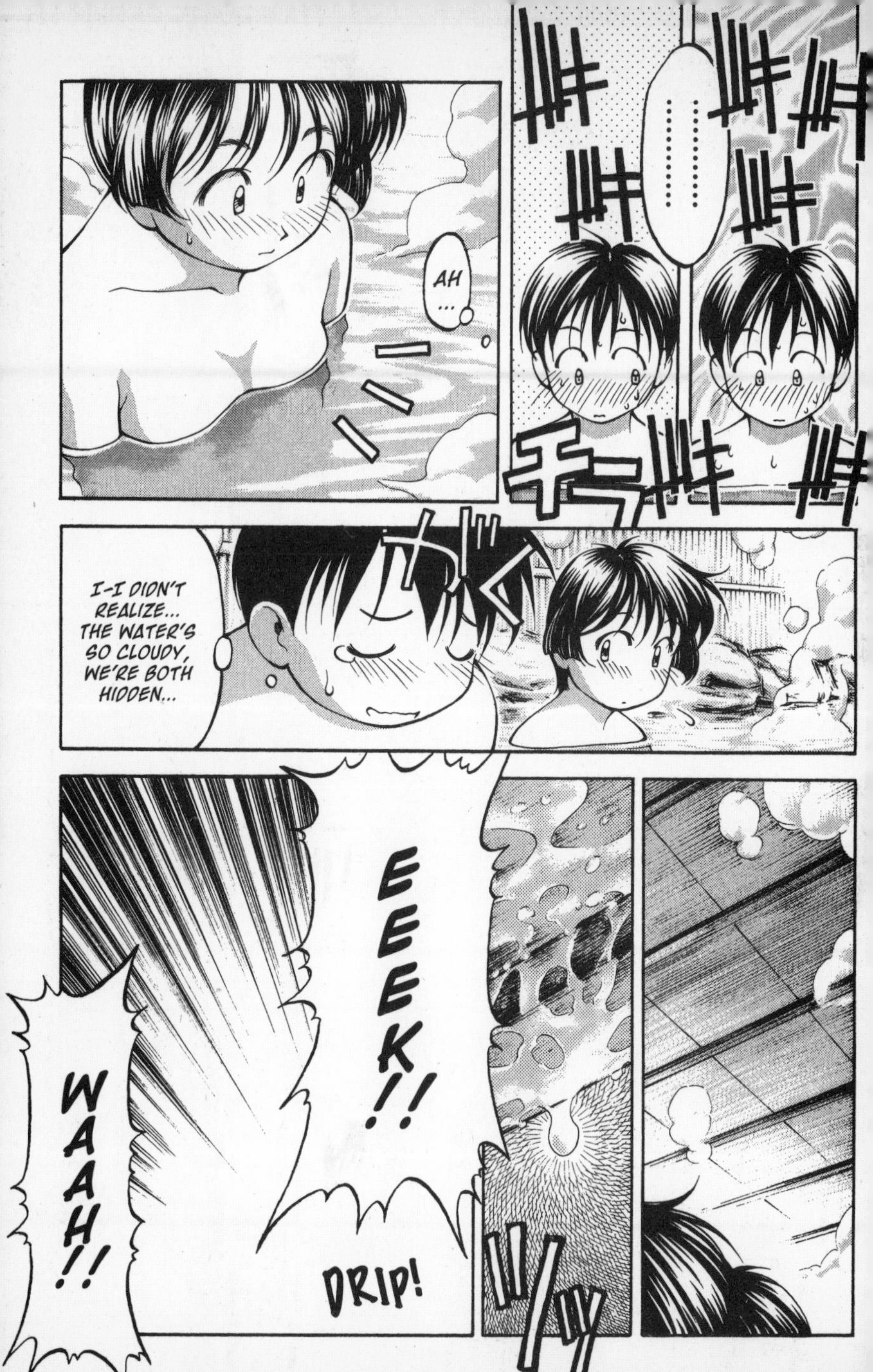
......
チラ
AH ...
I-I DIDN'T REALIZE... THE WATER'S SO CLOUDY, WE'RE BOTH HIDDEN...
EEEEK!!
DRIP!
WAAAH!!

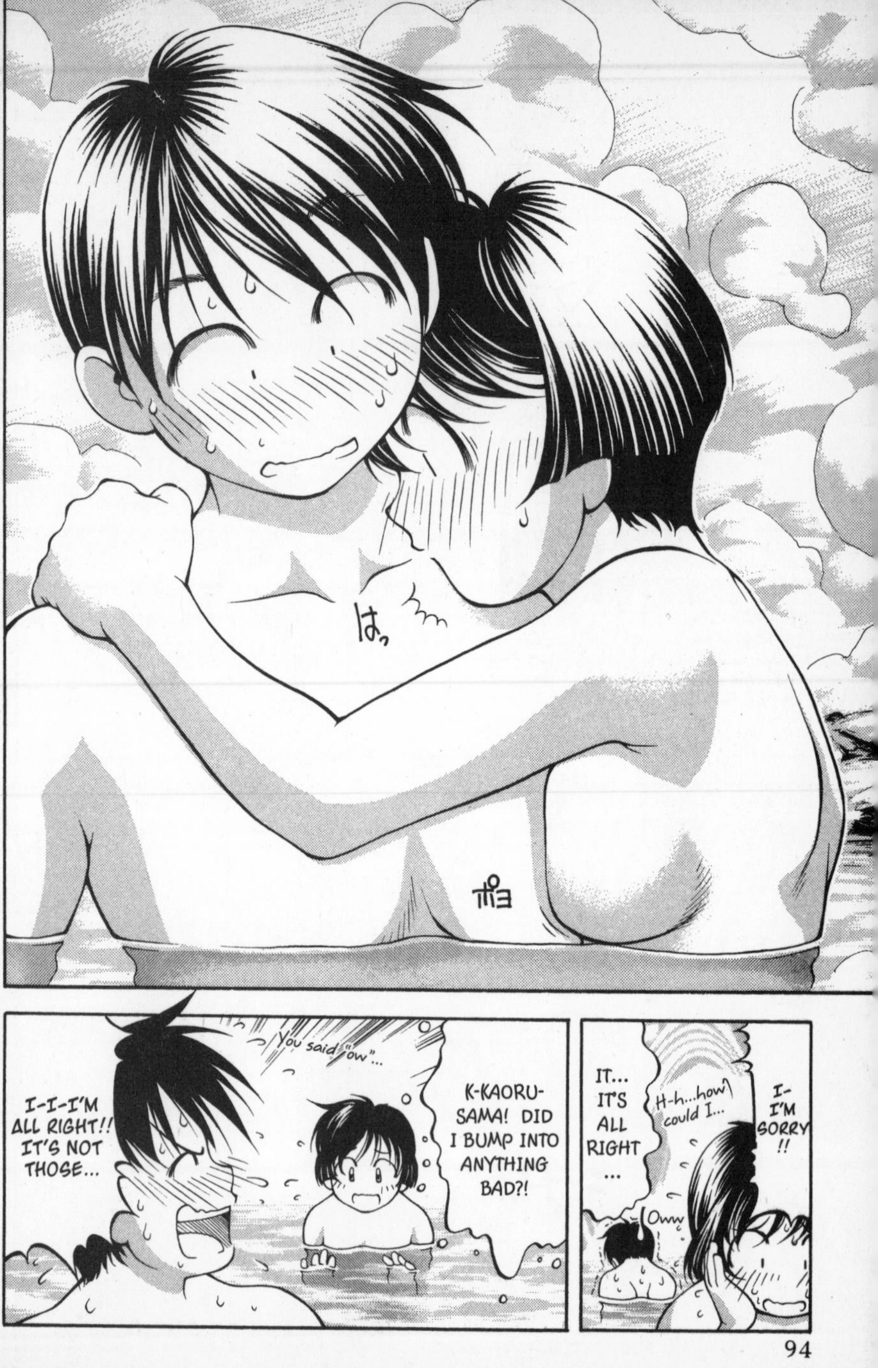
はっ
ポヨ
I- I'M SORRY !!
H-h...how could I...
IT... IT'S ALL RIGHT ...
Oww
K-KAORU-SAMA! DID I BUMP INTO ANYTHING BAD?!
You said "ow"...
I-I-I'M ALL RIGHT!! IT'S NOT THOSE...

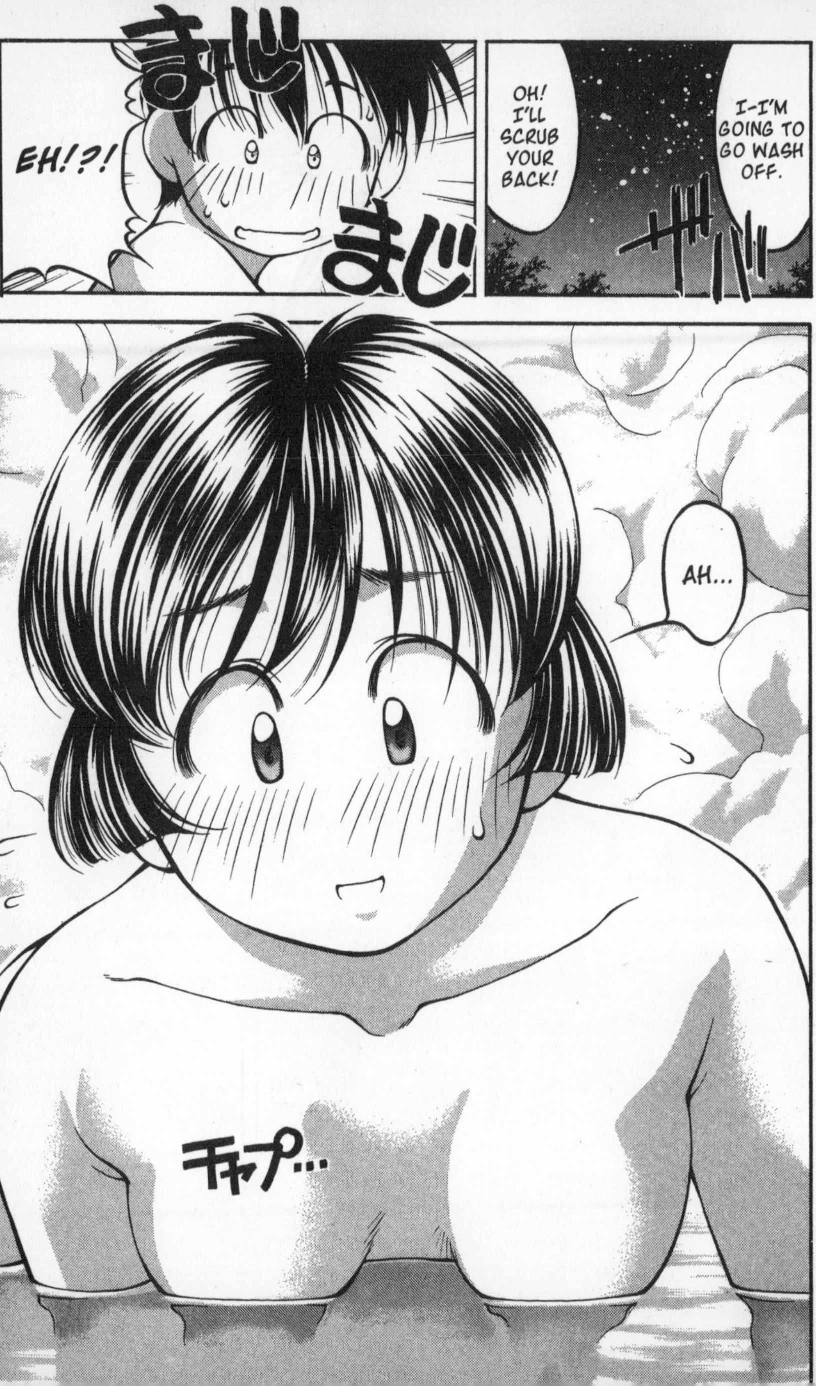
I-I'M GOING TO GO WASH OFF.
OH! I'LL SCRUB YOUR BACK!
ザバ
まじ
まじ
EH!?!
AH...
チャプ...

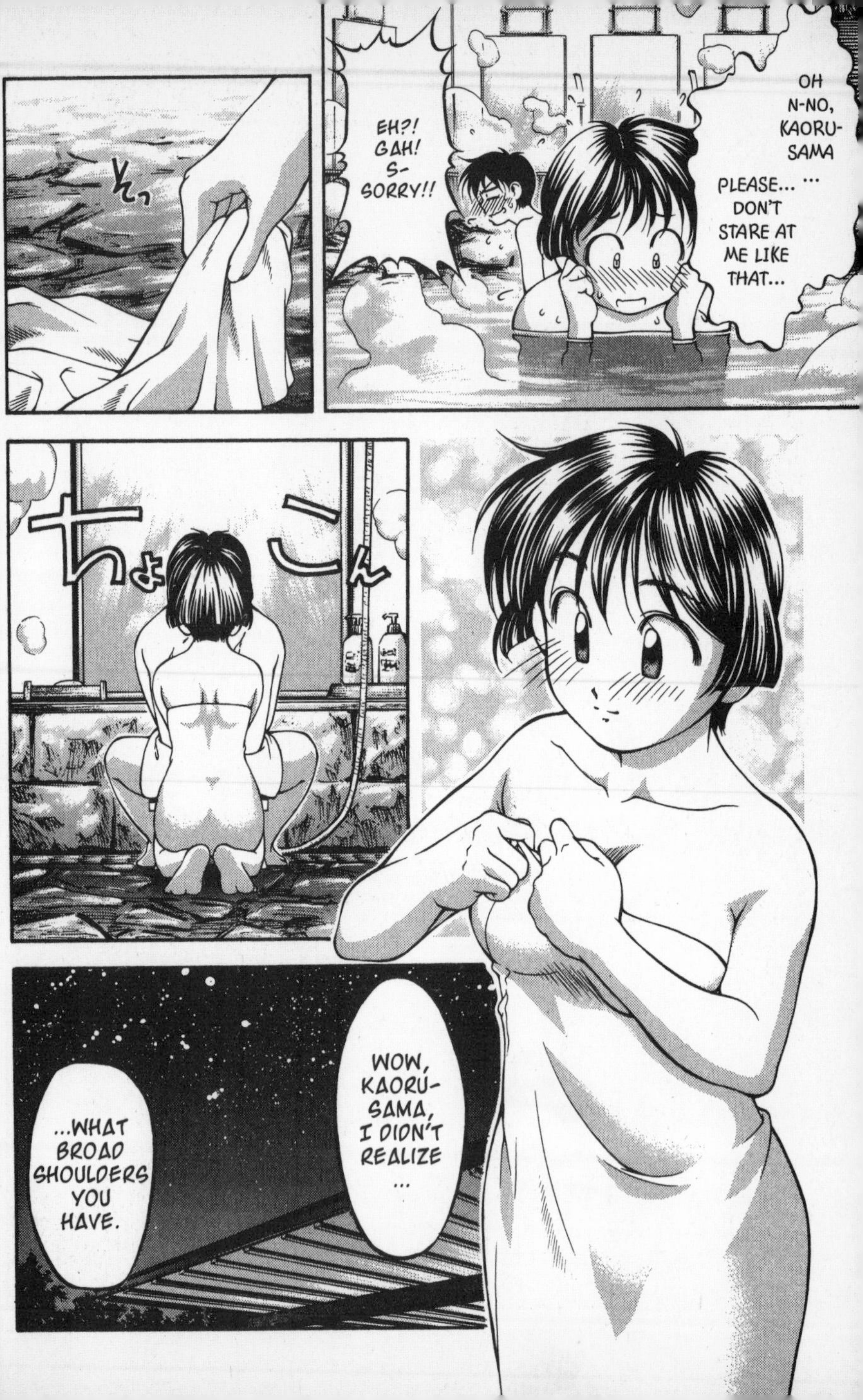
OH N-NO, KAORU-SAMA ...
PLEASE... DON'T STARE AT ME LIKE THAT...
EH?! GAH! S-SORRY!!
ちょこん
WOW, KAORU-SAMA, I DIDN'T REALIZE ...
...WHAT BROAD SHOULDERS YOU HAVE.

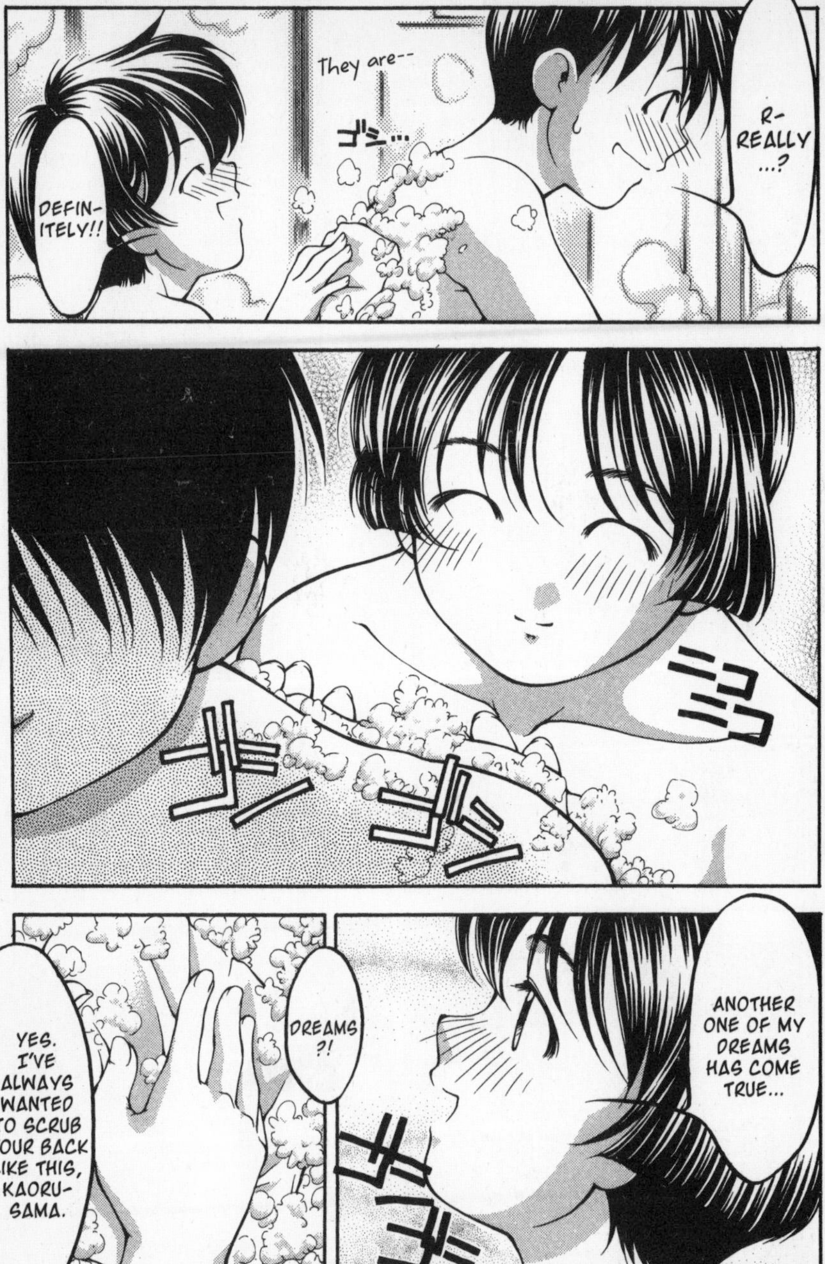
R-REALLY ...?
They are--
ゴシ...
DEFIN-ITELY!!
ニコニコ
ゴシゴシ
ANOTHER ONE OF MY DREAMS HAS COME TRUE...
DREAMS ?!
YES. I'VE ALWAYS WANTED TO SCRUB YOUR BACK LIKE THIS, KAORU-SAMA.

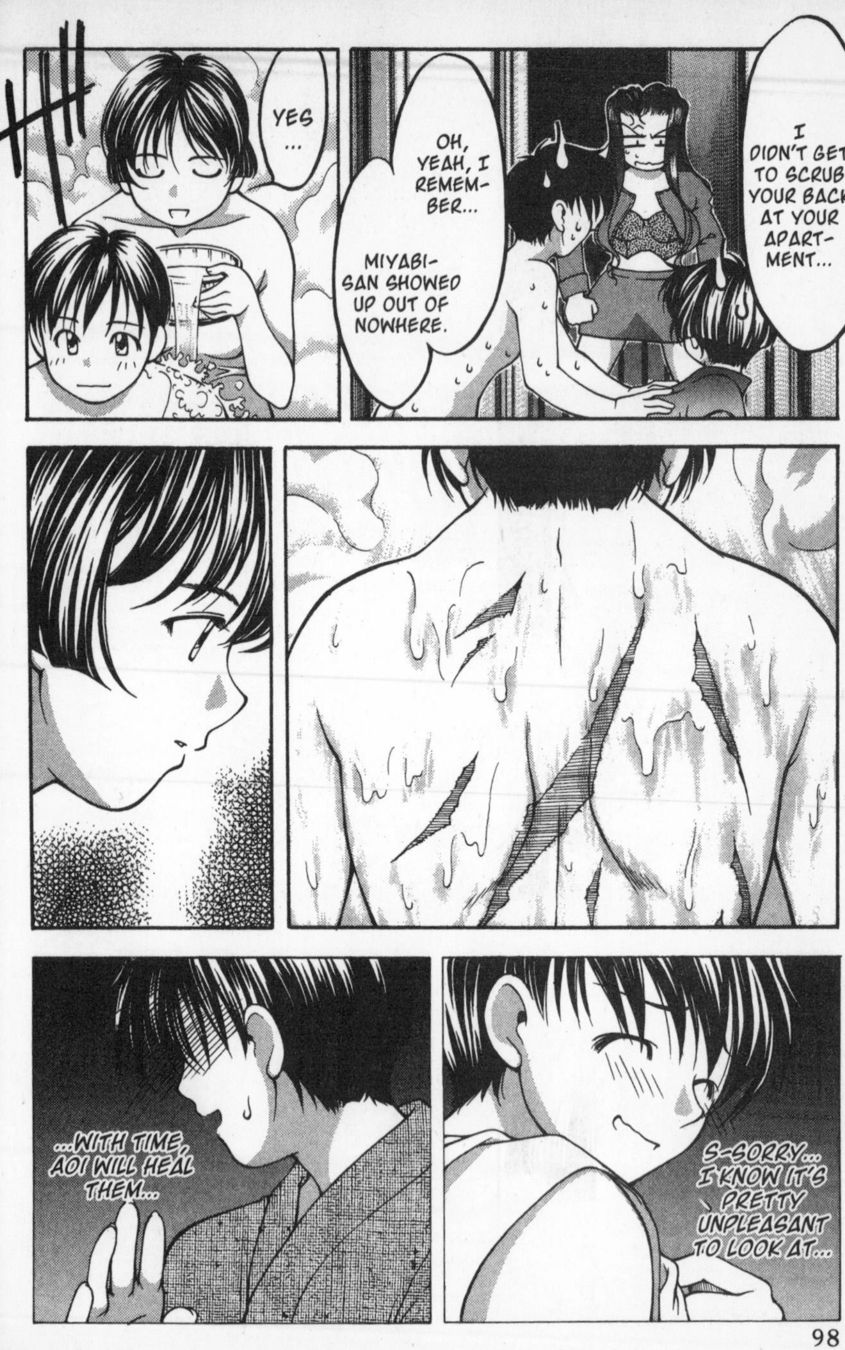
I DIDN'T GET TO SCRUB YOUR BACK AT YOUR APARTMENT...
OH, YEAH, I REMEMBER...
MIYABI-SAN SHOWED UP OUT OF NOWHERE.
YES ...
S-SORRY... I KNOW IT'S PRETTY UNPLEASANT TO LOOK AT...
...WITH TIME, AOI WILL HEAL THEM...

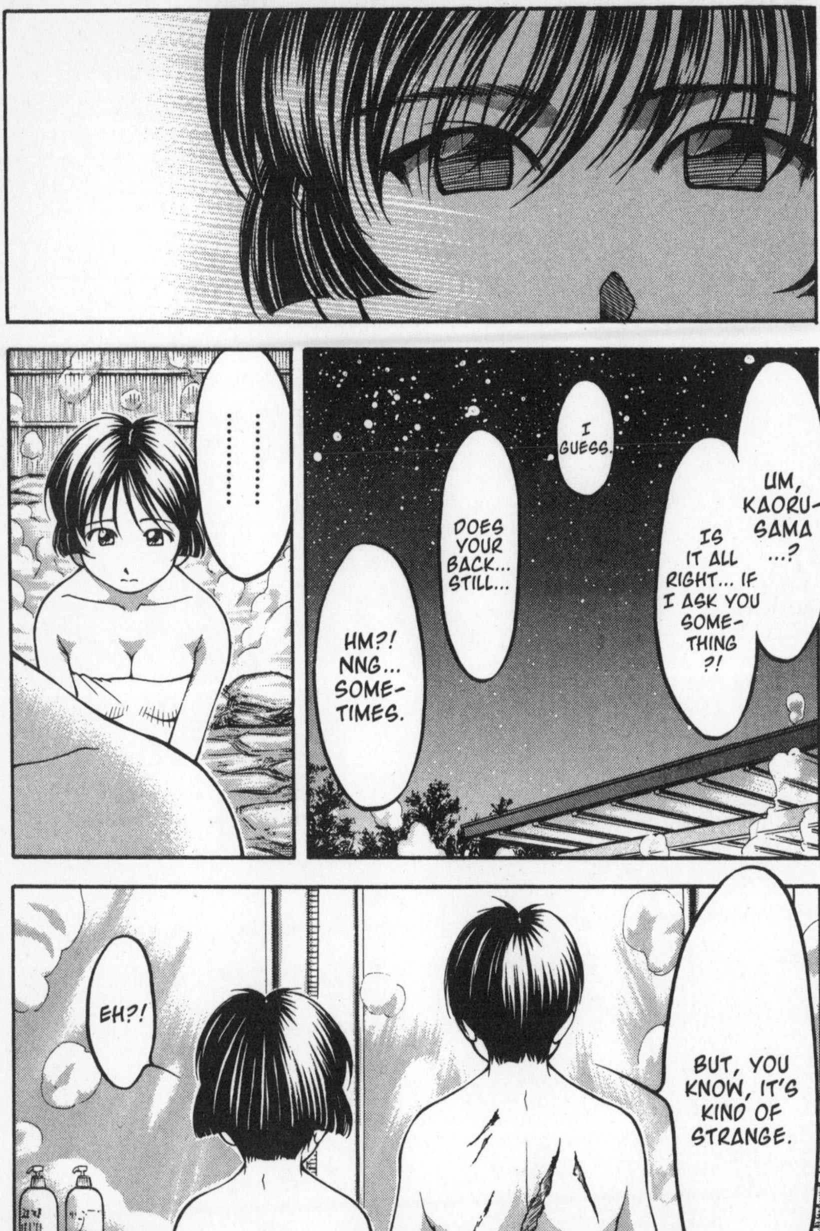
UM, KAORU-SAMA ...?
IS IT ALL RIGHT... IF I ASK YOU SOME-THING ?!
I GUESS.
DOES YOUR BACK... STILL...
HM?! NNG... SOME-TIMES.
......
BUT, YOU KNOW, IT'S KIND OF STRANGE.
EH?!

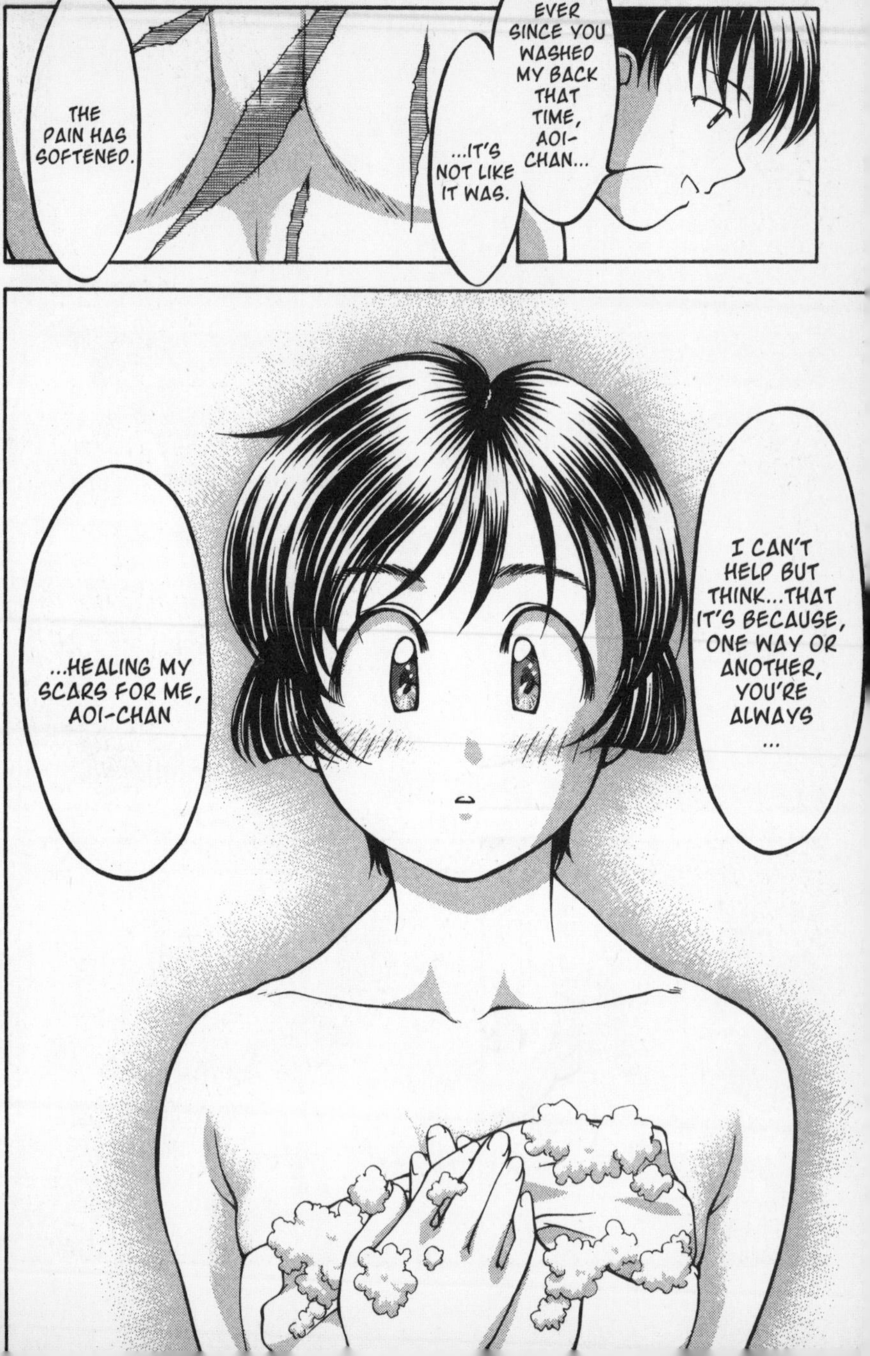
EVER SINCE YOU WASHED MY BACK THAT TIME, AOI-CHAN...
...IT'S NOT LIKE IT WAS.
THE PAIN HAS SOFTENED.
I CAN'T HELP BUT THINK...THAT IT'S BECAUSE, ONE WAY OR ANOTHER, YOU'RE ALWAYS ...
...HEALING MY SCARS FOR ME, AOI-CHAN

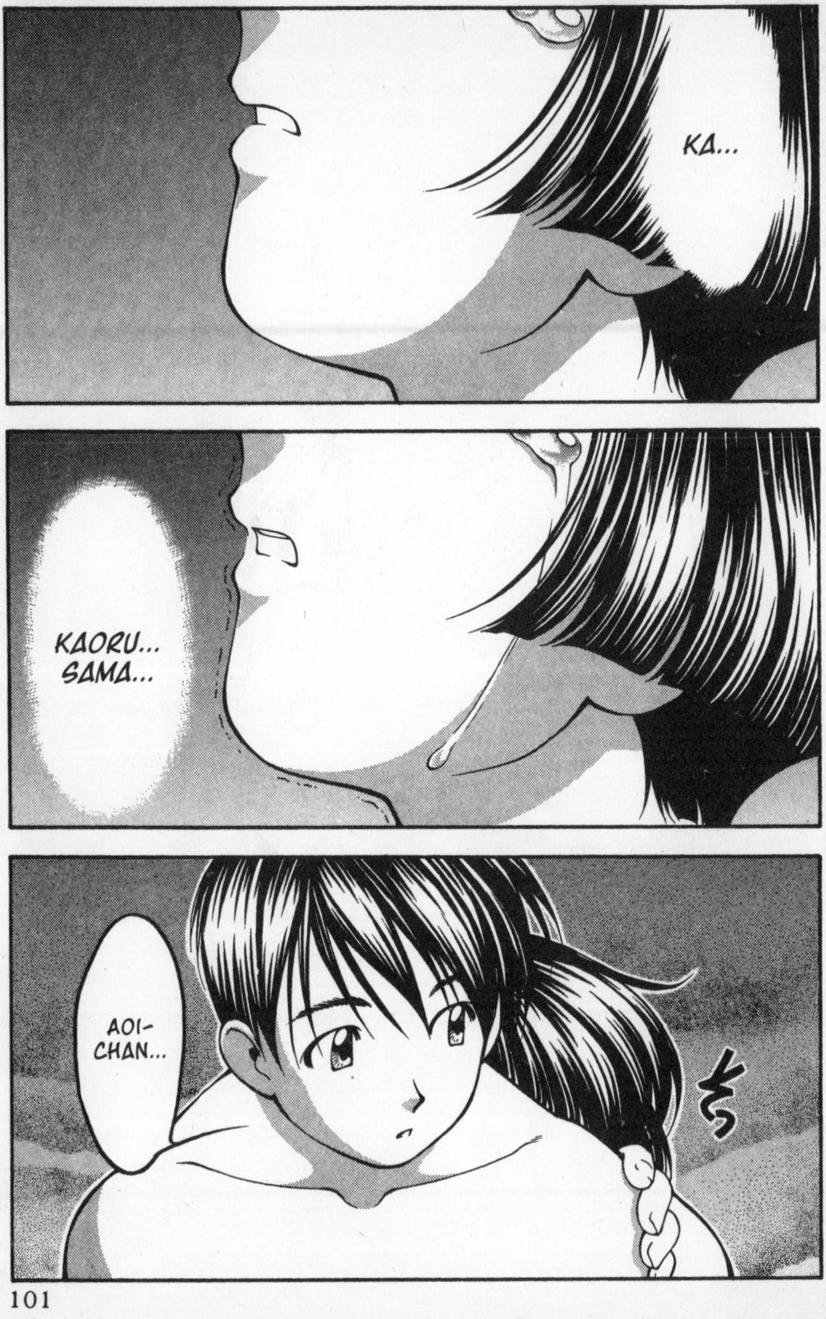
KA...
KAORU... SAMA...
AOI-CHAN...

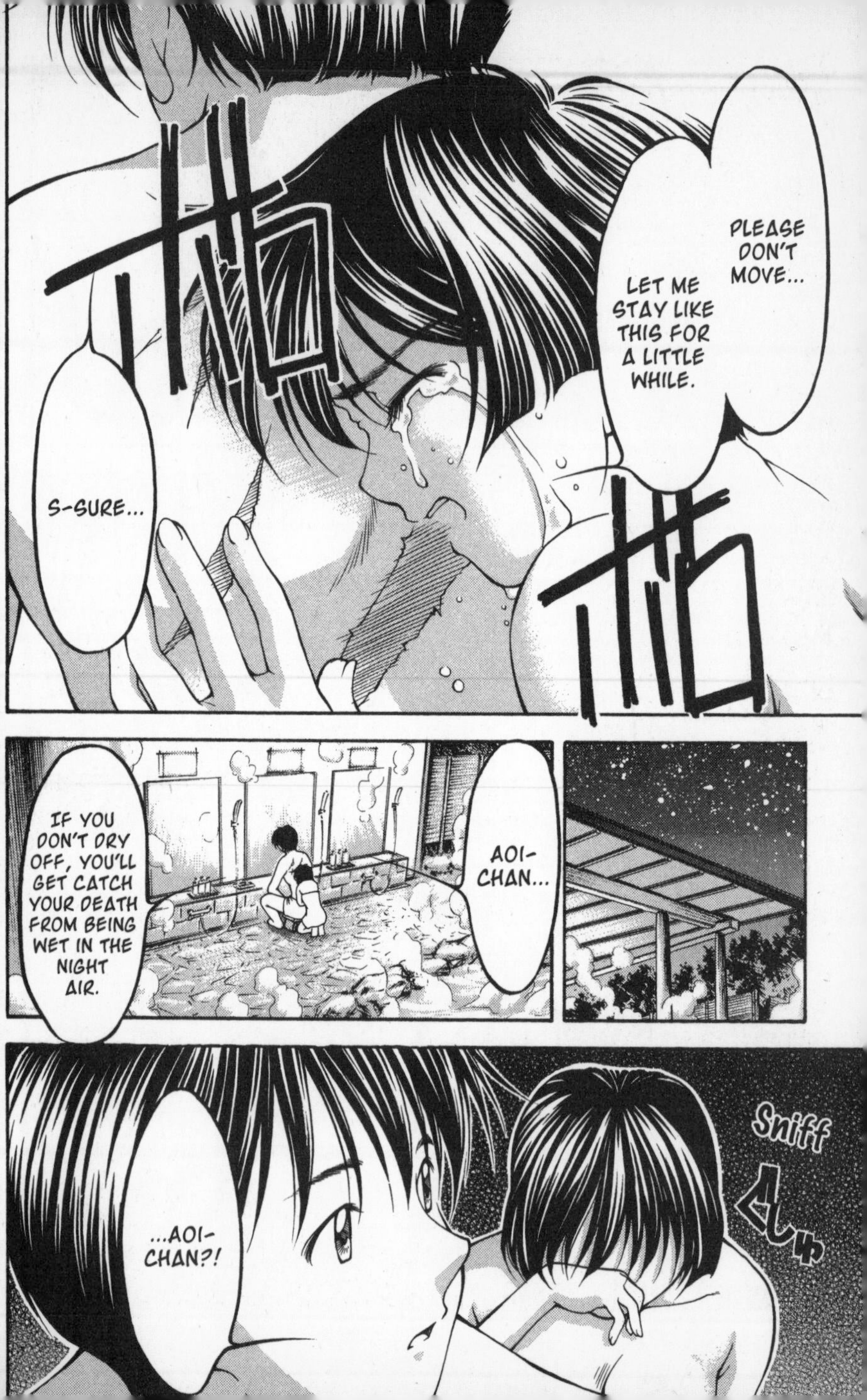
PLEASE DON'T MOVE... LET ME STAY LIKE THIS FOR A LITTLE WHILE.
S-SURE...
AOI-CHAN...
IF YOU DON'T DRY OFF, YOU'LL GET CATCH YOUR DEATH FROM BEING WET IN THE NIGHT AIR.
Sniff
...AOI-CHAN?!

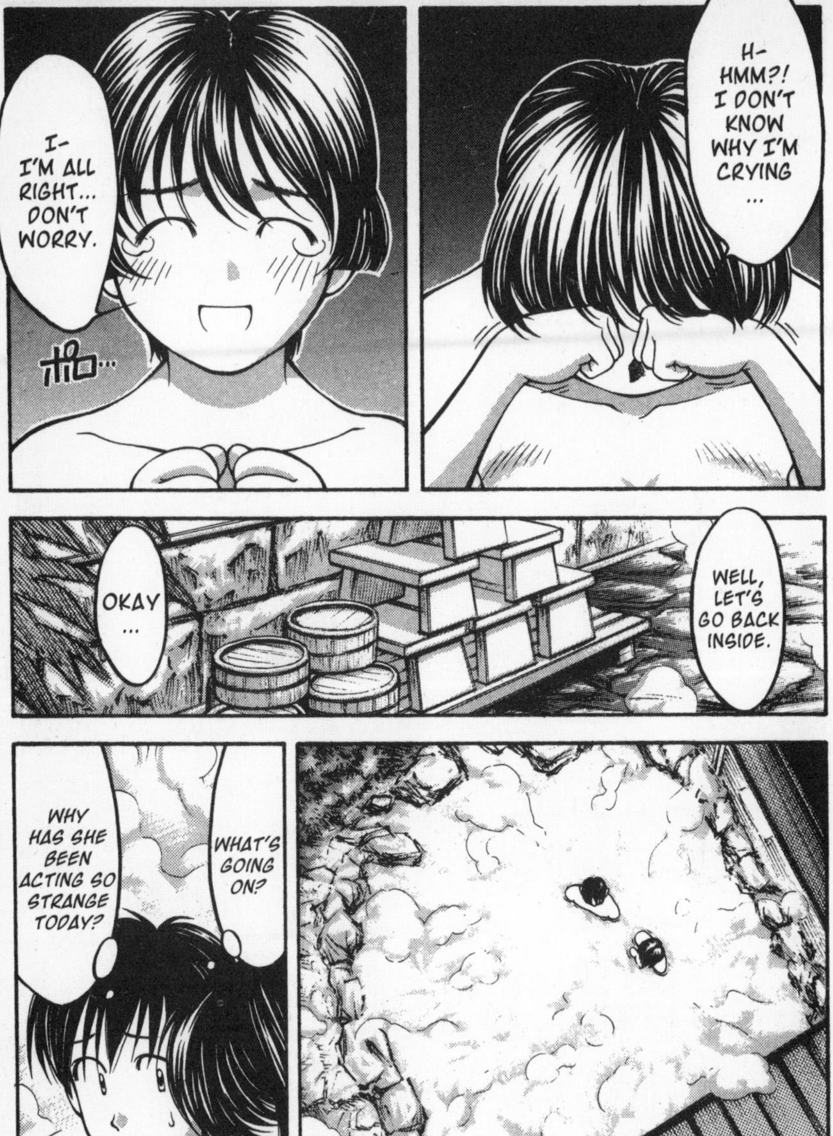
H-
HMM?!
I DON'T
KNOW
WHY I'M
CRYING
...
I-
I'M ALL
RIGHT...
DON'T
WORRY.
ポロ...
WELL,
LET'S
GO BACK
INSIDE.
OKAY
...
WHAT'S
GOING
ON?
WHY
HAS SHE
BEEN
ACTING SO
STRANGE
TODAY?

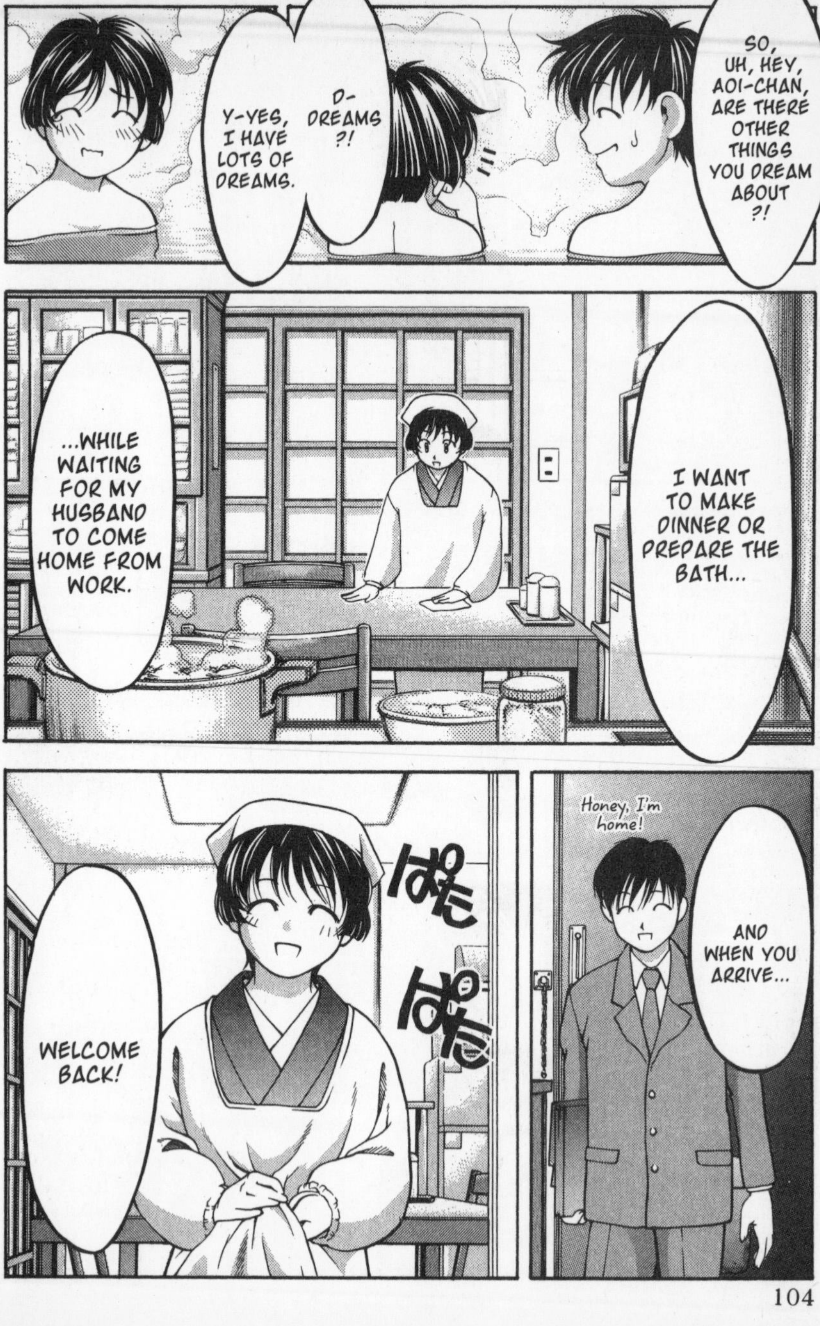
SO, UH, HEY, AOI-CHAN, ARE THERE OTHER THINGS YOU DREAM ABOUT?!
D-DREAMS?!
Y-YES, I HAVE LOTS OF DREAMS.
I WANT TO MAKE DINNER OR PREPARE THE BATH...
...WHILE WAITING FOR MY HUSBAND TO COME HOME FROM WORK.
Honey, I'm home!
AND WHEN YOU ARRIVE...
ぱた ぱた
WELCOME BACK!

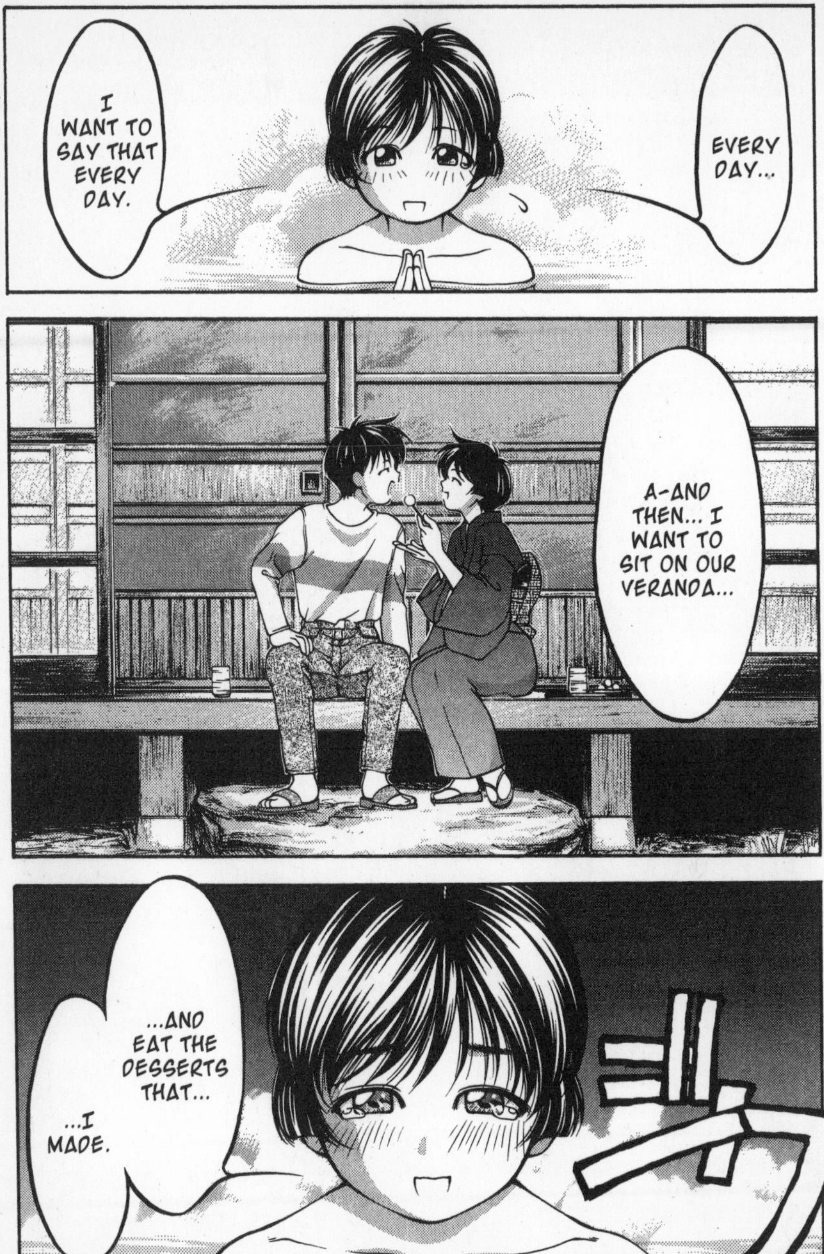
EVERY DAY...
I WANT TO SAY THAT EVERY DAY.
A-AND THEN... I WANT TO SIT ON OUR VERANDA...
...AND EAT THE DESSERTS THAT...
...I MADE.

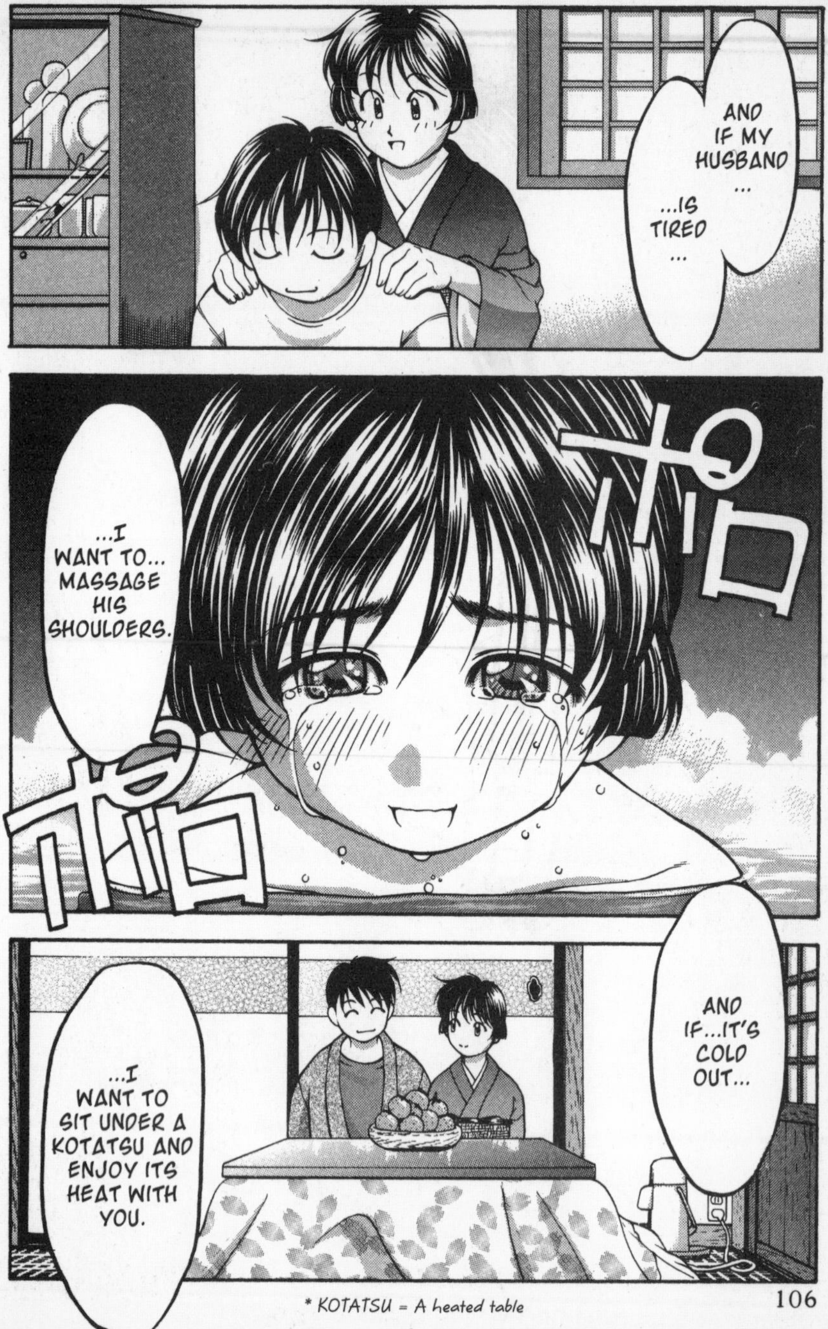
AND IF MY HUSBAND ...
...IS TIRED ...
ポロ
...I WANT TO... MASSAGE HIS SHOULDERS.
ポロ
AND IF...IT'S COLD OUT...
...I WANT TO SIT UNDER A KOTATSU AND ENJOY ITS HEAT WITH YOU.

* KOTATSU = A heated table

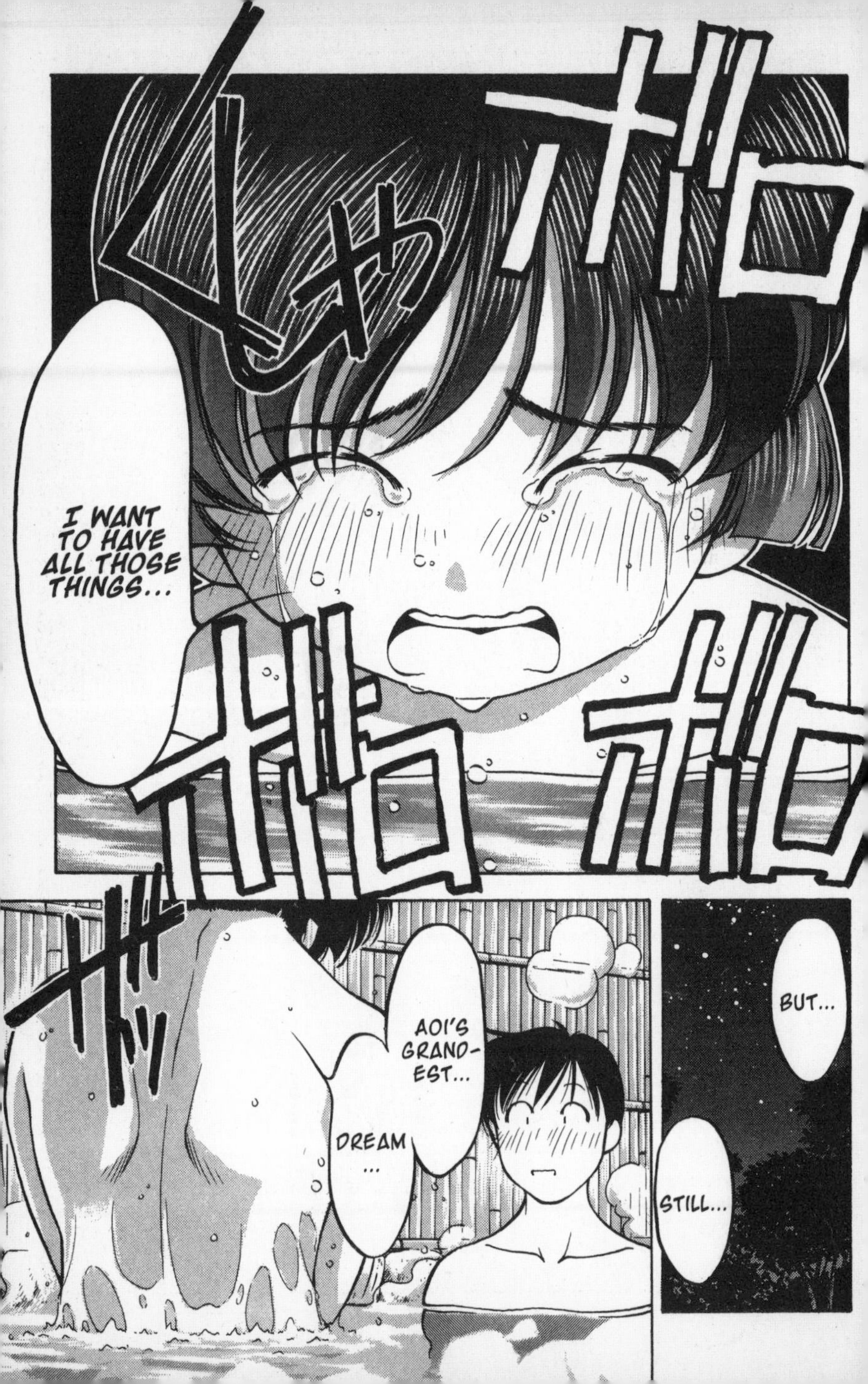
I WANT TO HAVE ALL THOSE THINGS...
BUT...
STILL...
AOI'S GRAND-EST...
DREAM ...

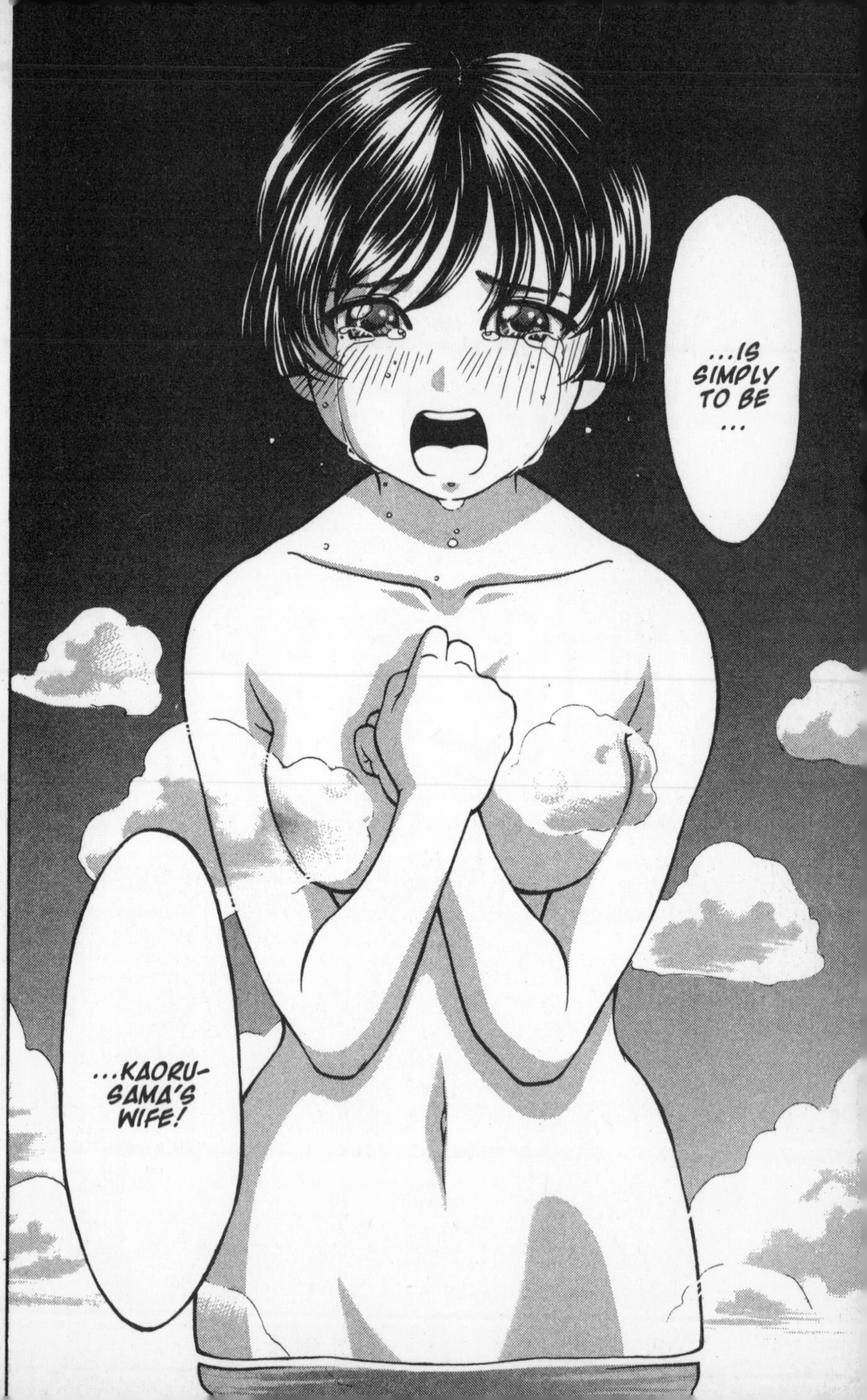
...IS SIMPLY TO BE ...
...KAORU-SAMA'S WIFE!

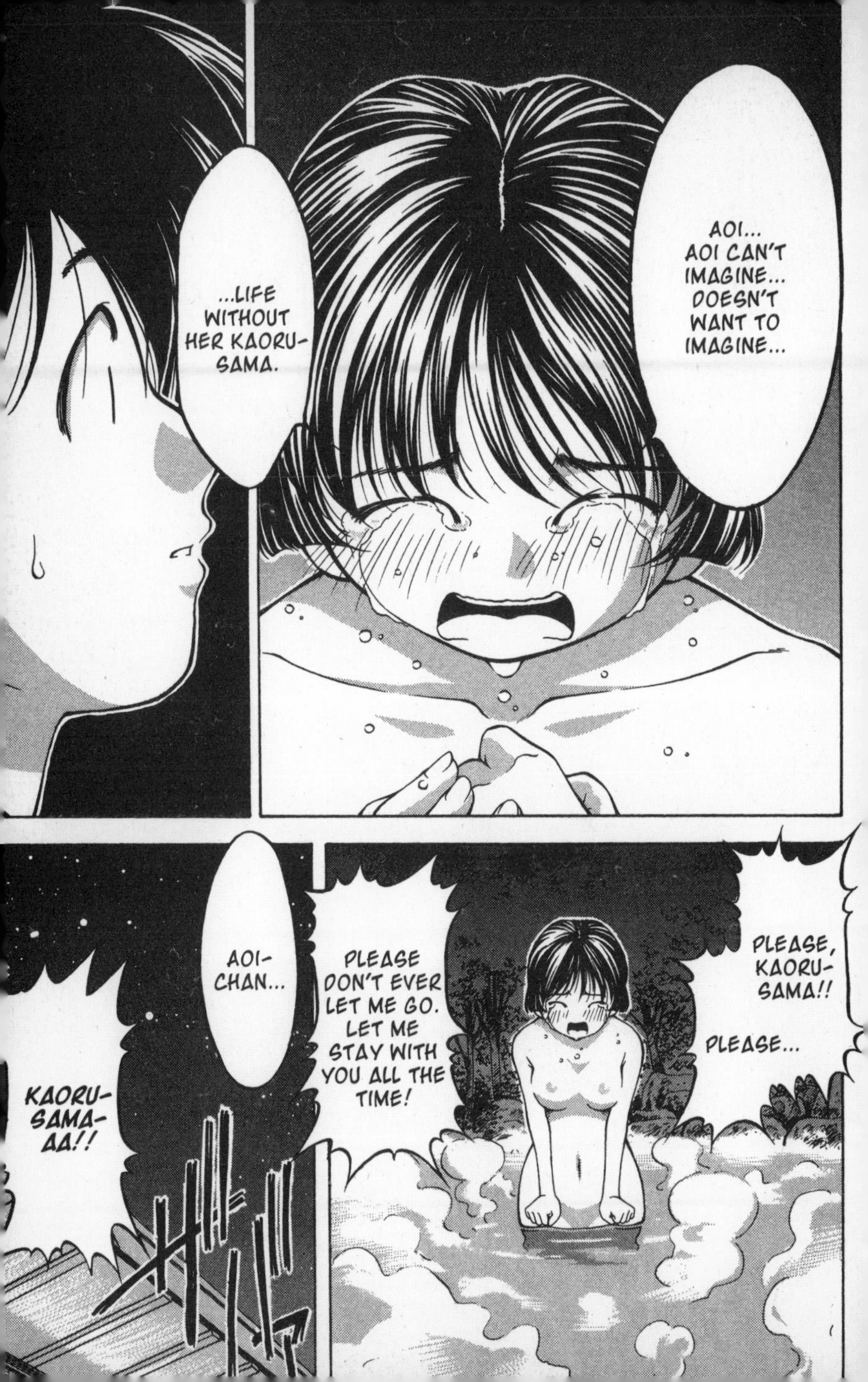
AOI... AOI CAN'T IMAGINE... DOESN'T WANT TO IMAGINE...
...LIFE WITHOUT HER KAORU-SAMA.
PLEASE, KAORU-SAMA!!
PLEASE...
PLEASE DON'T EVER LET ME GO. LET ME STAY WITH YOU ALL THE TIME!
AOI-CHAN...
KAORU-SAMA-AA!!

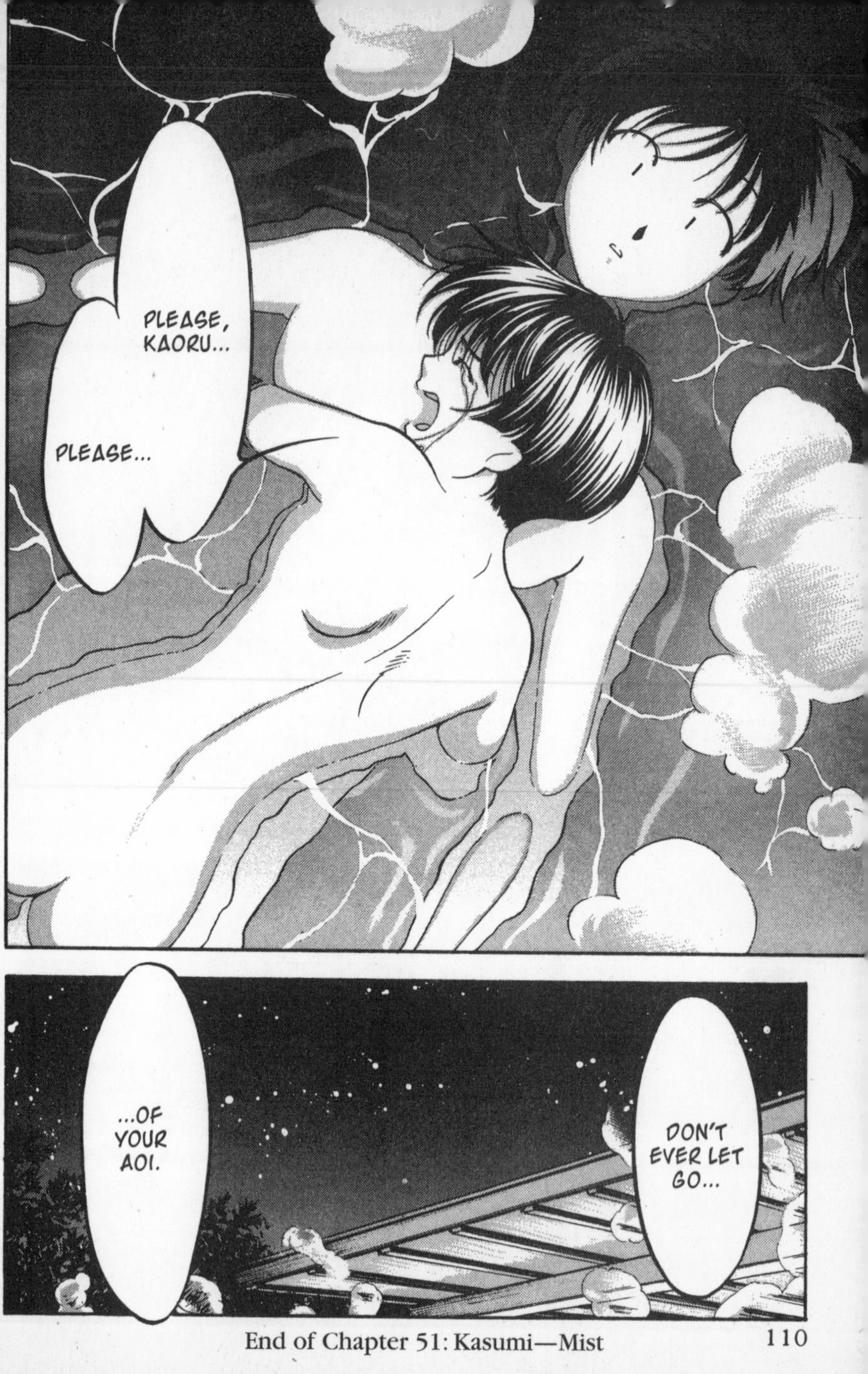
PLEASE, KAORU...
PLEASE...
DON'T EVER LET GO...
...OF YOUR AOI.

End of Chapter 51: Kasumi—Mist

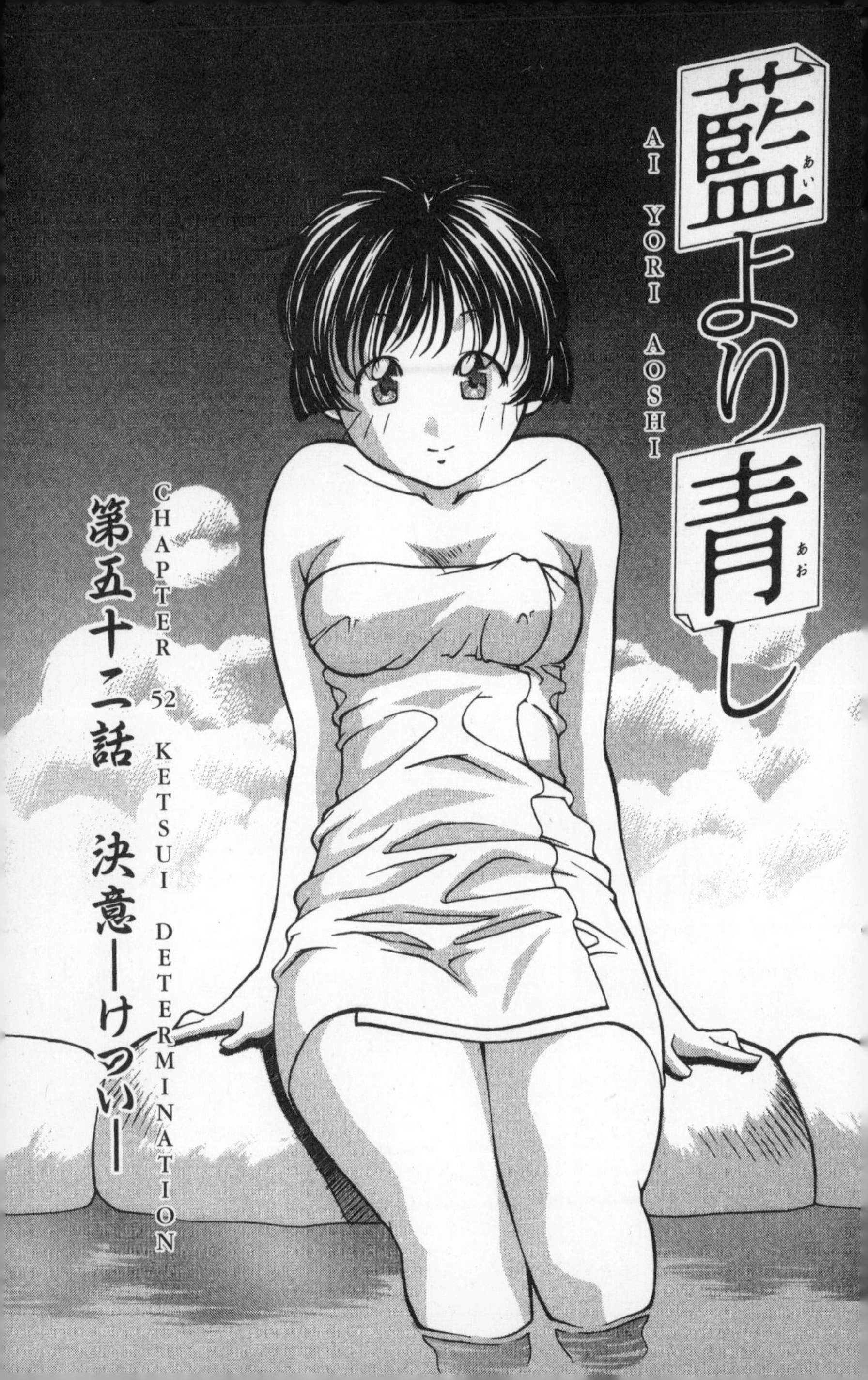
藍より青し
AI YORI AOSHI
第五十二話 決意—けつい—
CHAPTER 52 KETSUI DETERMINATION

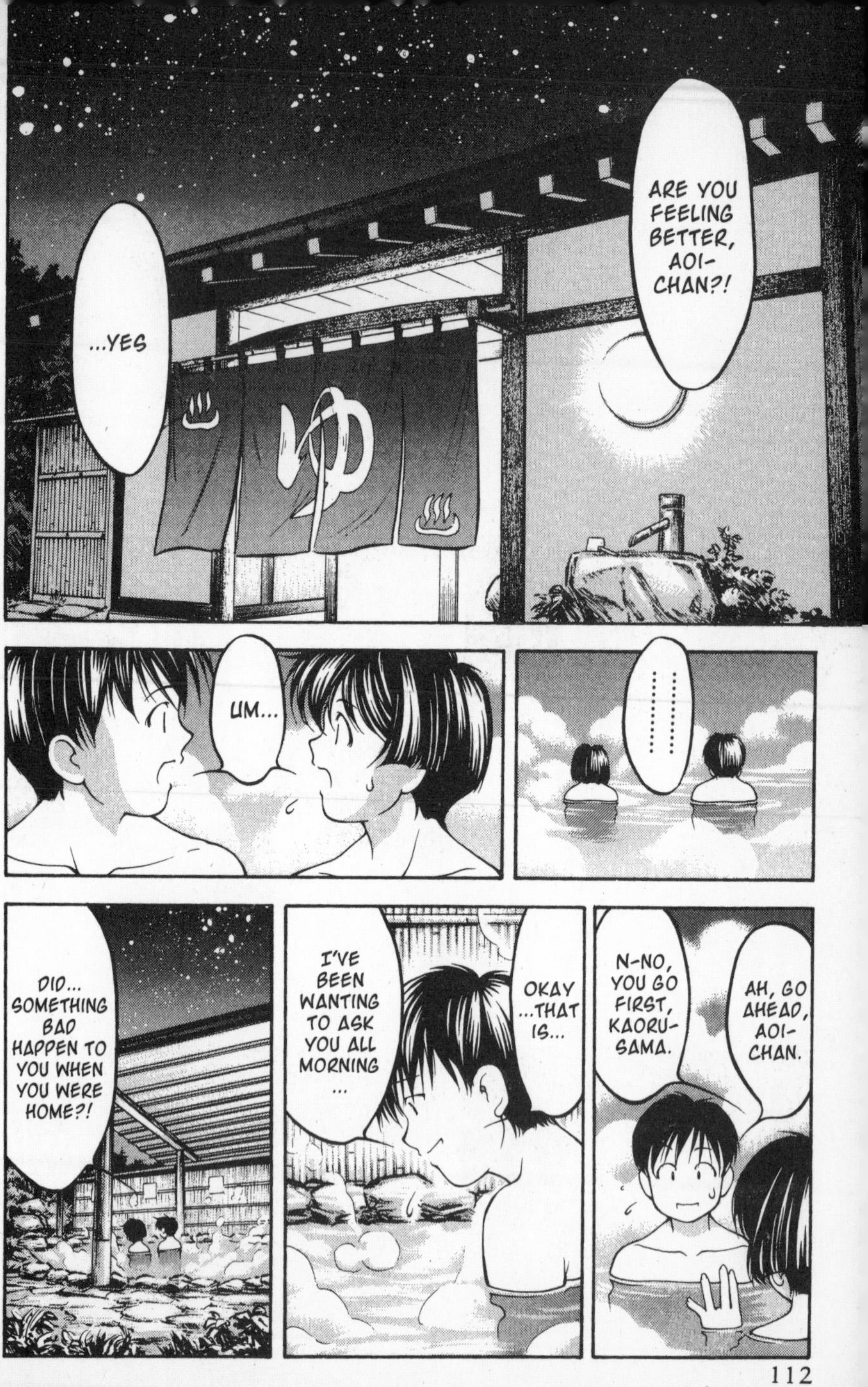
ARE YOU FEELING BETTER, AOI-CHAN?!
...YES
......
UM...
AH, GO AHEAD, AOI-CHAN.
N-NO, YOU GO FIRST, KAORU-SAMA.
OKAY ...THAT IS...
I'VE BEEN WANTING TO ASK YOU ALL MORNING ...
DID... SOMETHING BAD HAPPEN TO YOU WHEN YOU WERE HOME?!

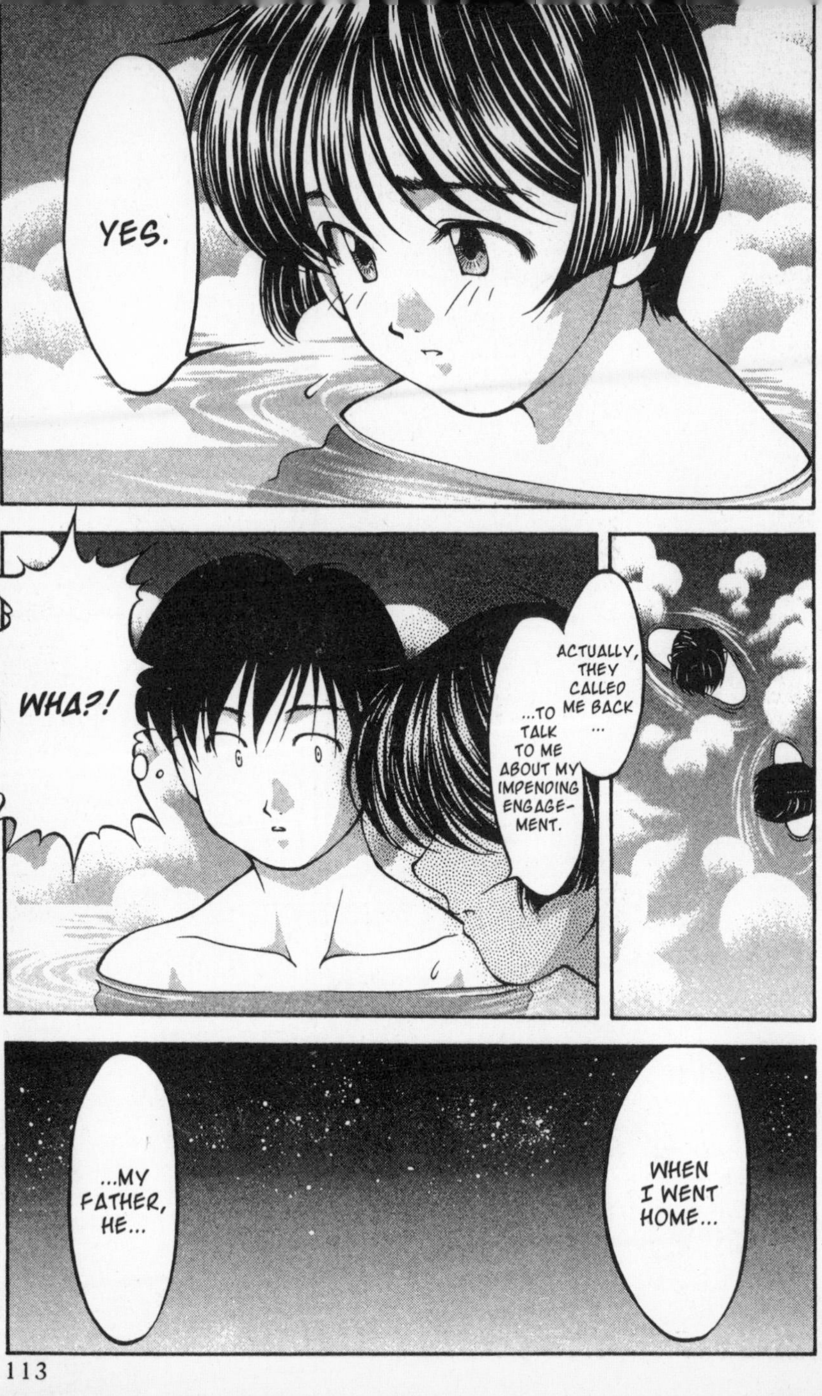
YES.
ACTUALLY, THEY CALLED ME BACK ...
...TO TALK TO ME ABOUT MY IMPENDING ENGAGE-MENT.
WHA?!
WHEN I WENT HOME...
...MY FATHER, HE...

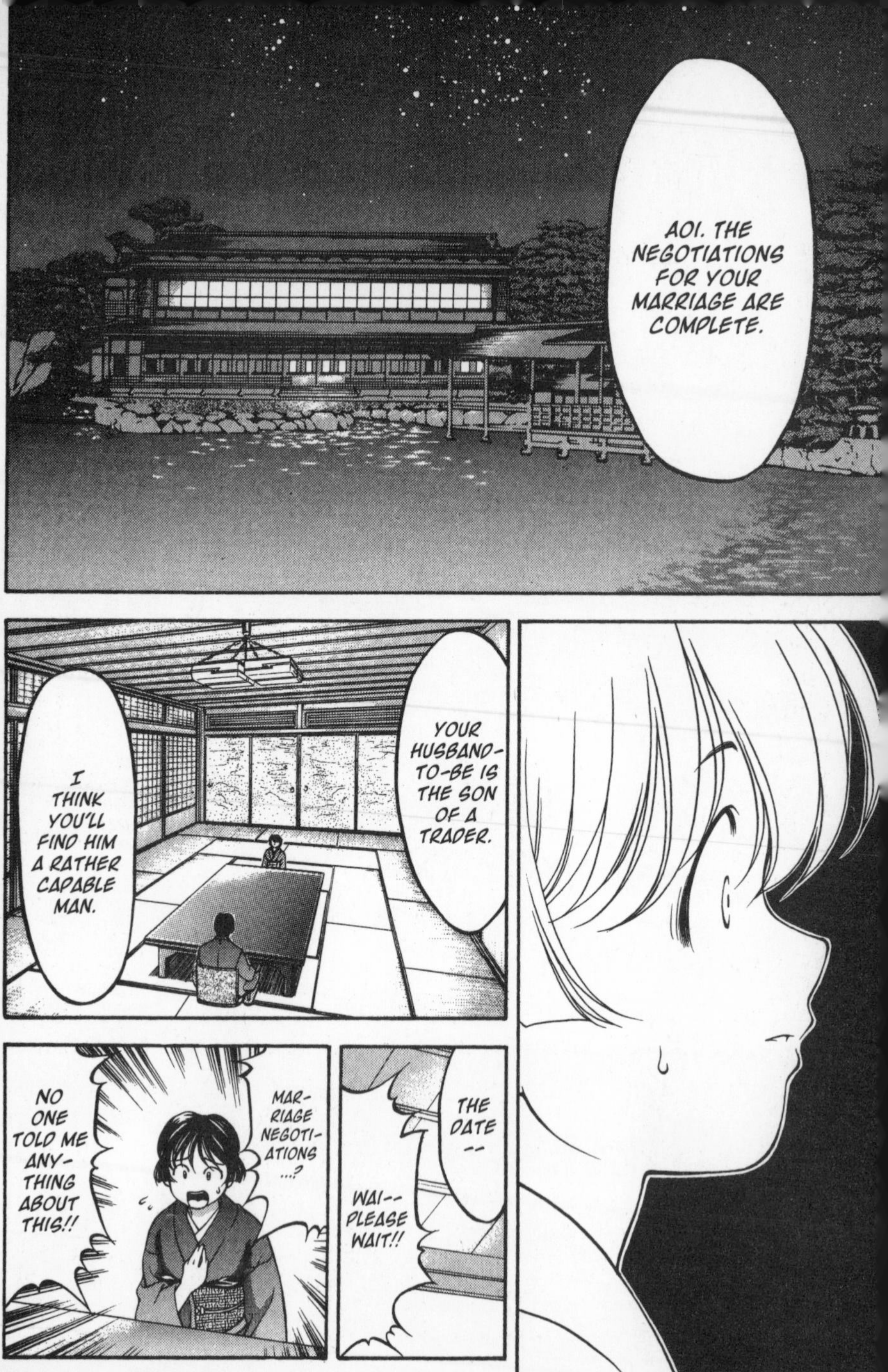
AOI. THE NEGOTIATIONS FOR YOUR MARRIAGE ARE COMPLETE.
YOUR HUSBAND-TO-BE IS THE SON OF A TRADER.
I THINK YOU'LL FIND HIM A RATHER CAPABLE MAN.
THE DATE --
WAI-- PLEASE WAIT!!
MAR-RIAGE NEGOTI-ATIONS ...?
NO ONE TOLD ME ANY-THING ABOUT THIS!!

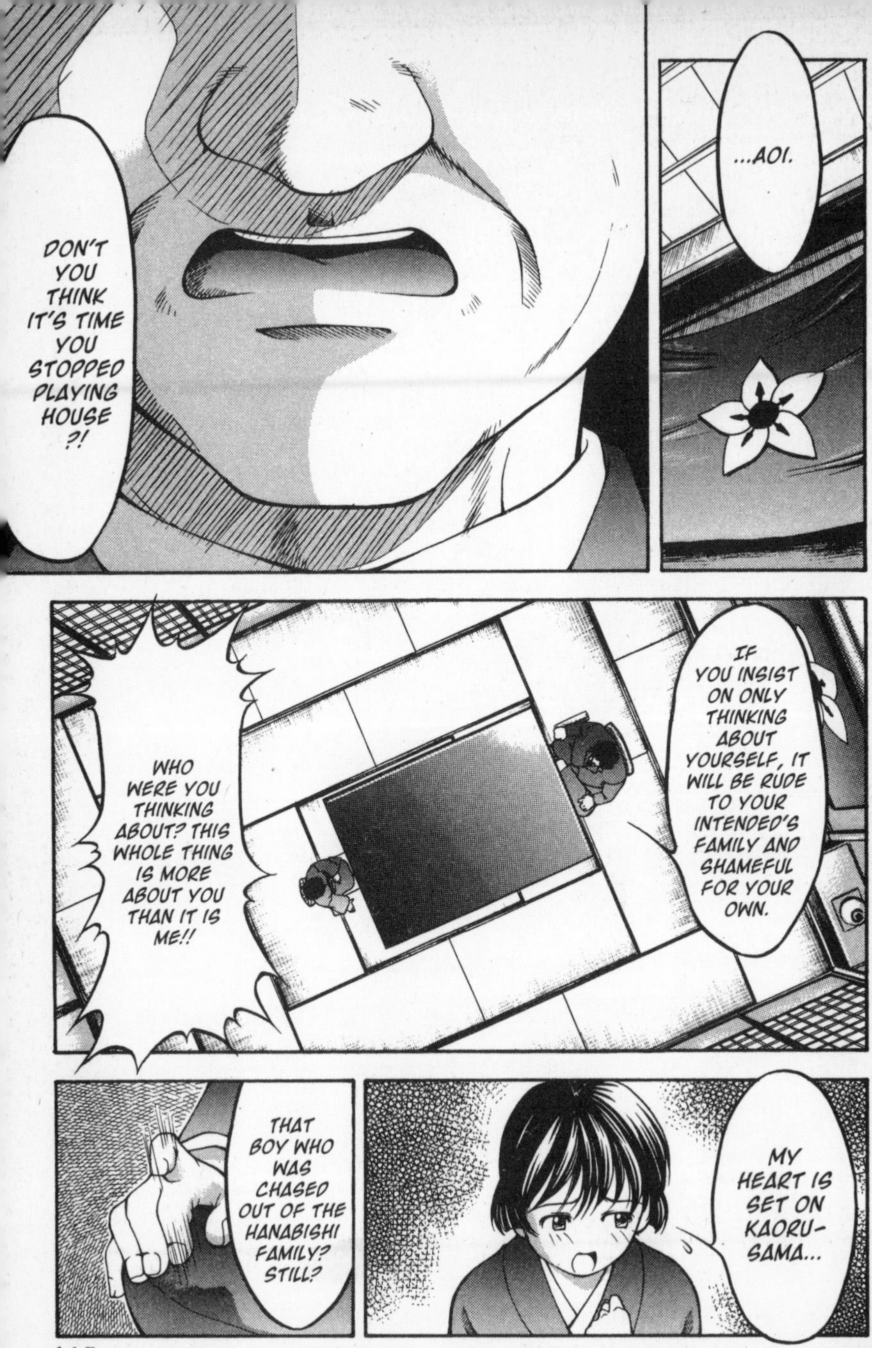
...AOI.
DON'T YOU THINK IT'S TIME YOU STOPPED PLAYING HOUSE ?!
IF YOU INSIST ON ONLY THINKING ABOUT YOURSELF, IT WILL BE RUDE TO YOUR INTENDED'S FAMILY AND SHAMEFUL FOR YOUR OWN.
WHO WERE YOU THINKING ABOUT? THIS WHOLE THING IS MORE ABOUT YOU THAN IT IS ME!!
MY HEART IS SET ON KAORU-SAMA...
THAT BOY WHO WAS CHASED OUT OF THE HANABISHI FAMILY? STILL?

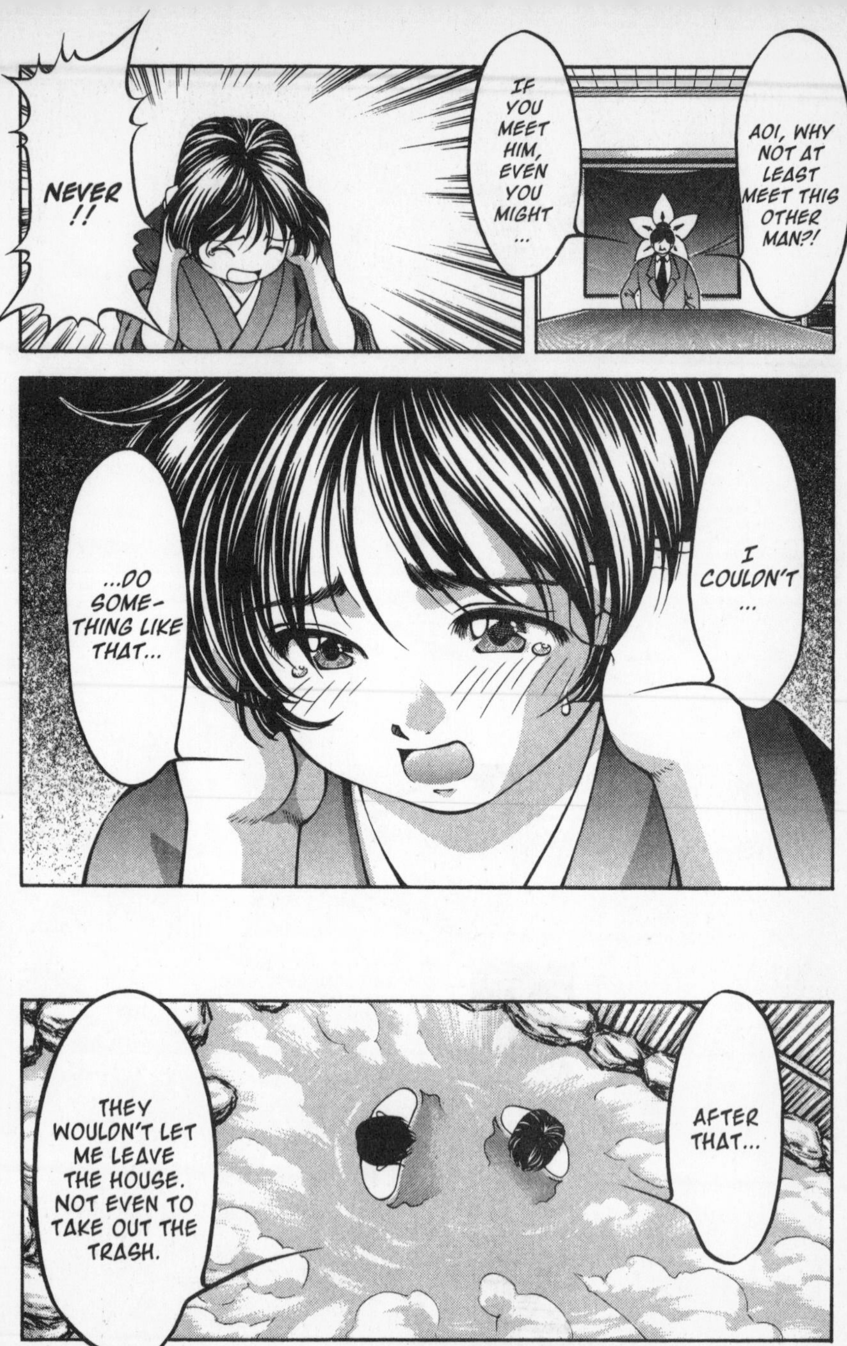
AOI, WHY NOT AT LEAST MEET THIS OTHER MAN?!
IF YOU MEET HIM, EVEN YOU MIGHT ...
NEVER !!
I COULDN'T ...
...DO SOME-THING LIKE THAT...
AFTER THAT...
THEY WOULDN'T LET ME LEAVE THE HOUSE. NOT EVEN TO TAKE OUT THE TRASH.

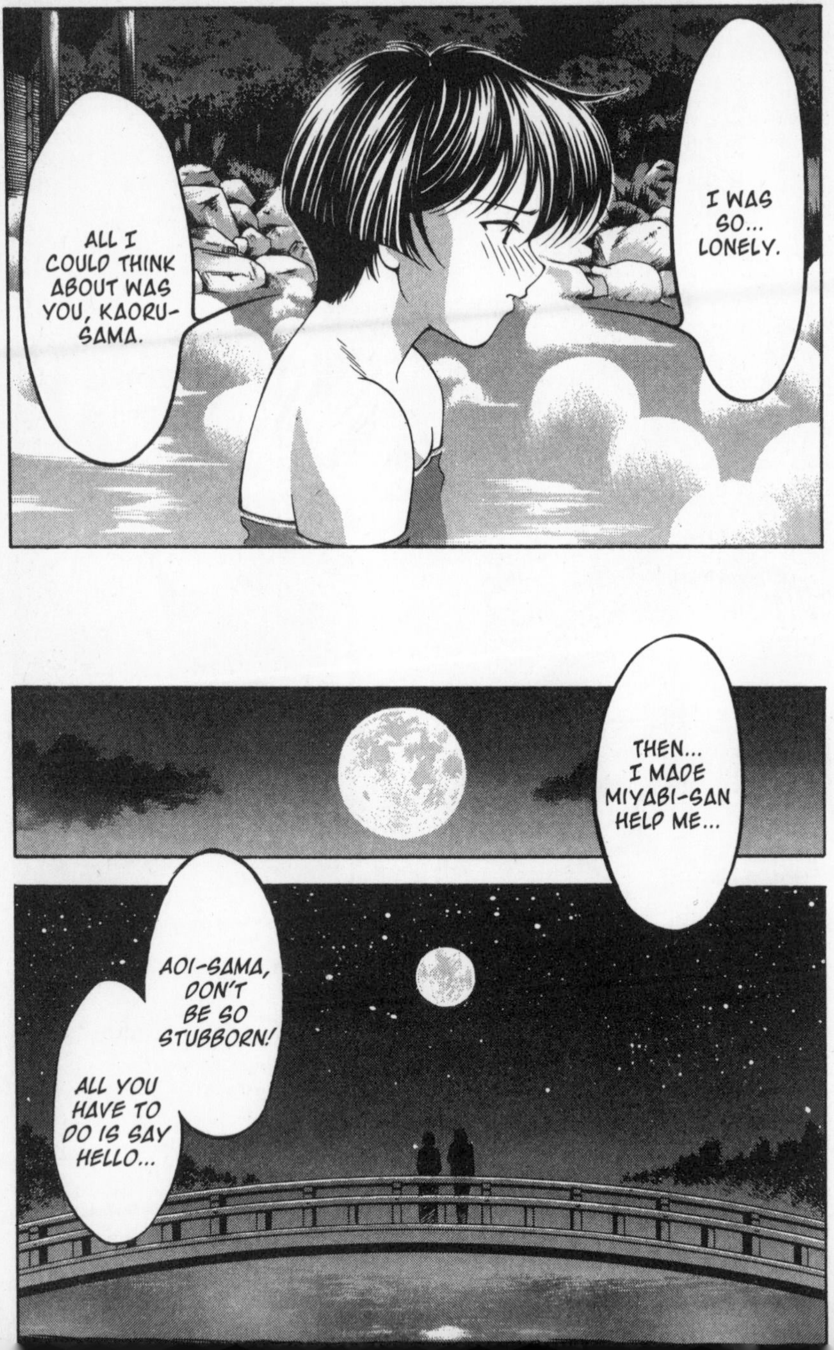
I WAS SO... LONELY.
ALL I COULD THINK ABOUT WAS YOU, KAORU-SAMA.
THEN... I MADE MIYABI-SAN HELP ME...
AOI-SAMA, DON'T BE SO STUBBORN!
ALL YOU HAVE TO DO IS SAY HELLO...

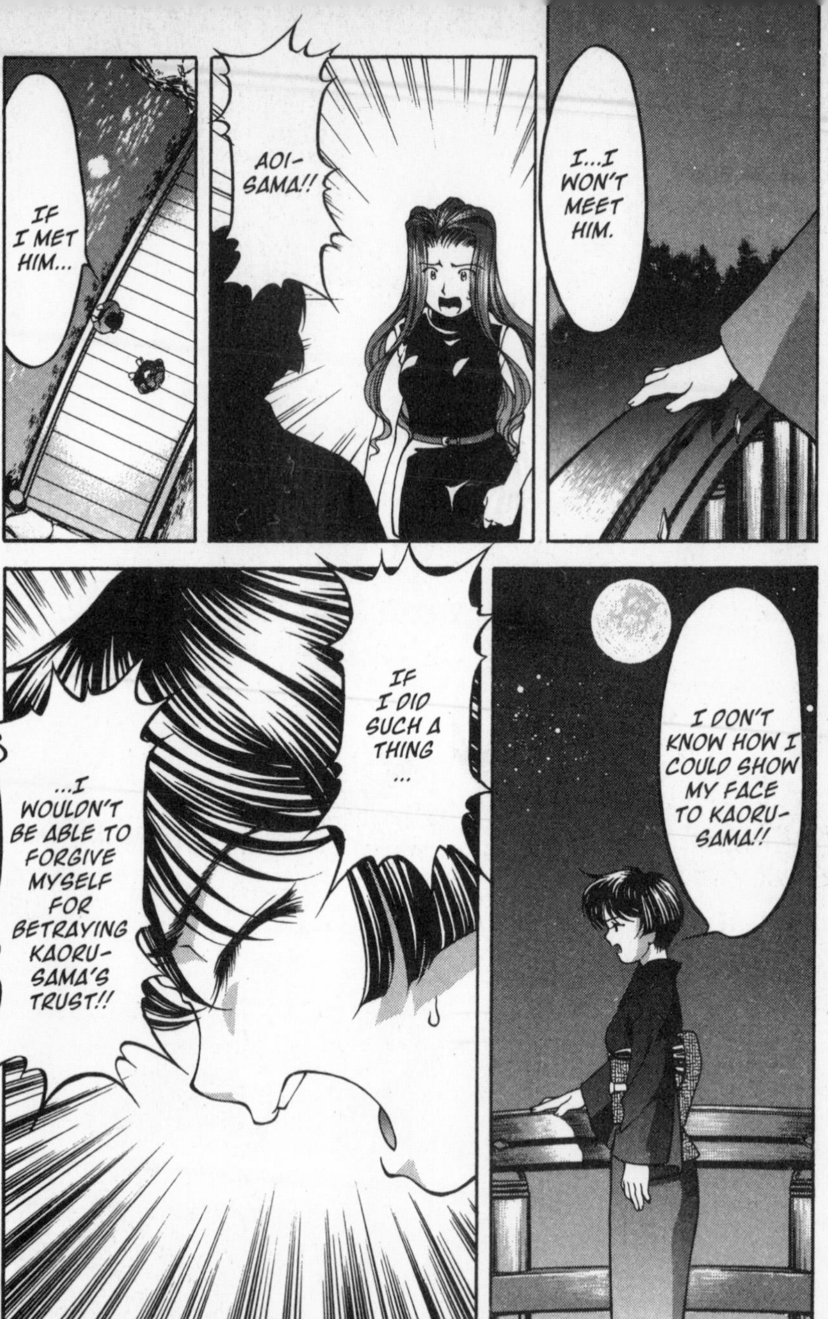
I...I WON'T MEET HIM.
AOI-SAMA!!
IF I MET HIM...
I DON'T KNOW HOW I COULD SHOW MY FACE TO KAORU-SAMA!!
IF I DID SUCH A THING ...
...I WOULDN'T BE ABLE TO FORGIVE MYSELF FOR BETRAYING KAORU-SAMA'S TRUST!!

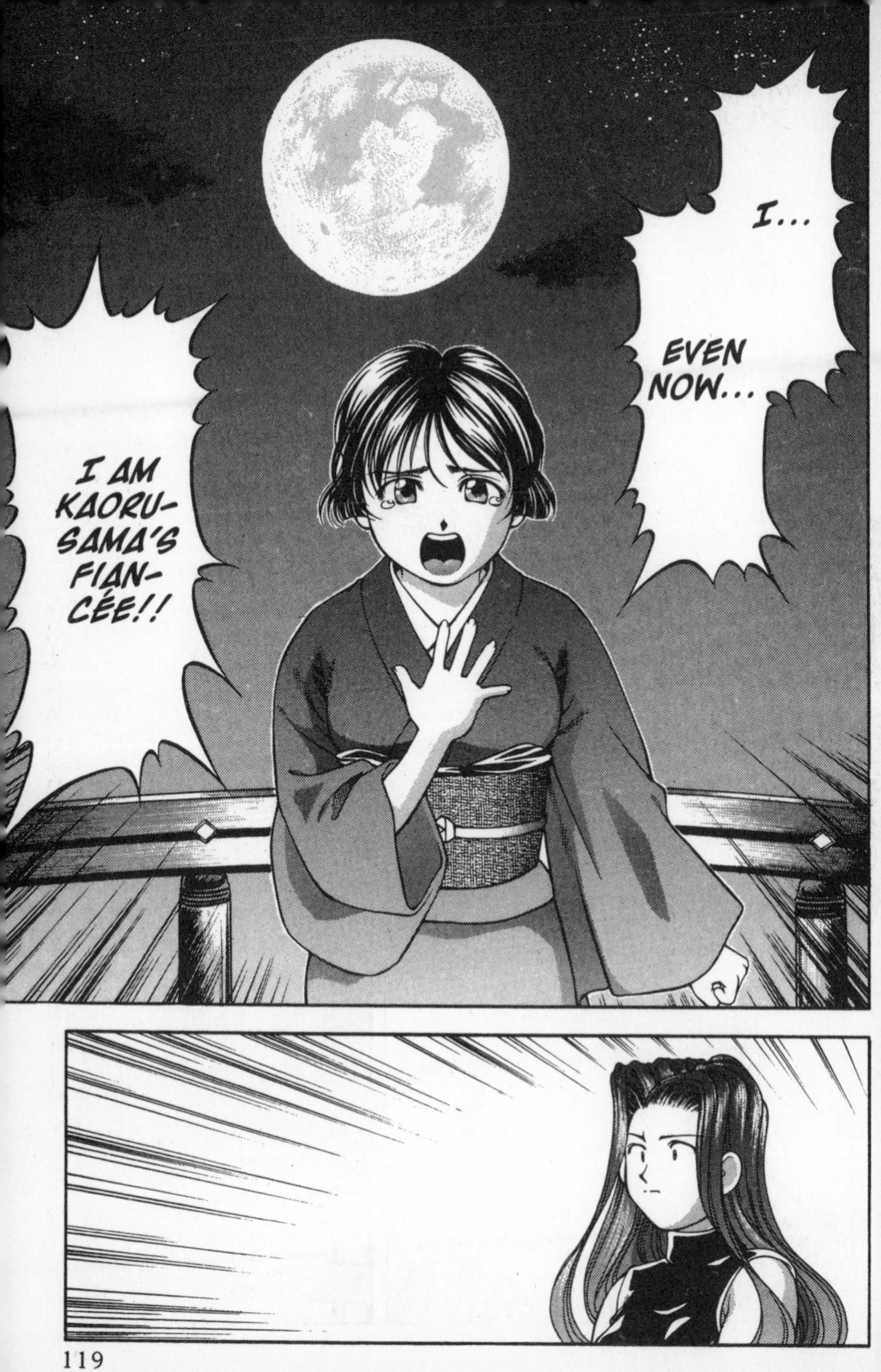
I...
EVEN NOW...
I AM KAORU-SAMA'S FIANCÉE!!

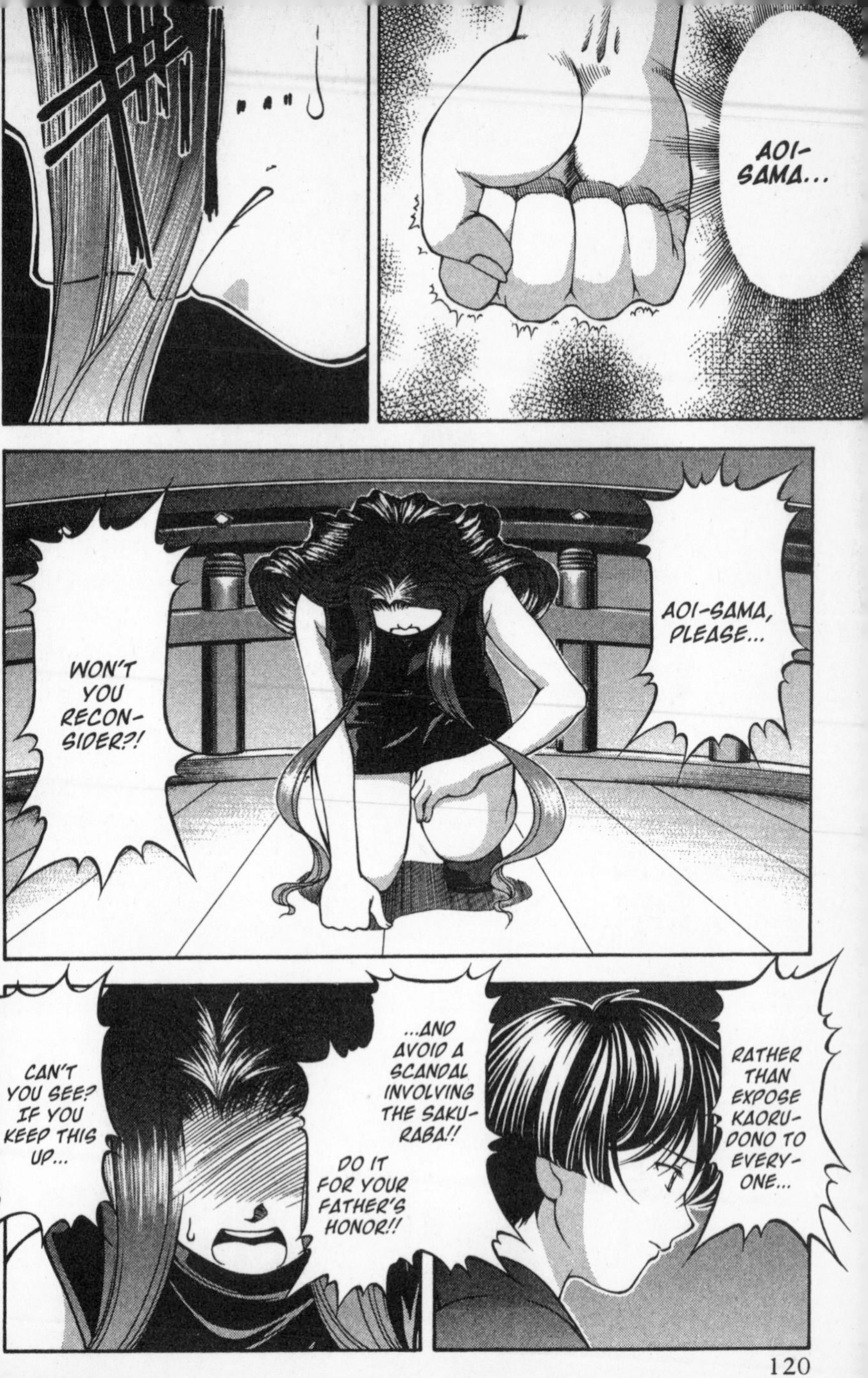
AOI-SAMA...
AOI-SAMA, PLEASE...
WON'T YOU RECONSIDER?!
RATHER THAN EXPOSE KAORU-DONO TO EVERYONE...
...AND AVOID A SCANDAL INVOLVING THE SAKURABA!!
DO IT FOR YOUR FATHER'S HONOR!!
CAN'T YOU SEE? IF YOU KEEP THIS UP...

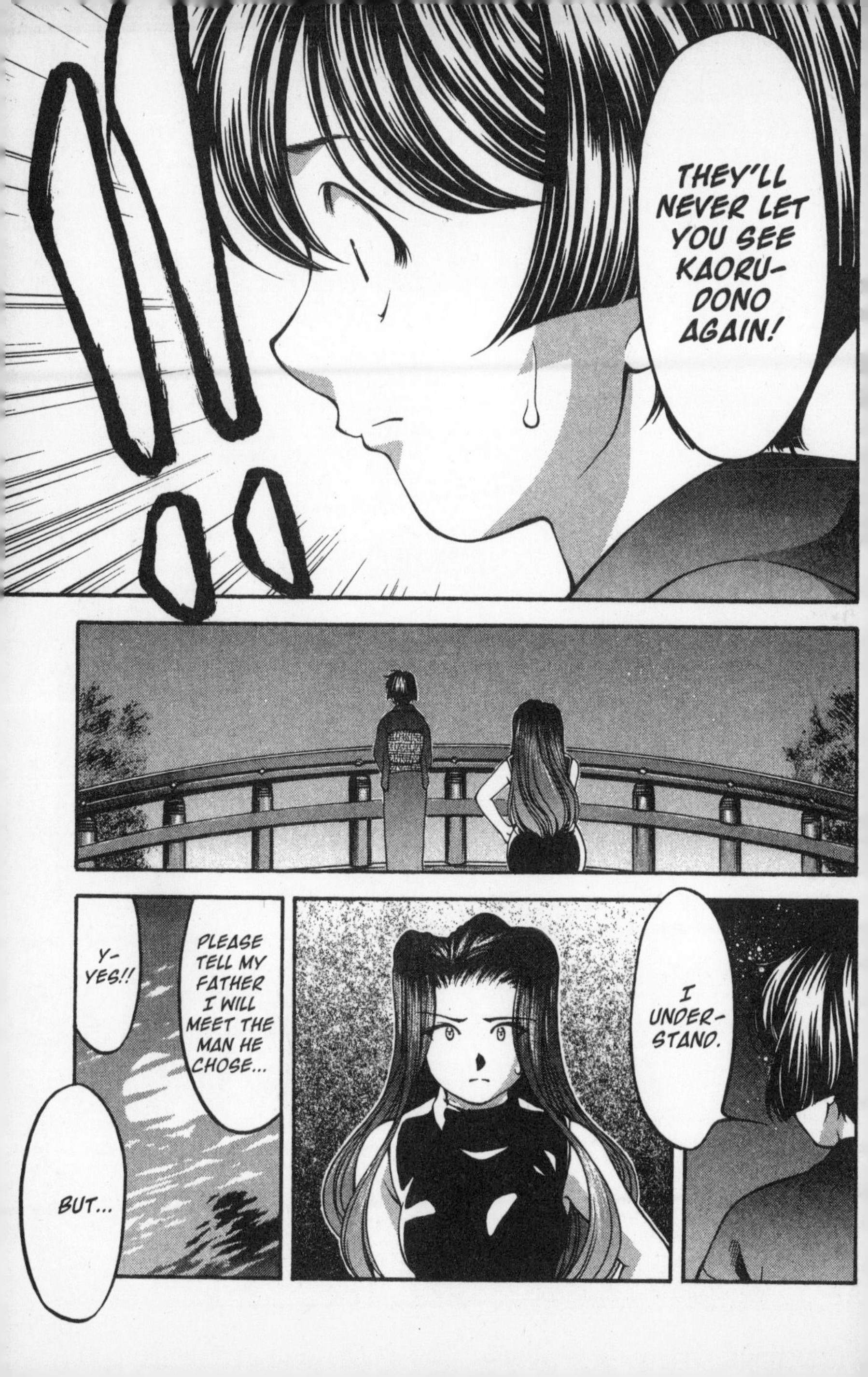
THEY'LL NEVER LET YOU SEE KAORU-DONO AGAIN!
I UNDER-STAND.
PLEASE TELL MY FATHER I WILL MEET THE MAN HE CHOSE...
Y-YES!!
BUT...

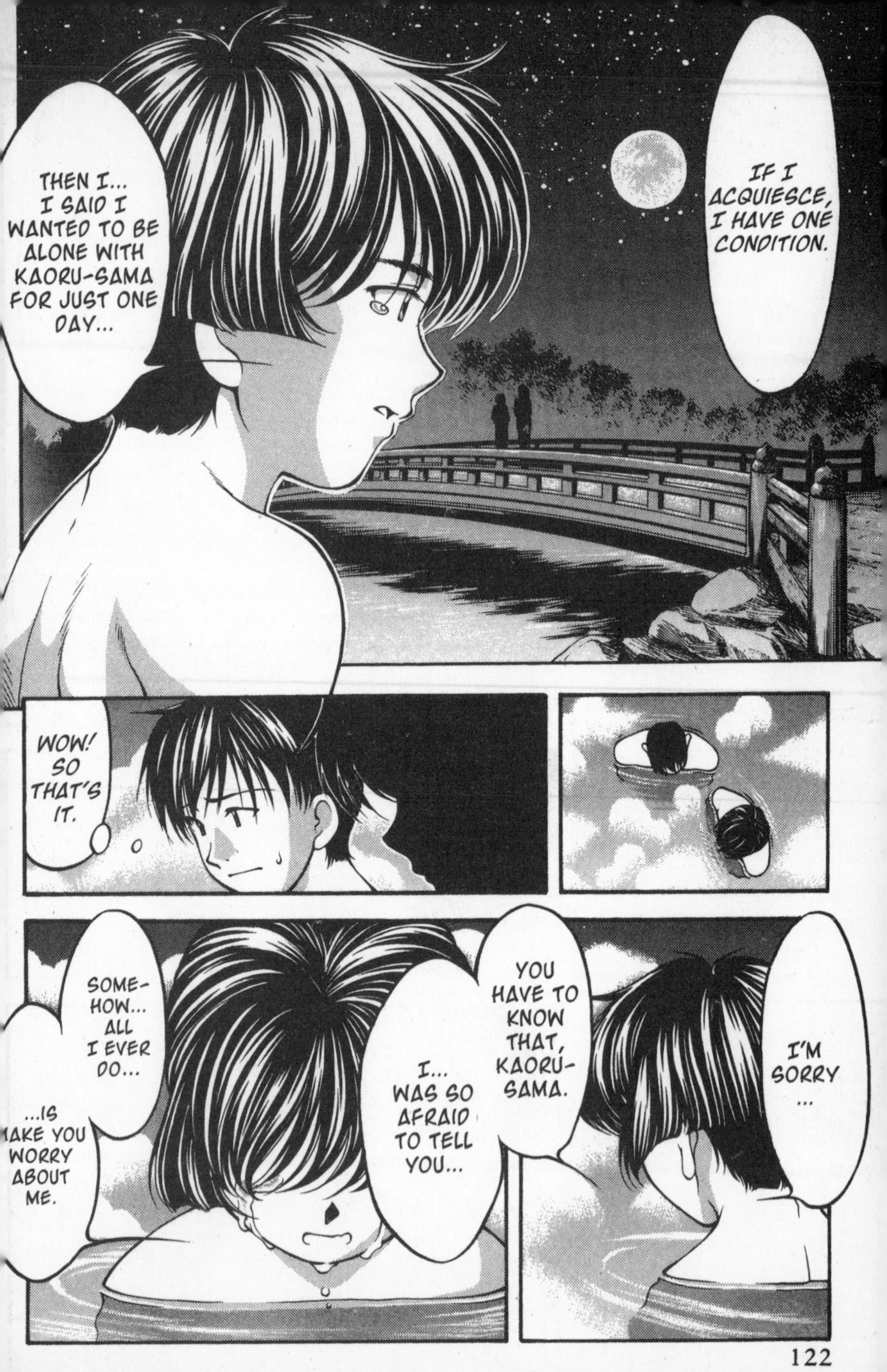
IF I ACQUIESCE, I HAVE ONE CONDITION.
THEN I... I SAID I WANTED TO BE ALONE WITH KAORU-SAMA FOR JUST ONE DAY...
WOW! SO THAT'S IT.
I'M SORRY ...
YOU HAVE TO KNOW THAT, KAORU-SAMA.
I... WAS SO AFRAID TO TELL YOU...
SOME-HOW... ALL I EVER DO...
...IS MAKE YOU WORRY ABOUT ME.

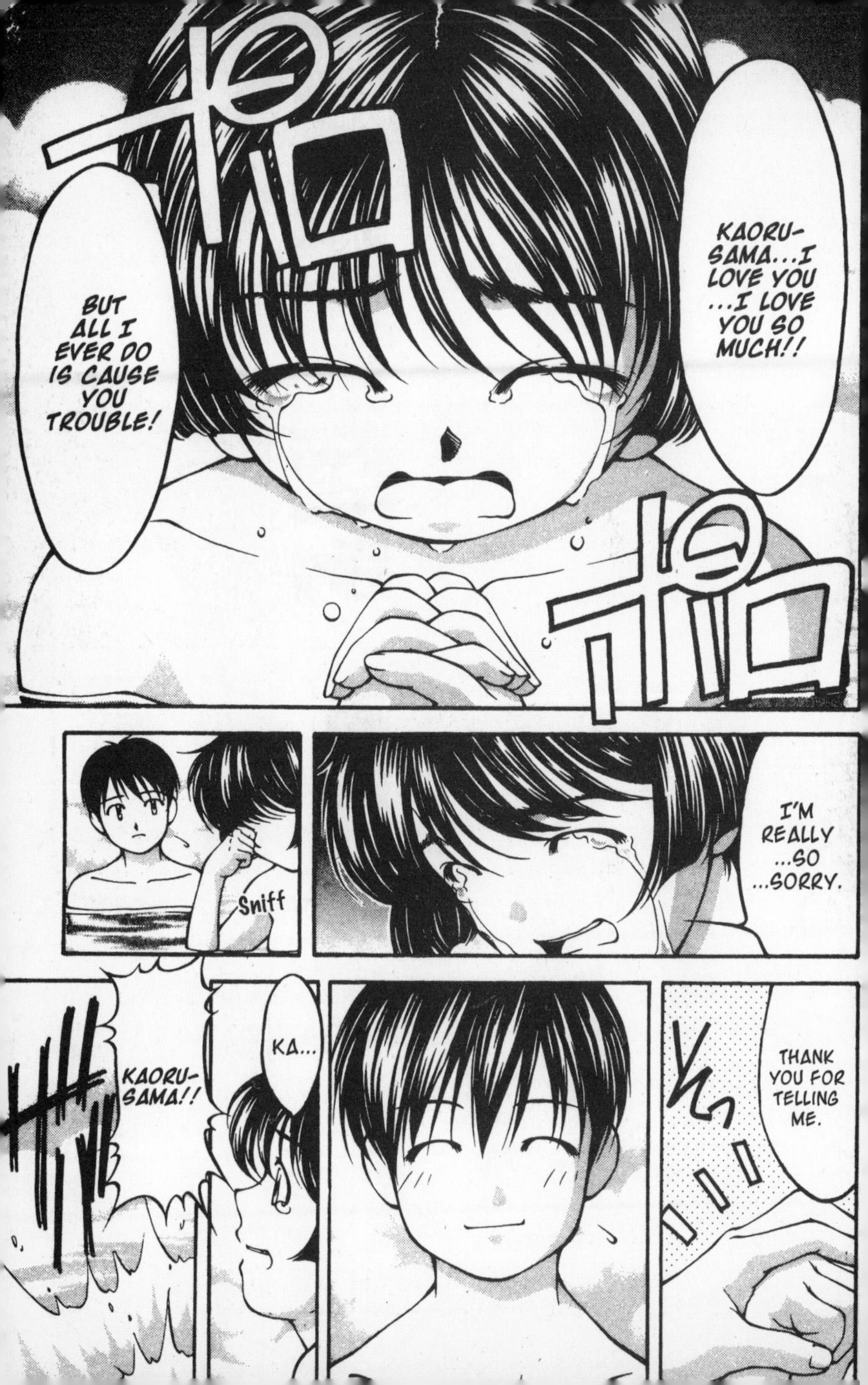
ポロ
KAORU-SAMA...I LOVE YOU ...I LOVE YOU SO MUCH!!
BUT ALL I EVER DO IS CAUSE YOU TROUBLE!
ポロ
I'M REALLY ...SO ...SORRY.
Sniff
THANK YOU FOR TELLING ME.
KA...
KAORU-SAMA!!

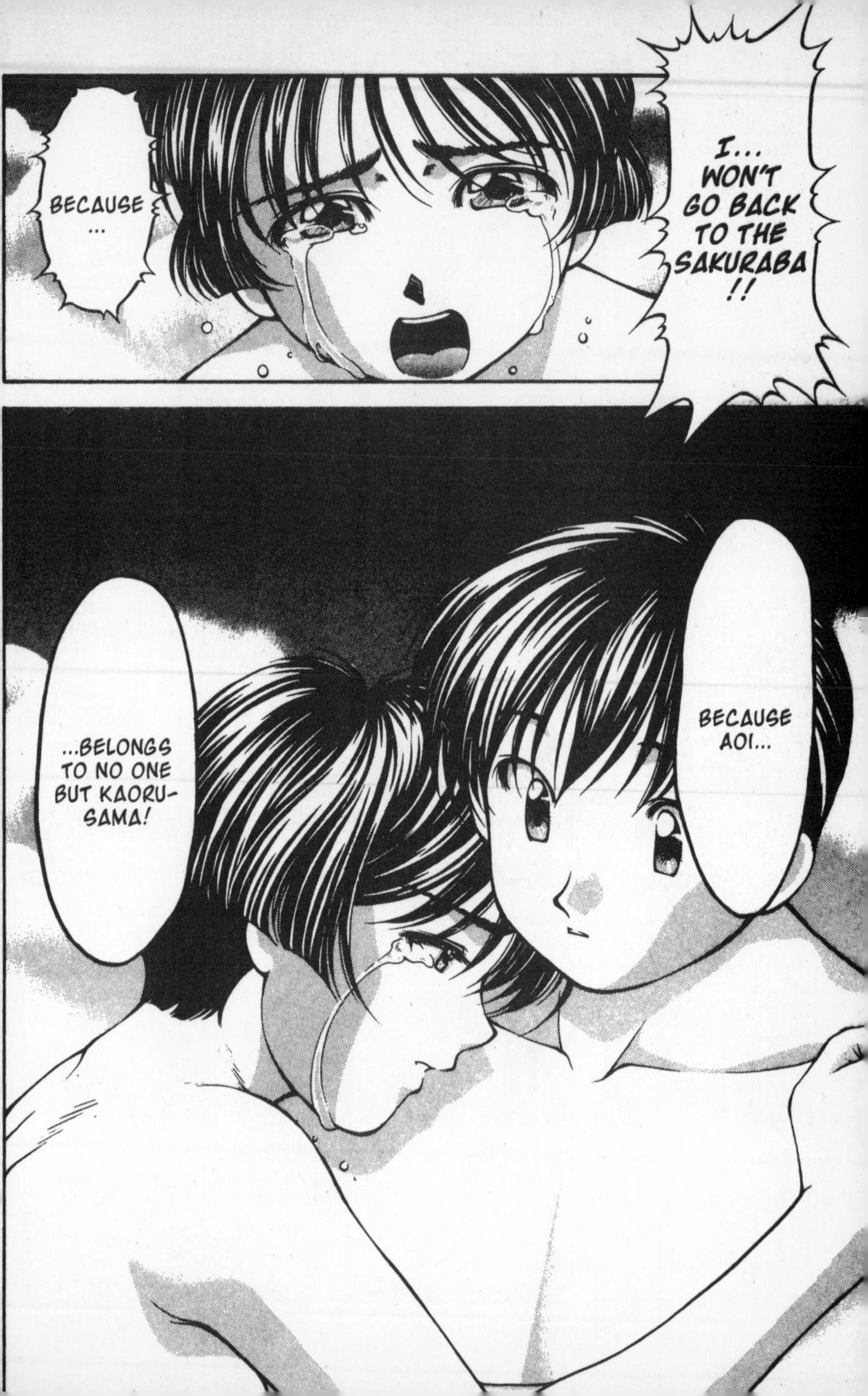
I... WON'T GO BACK TO THE SAKURABA!!
BECAUSE...
BECAUSE AOI...
...BELONGS TO NO ONE BUT KAORU-SAMA!

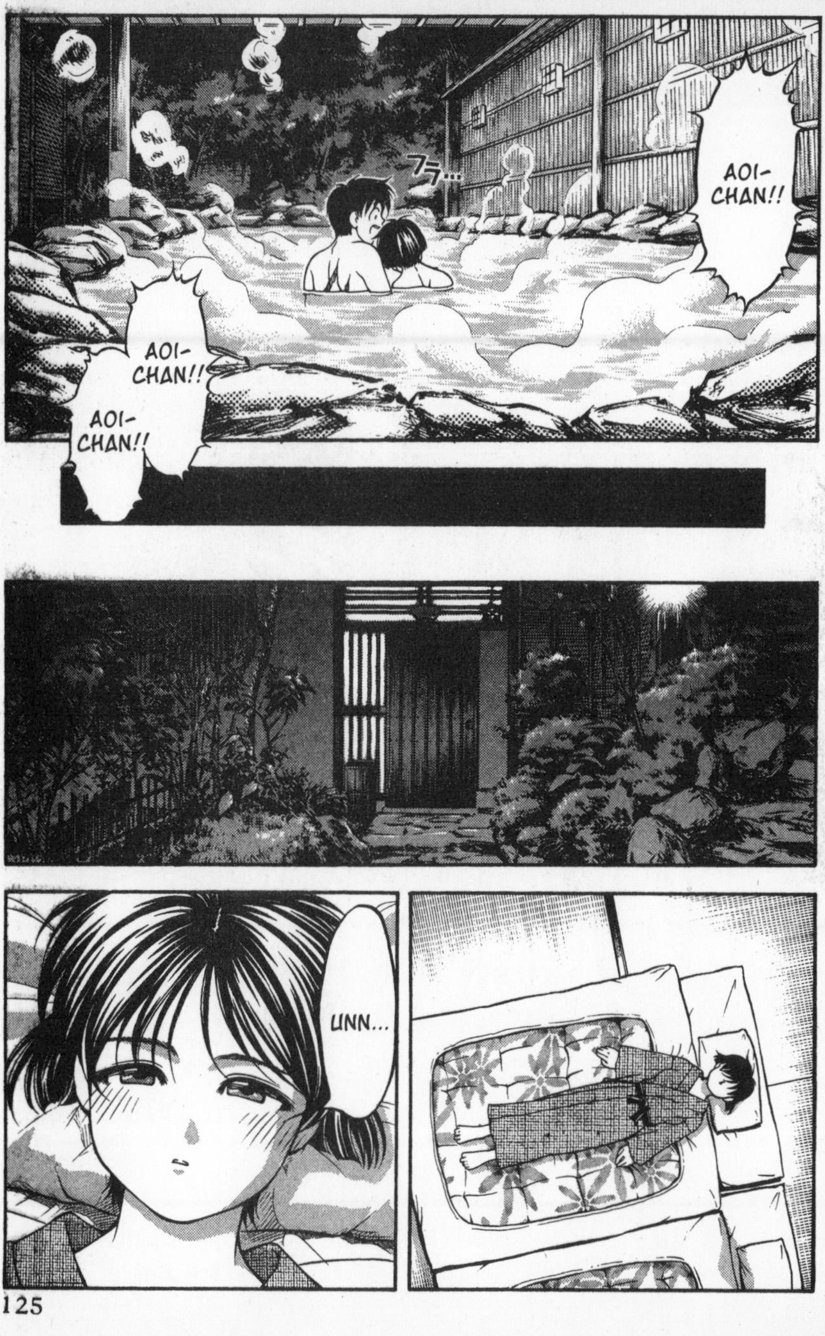
AOI-CHAN!!
フラ…
AOI-CHAN!!
AOI-CHAN!!
UNN...

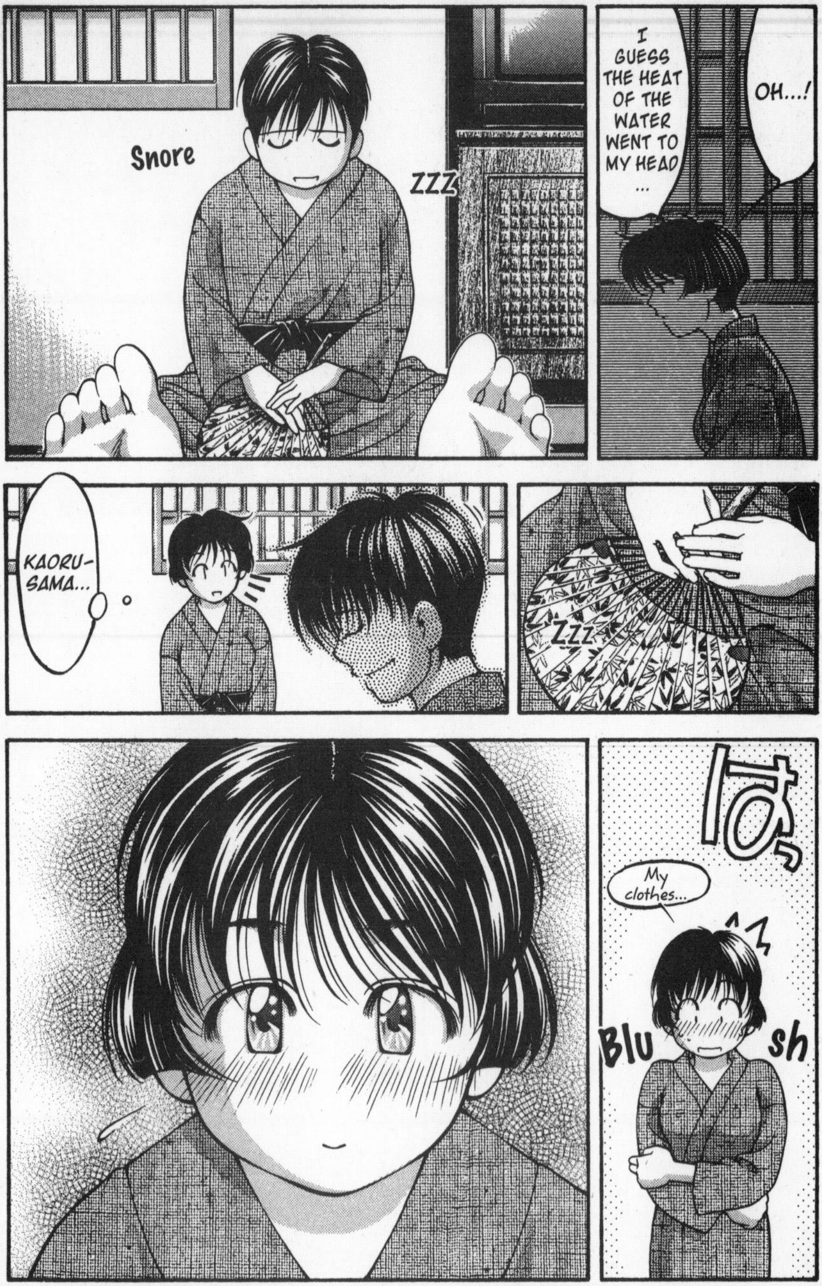

OH...!
I GUESS THE HEAT OF THE WATER WENT TO MY HEAD ...
ZZZ
Snore
ZZZ
KAORU-SAMA...
はっ
My clothes...
Blu sh

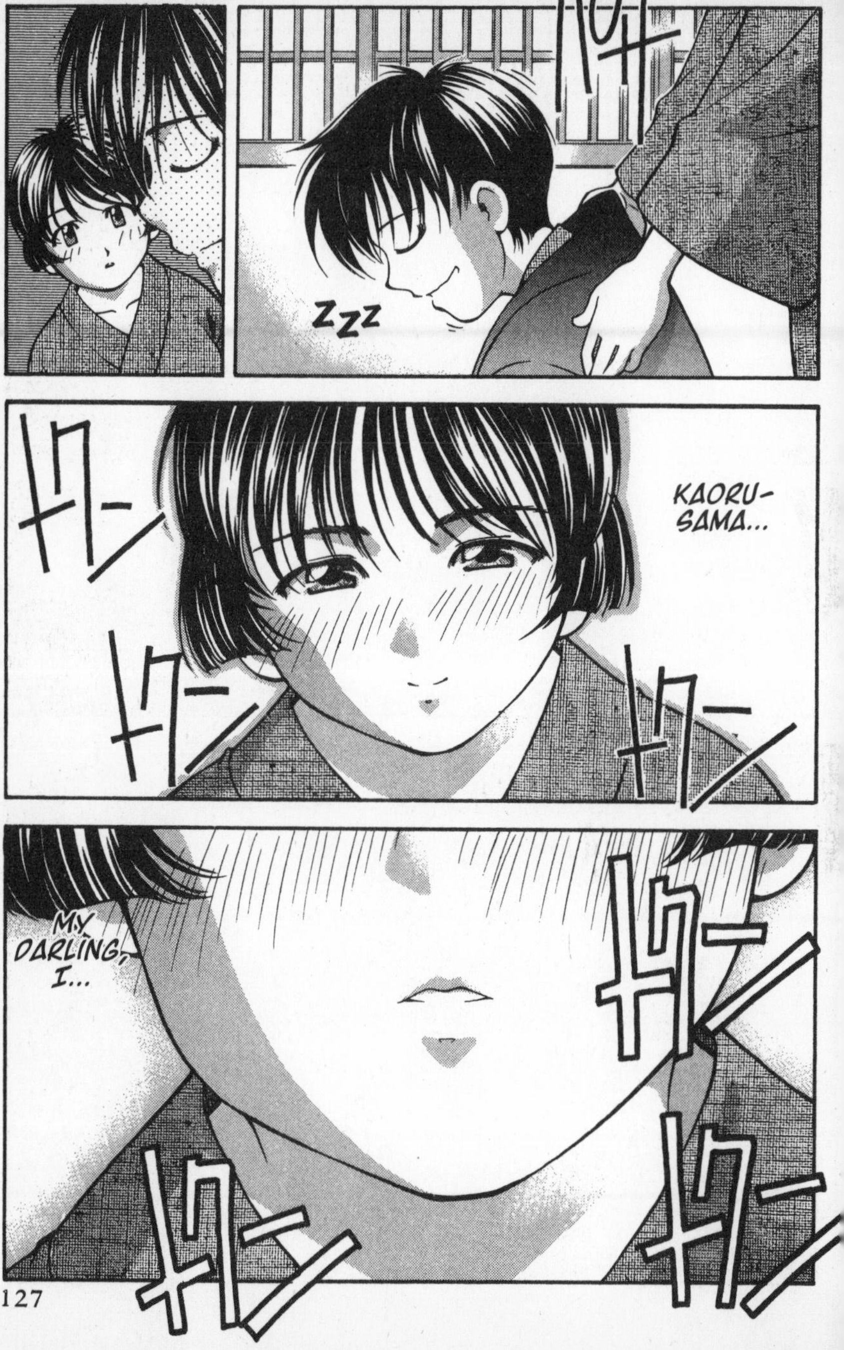
パサ
ZZZ
KAORU-SAMA...
トクーン
トクーン
トクーン
トクーン
MY DARLING, I...
トクン
トクーン

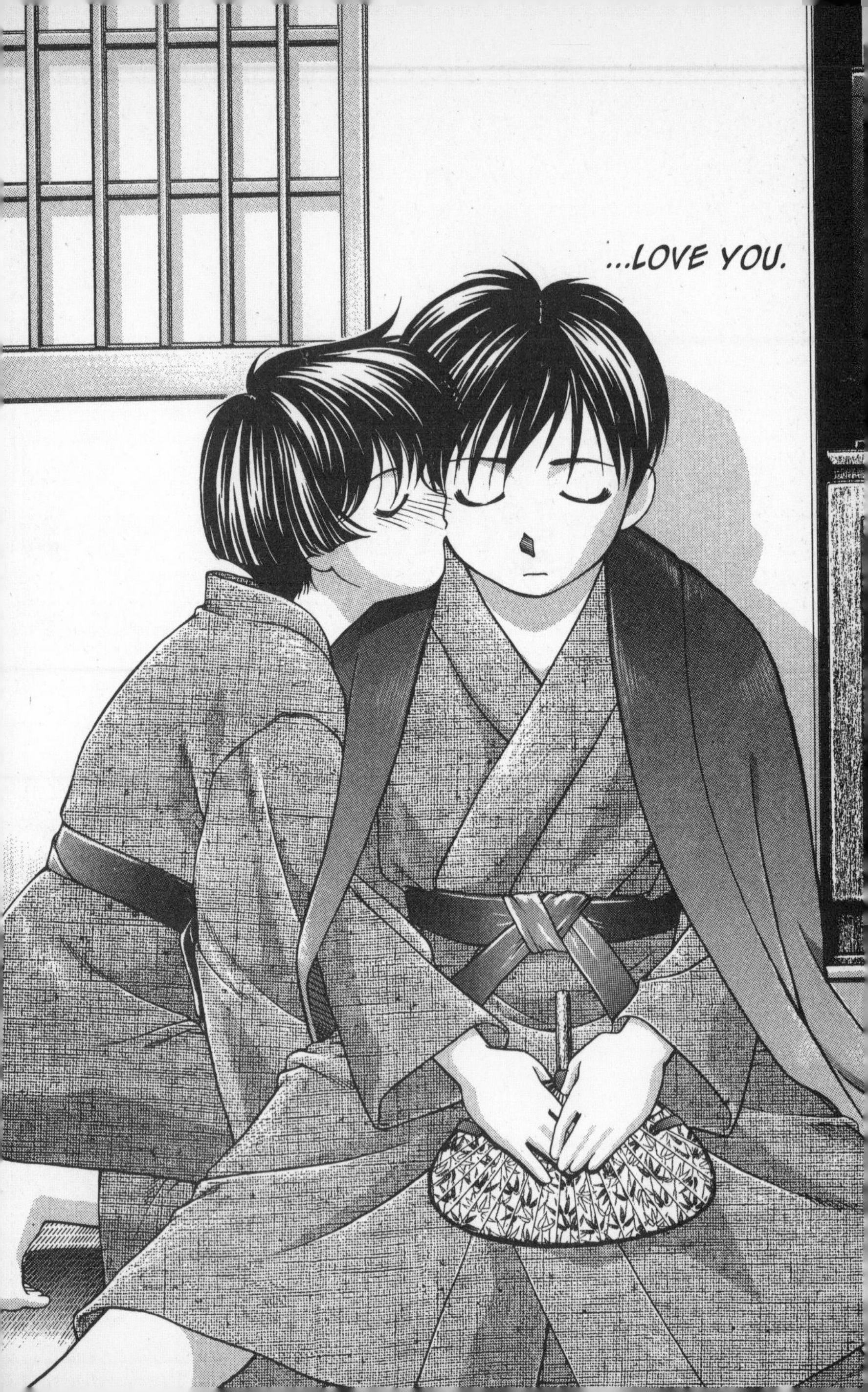
...LOVE YOU.

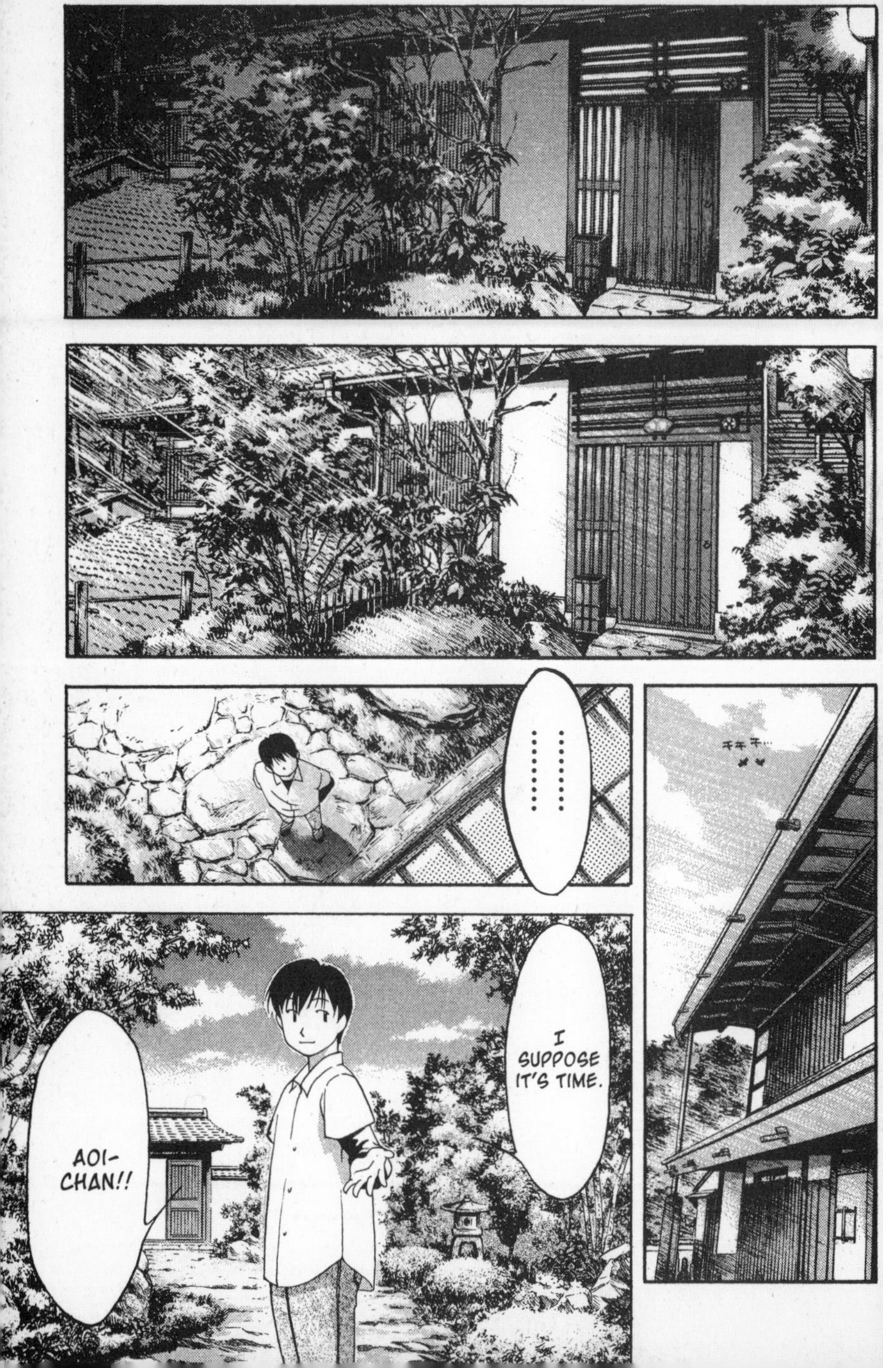
チチチ…
……
I SUPPOSE IT'S TIME.
AOI-CHAN!!

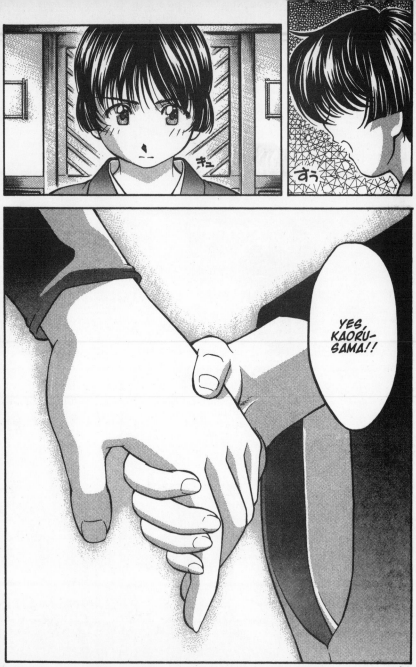

End of Chapter 52: Ketsui—Determination

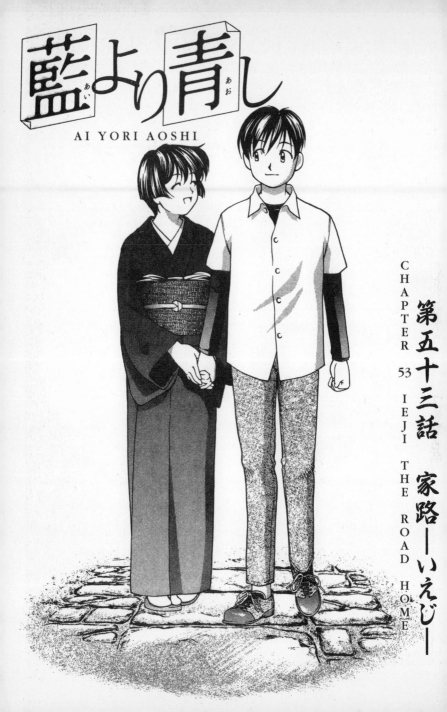

# 藍より青し

AI YORI AOSHI

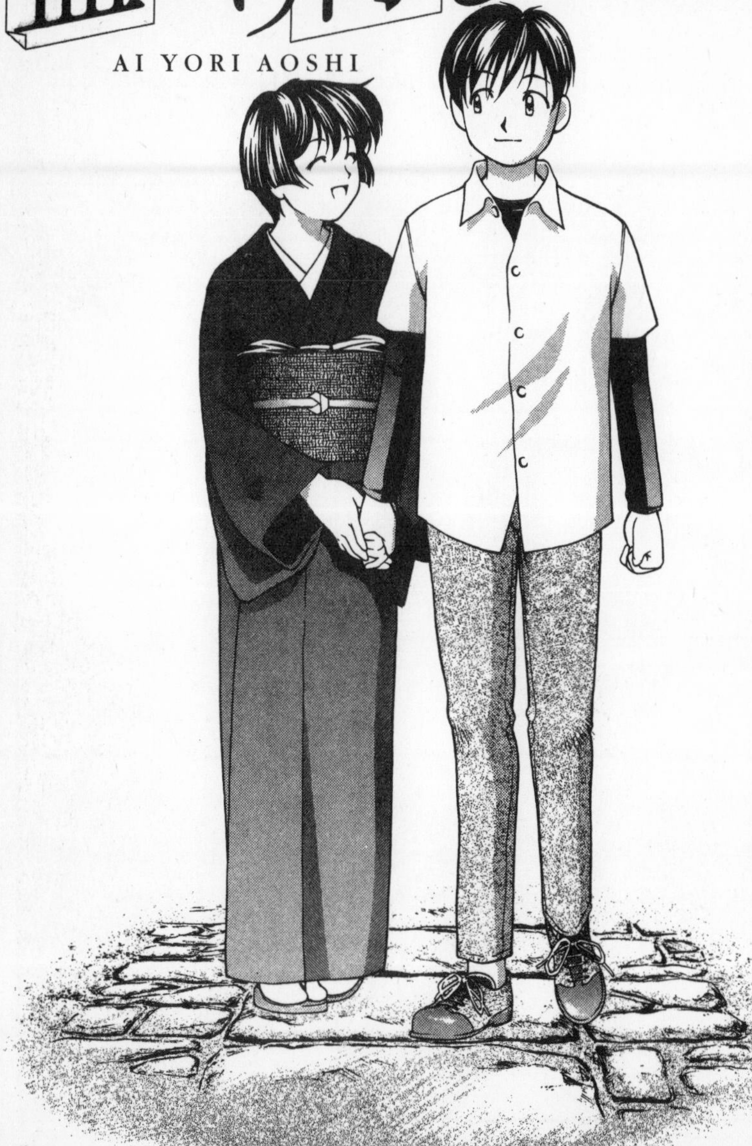

## 第五十三話 家路―いえじ―

CHAPTER 53 IEJI THE ROAD HOME

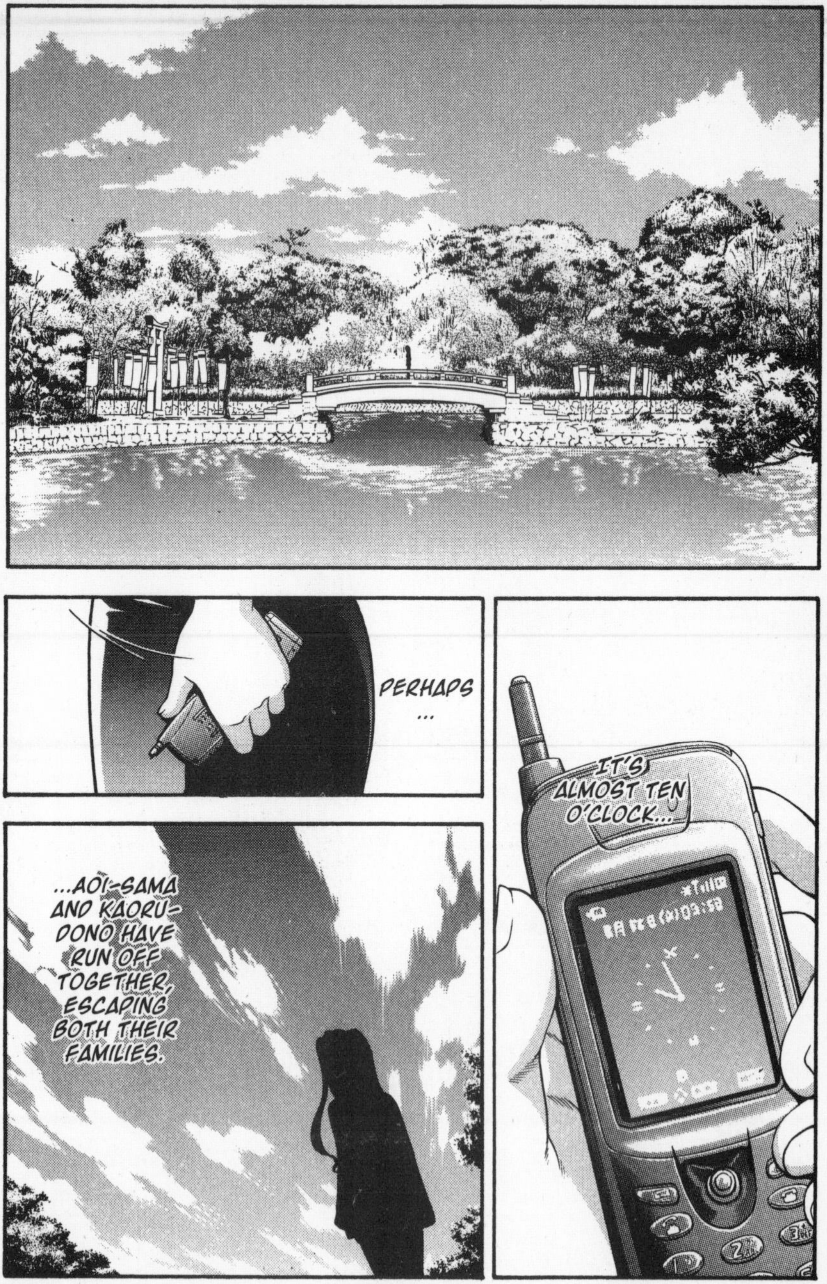
IT'S ALMOST TEN O'CLOCK...
PERHAPS...
...AOI-SAMA AND KAORU-DONO HAVE RUN OFF TOGETHER, ESCAPING BOTH THEIR FAMILIES.

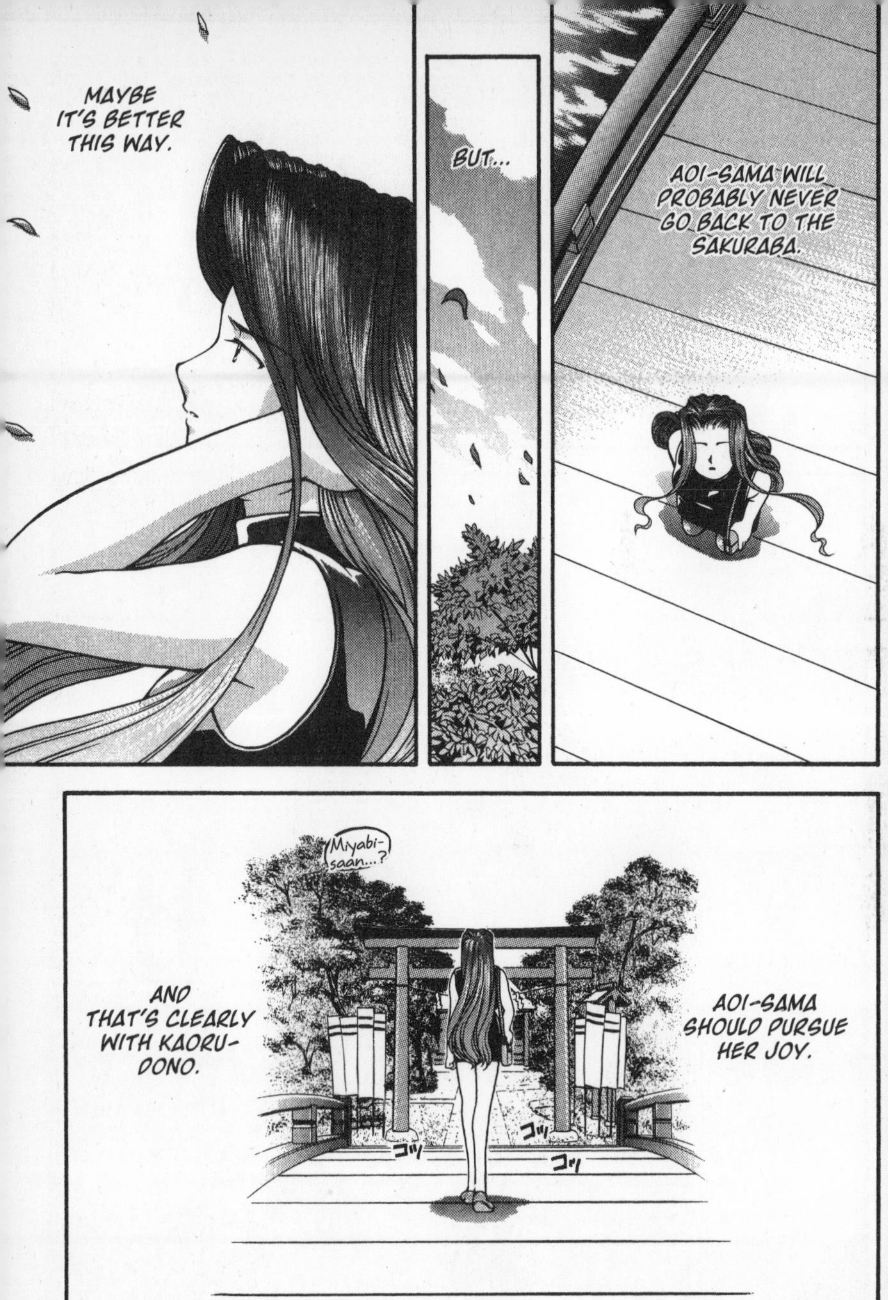
AOI-SAMA WILL PROBABLY NEVER GO BACK TO THE SAKURABA.
BUT...
MAYBE IT'S BETTER THIS WAY.
Miyabi-saan...?
AOI-SAMA SHOULD PURSUE HER JOY.
AND THAT'S CLEARLY WITH KAORU-DONO.
ゴッ
ゴッ
ゴッ

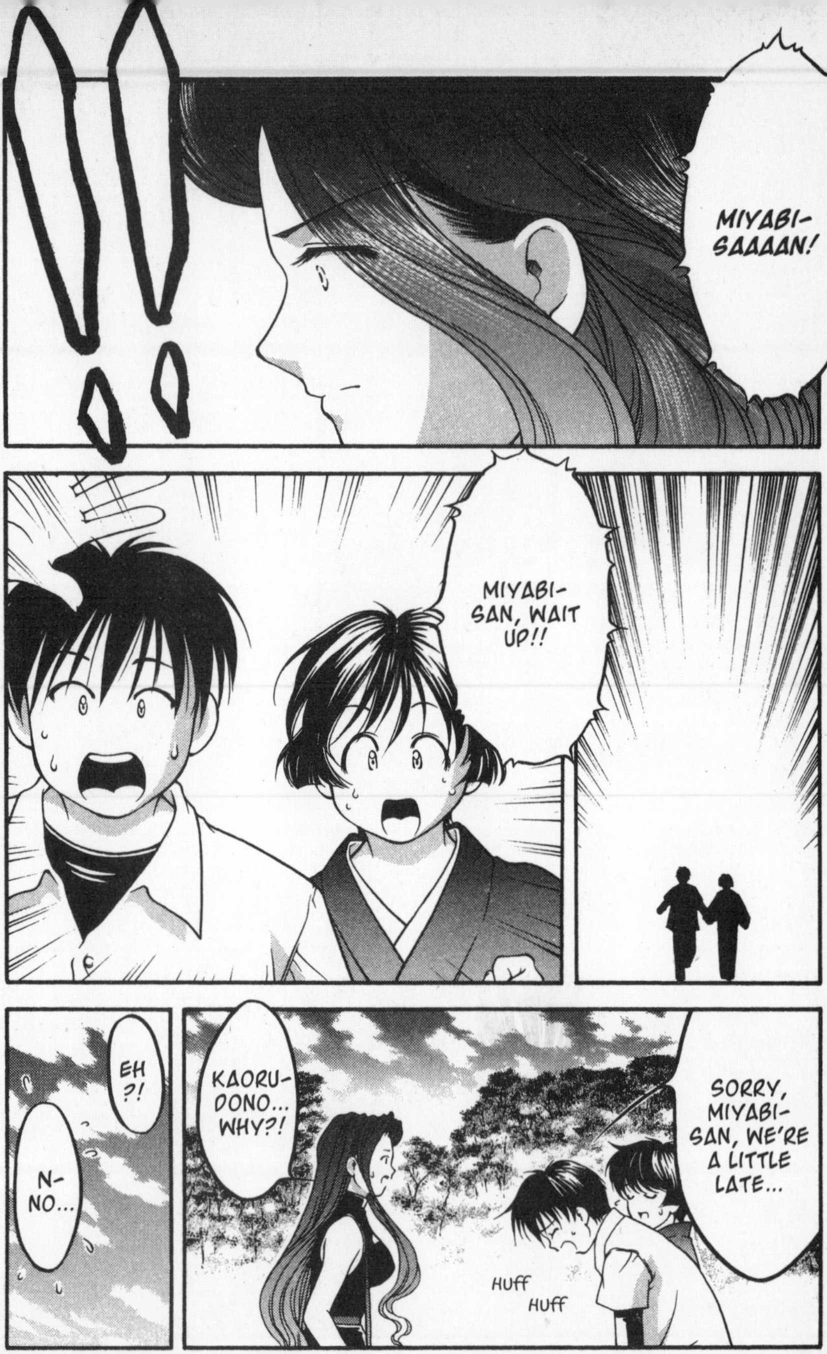
MIYABI-SAAAAN!
!!
MIYABI-SAN, WAIT UP!!
SORRY, MIYABI-SAN, WE'RE A LITTLE LATE...
KAORU-DONO... WHY?!
HUFF HUFF
EH?!
N-NO...

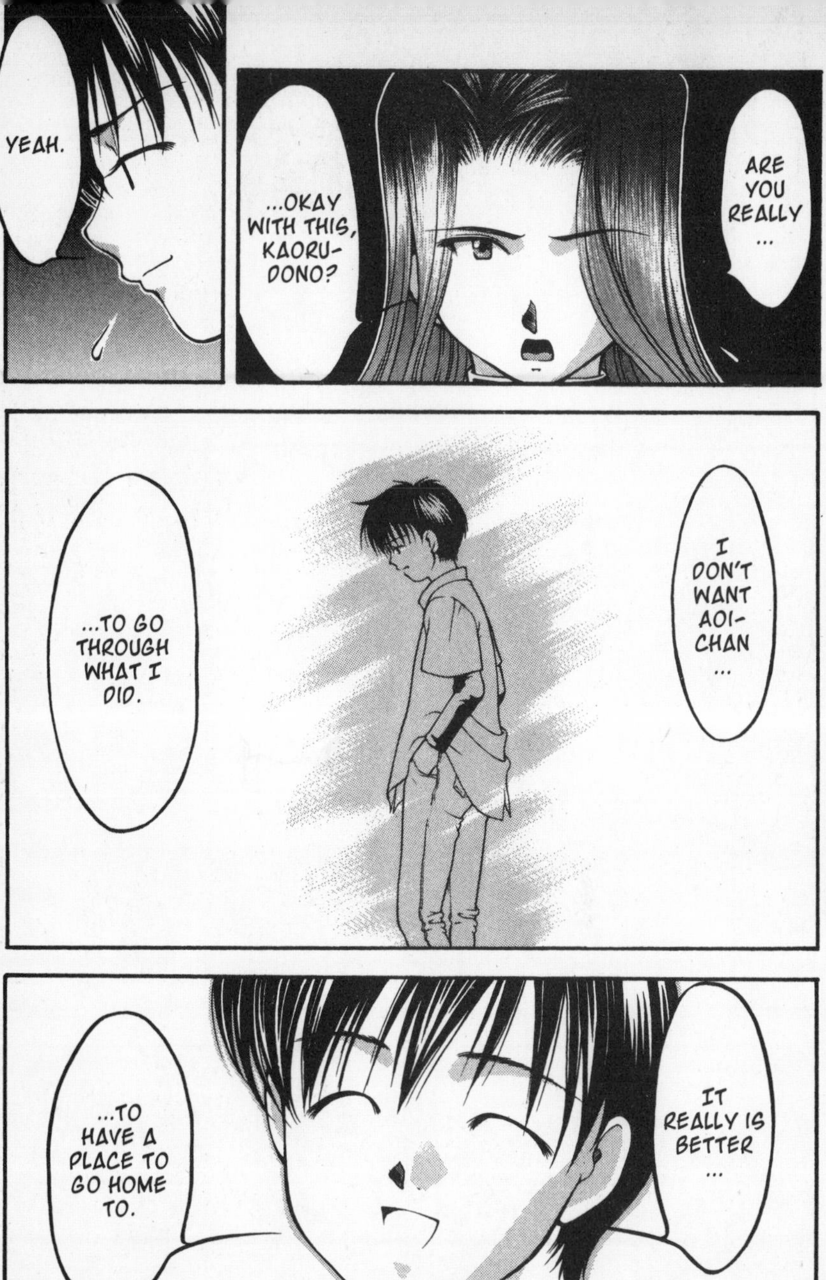
ARE YOU REALLY ...
...OKAY WITH THIS, KAORU-DONO?
YEAH.
I DON'T WANT AOI-CHAN ...
...TO GO THROUGH WHAT I DID.
IT REALLY IS BETTER ...
...TO HAVE A PLACE TO GO HOME TO.

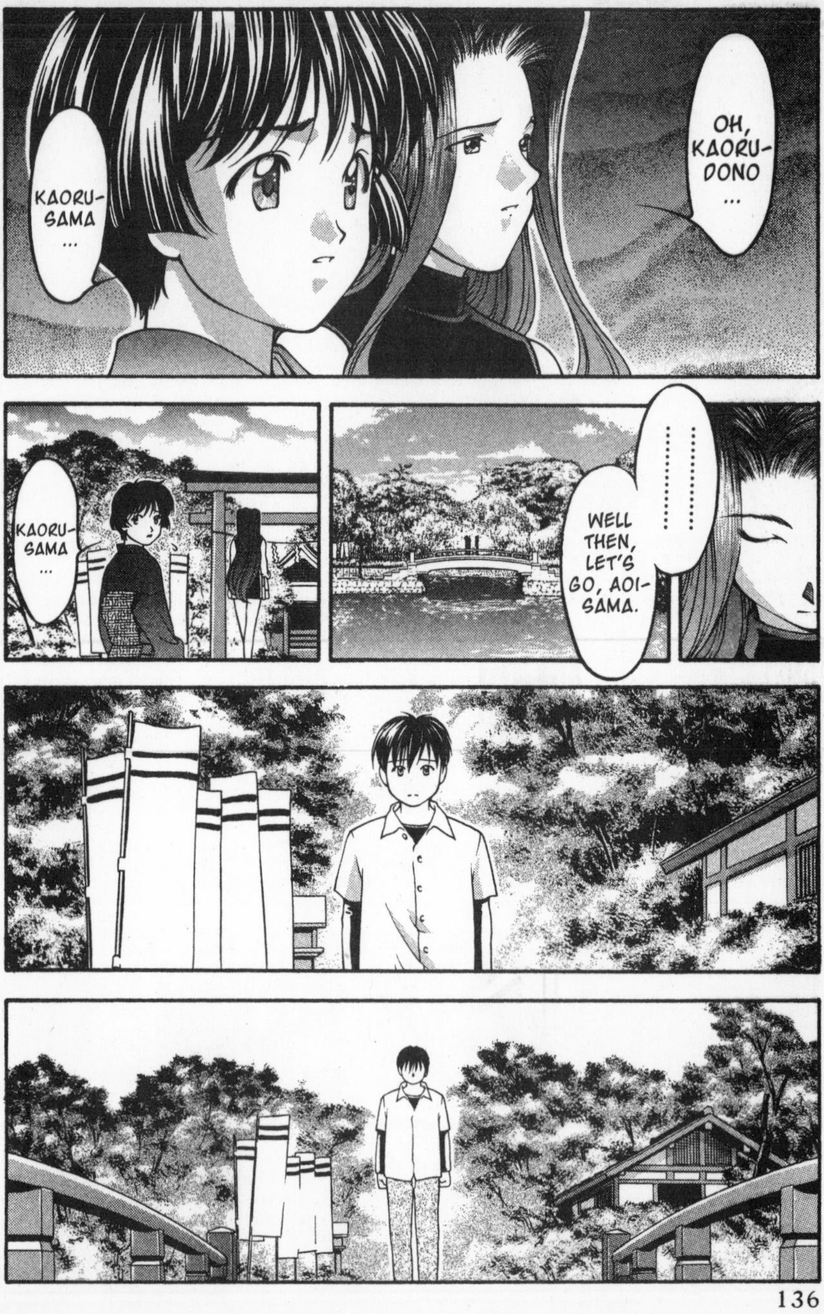
OH, KAORU-DONO ...
KAORU-SAMA ...
.........
WELL THEN, LET'S GO, AOI-SAMA.
KAORU-SAMA ...

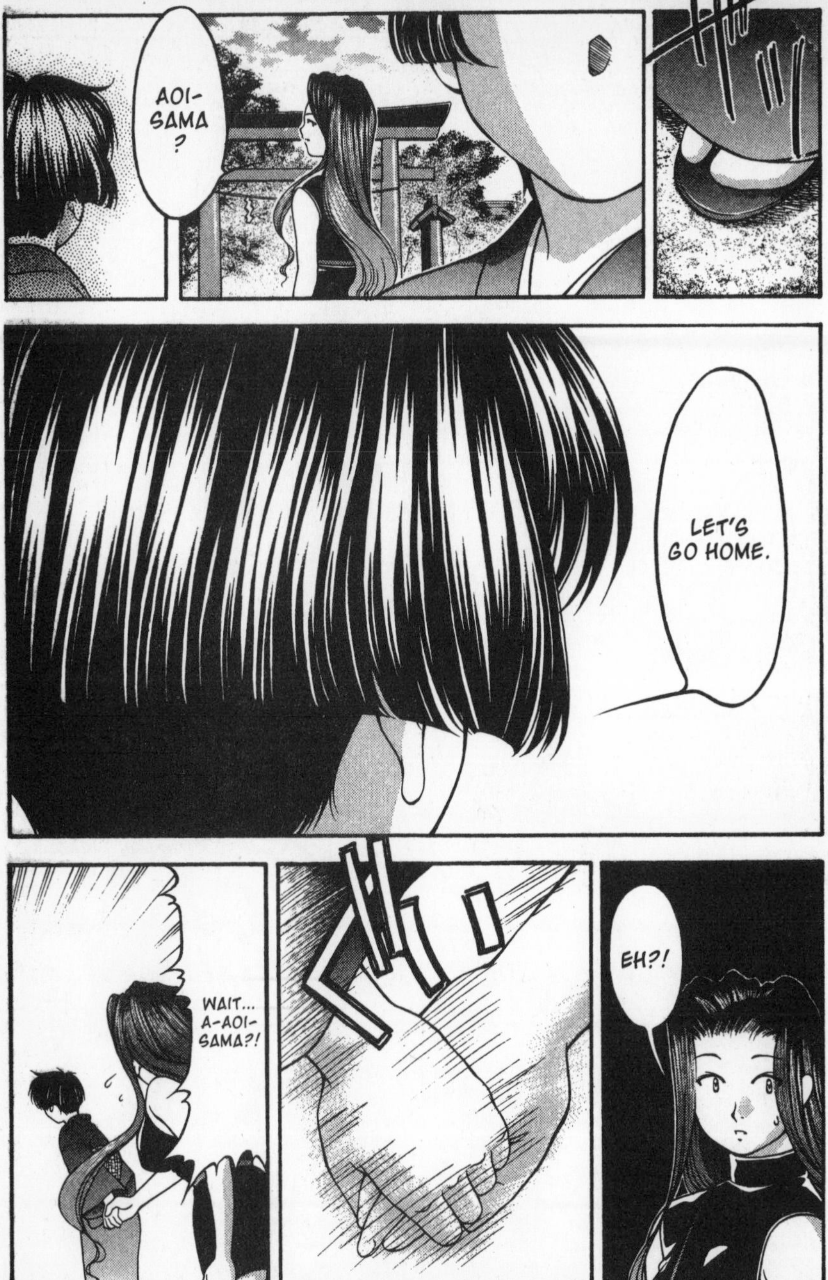
AOI-SAMA?
LET'S GO HOME.
EH?!
WAIT... A-AOI-SAMA?!

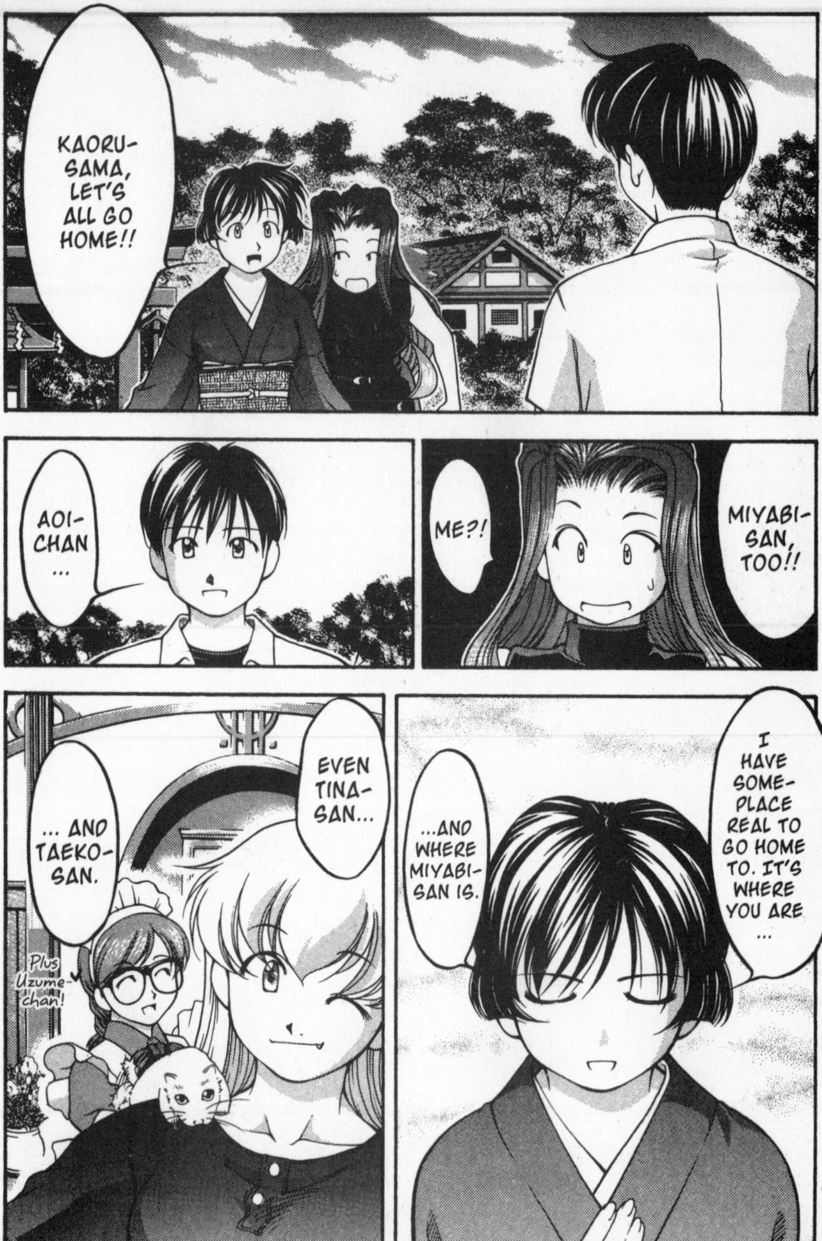
KAORU-SAMA, LET'S ALL GO HOME!!
MIYABI-SAN, TOO!!
ME?!
AOI-CHAN ...
I HAVE SOME-PLACE REAL TO GO HOME TO. IT'S WHERE YOU ARE ...
...AND WHERE MIYABI-SAN IS.
EVEN TINA-SAN...
... AND TAEKO-SAN.
Plus Uzume-chan!

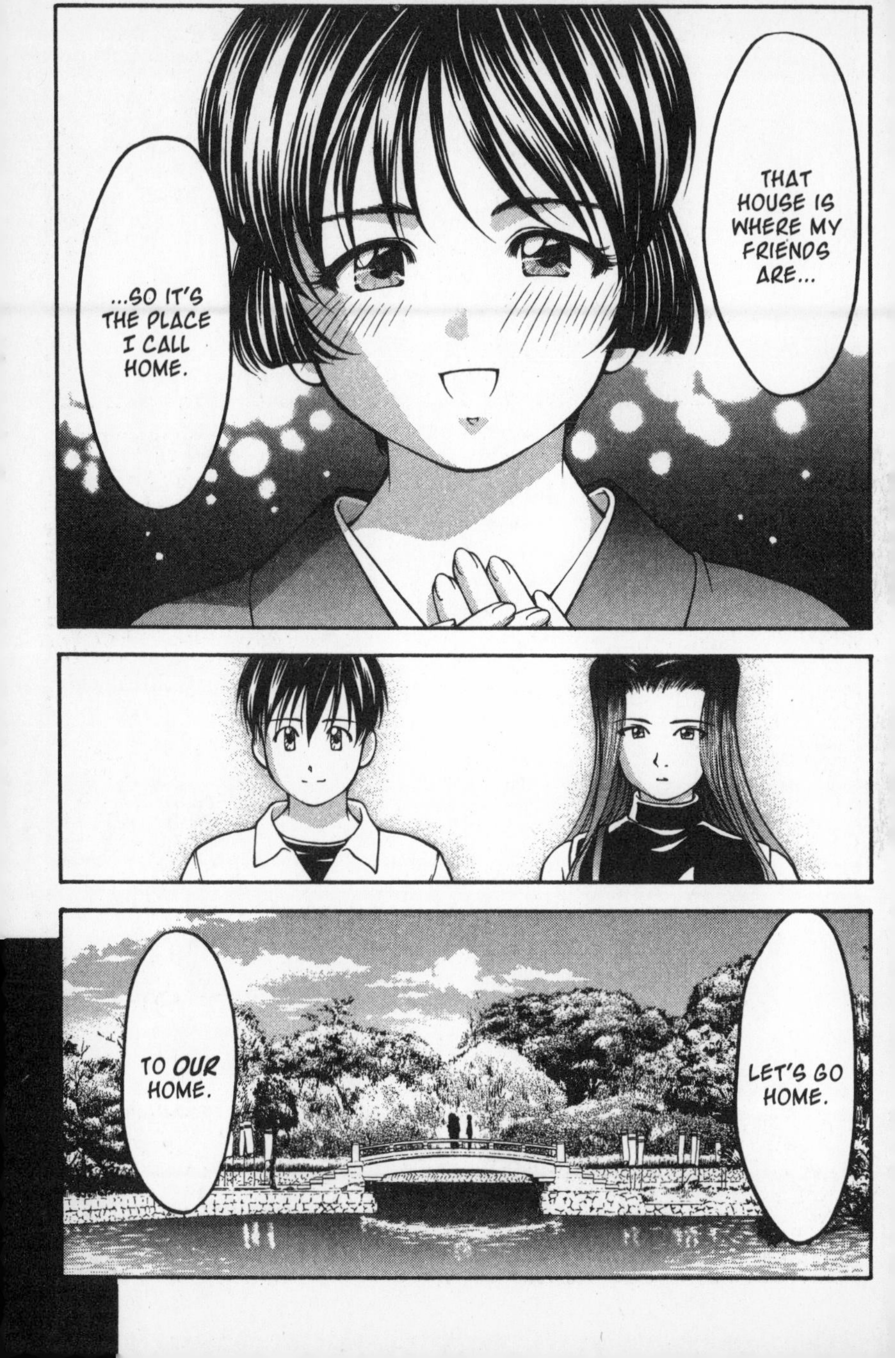
THAT HOUSE IS WHERE MY FRIENDS ARE...
...SO IT'S THE PLACE I CALL HOME.
LET'S GO HOME.
TO *OUR* HOME.

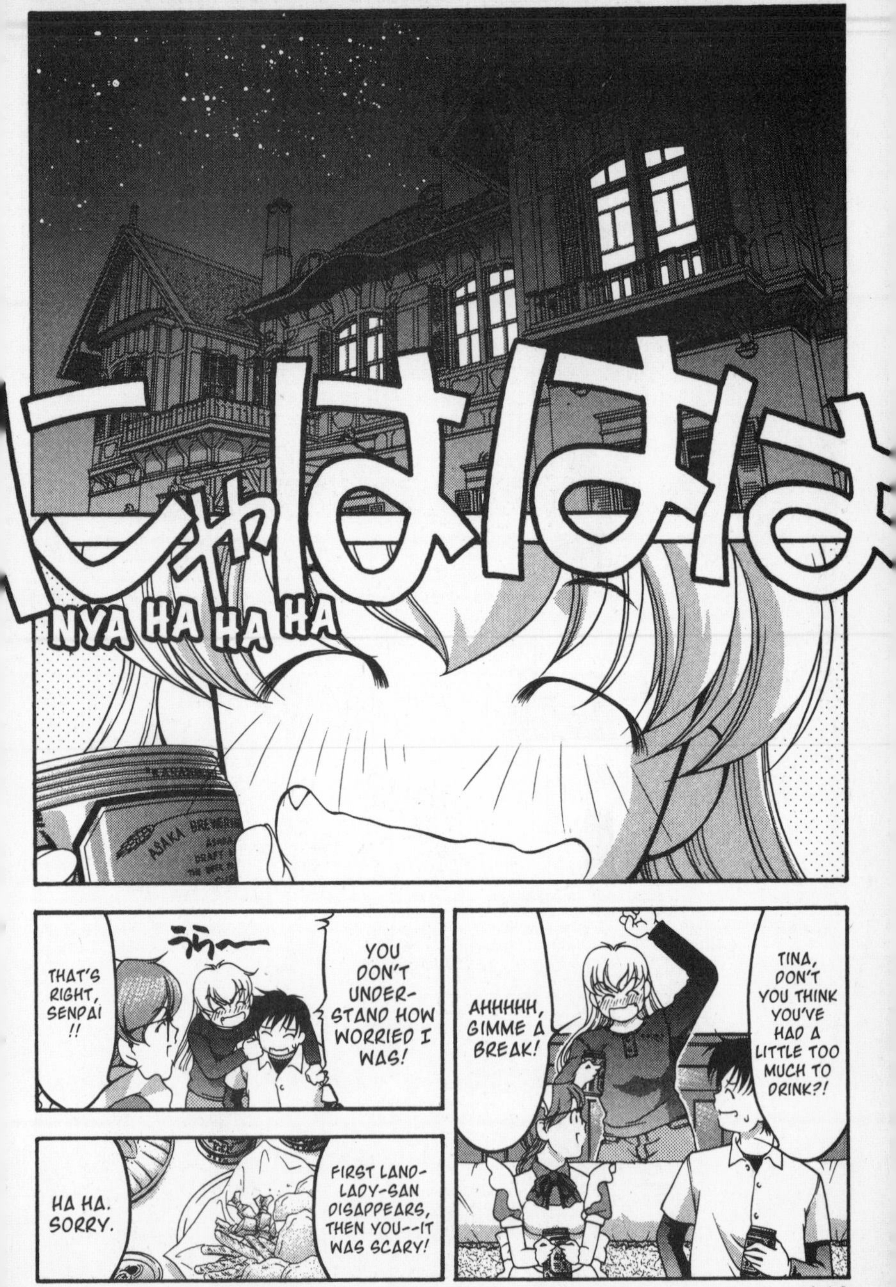
にゃははは
NYA HA HA HA
TINA, DON'T YOU THINK YOU'VE HAD A LITTLE TOO MUCH TO DRINK?!
AHHHHH, GIMME A BREAK!
YOU DON'T UNDER-STAND HOW WORRIED I WAS!
うら〜
THAT'S RIGHT, SENPAI !!
FIRST LAND-LADY-SAN DISAPPEARS, THEN YOU--IT WAS SCARY!
HA HA. SORRY.

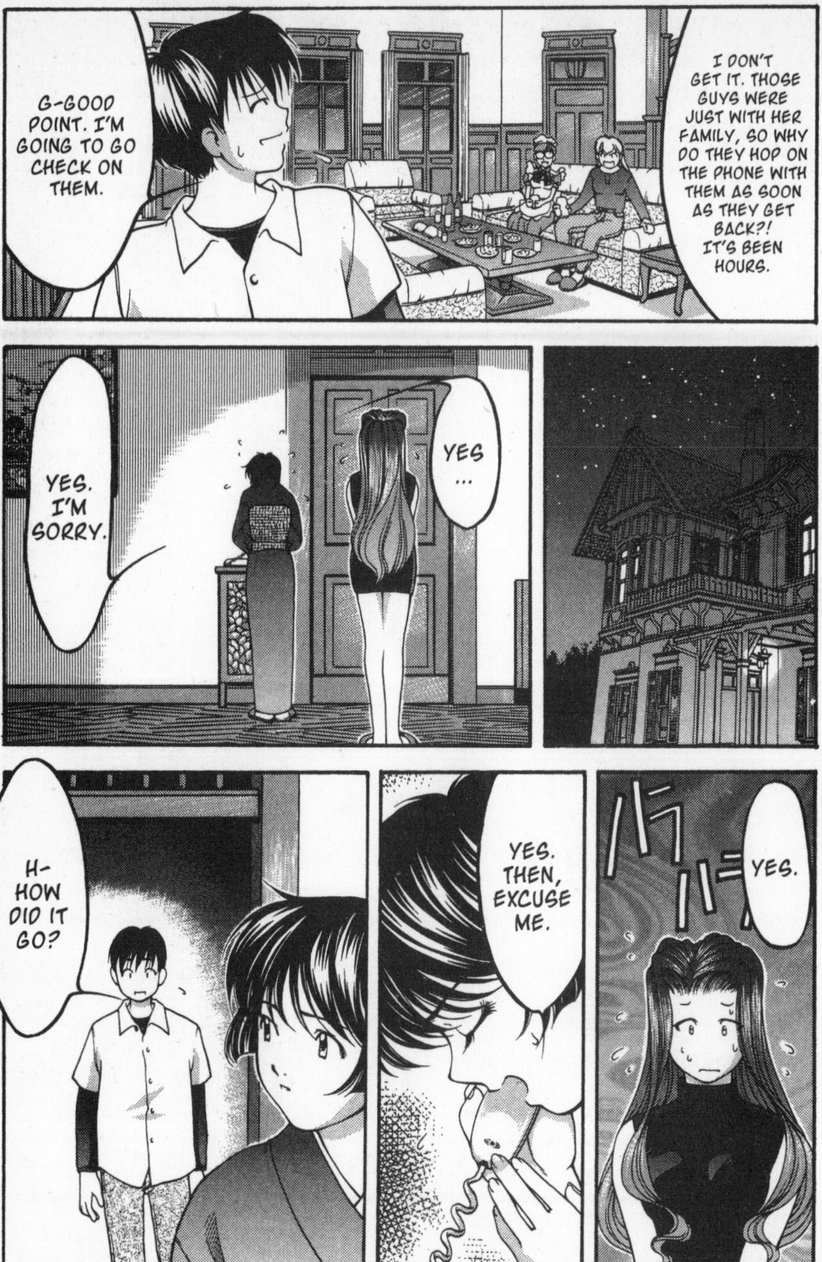
I DON'T GET IT. THOSE GUYS WERE JUST WITH HER FAMILY, SO WHY DO THEY HOP ON THE PHONE WITH THEM AS SOON AS THEY GET BACK?! IT'S BEEN HOURS.
G-GOOD POINT. I'M GOING TO GO CHECK ON THEM.
YES ...
YES. I'M SORRY.
YES.
YES. THEN, EXCUSE ME.
H-HOW DID IT GO?

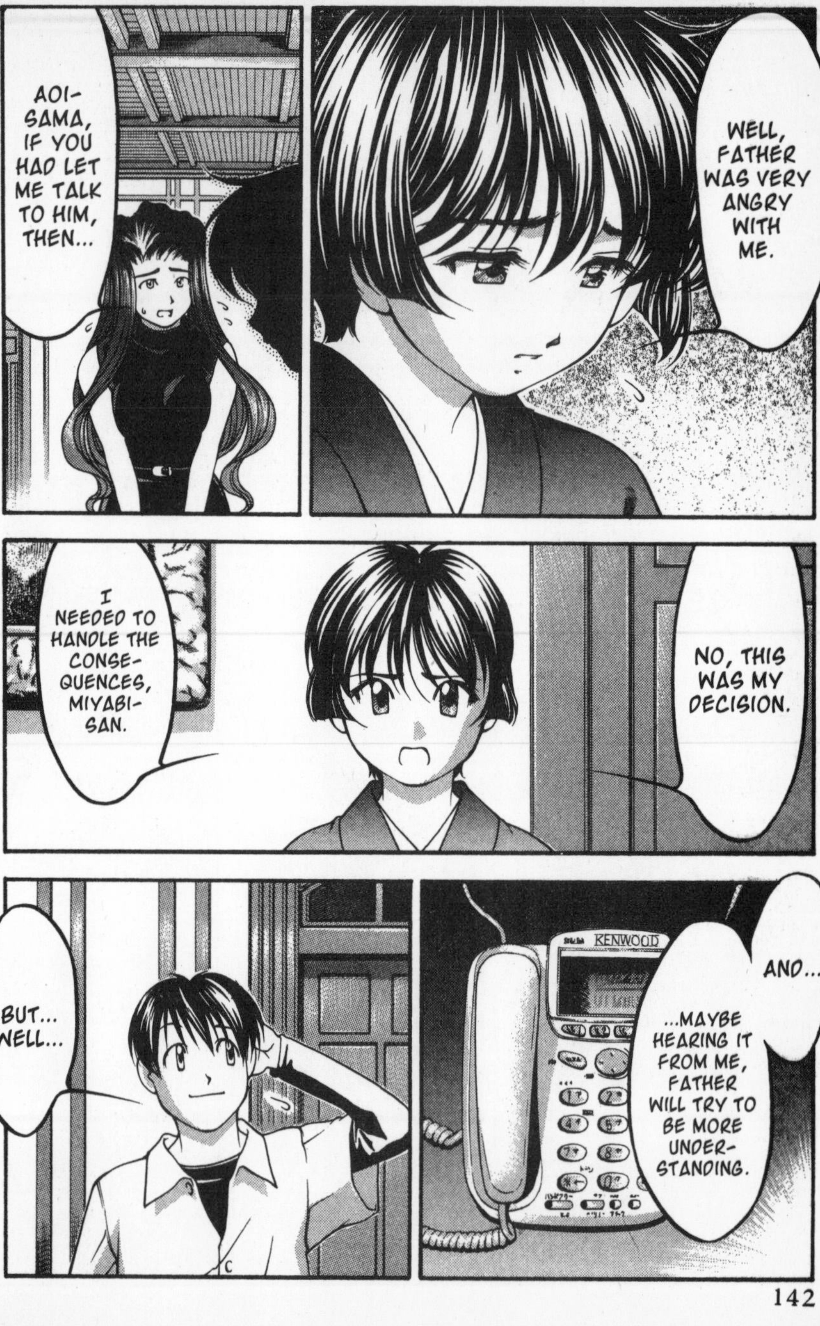
WELL, FATHER WAS VERY ANGRY WITH ME.
AOI-SAMA, IF YOU HAD LET ME TALK TO HIM, THEN...
NO, THIS WAS MY DECISION.
I NEEDED TO HANDLE THE CONSE-QUENCES, MIYABI-SAN.
AND...
...MAYBE HEARING IT FROM ME, FATHER WILL TRY TO BE MORE UNDER-STANDING.
KENWOOD
BUT... WELL...

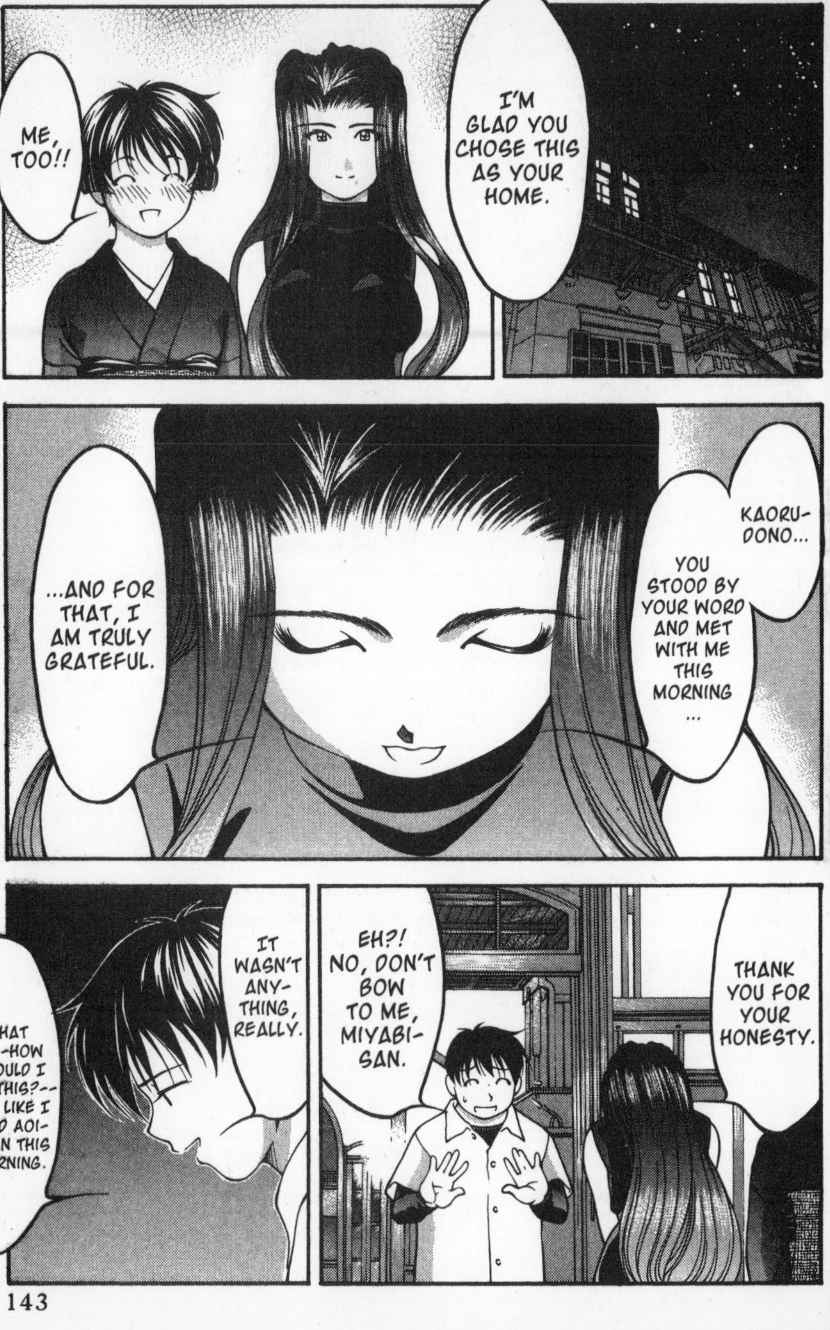

I'M GLAD YOU CHOSE THIS AS YOUR HOME.
ME, TOO!!
KAORU-DONO... YOU STOOD BY YOUR WORD AND MET WITH ME THIS MORNING...
...AND FOR THAT, I AM TRULY GRATEFUL.
THANK YOU FOR YOUR HONESTY.
EH?! NO, DON'T BOW TO ME, MIYABI-SAN.
IT WASN'T ANYTHING, REALLY.
THAT IS--HOW SHOULD I PUT THIS?--IT'S LIKE I TOLD AOI-CHAN THIS MORNING.

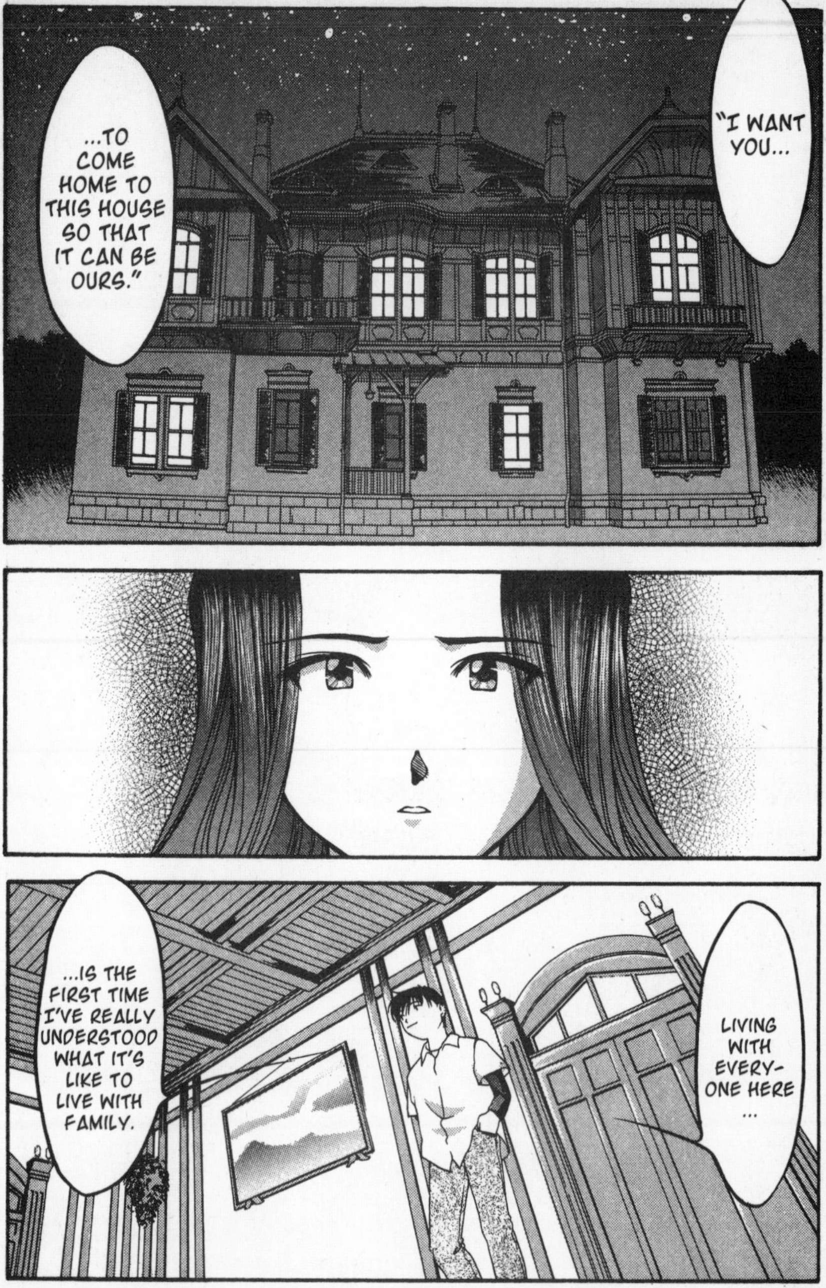
"I WANT YOU...
...TO COME HOME TO THIS HOUSE SO THAT IT CAN BE OURS."
LIVING WITH EVERY-ONE HERE ...
...IS THE FIRST TIME I'VE REALLY UNDERSTOOD WHAT IT'S LIKE TO LIVE WITH FAMILY.

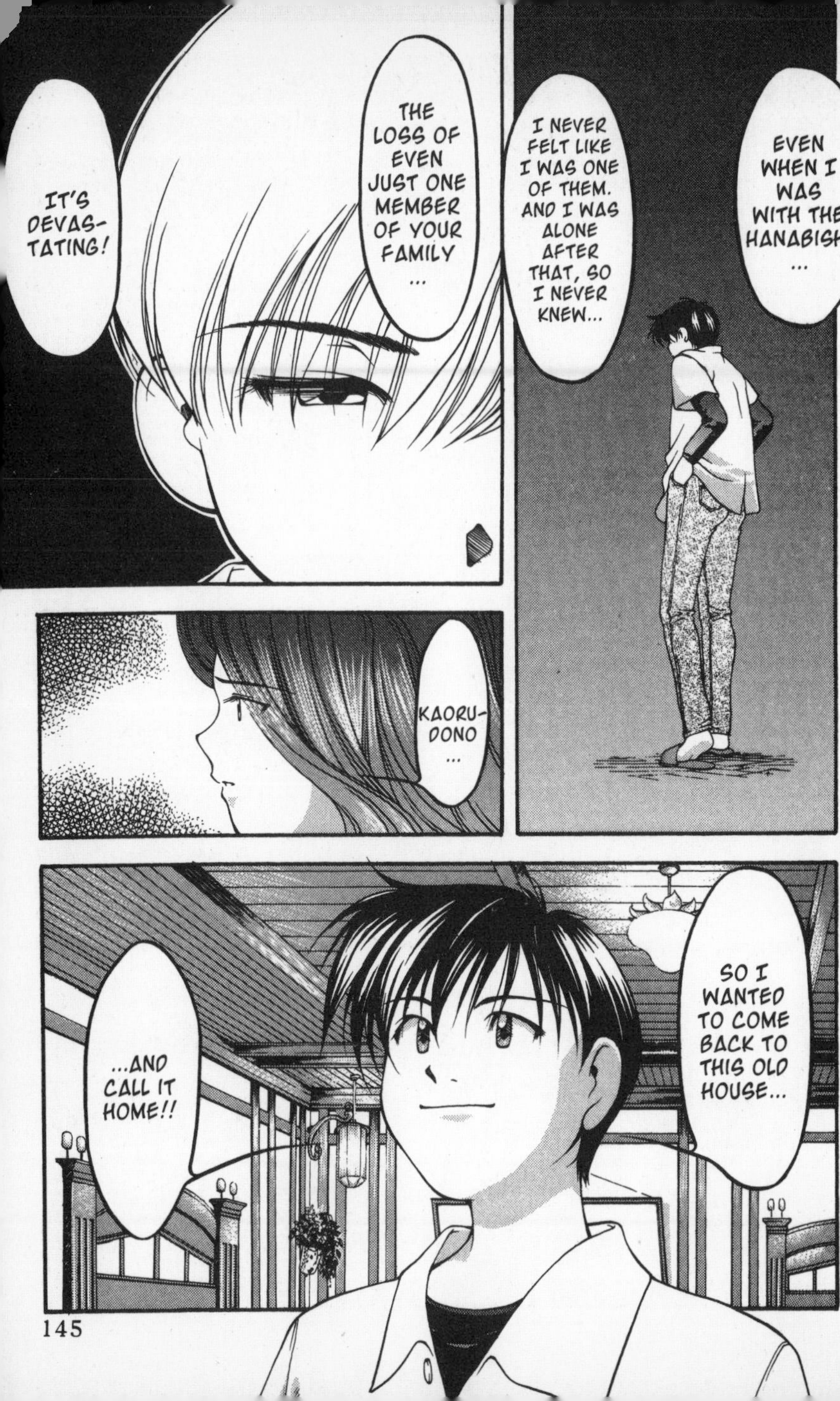
EVEN WHEN I WAS WITH THE HANABISHI ...
I NEVER FELT LIKE I WAS ONE OF THEM. AND I WAS ALONE AFTER THAT, SO I NEVER KNEW...
THE LOSS OF EVEN JUST ONE MEMBER OF YOUR FAMILY ...
IT'S DEVAS-TATING!
KAORU-DONO ...
SO I WANTED TO COME BACK TO THIS OLD HOUSE...
...AND CALL IT HOME!!

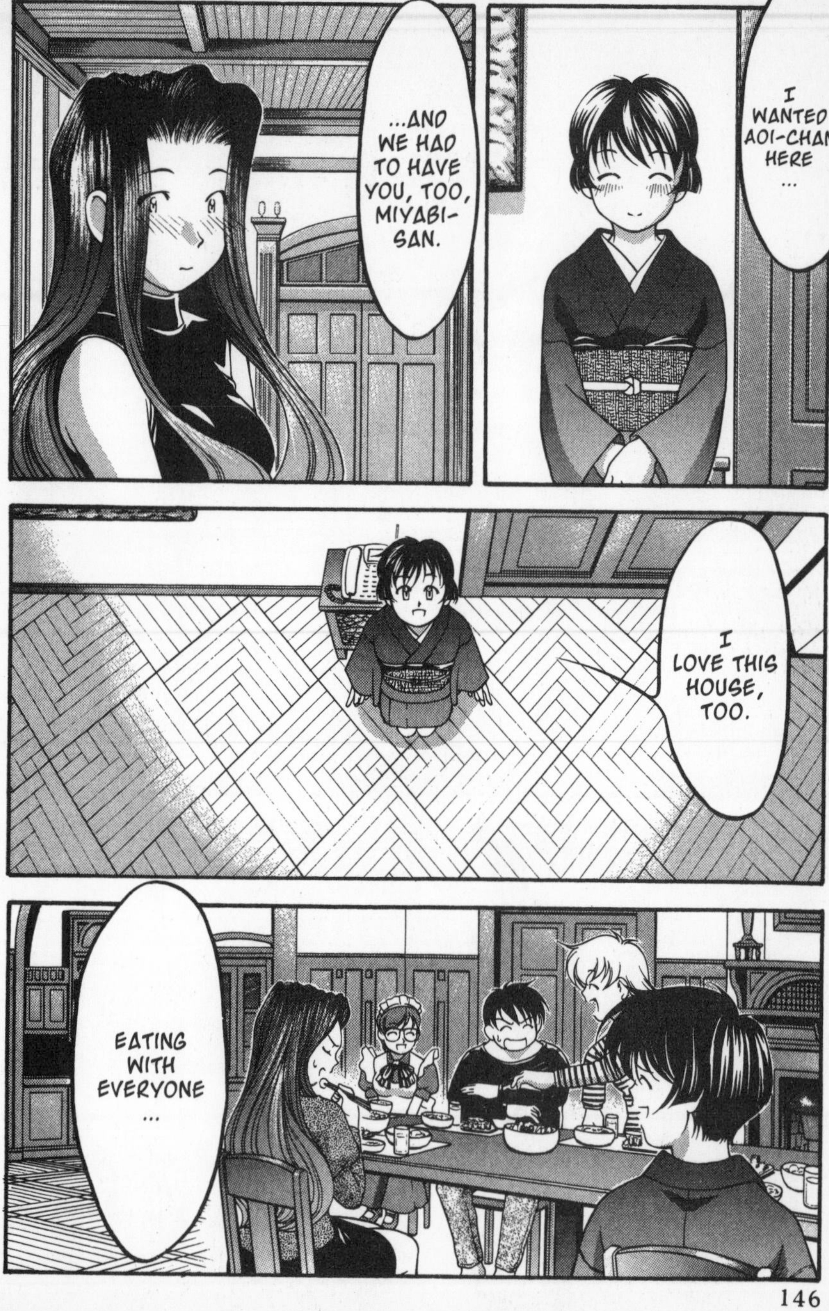
I WANTED AOI-CHAN HERE ...
...AND WE HAD TO HAVE YOU, TOO, MIYABI-SAN.
I LOVE THIS HOUSE, TOO.
EATING WITH EVERYONE ...

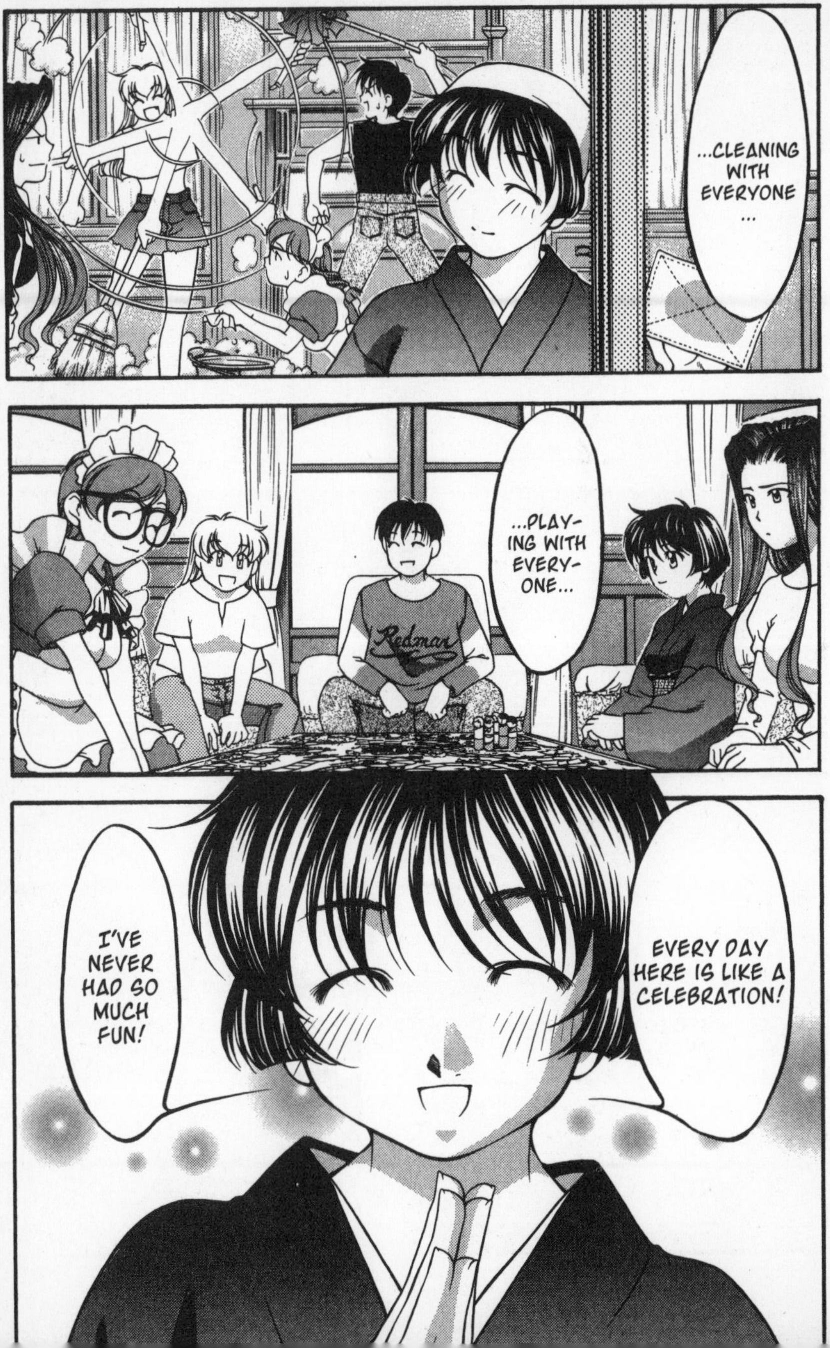
...CLEANING WITH EVERYONE ...
...PLAY-ING WITH EVERY-ONE...
Redman
EVERY DAY HERE IS LIKE A CELEBRATION!
I'VE NEVER HAD SO MUCH FUN!

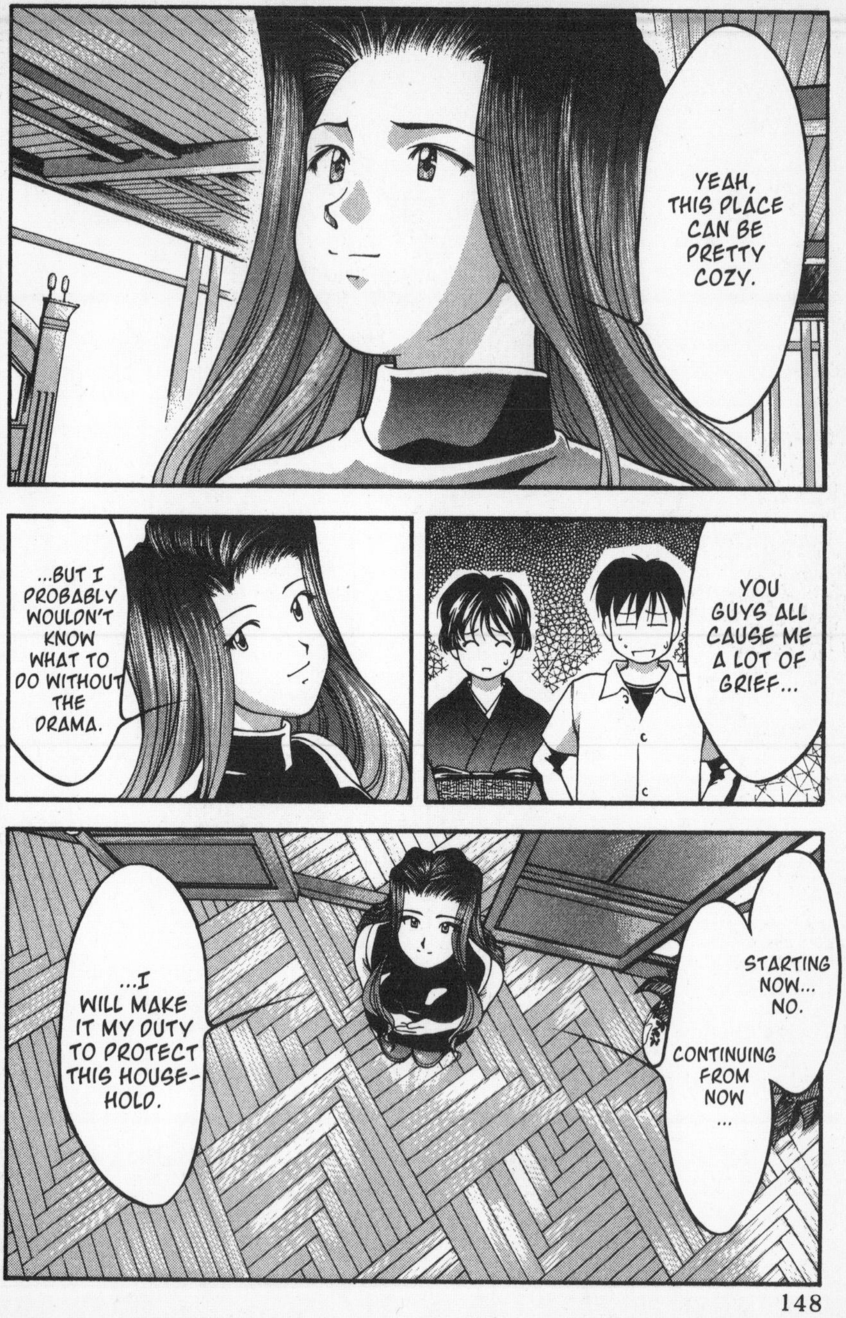
YEAH, THIS PLACE CAN BE PRETTY COZY.
YOU GUYS ALL CAUSE ME A LOT OF GRIEF...
...BUT I PROBABLY WOULDN'T KNOW WHAT TO DO WITHOUT THE DRAMA.
STARTING NOW... NO.
CONTINUING FROM NOW...
...I WILL MAKE IT MY DUTY TO PROTECT THIS HOUSE-HOLD.

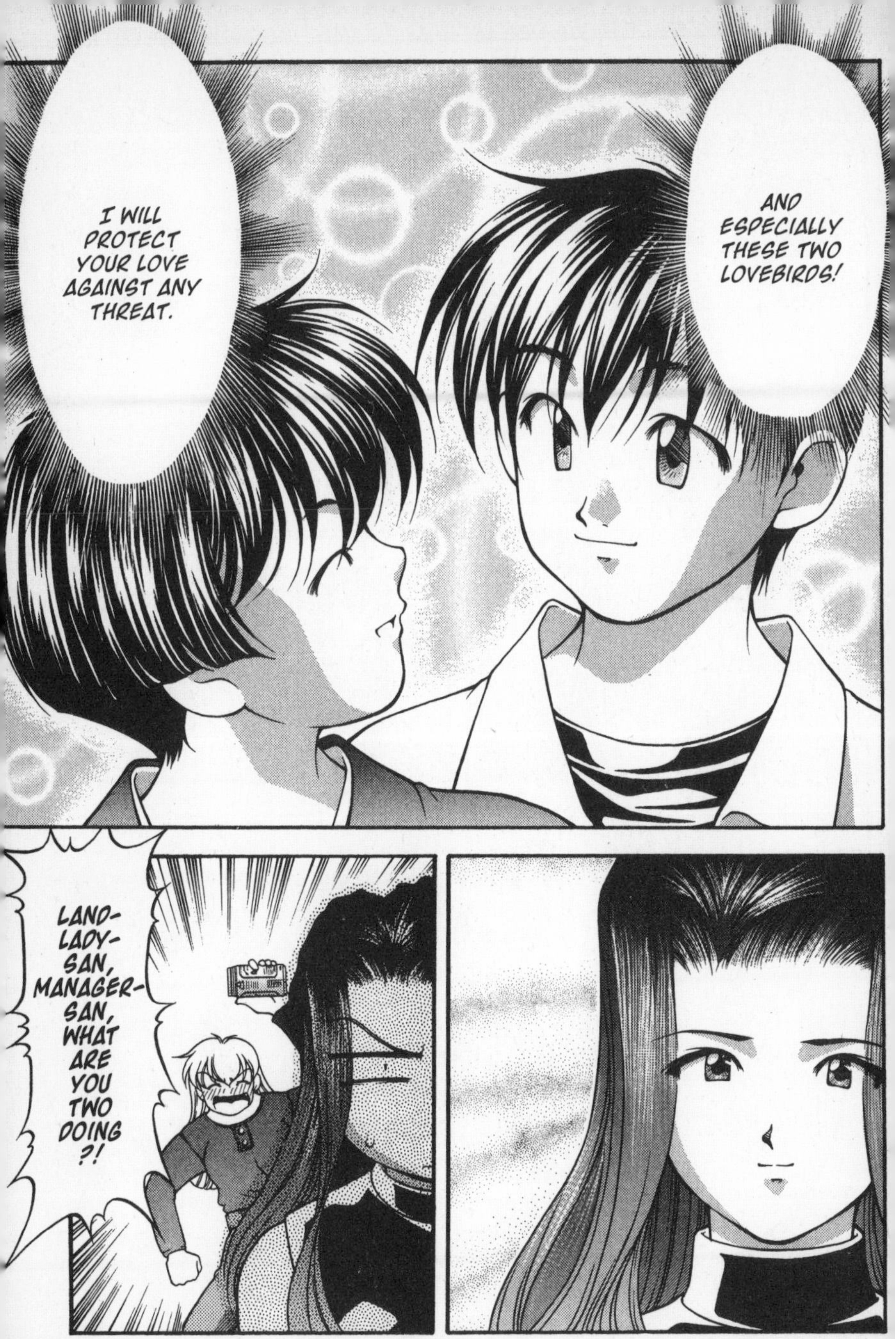
AND ESPECIALLY THESE TWO LOVEBIRDS!
I WILL PROTECT YOUR LOVE AGAINST ANY THREAT.
LAND-LADY-SAN, MANAGER-SAN, WHAT ARE YOU TWO DOING?!

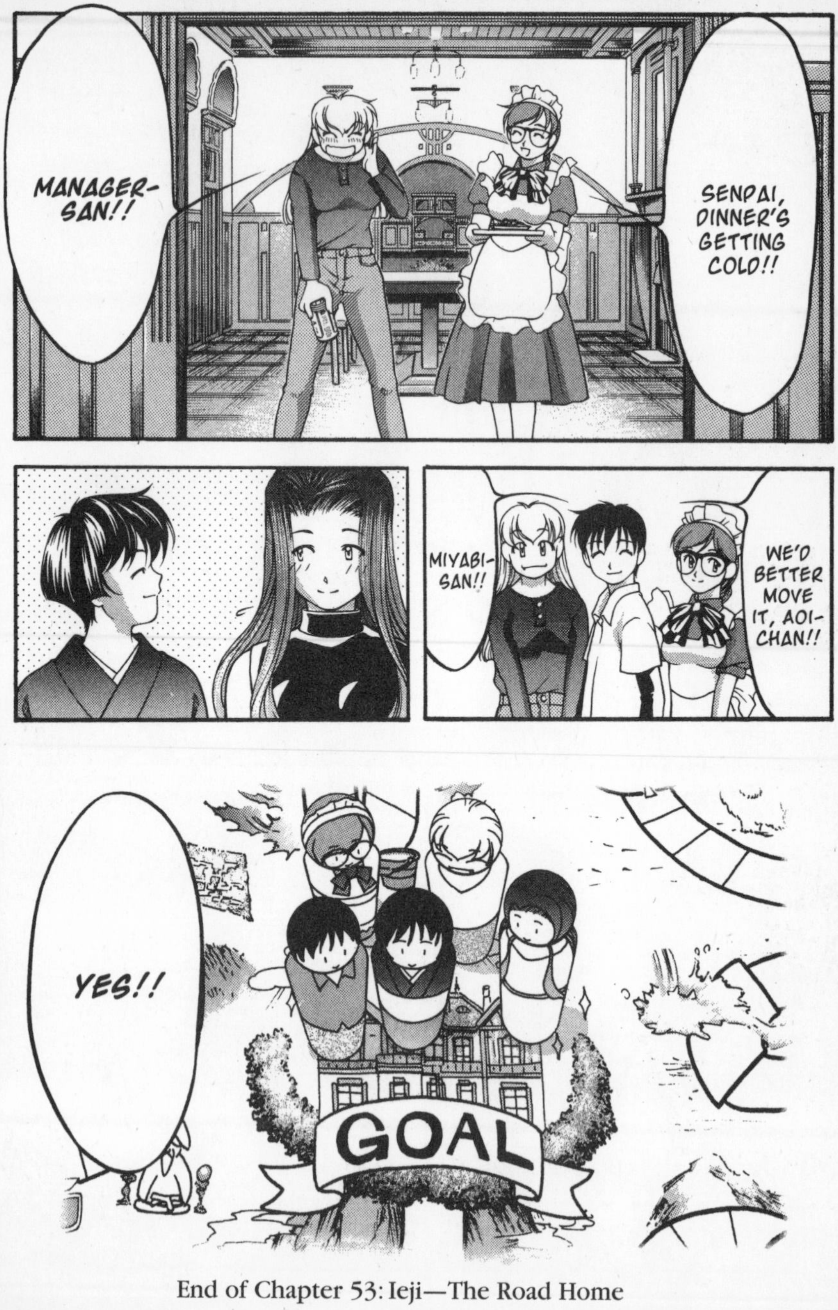
SENPAI, DINNER'S GETTING COLD!!
MANAGER-SAN!!
WE'D BETTER MOVE IT, AOI-CHAN!!
MIYABI-SAN!!
YES!!
GOAL

End of Chapter 53: Ieji—The Road Home

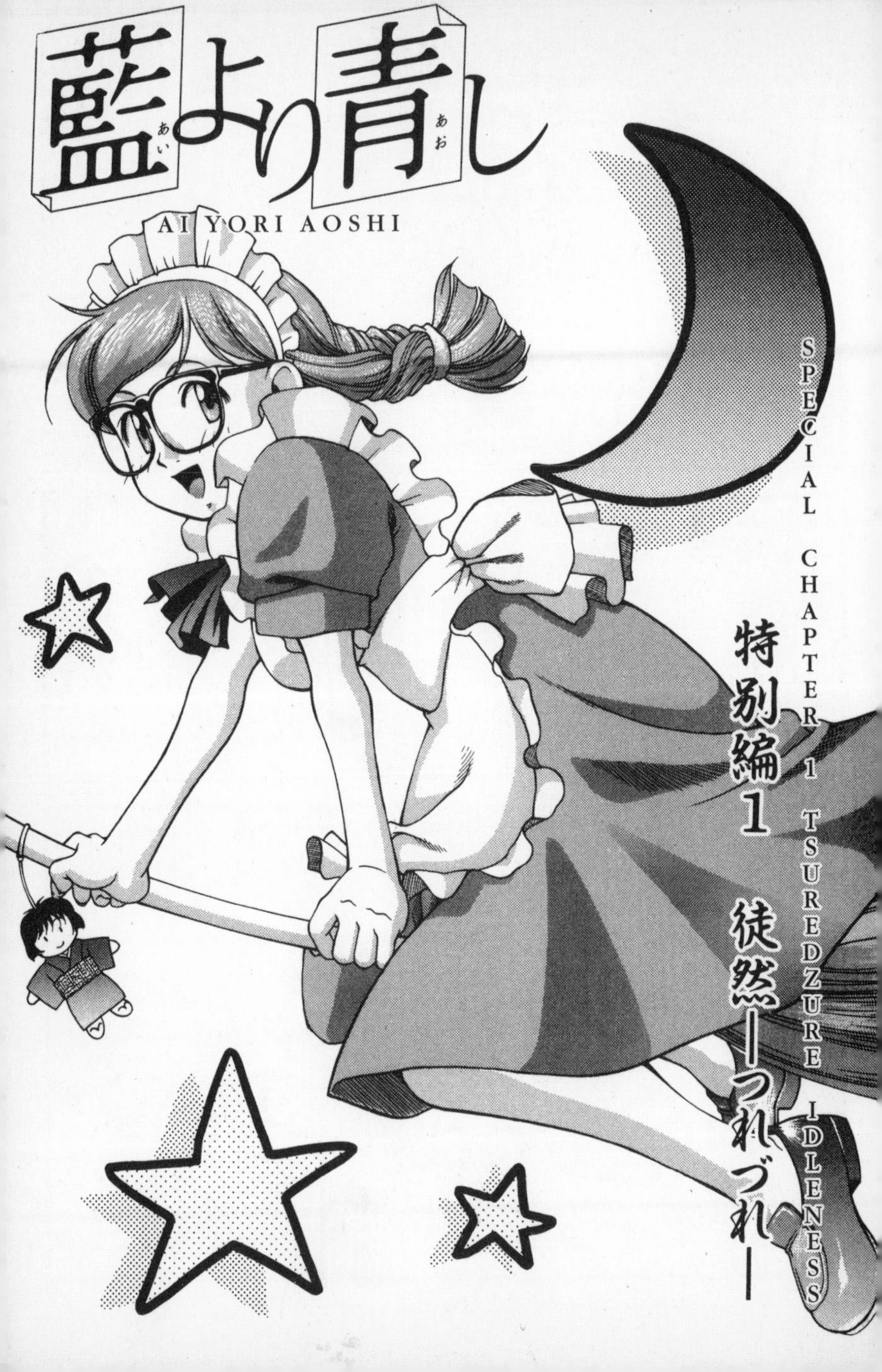
藍(あい)より青(あお)し
AI YORI AOSHI
SPECIAL CHAPTER 1 TSUREDZURE IDLENESS
特別編1 徒然—つれづれ—

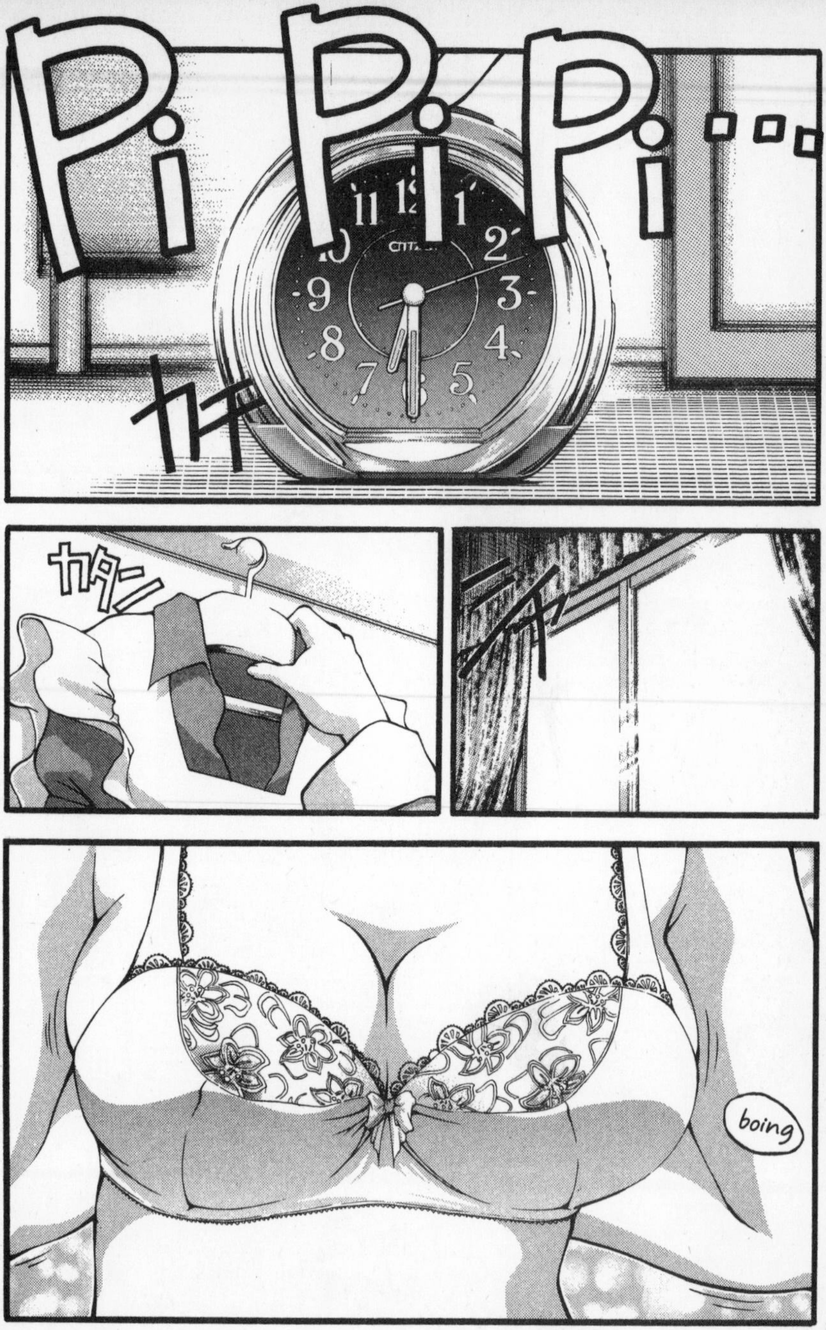
Pi Pi Pi...
カチ
カタン
シャ
boing

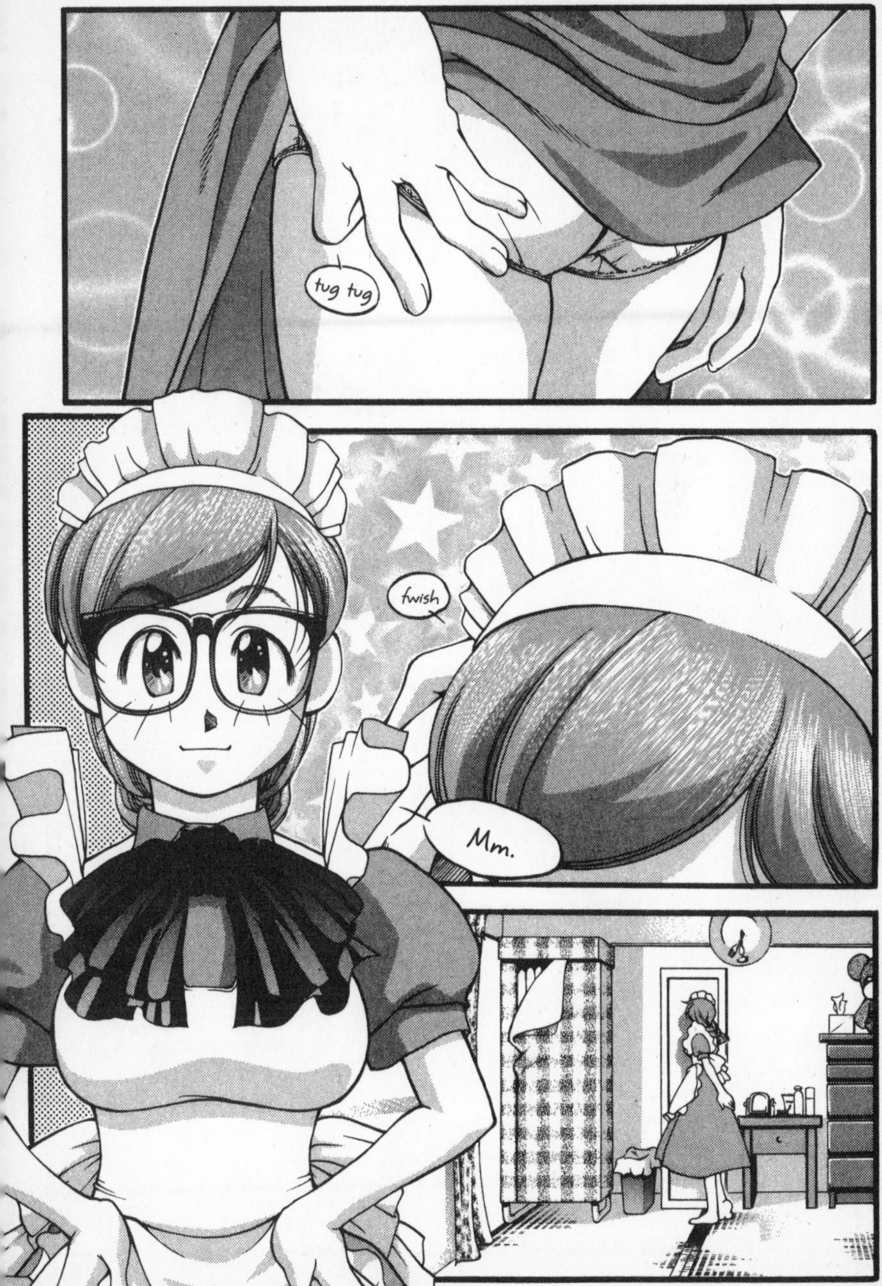
tug tug
fwish
Mm.

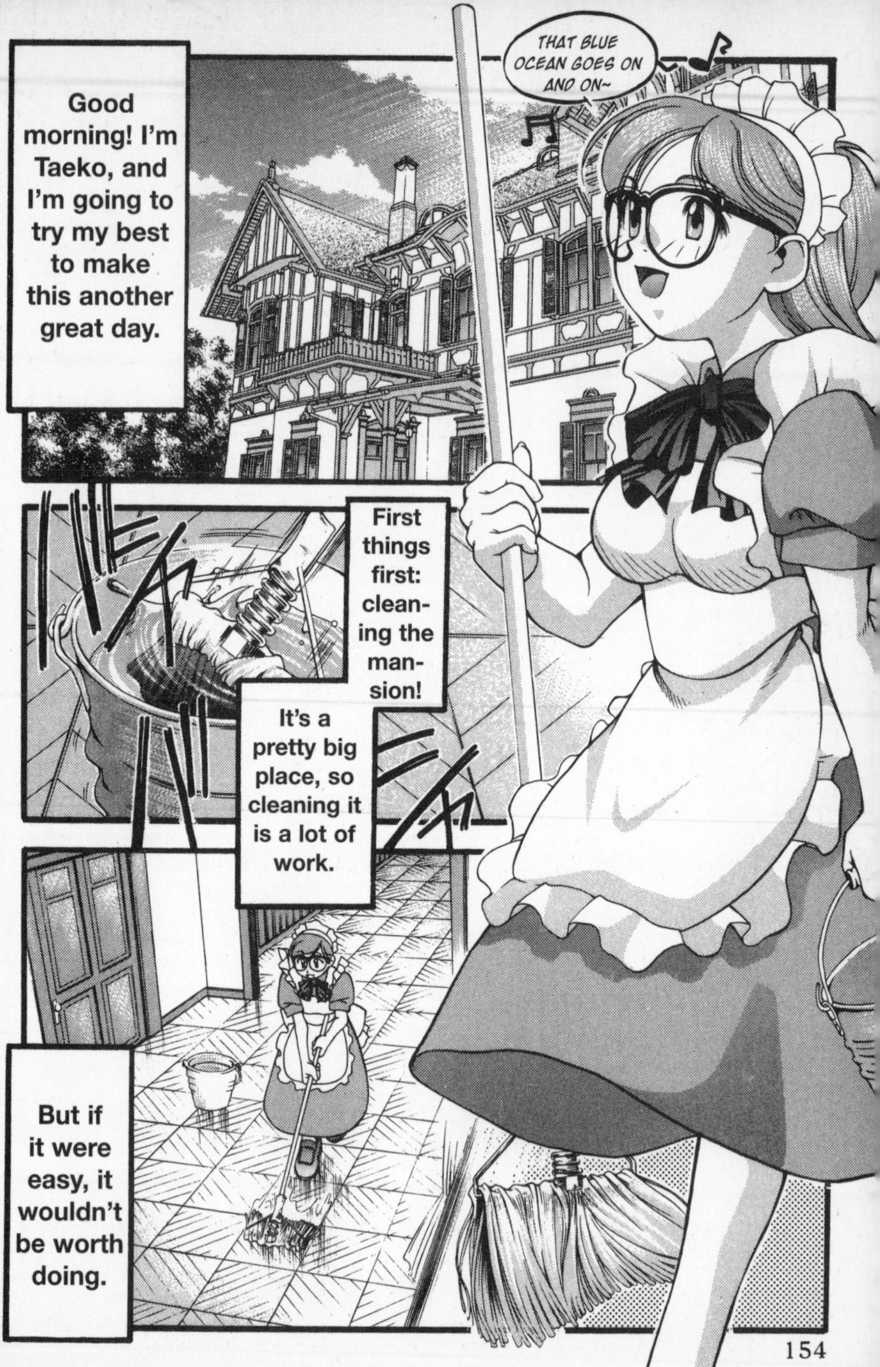
THAT BLUE OCEAN GOES ON AND ON~
Good morning! I'm Taeko, and I'm going to try my best to make this another great day.
First things first: clean-ing the man-sion!
It's a pretty big place, so cleaning it is a lot of work.
But if it were easy, it wouldn't be worth doing.

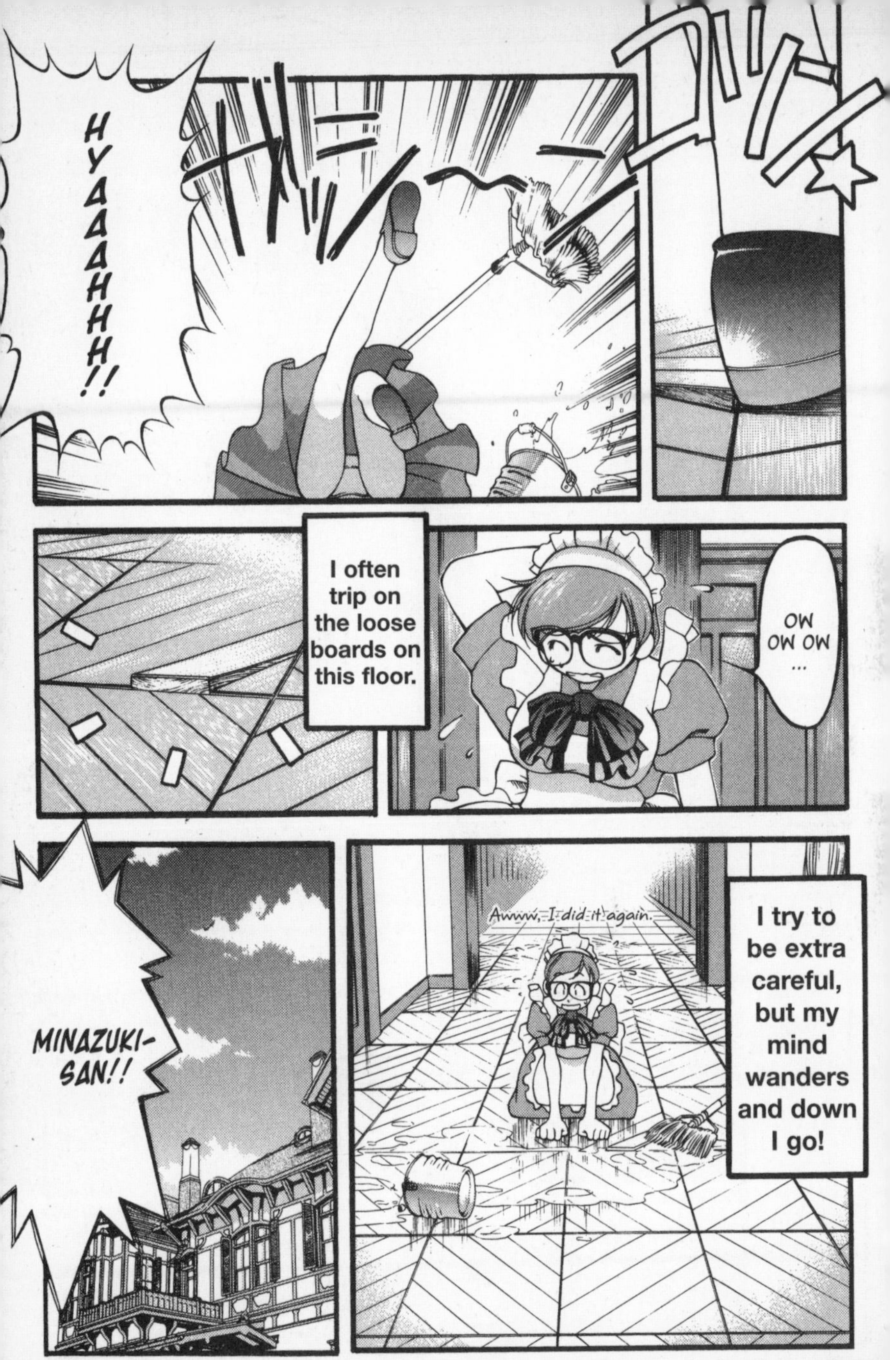

HYAAAAHHHH!!
OW OW OW ...
I often trip on the loose boards on this floor.
I try to be extra careful, but my mind wanders and down I go!
Awww, I did it again.
MINAZUKI-SAN!!

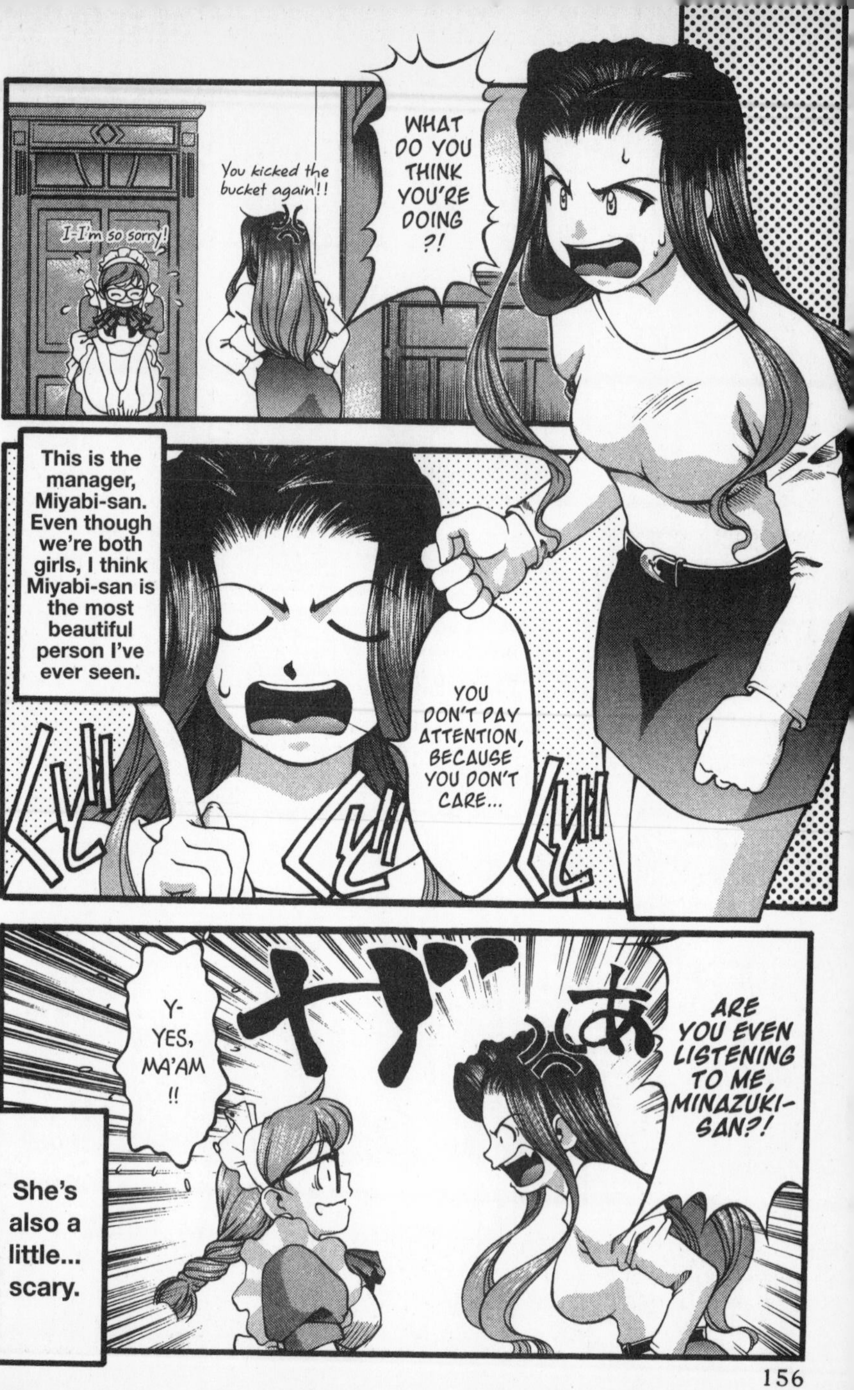

WHAT DO YOU THINK YOU'RE DOING ?!
You kicked the bucket again!!
I-I'm so sorry!
YOU DON'T PAY ATTENTION, BECAUSE YOU DON'T CARE...
This is the manager, Miyabi-san. Even though we're both girls, I think Miyabi-san is the most beautiful person I've ever seen.
ARE YOU EVEN LISTENING TO ME, MINAZUKI-SAN?!
Y-YES, MA'AM !!
She's also a little... scary.

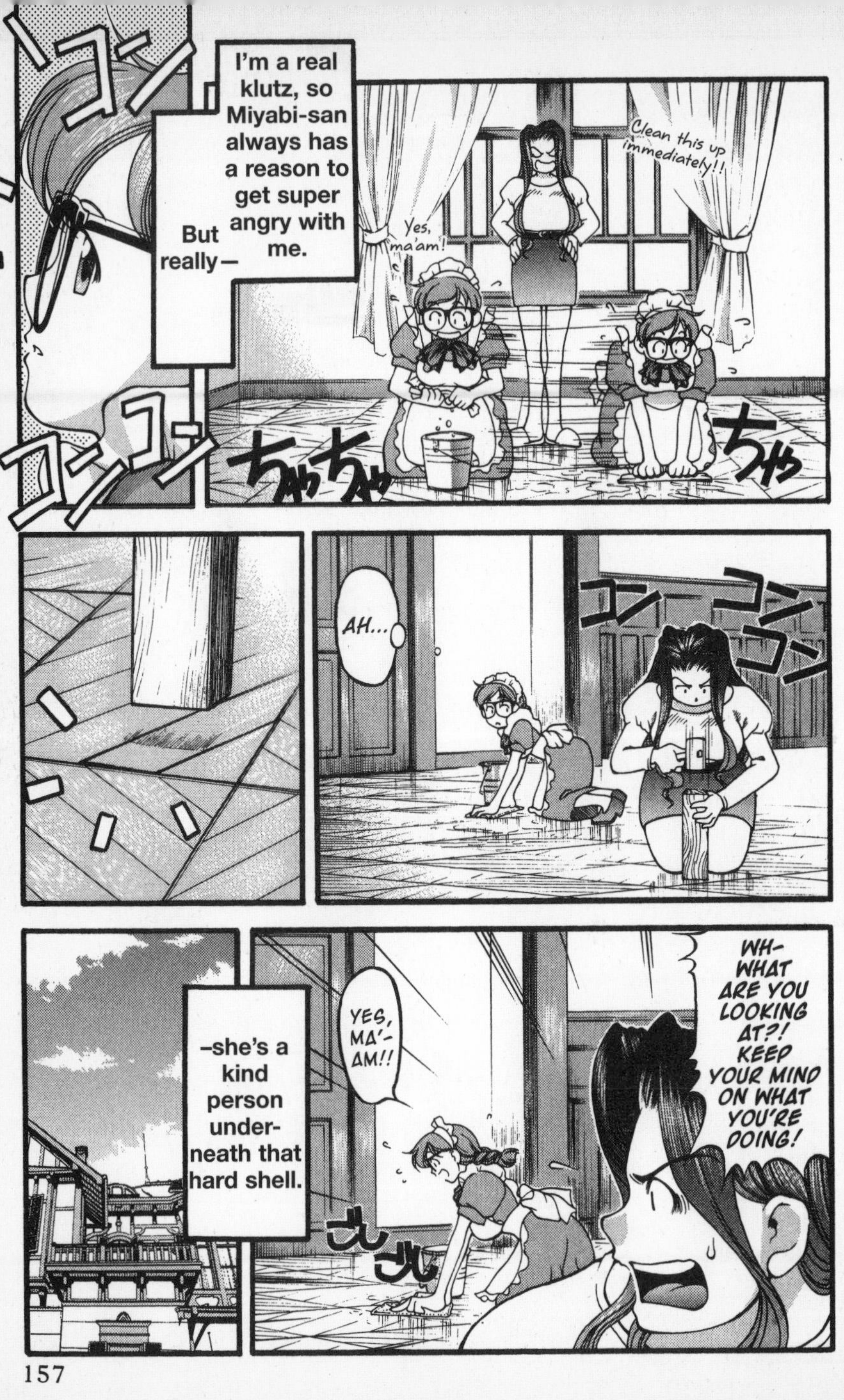
Clean this up immediately!!
Yes, ma'am!
I'm a real klutz, so Miyabi-san always has a reason to get super angry with me.
ちゃっちゃっ
ちゃっ
But really—
AH...
WH-WHAT ARE YOU LOOKING AT?! KEEP YOUR MIND ON WHAT YOU'RE DOING!
YES, MA'-AM!!
–she's a kind person under-neath that hard shell.

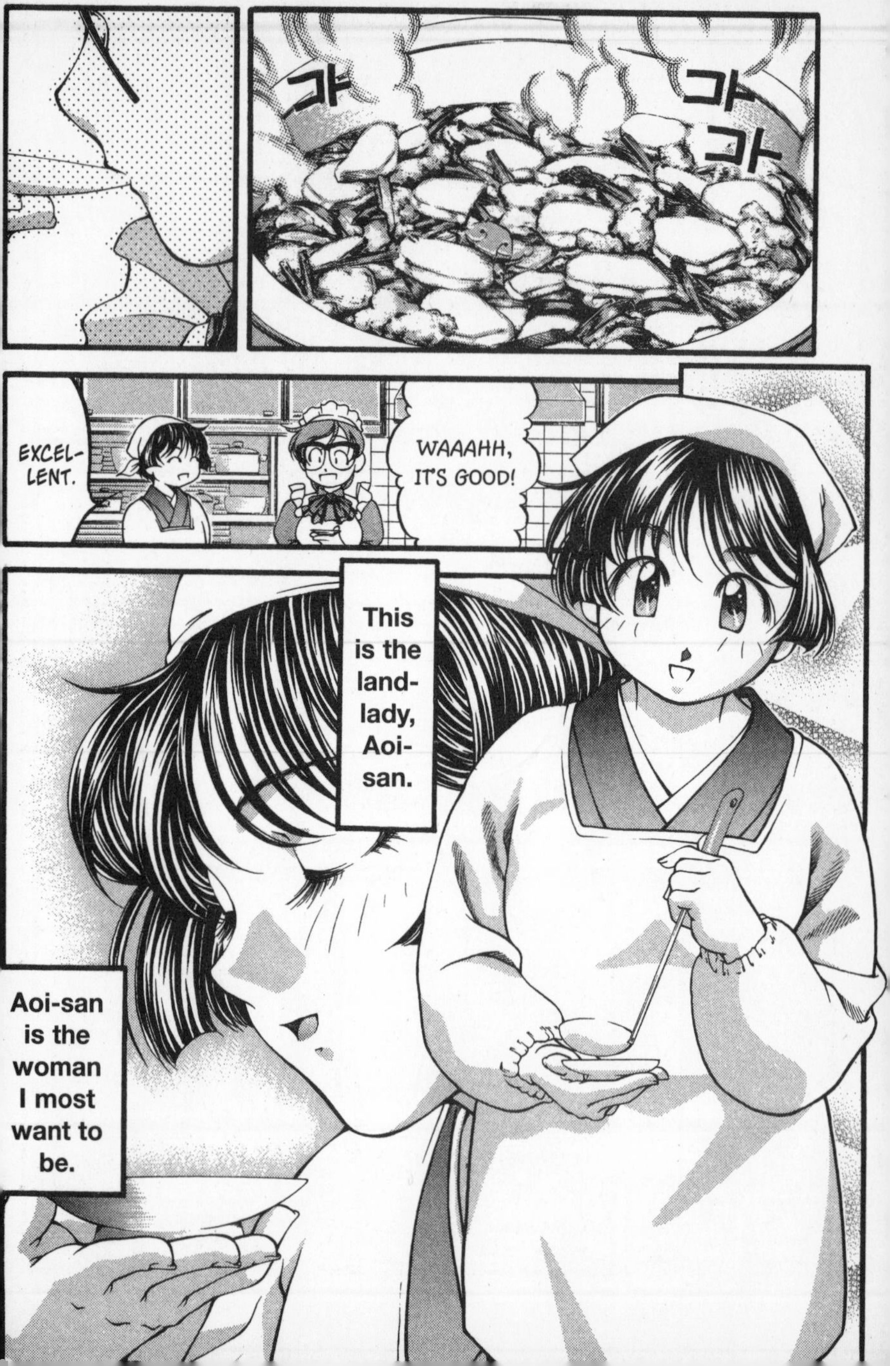
WAAAHH, IT'S GOOD!
EXCEL-LENT.
This is the land-lady, Aoi-san.
Aoi-san is the woman I most want to be.

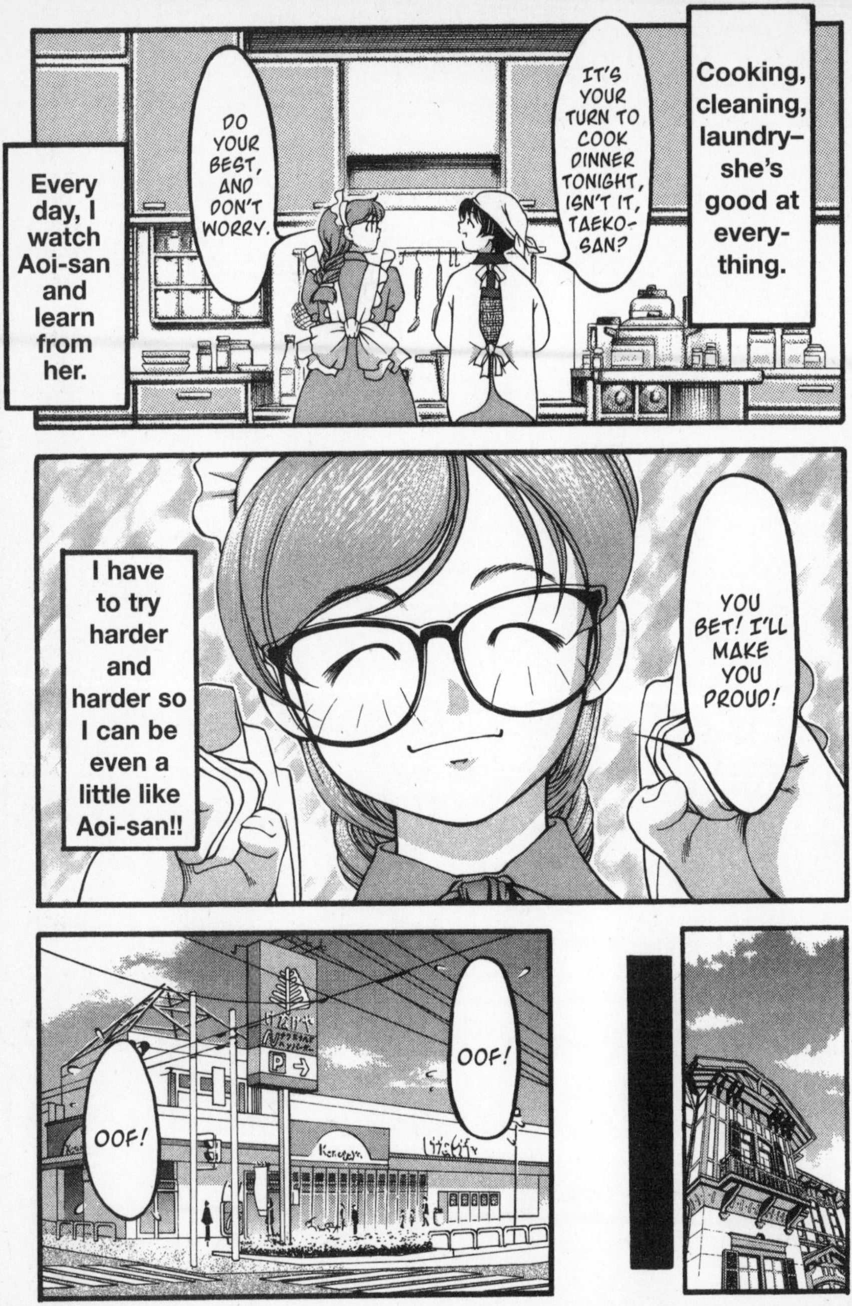
Cooking, cleaning, laundry–she's good at every-thing.
IT'S YOUR TURN TO COOK DINNER TONIGHT, ISN'T IT, TAEKO-SAN?
DO YOUR BEST, AND DON'T WORRY.
Every day, I watch Aoi-san and learn from her.
YOU BET! I'LL MAKE YOU PROUD!
I have to try harder and harder so I can be even a little like Aoi-san!!
OOF!
OOF!

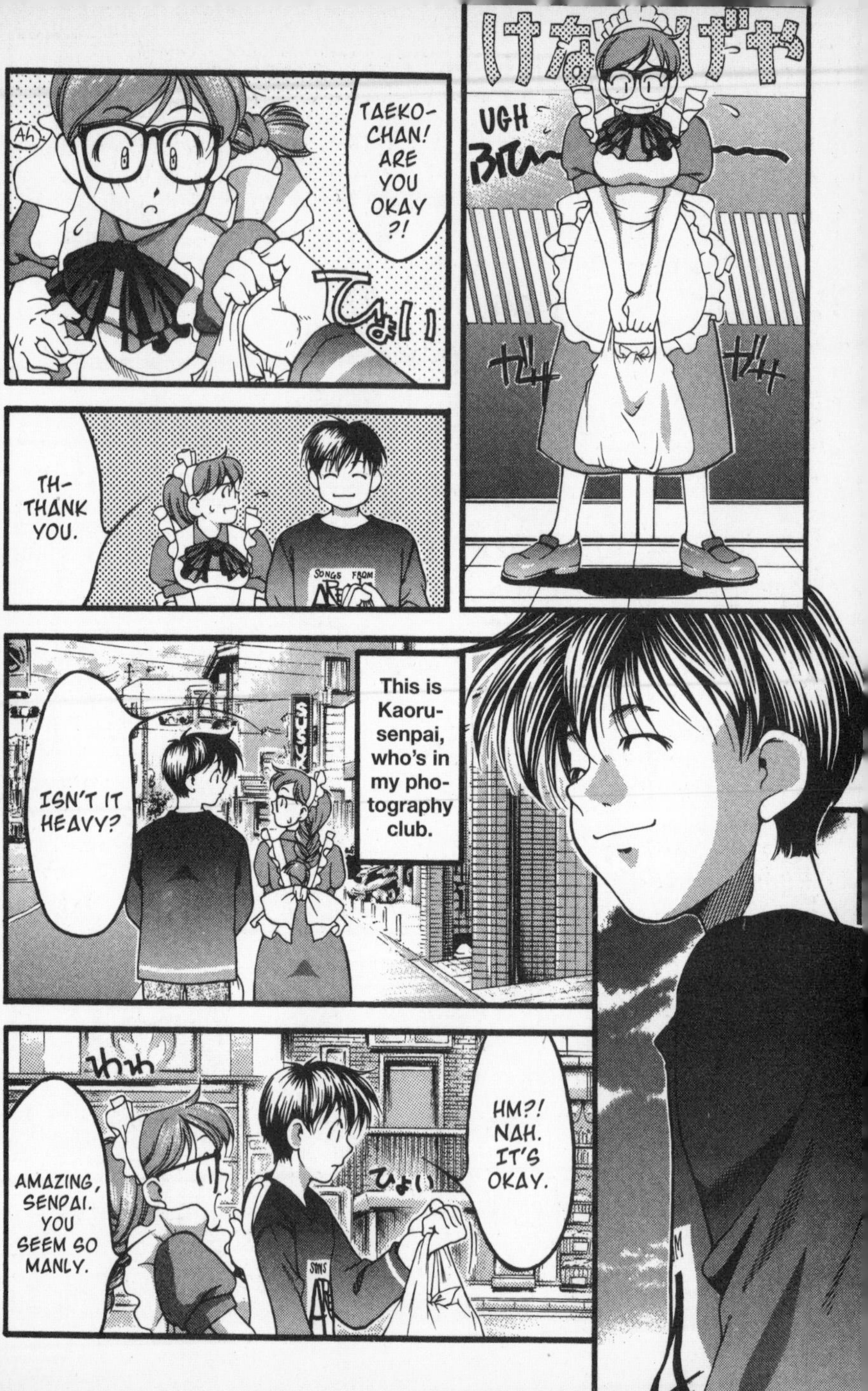
UGH
Ah
TAEKO-CHAN! ARE YOU OKAY?!
ひょい
TH-THANK YOU.
This is Kaoru-senpai, who's in my photography club.
ISN'T IT HEAVY?
HM?! NAH. IT'S OKAY.
ひょい
AMAZING, SENPAI. YOU SEEM SO MANLY.

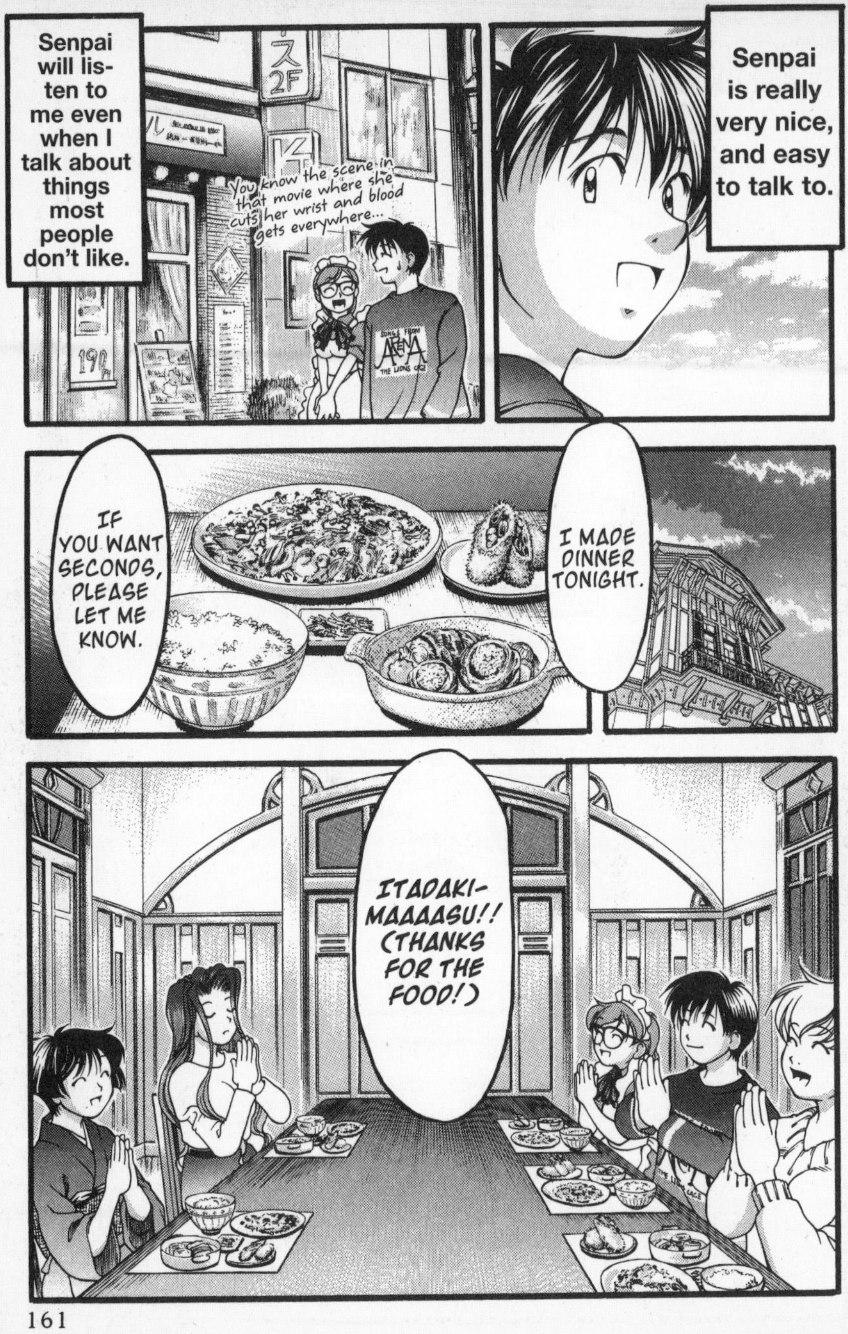
Senpai is really very nice, and easy to talk to.
Senpai will lis-ten to me even when I talk about things most people don't like.
You know the scene in that movie where she cuts her wrist and blood gets everywhere...
I MADE DINNER TONIGHT.
IF YOU WANT SECONDS, PLEASE LET ME KNOW.
ITADAKI-MAAAASU!! (THANKS FOR THE FOOD!)

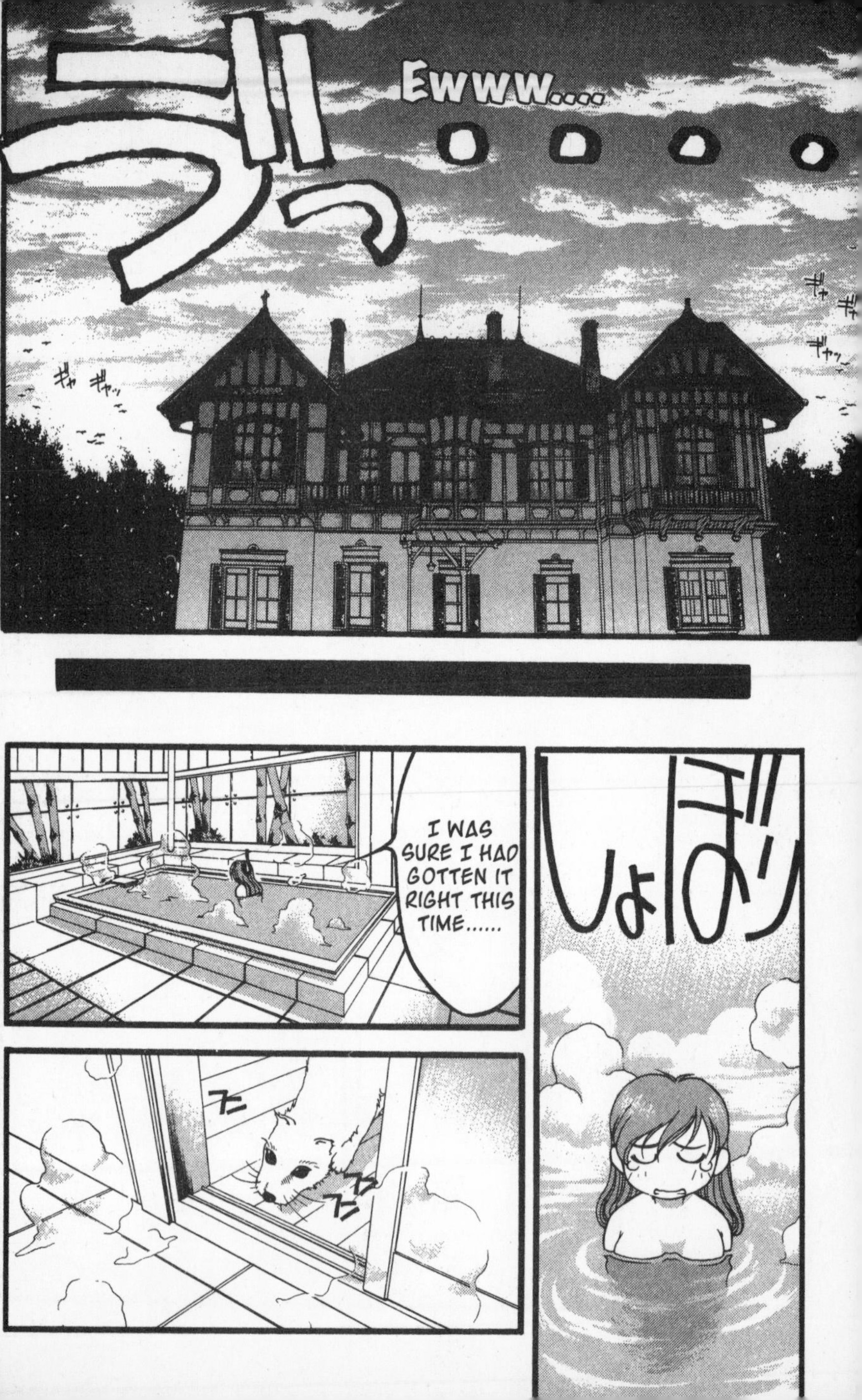
うっ
Ewww....
ギャ ギャッ
しょぼり
I WAS SURE I HAD GOTTEN IT RIGHT THIS TIME......

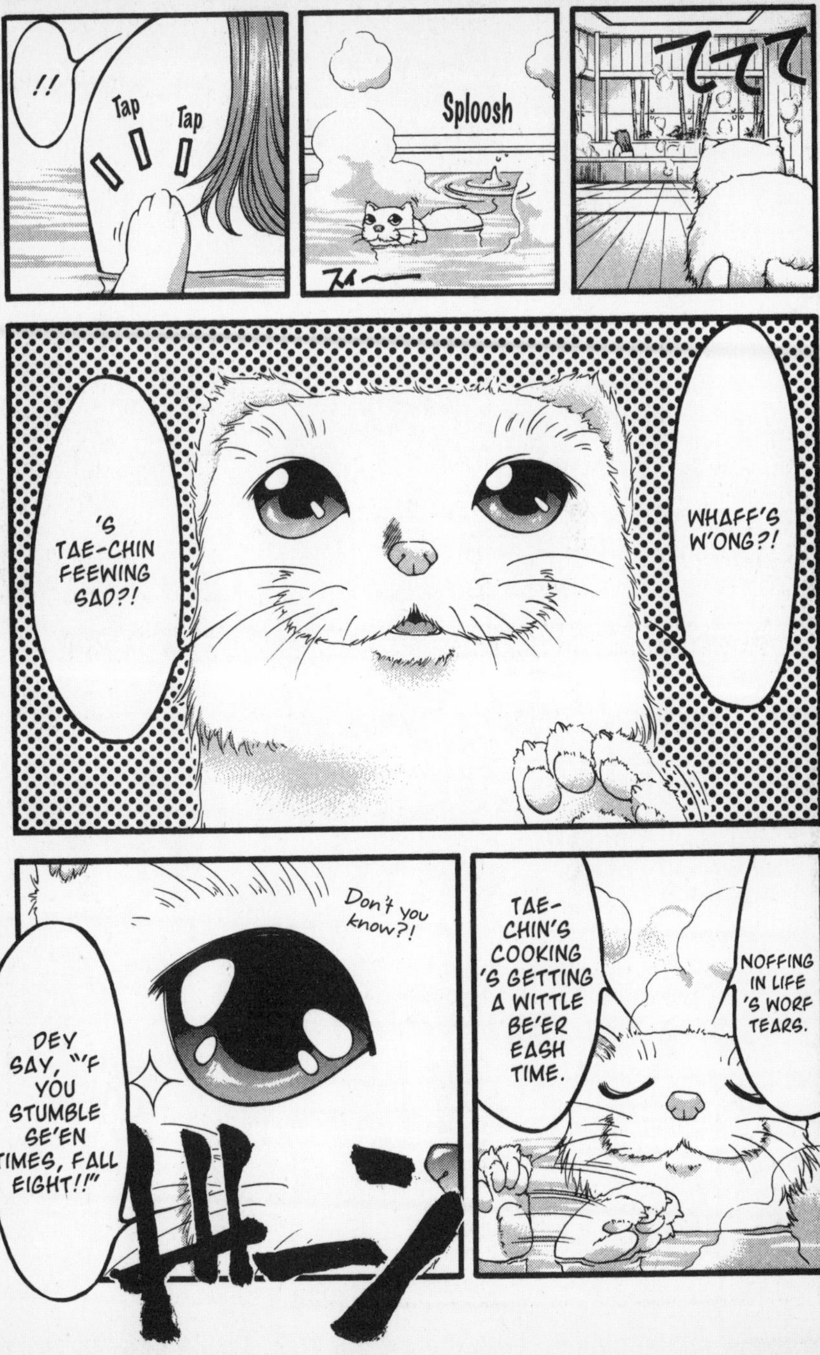
ててて
Sploosh
スィー
!!
Tap
Tap
WHAFF'S W'ONG?!
'S TAE-CHIN FEEWING SAD?!
NOFFING IN LIFE 'S WORF TEARS.
TAE-CHIN'S COOKING 'S GETTING A WITTLE BE'ER EASH TIME.
Don't you know?!
DEY SAY, "'F YOU STUMBLE SE'EN TIMES, FALL EIGHT!!"

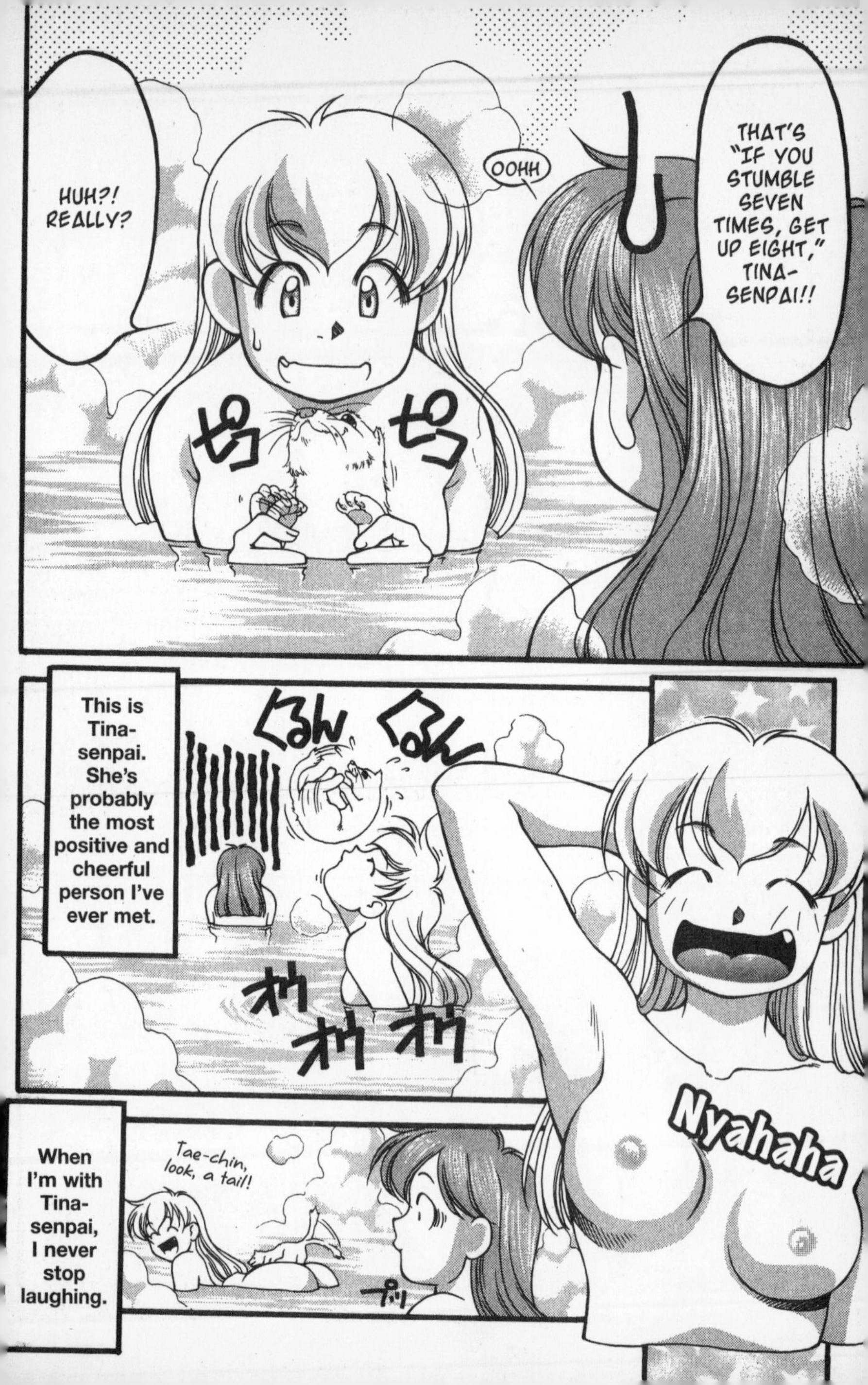
THAT'S "IF YOU STUMBLE SEVEN TIMES, GET UP EIGHT," TINA-SENPAI!!
OOHH
HUH?! REALLY?
ぴこ ぴこ
くるん くるん
This is Tina-senpai. She's probably the most positive and cheerful person I've ever met.
オウ オウ オウ
Nyahaha
When I'm with Tina-senpai, I never stop laughing.
Tae-chin, look, a tail!
ぷい

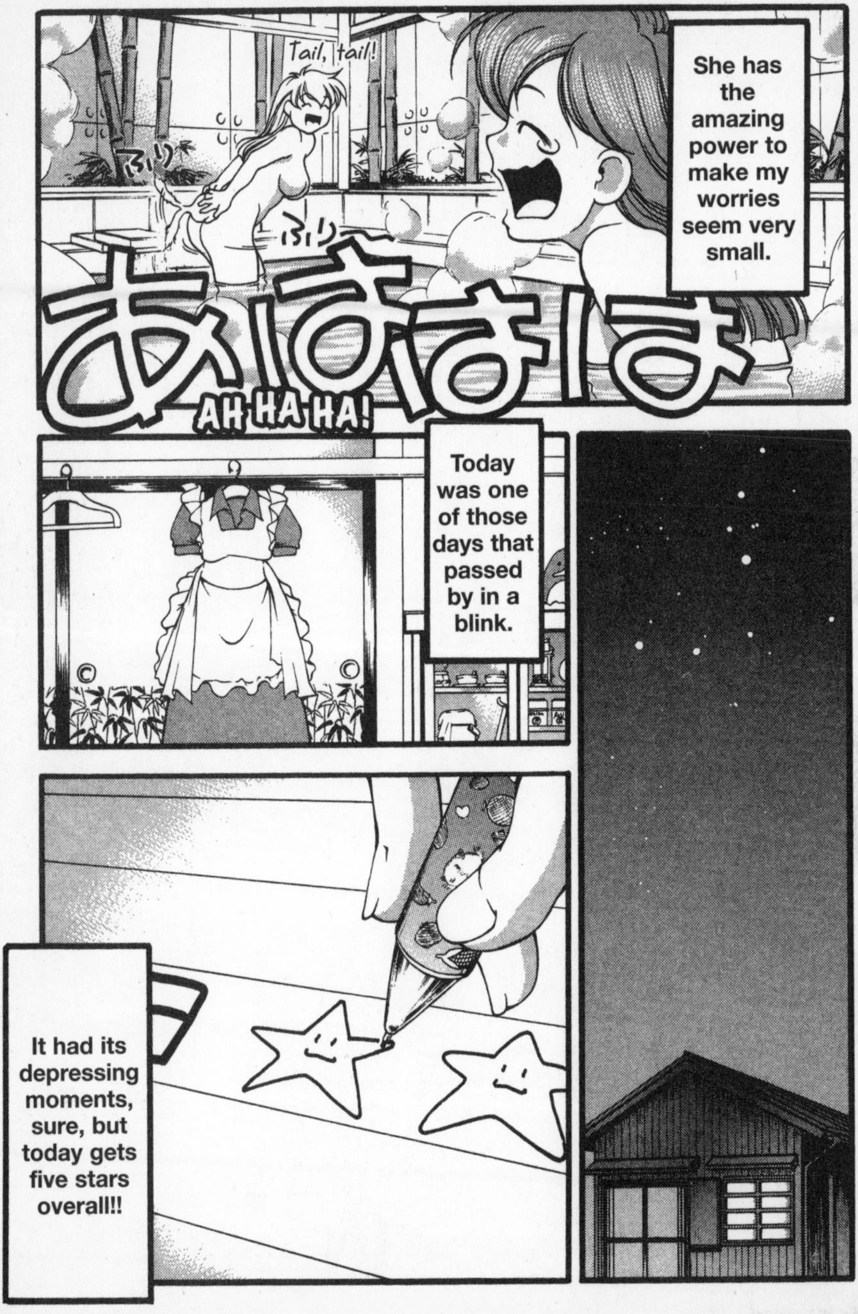
She has the amazing power to make my worries seem very small.
Tail, tail!
ふり
ふり
あははは
AH HA HA!
Today was one of those days that passed by in a blink.
It had its depressing moments, sure, but today gets five stars overall!!

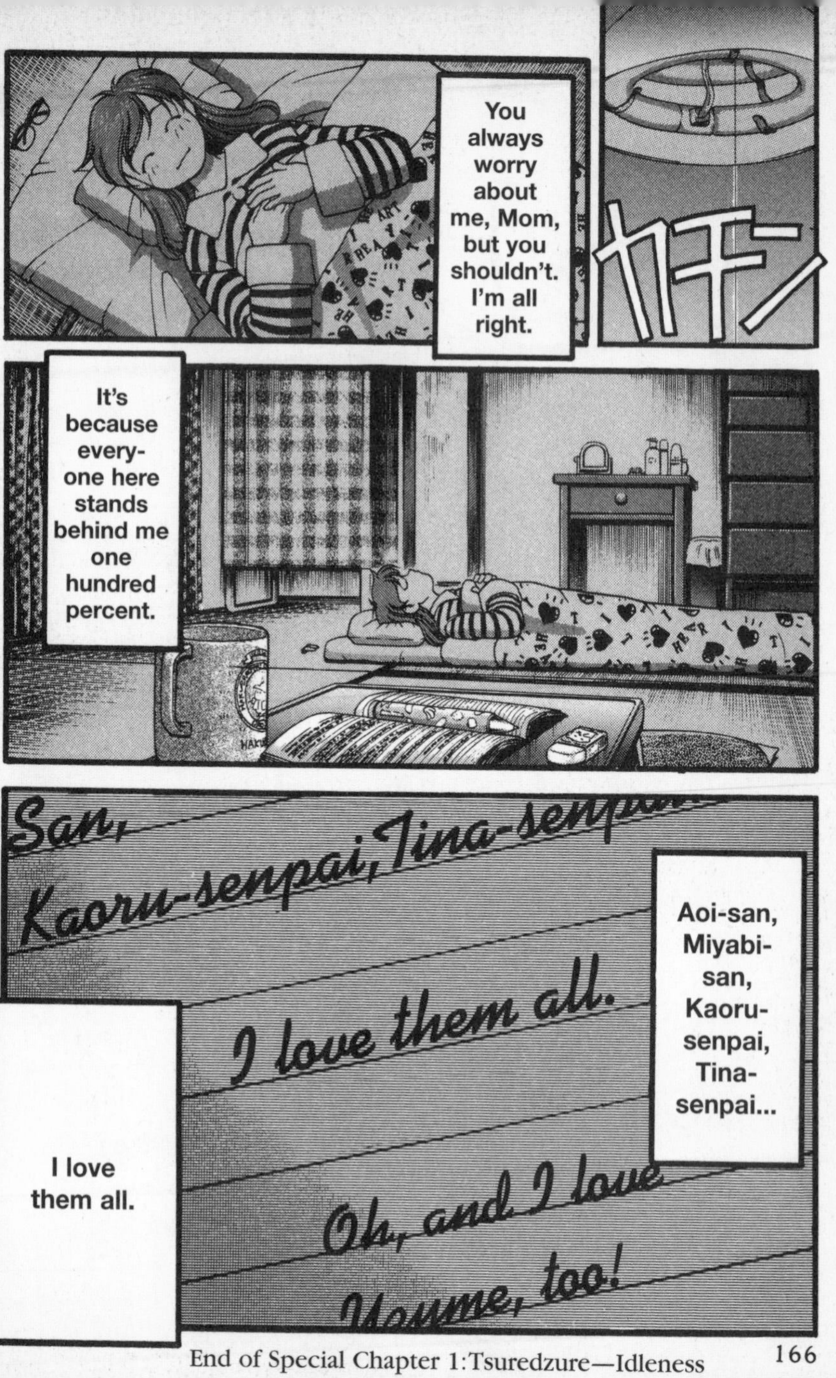
カチーン
You always worry about me, Mom, but you shouldn't. I'm all right.
It's because every-one here stands behind me one hundred percent.
Aoi-san, Miyabi-san, Kaoru-senpai, Tina-senpai...
San,
Kaoru-senpai, Tina-senpai
I love them all.
Oh, and I love
too!
I love them all.

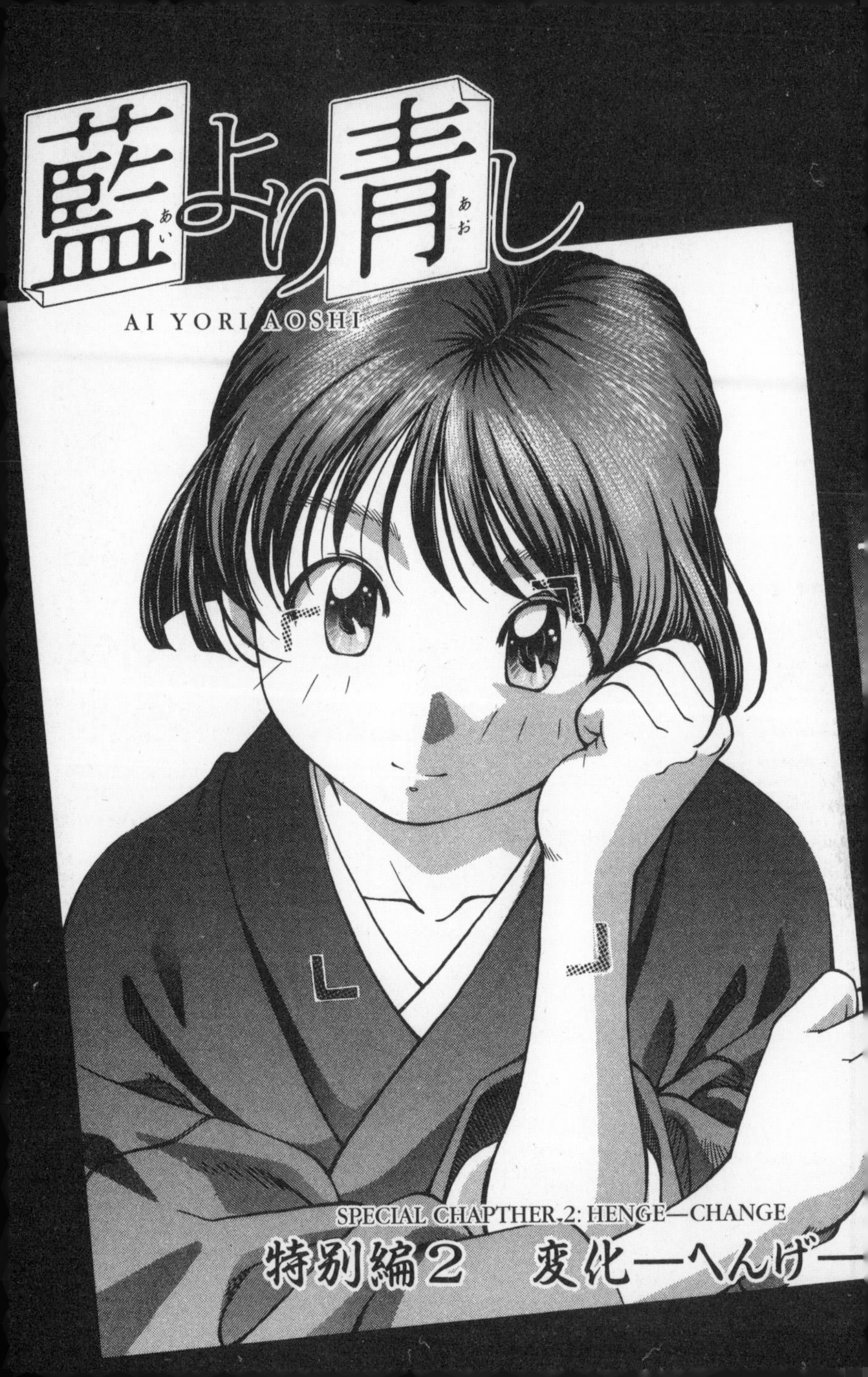
藍(あい)より青(あお)し
AI YORI AOSHI
SPECIAL CHAPTHER 2: HENGE—CHANGE
特別編2　変化—へんげ—

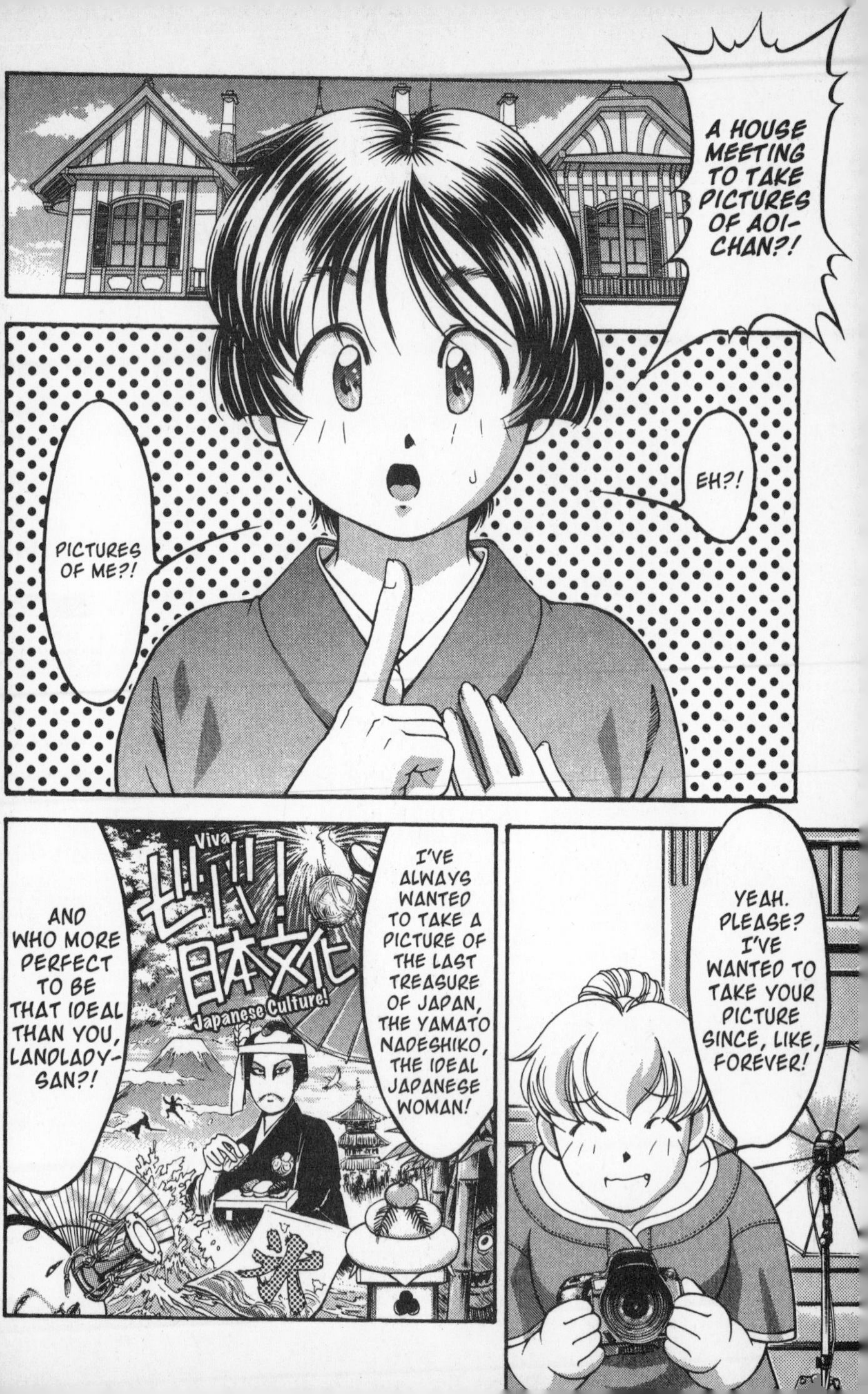
A HOUSE MEETING TO TAKE PICTURES OF AOI-CHAN?!
EH?!
PICTURES OF ME?!
YEAH. PLEASE? I'VE WANTED TO TAKE YOUR PICTURE SINCE, LIKE, FOREVER!
I'VE ALWAYS WANTED TO TAKE A PICTURE OF THE LAST TREASURE OF JAPAN, THE YAMATO NADESHIKO, THE IDEAL JAPANESE WOMAN!
Viva ビバ！日本文化 Japanese Culture!
AND WHO MORE PERFECT TO BE THAT IDEAL THAN YOU, LANDLADY-SAN?!

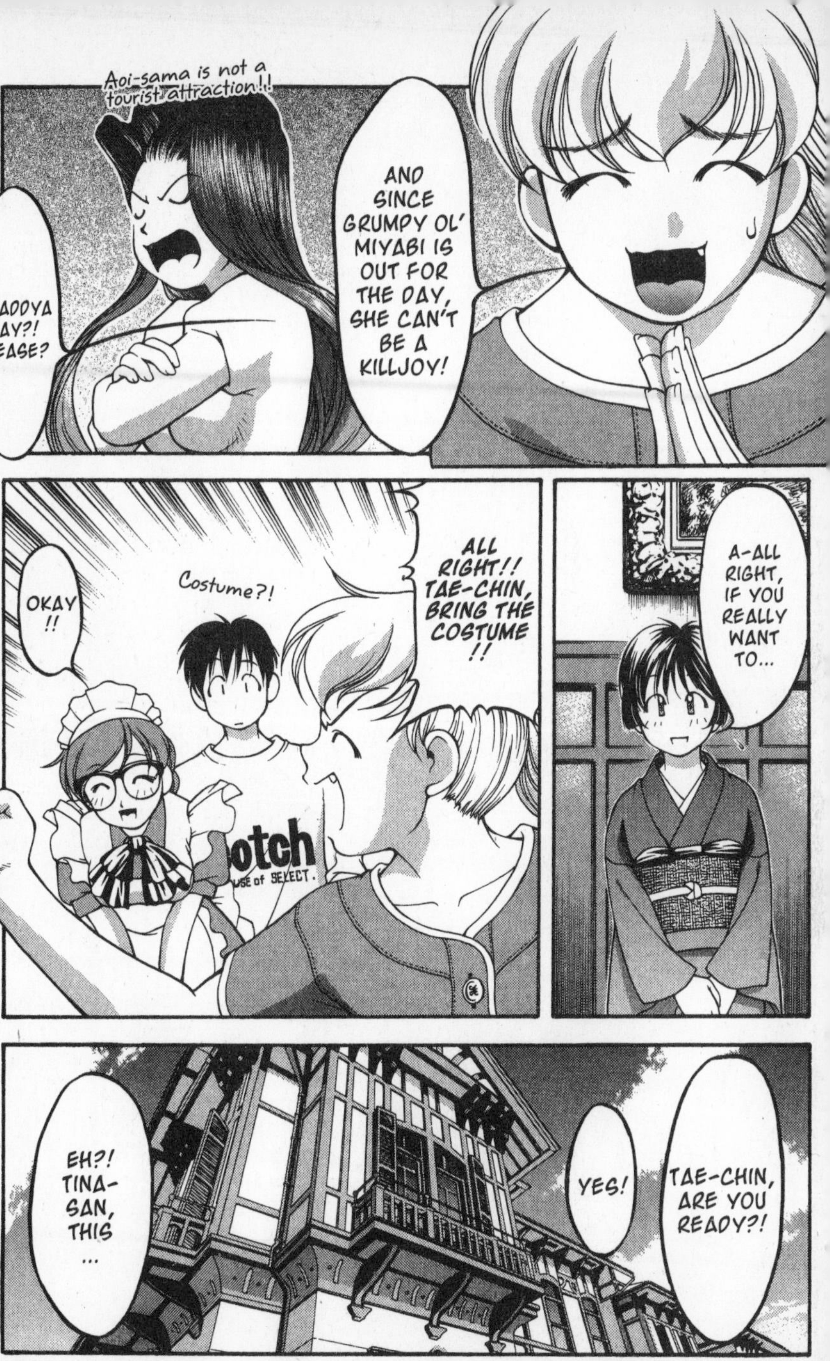
AND SINCE GRUMPY OL' MIYABI IS OUT FOR THE DAY, SHE CAN'T BE A KILLJOY!
Aoi-sama is not a tourist attraction!!
WHADDYA SAY?! PLEASE?
A-ALL RIGHT, IF YOU REALLY WANT TO...
ALL RIGHT!! TAE-CHIN, BRING THE COSTUME!!
Costume?!
OKAY!!
TAE-CHIN, ARE YOU READY?!
YES!
EH?! TINA-SAN, THIS ...

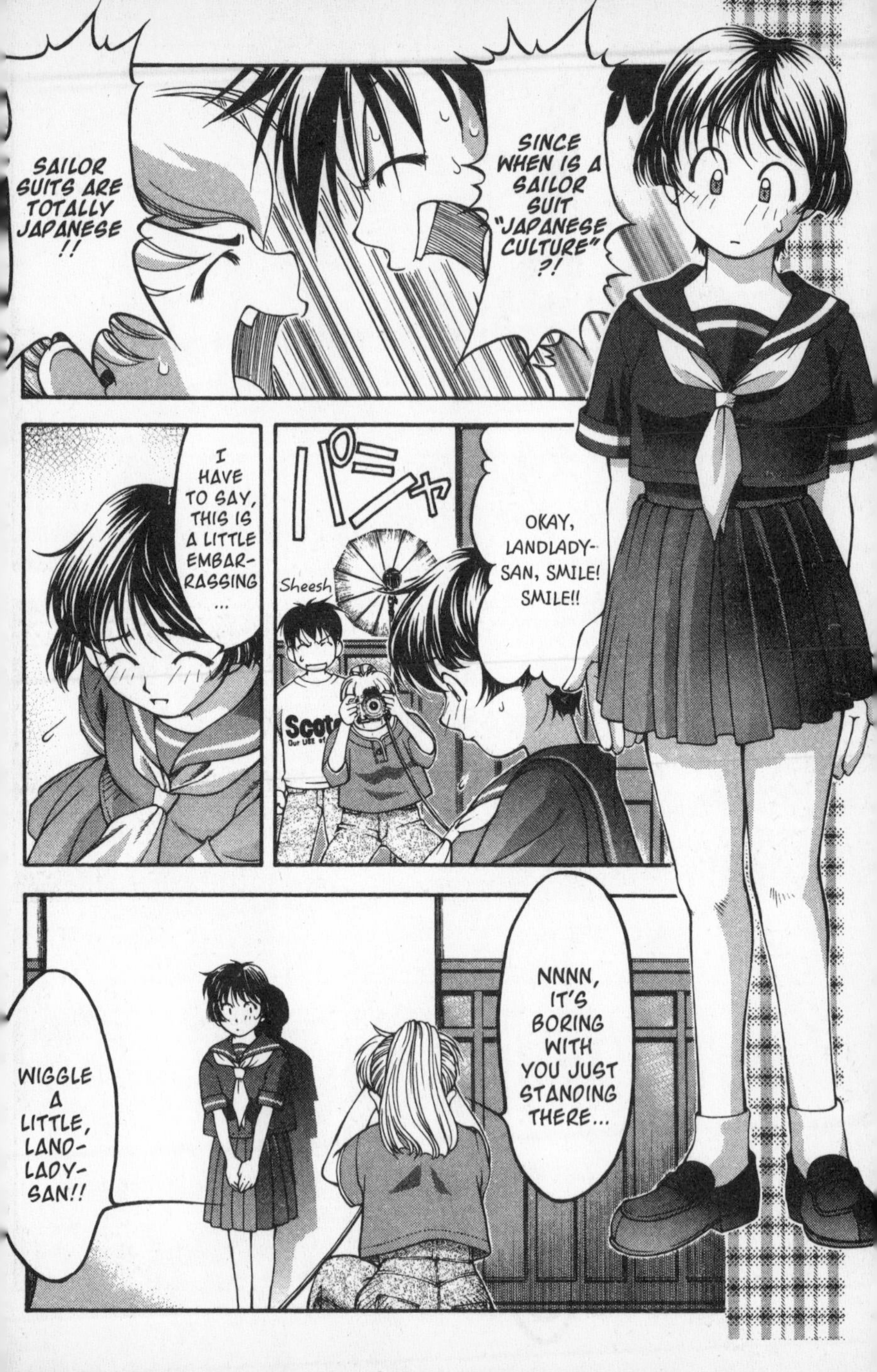
SINCE WHEN IS A SAILOR SUIT "JAPANESE CULTURE"?!
SAILOR SUITS ARE TOTALLY JAPANESE!!
パシャ
Sheesh
OKAY, LANDLADY-SAN, SMILE! SMILE!!
I HAVE TO SAY, THIS IS A LITTLE EMBARRASSING...
NNNN, IT'S BORING WITH YOU JUST STANDING THERE...
WIGGLE A LITTLE, LANDLADY-SAN!!

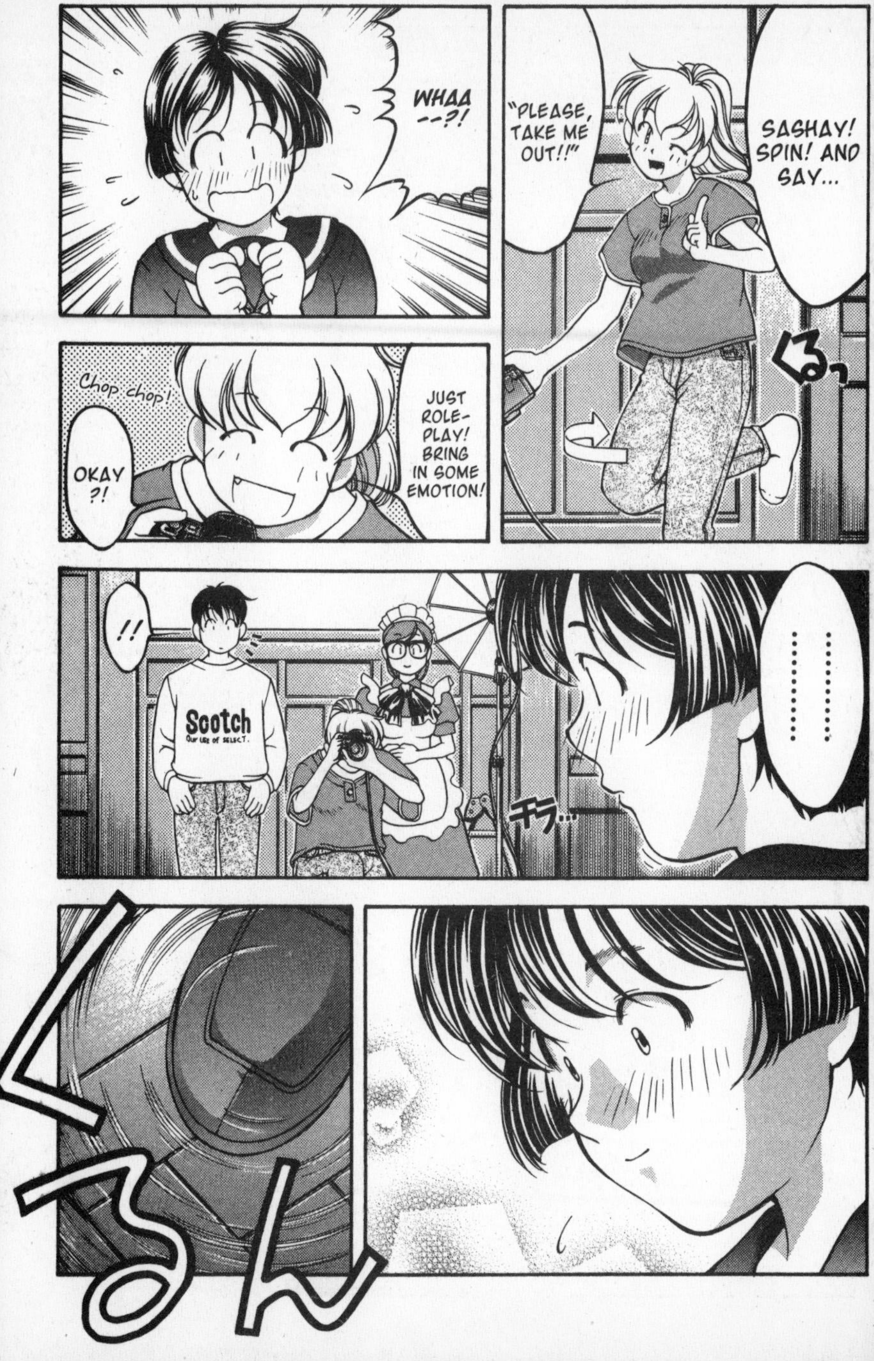
SASHAY! SPIN! AND SAY...
"PLEASE, TAKE ME OUT!!"
くるっ
WHAA --?!
JUST ROLE-PLAY! BRING IN SOME EMOTION!
Chop chop!
OKAY ?!
......
チラ...
!!
Scotch
くるん

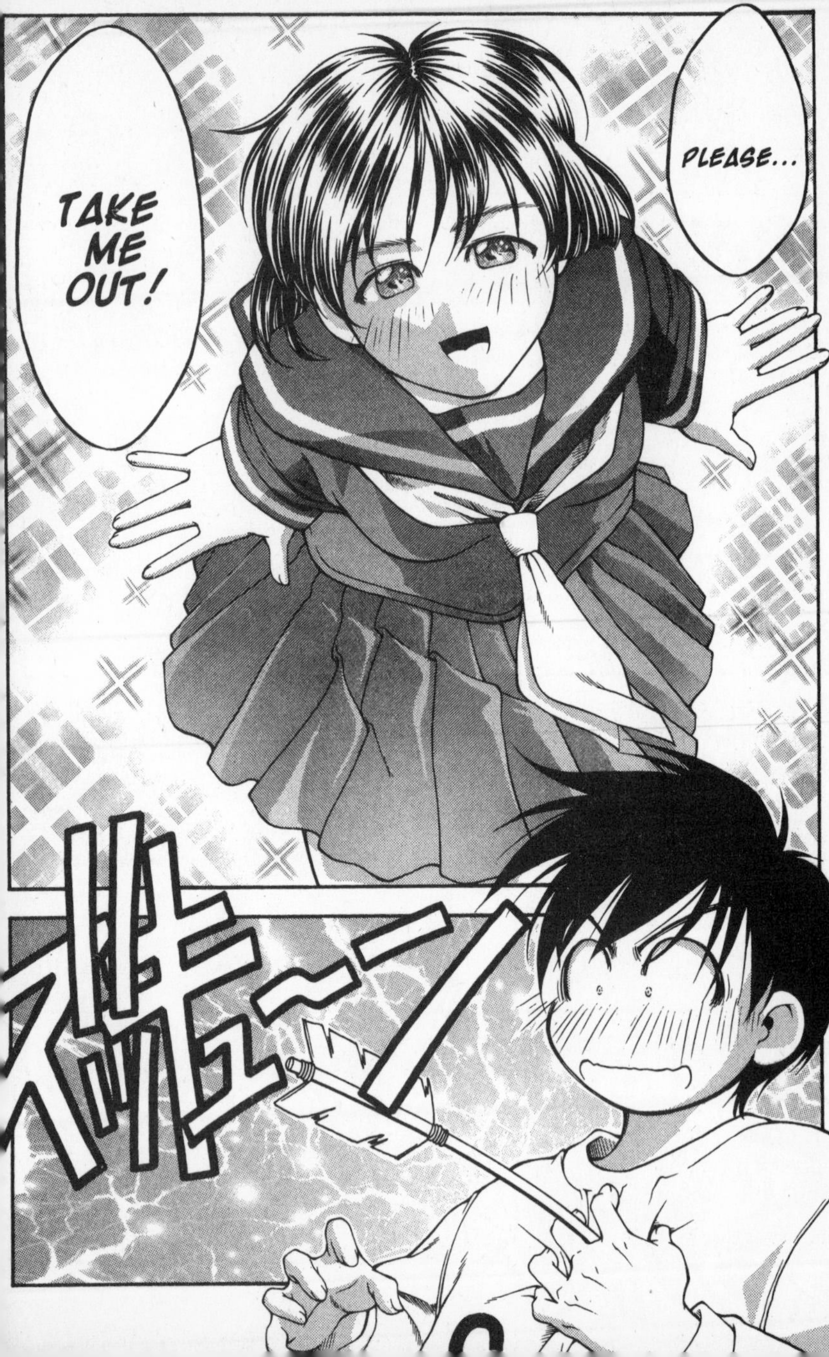
PLEASE...
TAKE ME OUT!
ズッキュ～ン

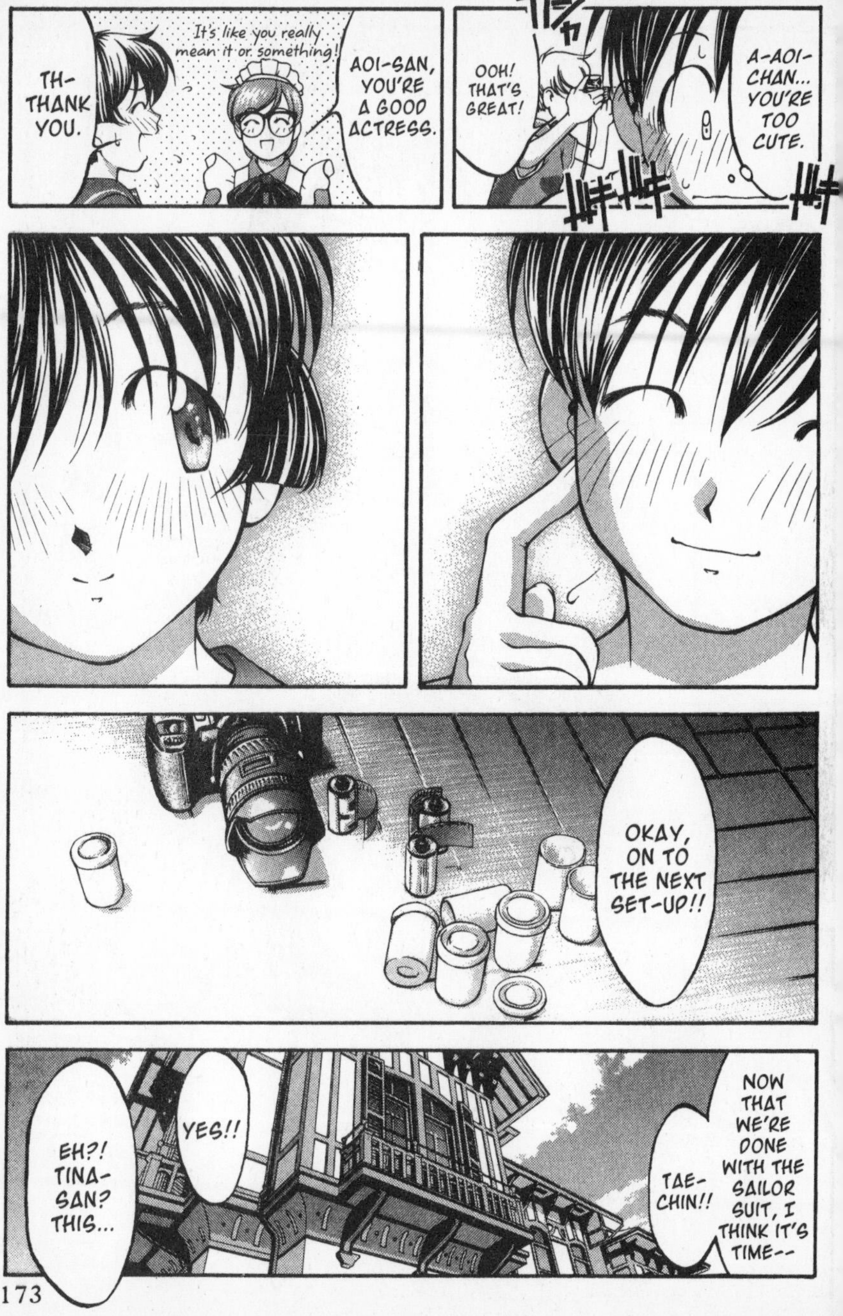
A-AOI-CHAN... YOU'RE TOO CUTE.
OOH! THAT'S GREAT!
AOI-SAN, YOU'RE A GOOD ACTRESS.
It's like you really mean it or something!
TH-THANK YOU.
OKAY, ON TO THE NEXT SET-UP!!
NOW THAT WE'RE DONE WITH THE SAILOR SUIT, I THINK IT'S TIME--
TAE-CHIN!!
YES!!
EH?! TINA-SAN? THIS...

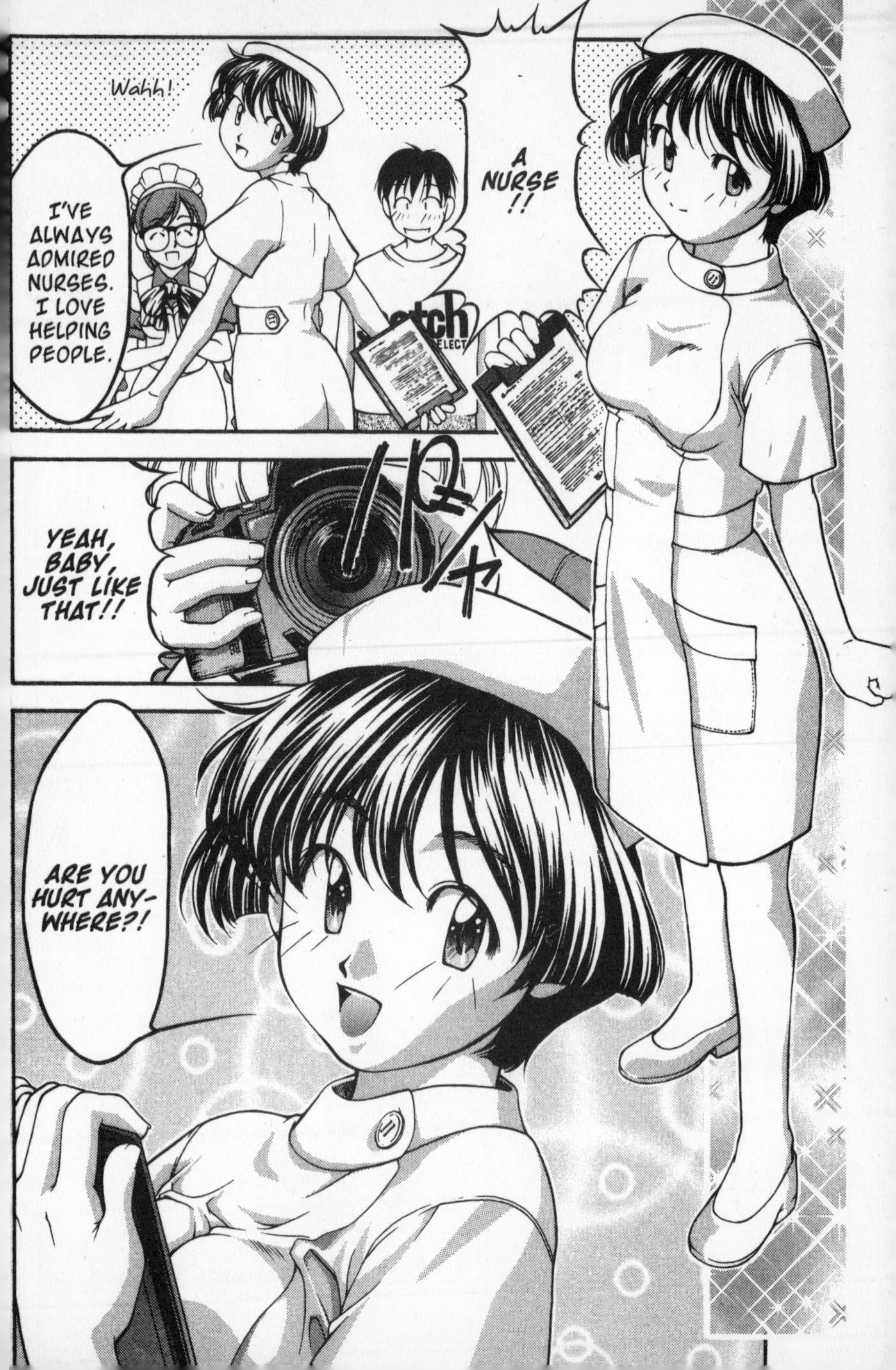
A NURSE!!
Wahh!
I'VE ALWAYS ADMIRED NURSES. I LOVE HELPING PEOPLE.
YEAH, BABY, JUST LIKE THAT!!
ARE YOU HURT ANY-WHERE?!

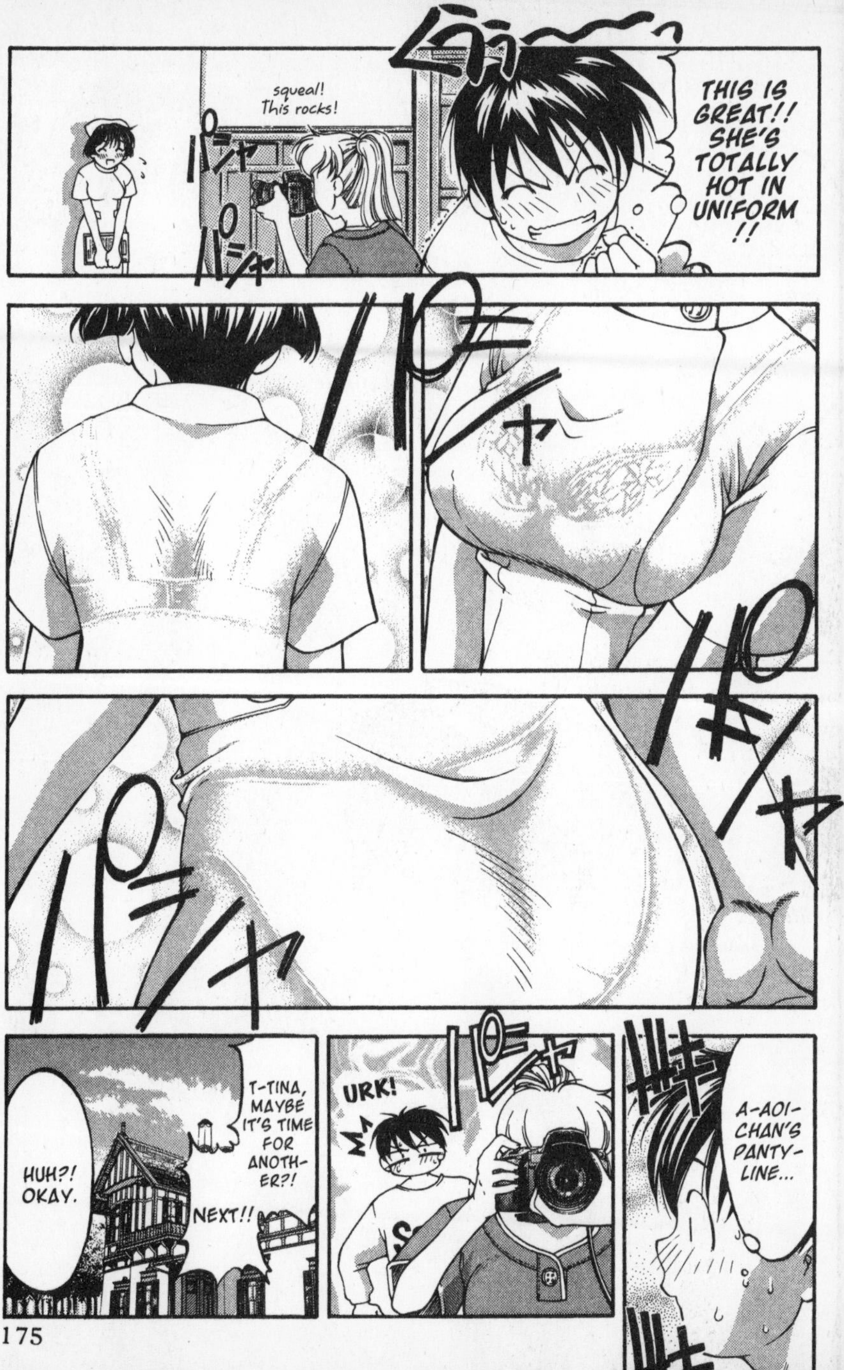
THIS IS GREAT!! SHE'S TOTALLY HOT IN UNIFORM!!
squeal! This rocks!
A-AOI-CHAN'S PANTY-LINE...
URK!
T-TINA, MAYBE IT'S TIME FOR ANOTHER?!
HUH?! OKAY.
NEXT!!

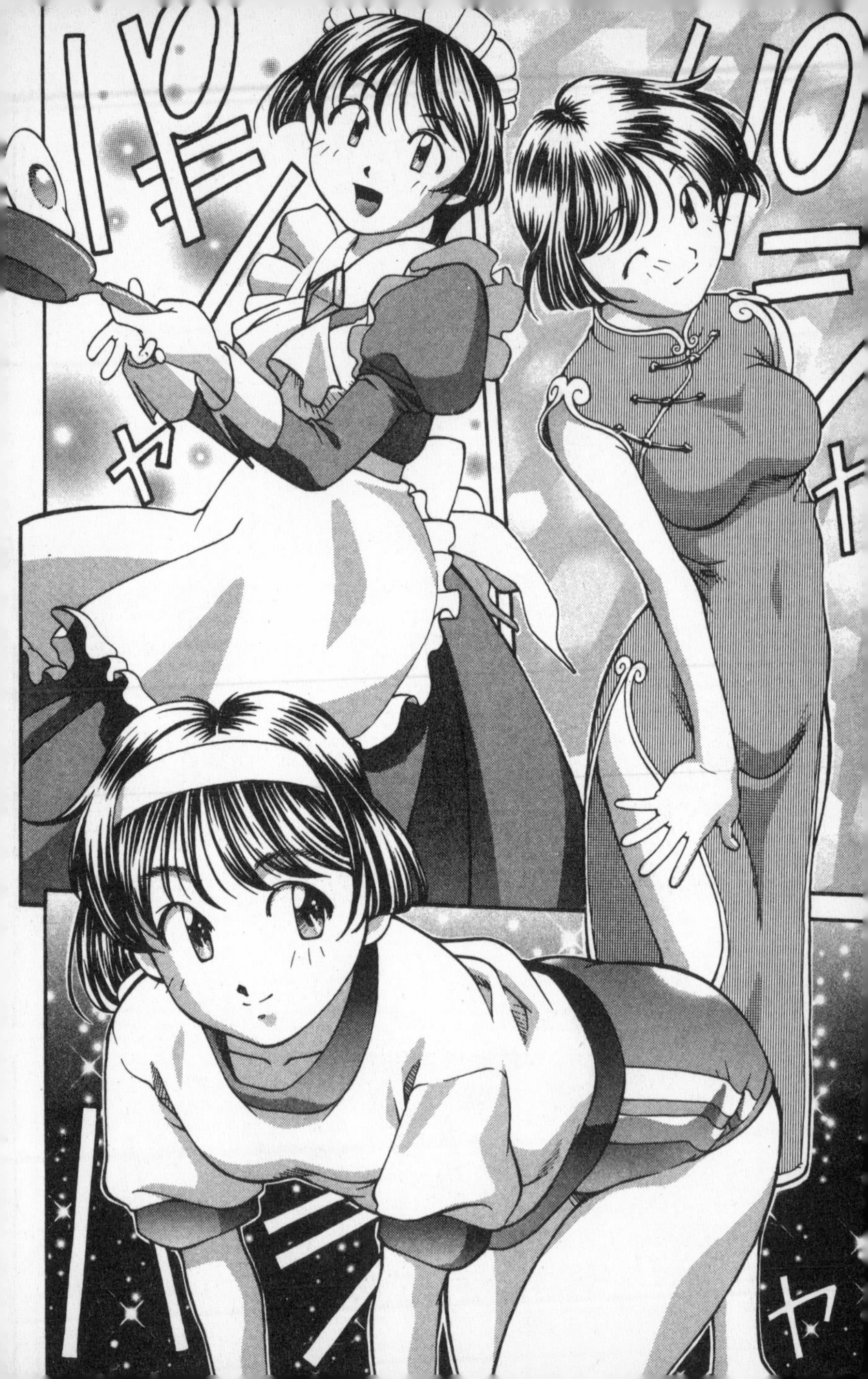

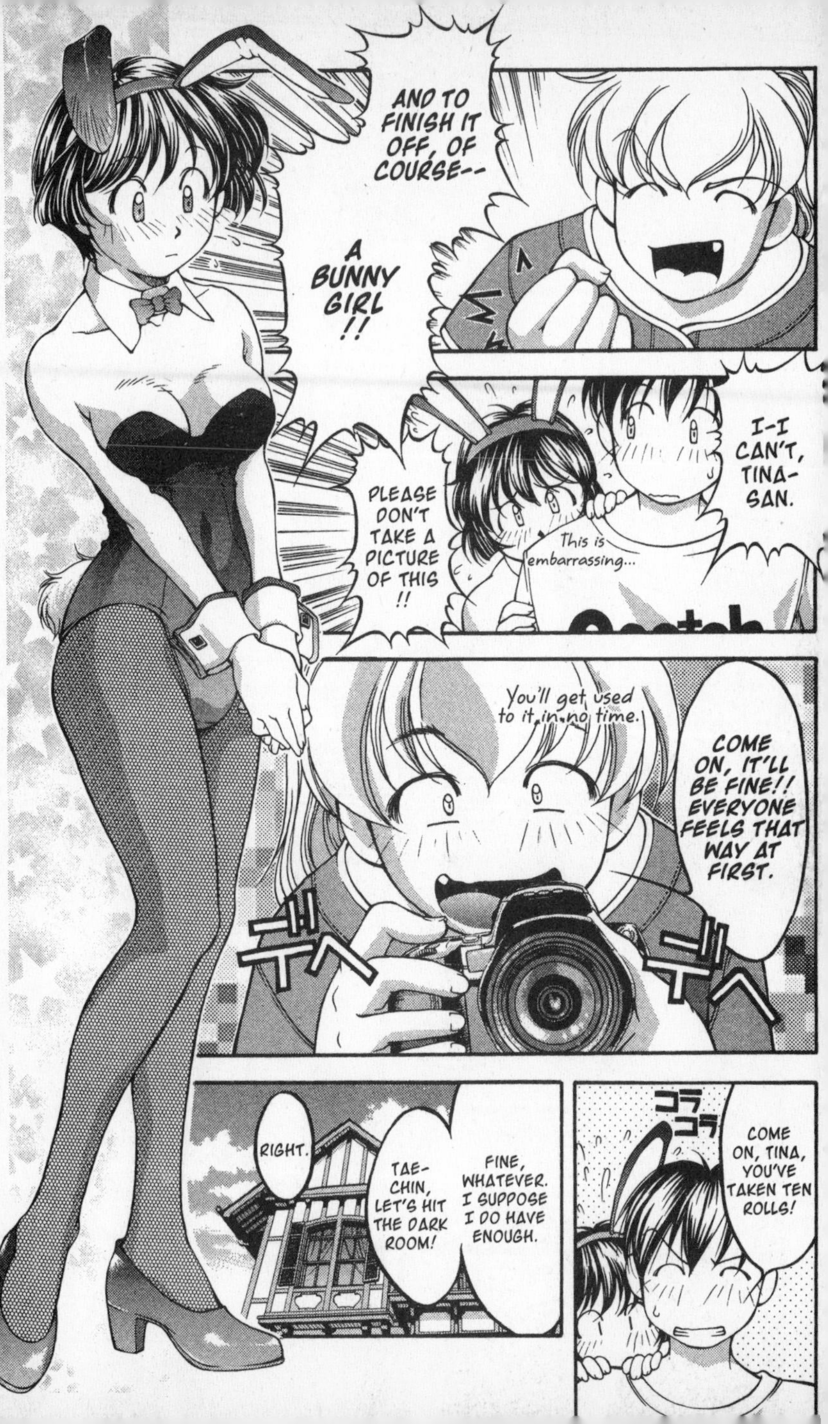
AND TO FINISH IT OFF, OF COURSE--
A BUNNY GIRL !!
I-I CAN'T, TINA-SAN.
PLEASE DON'T TAKE A PICTURE OF THIS !!
This is embarrassing...
COME ON, IT'LL BE FINE!! EVERYONE FEELS THAT WAY AT FIRST.
You'll get used to it in no time.
コラ コラ
COME ON, TINA, YOU'VE TAKEN TEN ROLLS!
FINE, WHATEVER. I SUPPOSE I DO HAVE ENOUGH.
TAE-CHIN, LET'S HIT THE DARK ROOM!
RIGHT.

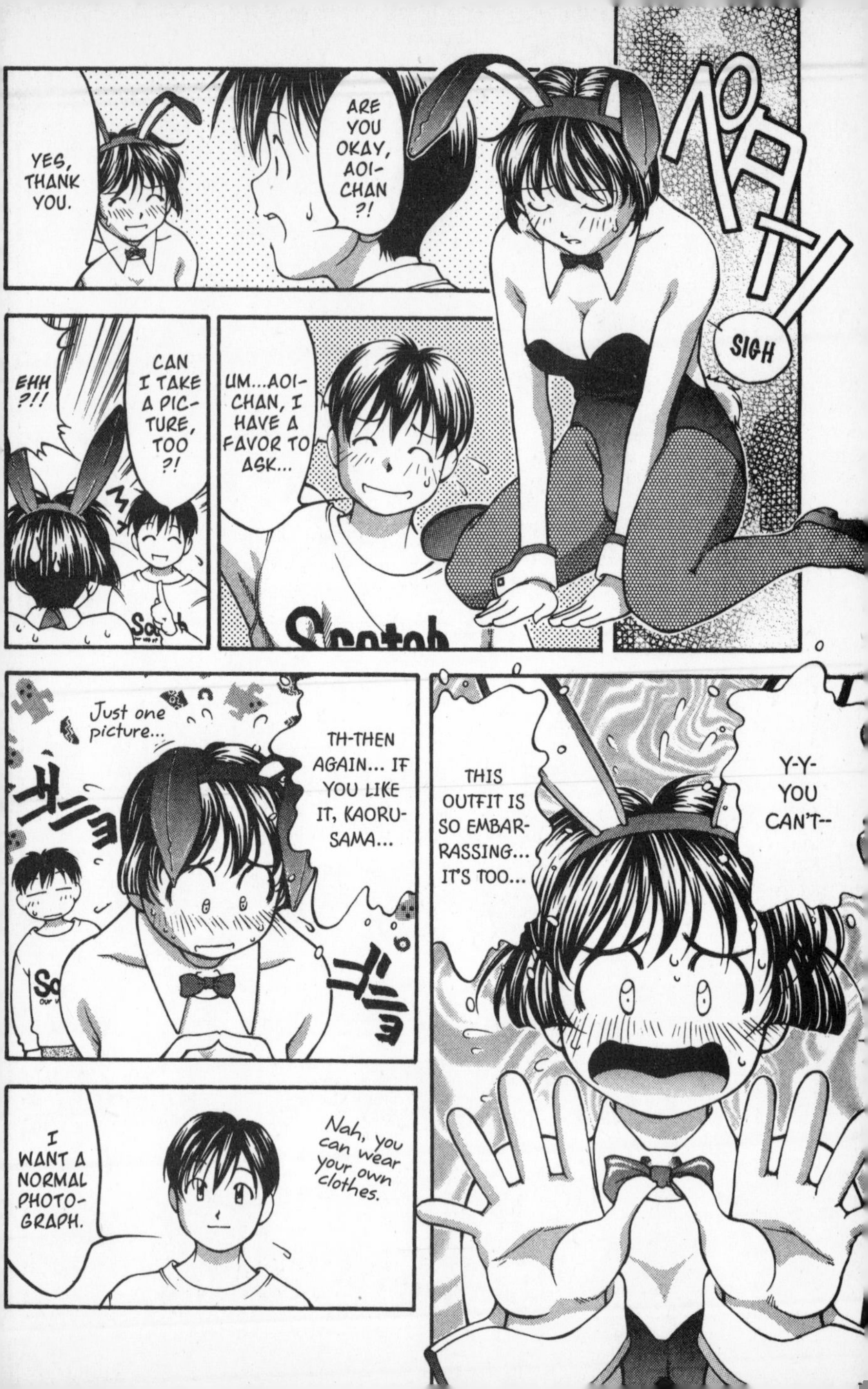
SIGH
ARE YOU OKAY, AOI-CHAN?!
YES, THANK YOU.
UM...AOI-CHAN, I HAVE A FAVOR TO ASK...
CAN I TAKE A PICTURE, TOO?!
EHH?!!
Y-Y-YOU CAN'T--
THIS OUTFIT IS SO EMBARRASSING... IT'S TOO...
TH-THEN AGAIN... IF YOU LIKE IT, KAORU-SAMA...
Just one picture...
Nah, you can wear your own clothes.
I WANT A NORMAL PHOTOGRAPH.

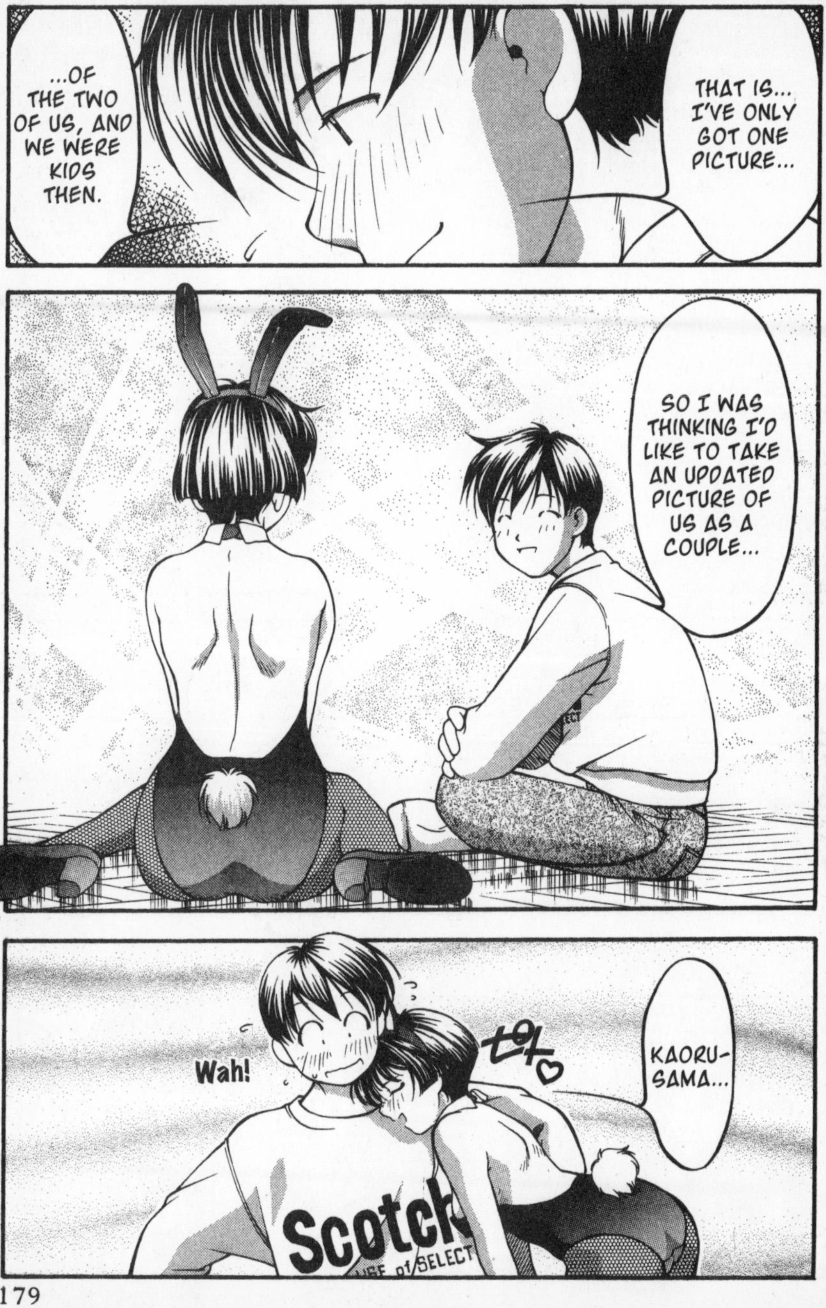
THAT IS... I'VE ONLY GOT ONE PICTURE...
...OF THE TWO OF US, AND WE WERE KIDS THEN.
SO I WAS THINKING I'D LIKE TO TAKE AN UPDATED PICTURE OF US AS A COUPLE...
KAORU-SAMA...
Wah!
Scotch

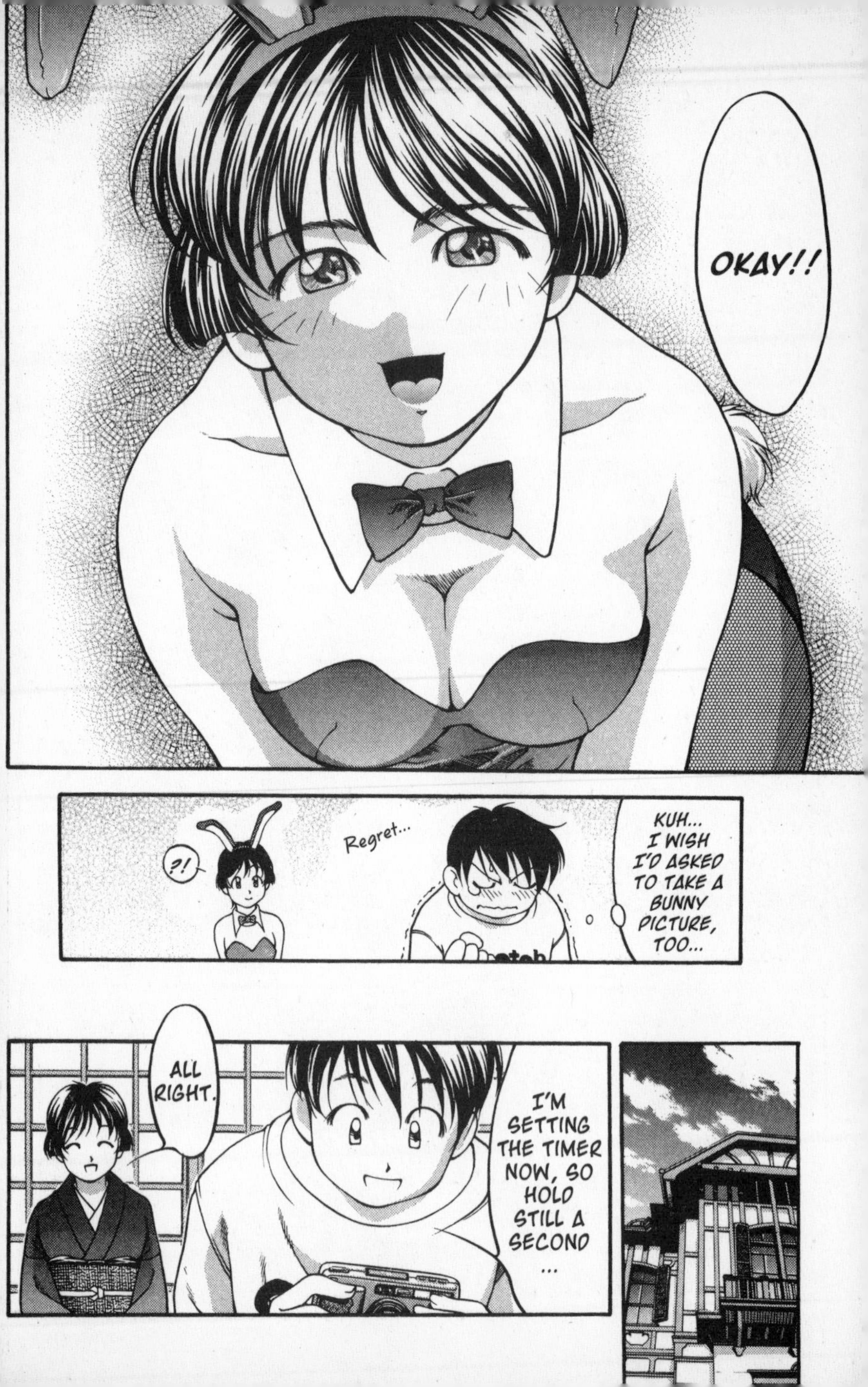
OKAY!!
KUH... I WISH I'D ASKED TO TAKE A BUNNY PICTURE, TOO...
Regret...
?!
I'M SETTING THE TIMER NOW, SO HOLD STILL A SECOND ...
ALL RIGHT.

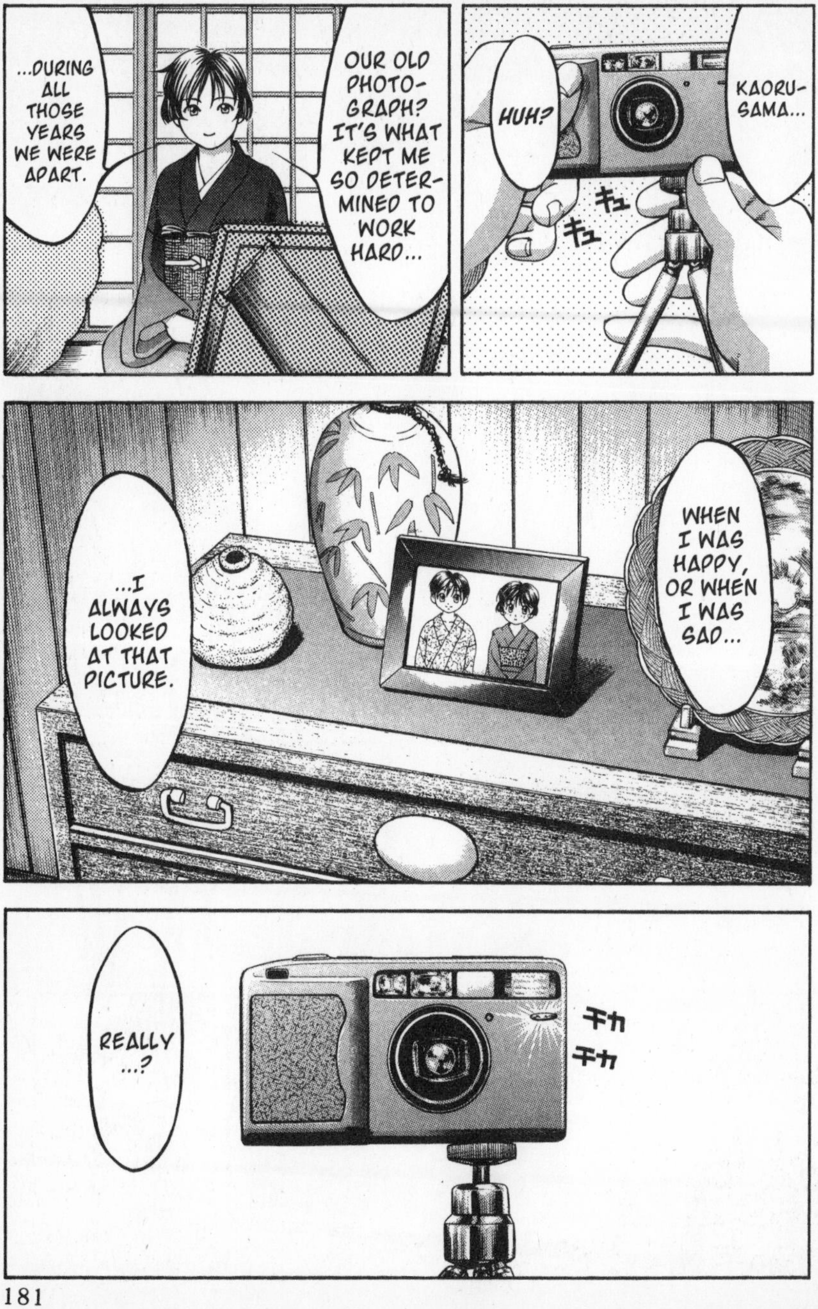
KAORU-SAMA...
HUH?
キュ
キュ
OUR OLD PHOTOGRAPH? IT'S WHAT KEPT ME SO DETERMINED TO WORK HARD...
...DURING ALL THOSE YEARS WE WERE APART.
WHEN I WAS HAPPY, OR WHEN I WAS SAD...
...I ALWAYS LOOKED AT THAT PICTURE.
チカ
チカ
REALLY ...?

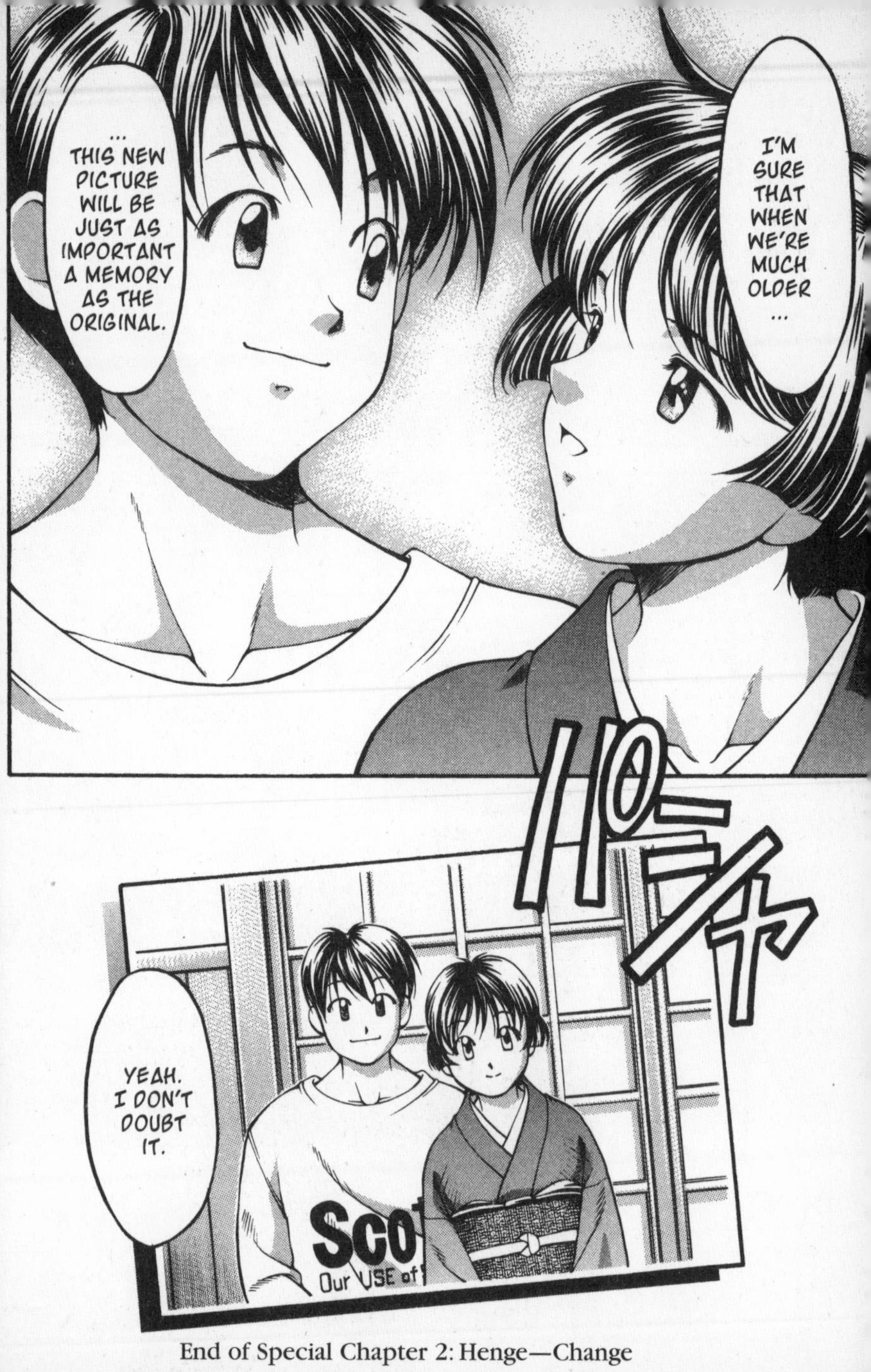
I'M SURE THAT WHEN WE'RE MUCH OLDER ...
... THIS NEW PICTURE WILL BE JUST AS IMPORTANT A MEMORY AS THE ORIGINAL.
パーシャ
YEAH. I DON'T DOUBT IT.
SCO
Our USE of

End of Special Chapter 2: Henge—Change

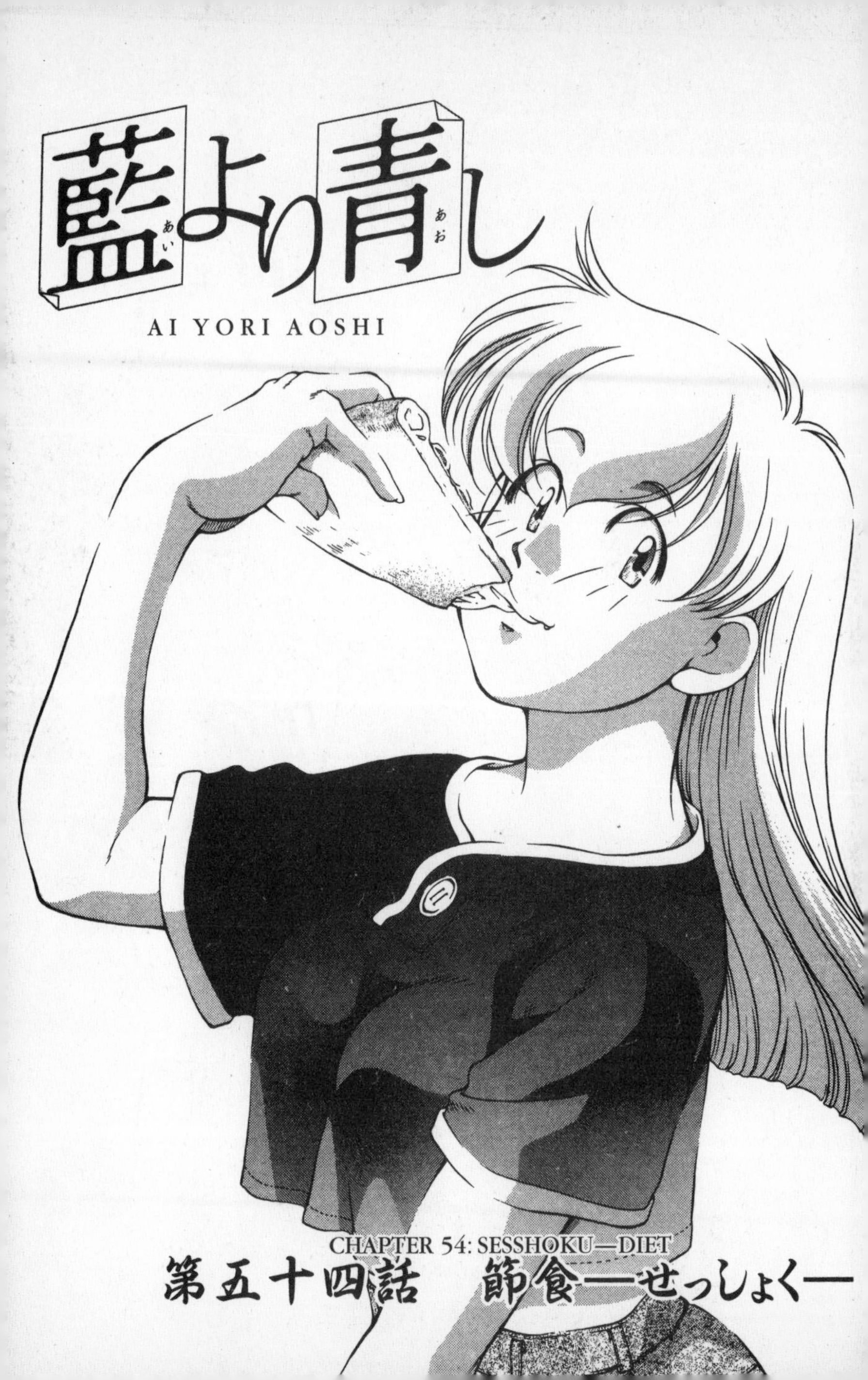
藍(あい)より青(あお)し
AI YORI AOSHI
CHAPTER 54: SESSHOKU—DIET
第五十四話　節食—せっしょく—

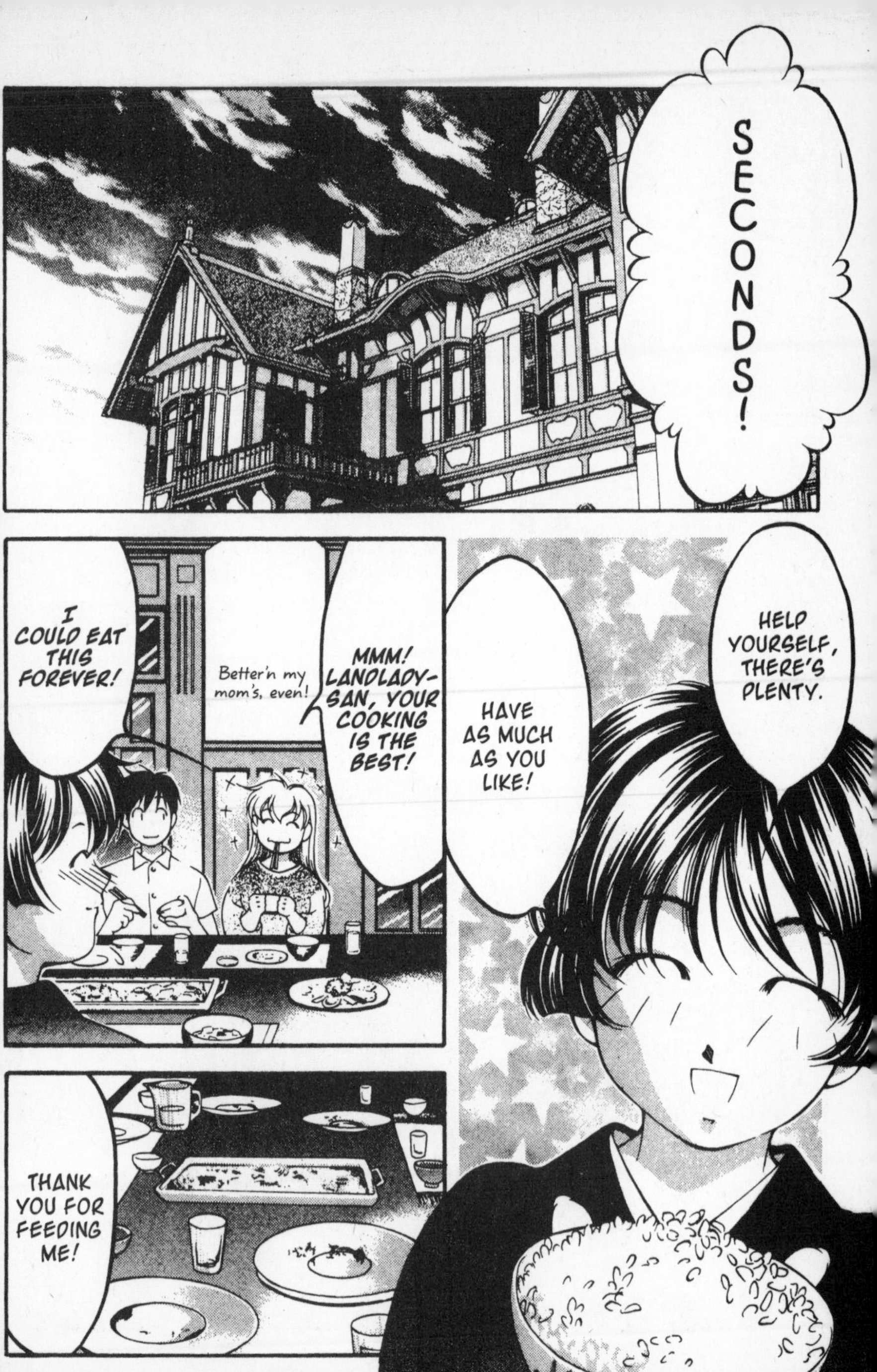
SECONDS!
HELP YOURSELF, THERE'S PLENTY.
HAVE AS MUCH AS YOU LIKE!
MMM! LANDLADY-SAN, YOUR COOKING IS THE BEST!
Better'n my mom's, even!
I COULD EAT THIS FOREVER!
THANK YOU FOR FEEDING ME!

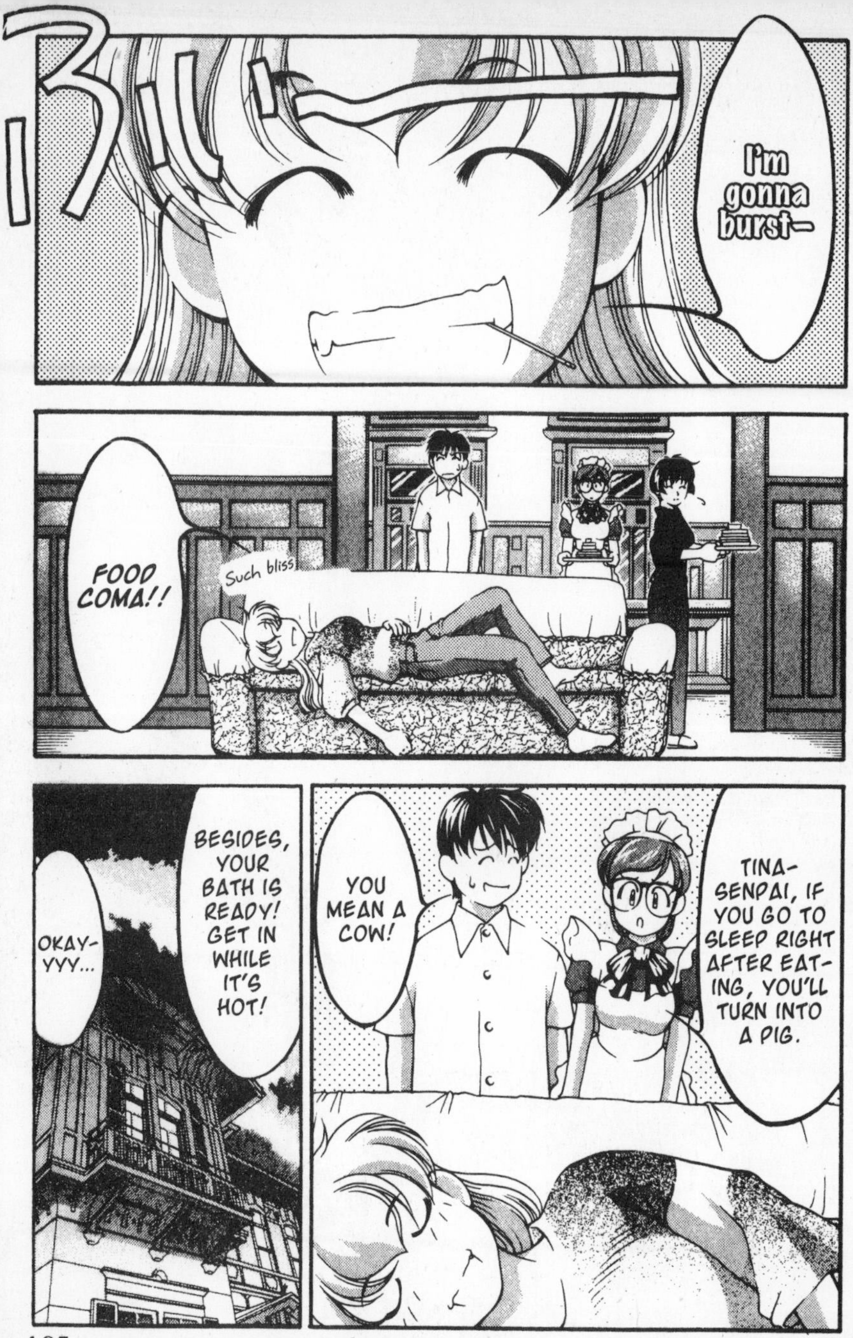
I'm gonna burst—
FOOD COMA!!
Such bliss
TINA-SENPAI, IF YOU GO TO SLEEP RIGHT AFTER EATING, YOU'LL TURN INTO A PIG.
YOU MEAN A COW!
BESIDES, YOUR BATH IS READY! GET IN WHILE IT'S HOT!
OKAY-YYY...

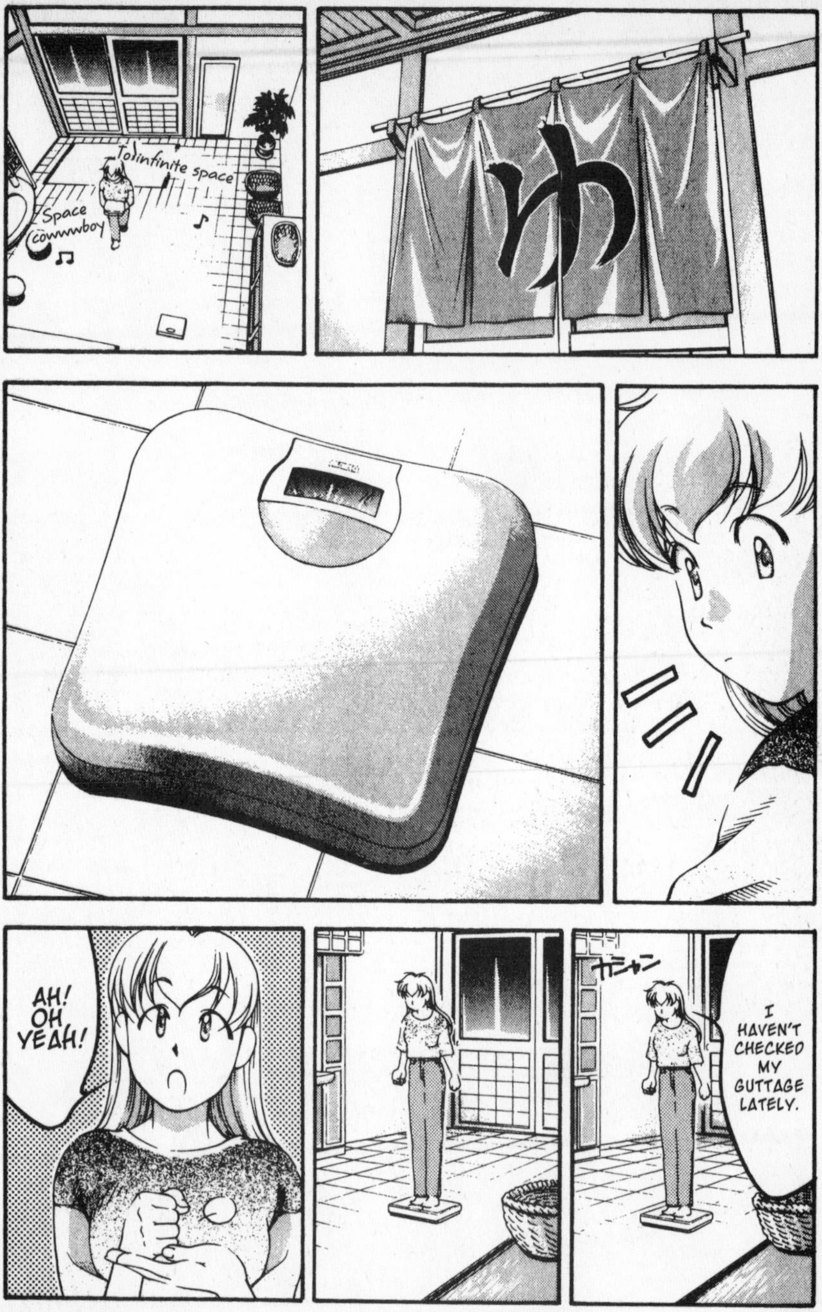
ゆ
To infinite space
Space cowwwboy
ガシャン
I HAVEN'T CHECKED MY GUTTAGE LATELY.
AH! OH YEAH!

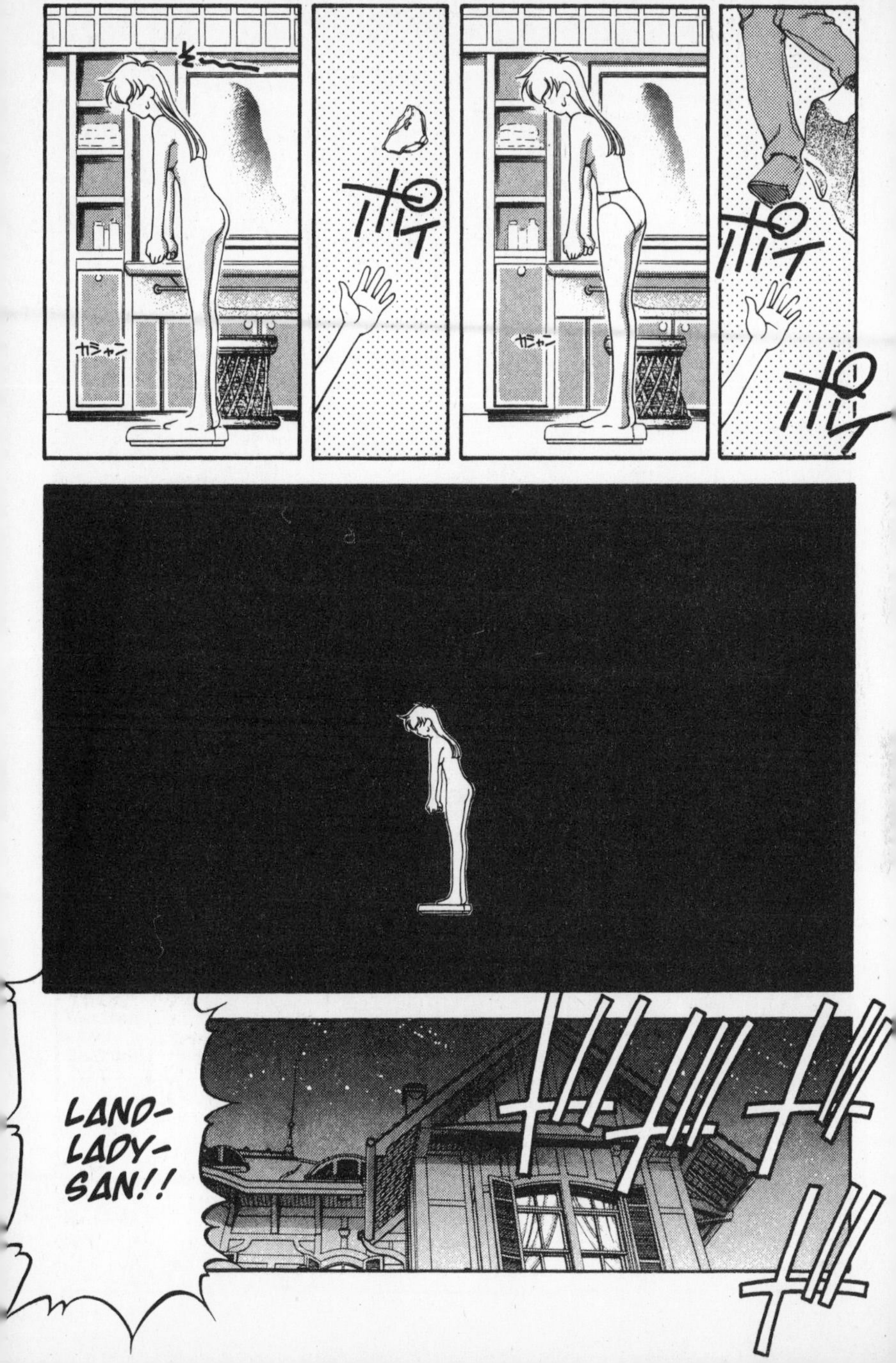
ポイ
ポイ
カシャン
ポイ
カシャン
LAND-
LADY-
SAN!!

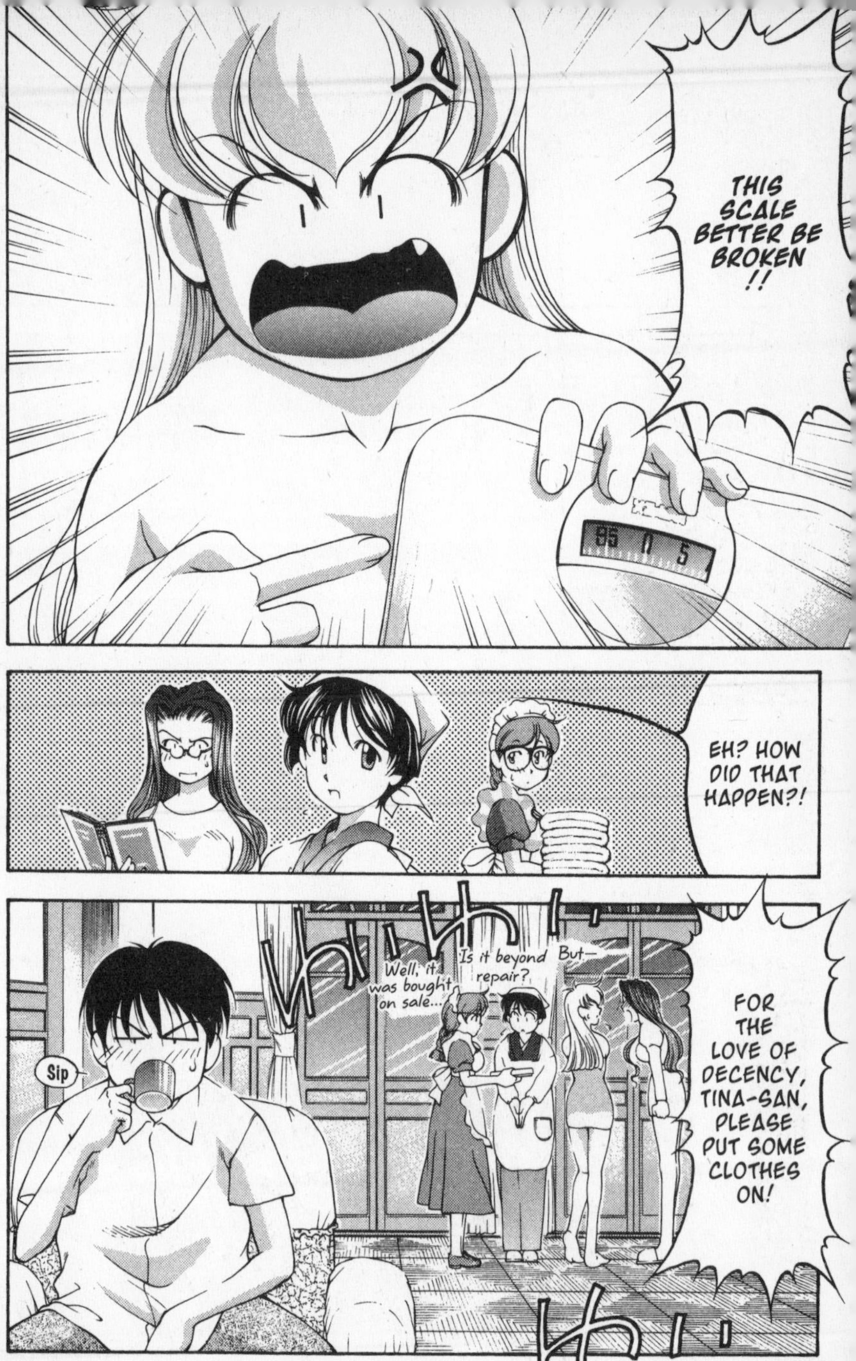
THIS SCALE BETTER BE BROKEN !!
EH? HOW DID THAT HAPPEN?!
FOR THE LOVE OF DECENCY, TINA-SAN, PLEASE PUT SOME CLOTHES ON!
But—
Is it beyond repair?
Well, it was bought on sale...
Sip

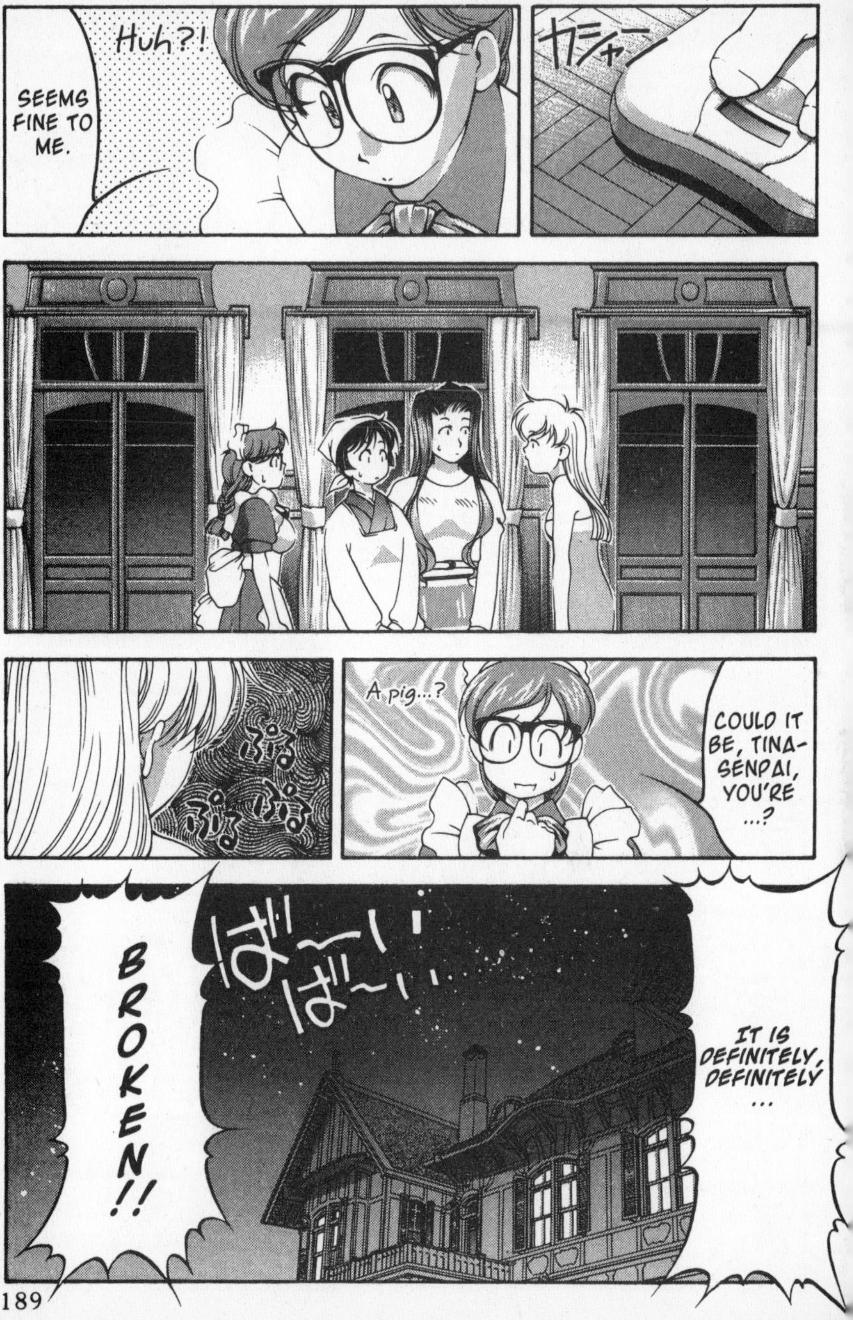
カシャー
Huh?!
SEEMS FINE TO ME.
COULD IT BE, TINA-SENPAI, YOU'RE ...?
A pig...?
ぷる ぷる ぷる
IT IS DEFINITELY, DEFINITELY ...
ば～い ば～い
BROKEN!!

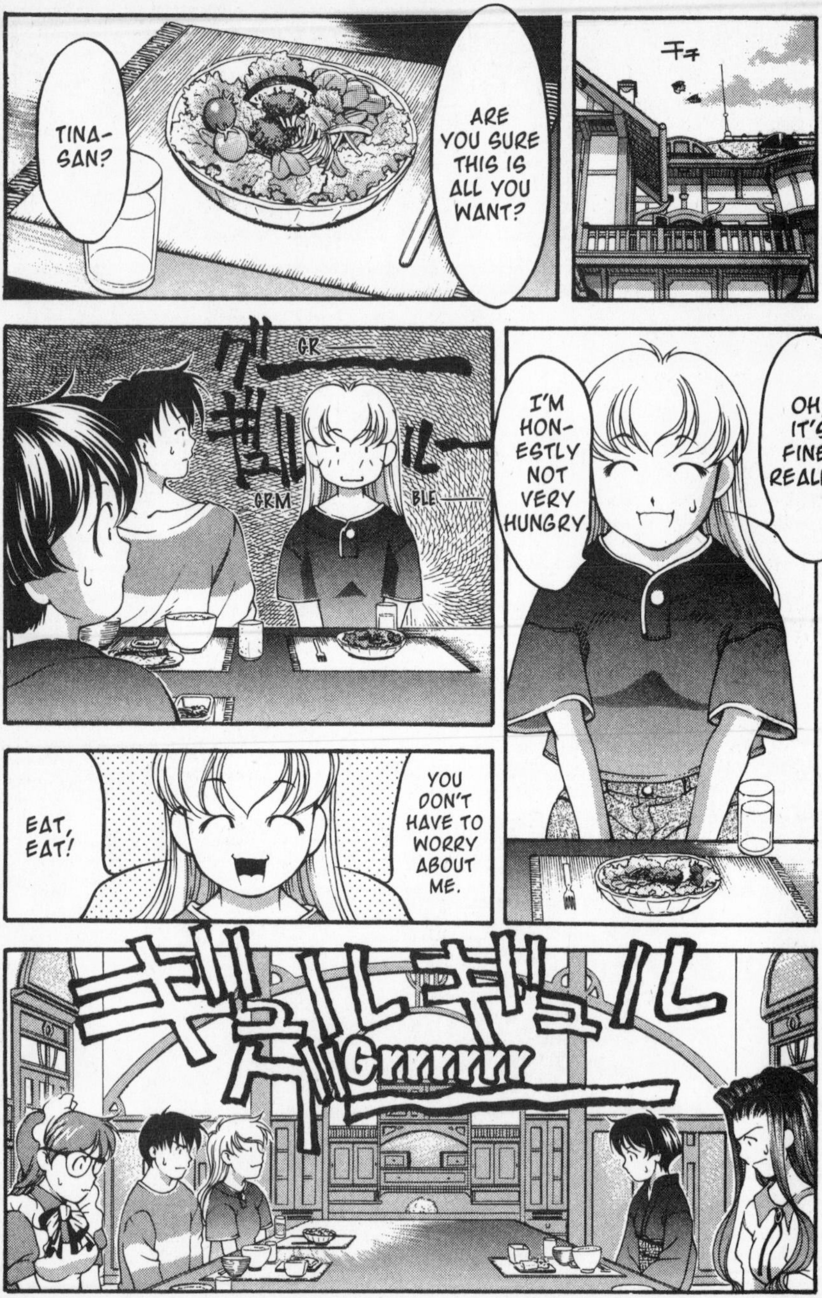
ARE YOU SURE THIS IS ALL YOU WANT?
TINA-SAN?
OH, IT'S FINE, REALLY.
I'M HON-ESTLY NOT VERY HUNGRY.
GR—
GRM
BLE—
YOU DON'T HAVE TO WORRY ABOUT ME.
EAT, EAT!
Grrrrrrr

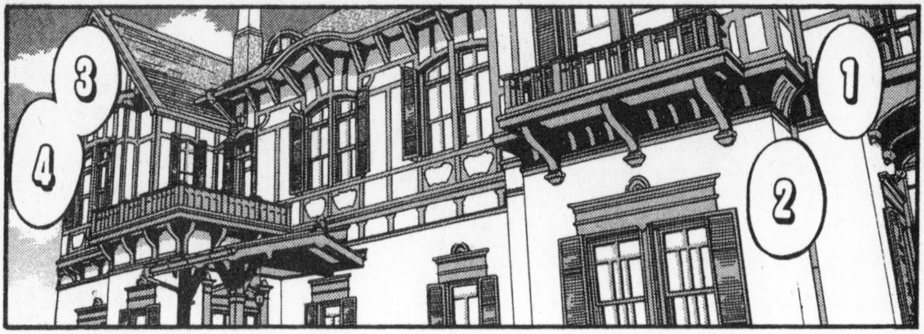
1
2
3
4
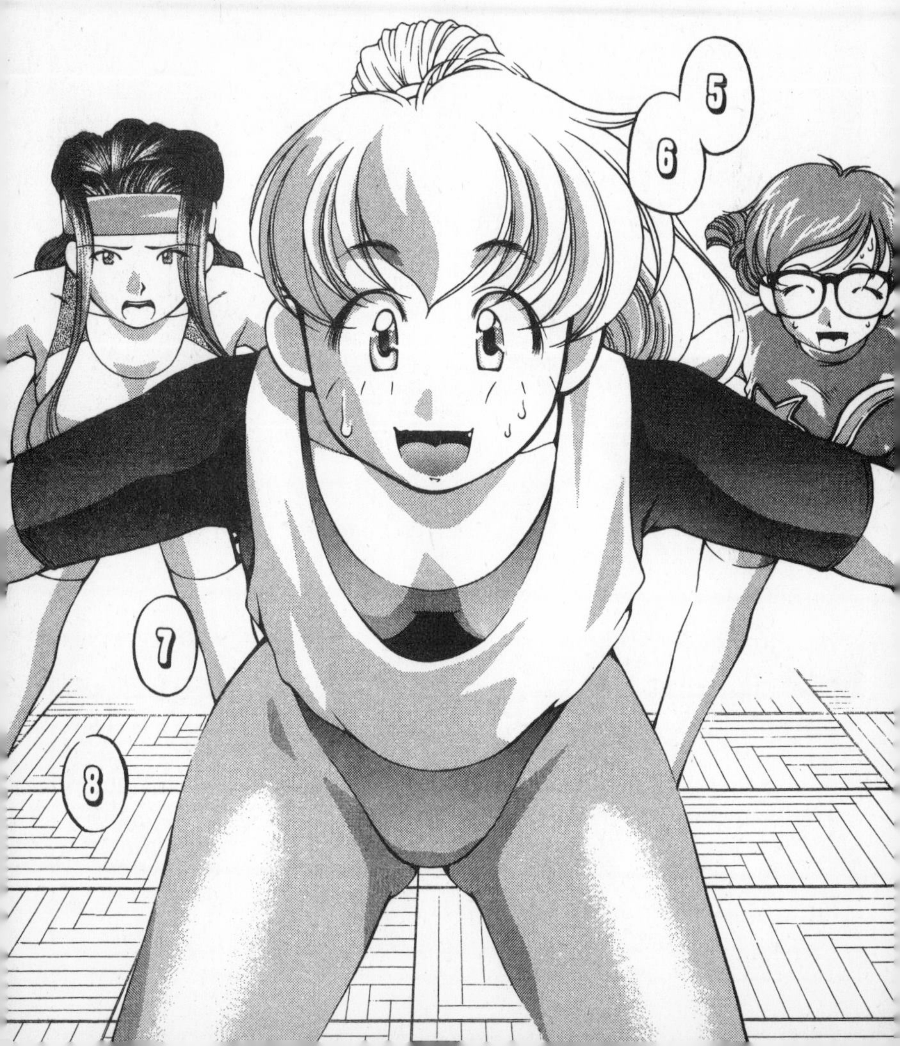
5
6
7
8

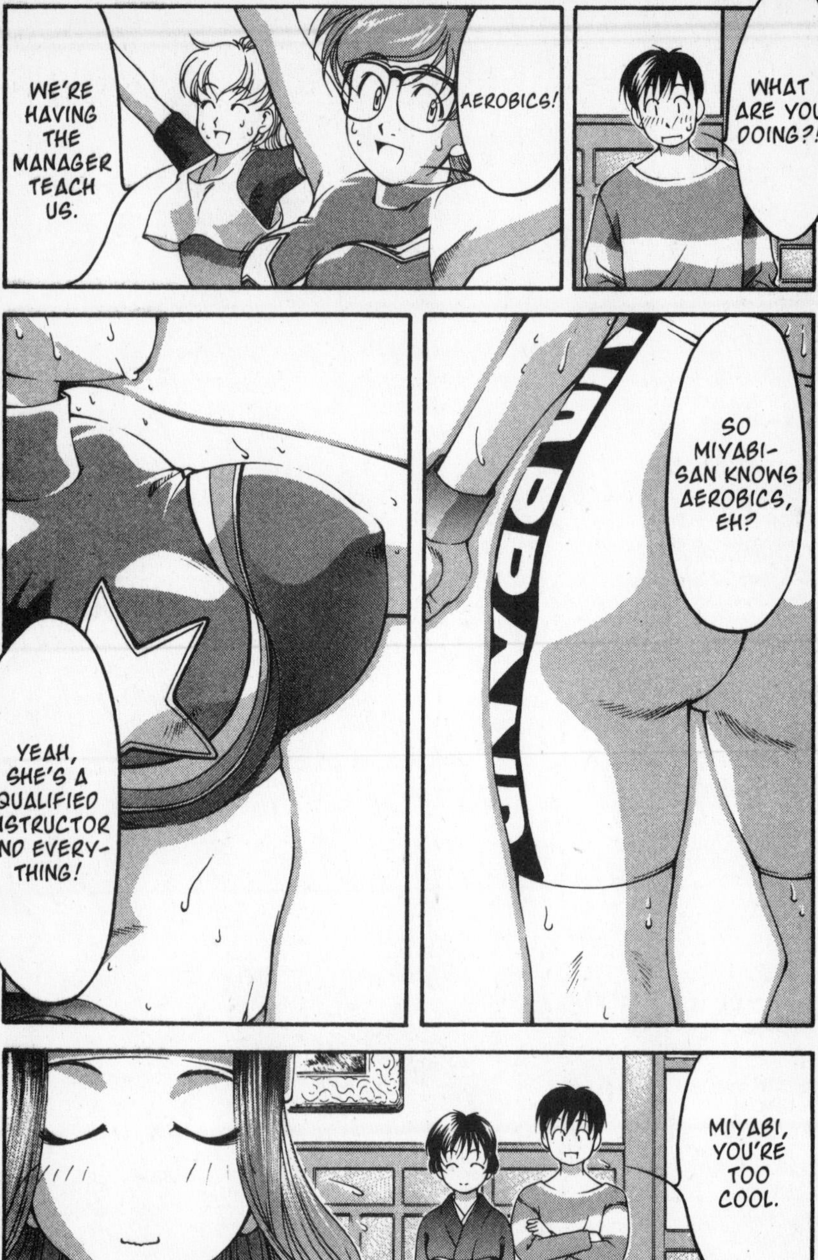
WHAT ARE YOU DOING?!
AEROBICS!
WE'RE HAVING THE MANAGER TEACH US.
SO MIYABI-SAN KNOWS AEROBICS, EH?
YEAH, SHE'S A QUALIFIED INSTRUCTOR AND EVERY-THING!
MIYABI, YOU'RE TOO COOL.

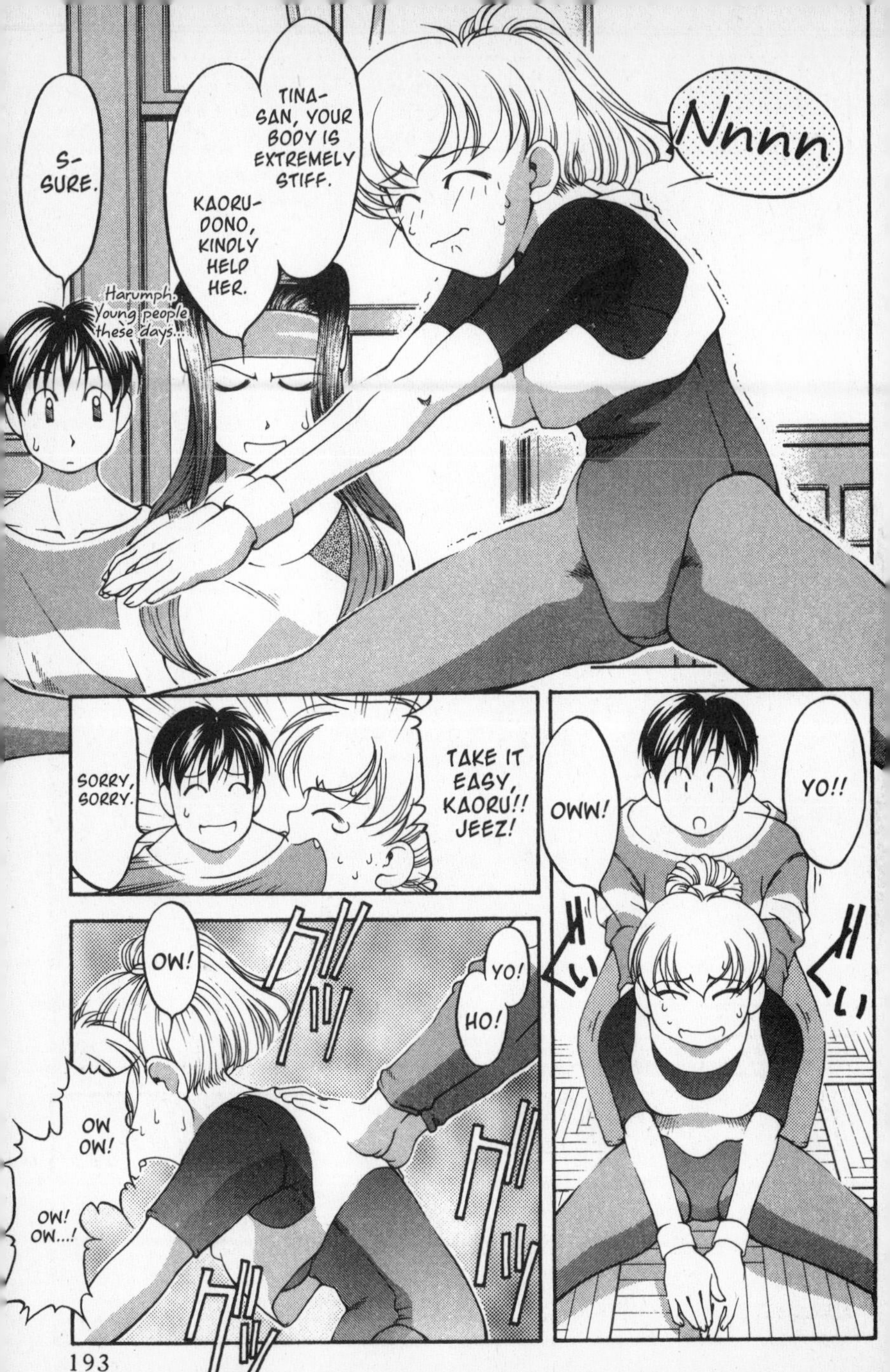
Nnnn
Tina-san, your body is extremely stiff.
Kaoru-dono, kindly help her.
S-sure.
Harumph. Young people these days...
YO!!
OWW!
Take it easy, Kaoru!! Jeez!
Sorry, sorry.
YO!
HO!
OW!
OW OW!
OW! OW...!

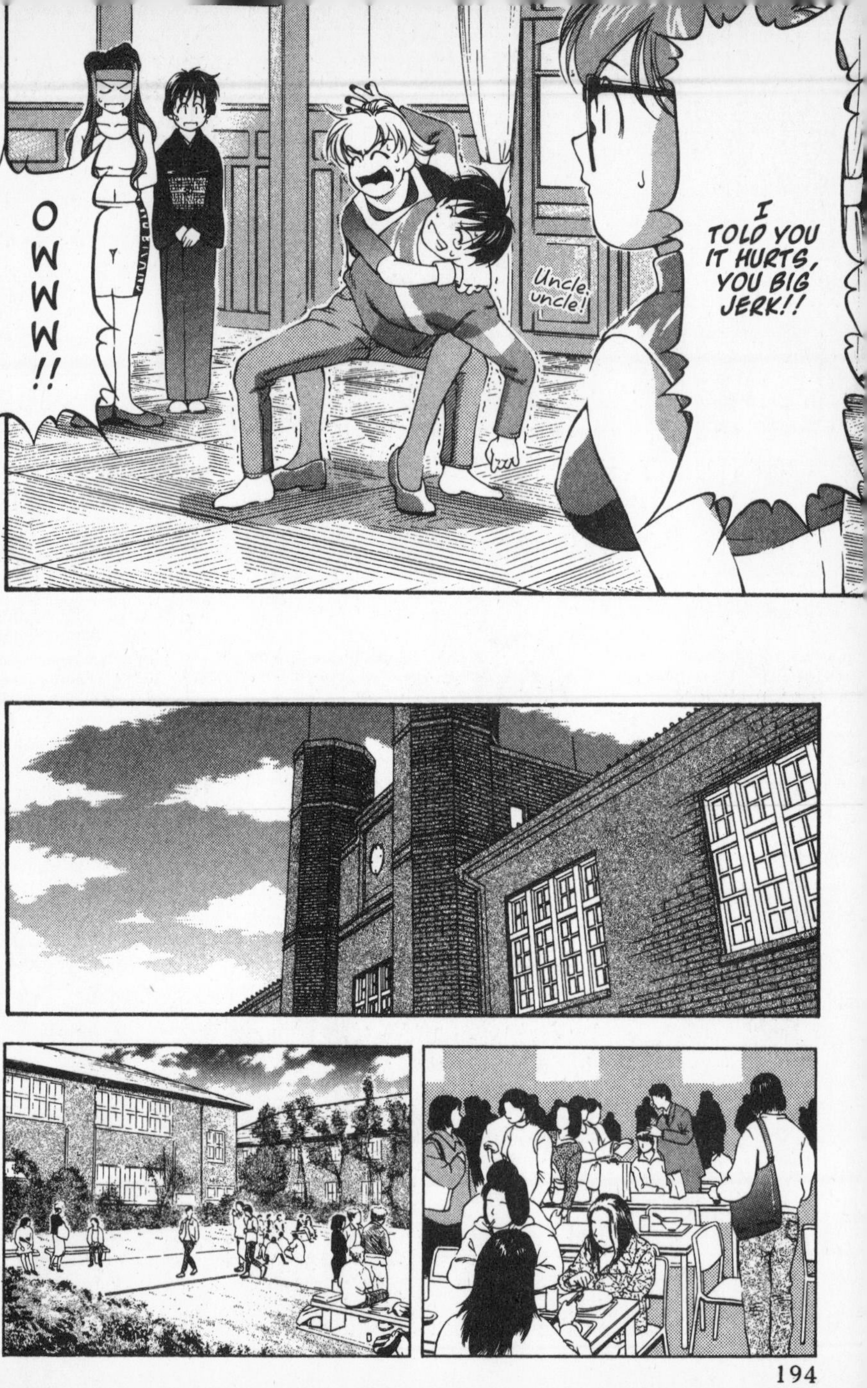
I TOLD YOU IT HURTS, YOU BIG JERK!!
Uncle uncle!
OWWW!!

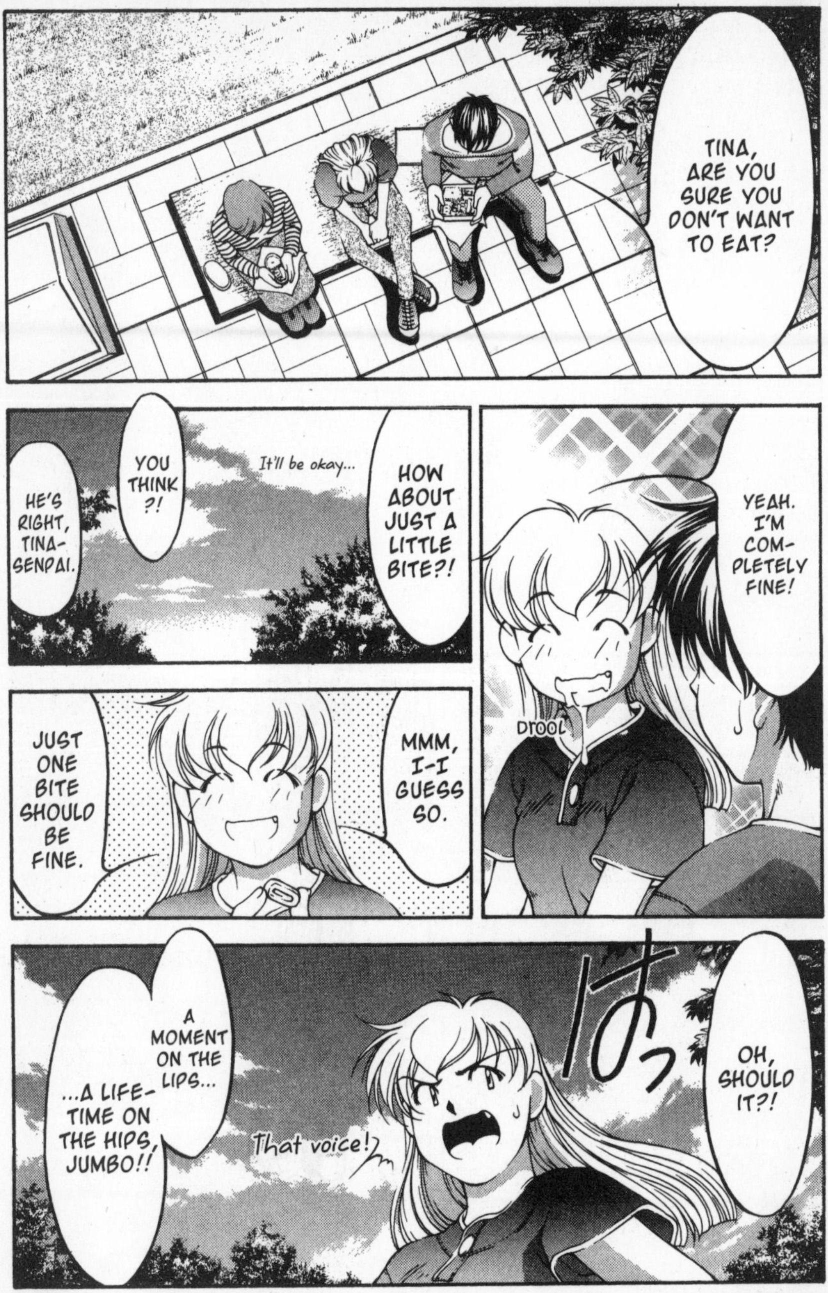
TINA, ARE YOU SURE YOU DON'T WANT TO EAT?
YEAH. I'M COM-PLETELY FINE!
Drool
HOW ABOUT JUST A LITTLE BITE?!
It'll be okay...
YOU THINK?!
HE'S RIGHT, TINA-SENPAI.
MMM, I-I GUESS SO.
JUST ONE BITE SHOULD BE FINE.
OH, SHOULD IT?!
はっ
That voice!
A MOMENT ON THE LIPS...
...A LIFE-TIME ON THE HIPS, JUMBO!!

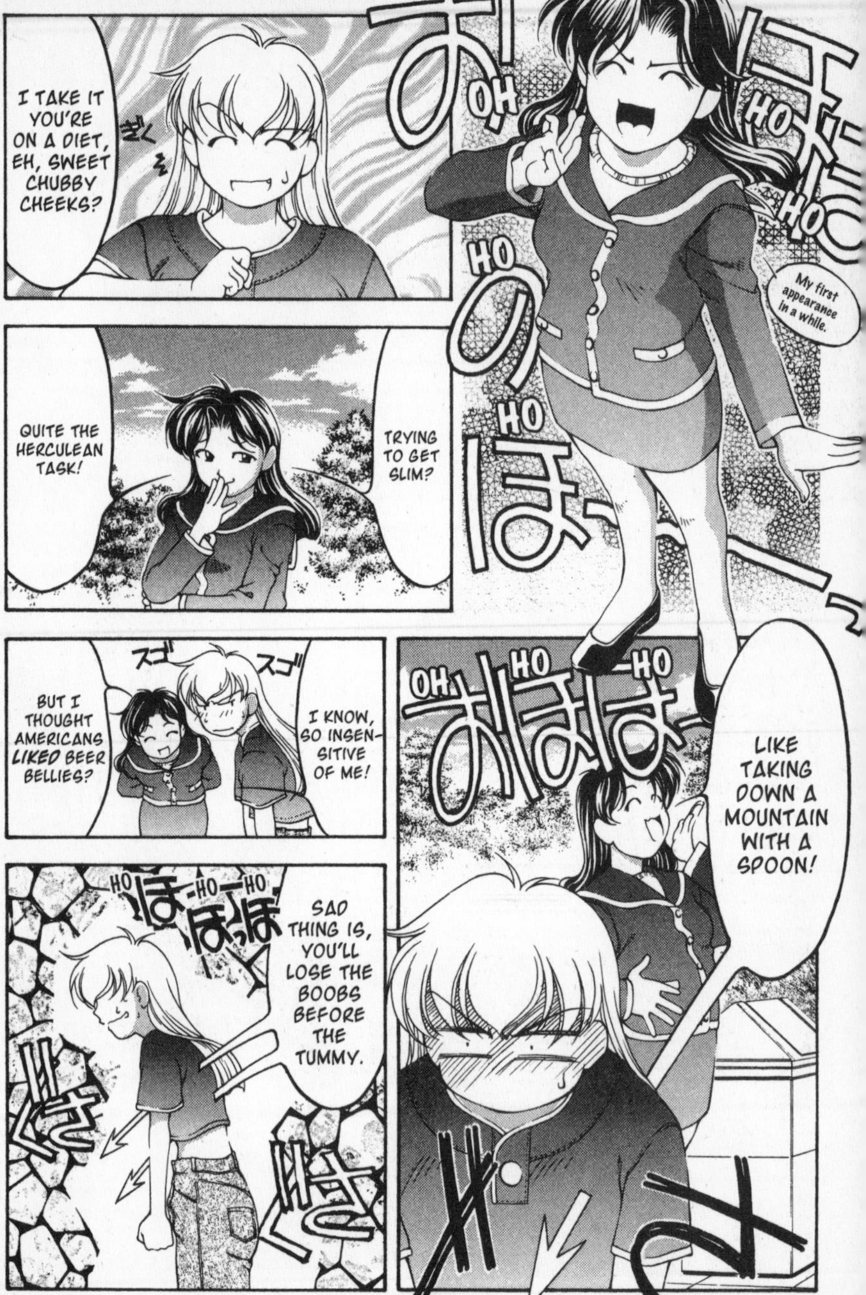
OH HO HO HO HO
おーほほのほーっ
My first appearance in a while.
ぎく
I TAKE IT YOU'RE ON A DIET, EH, SWEET CHUBBY CHEEKS?
TRYING TO GET SLIM?
QUITE THE HERCULEAN TASK!
OH HO HO HO
おほほほ
LIKE TAKING DOWN A MOUNTAIN WITH A SPOON!
スゴ スゴ
I KNOW, SO INSENSITIVE OF ME!
BUT I THOUGHT AMERICANS *LIKED* BEER BELLIES?
HO HO HO
SAD THING IS, YOU'LL LOSE THE BOOBS BEFORE THE TUMMY.

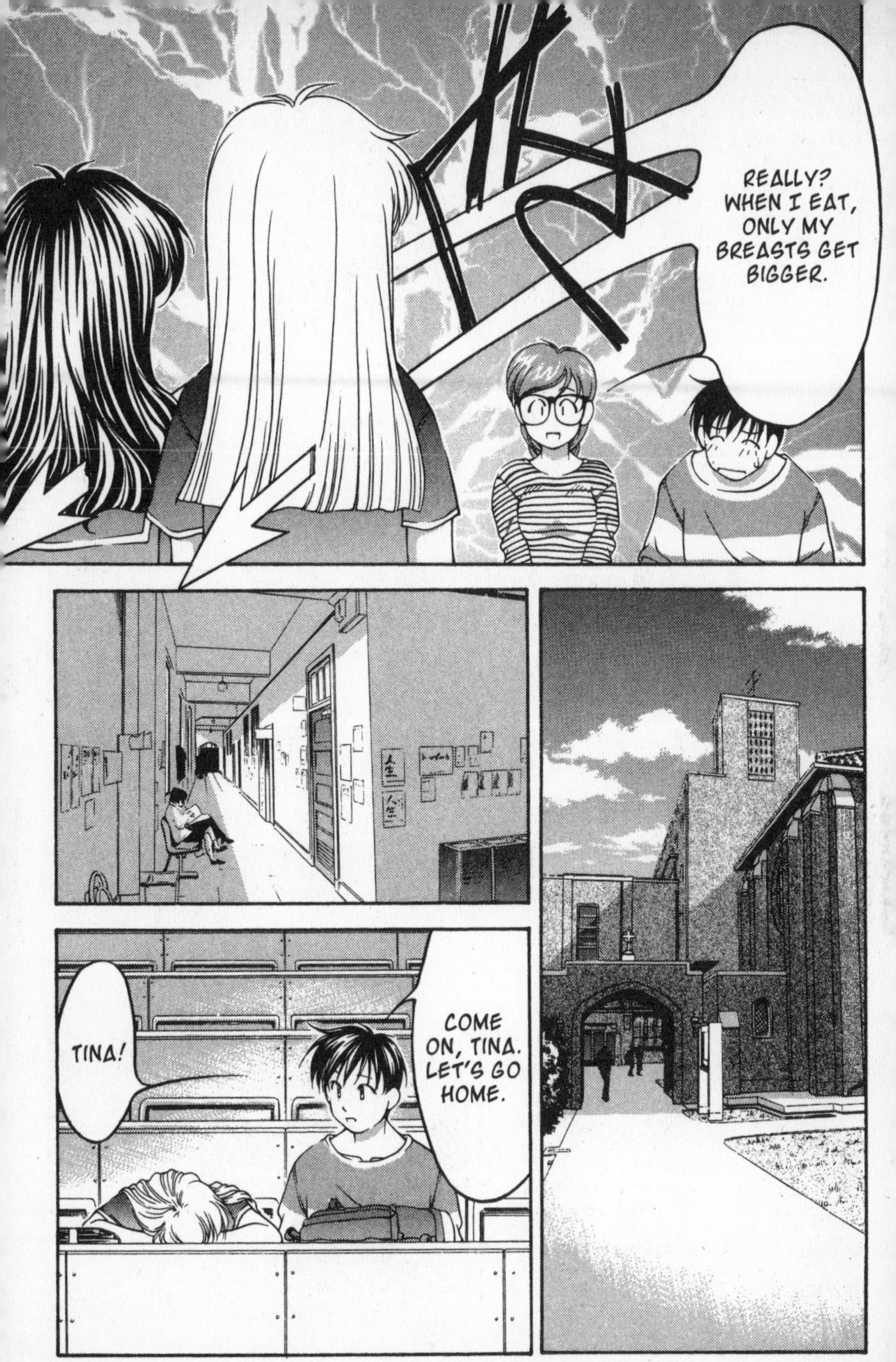
REALLY? WHEN I EAT, ONLY MY BREASTS GET BIGGER.
COME ON, TINA. LET'S GO HOME.
TINA!

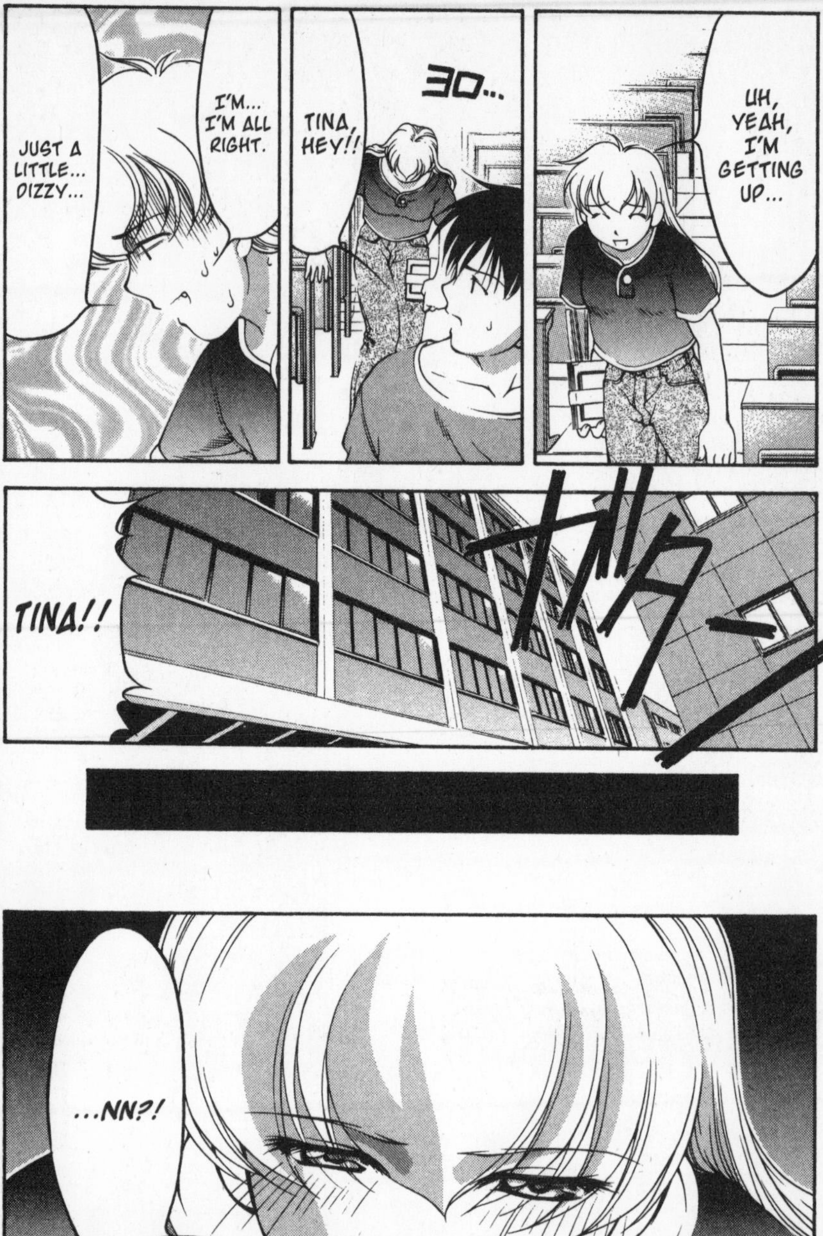
UH, YEAH, I'M GETTING UP...
30...
TINA, HEY!!
I'M... I'M ALL RIGHT.
JUST A LITTLE... DIZZY...
TINA!!
...NN?!

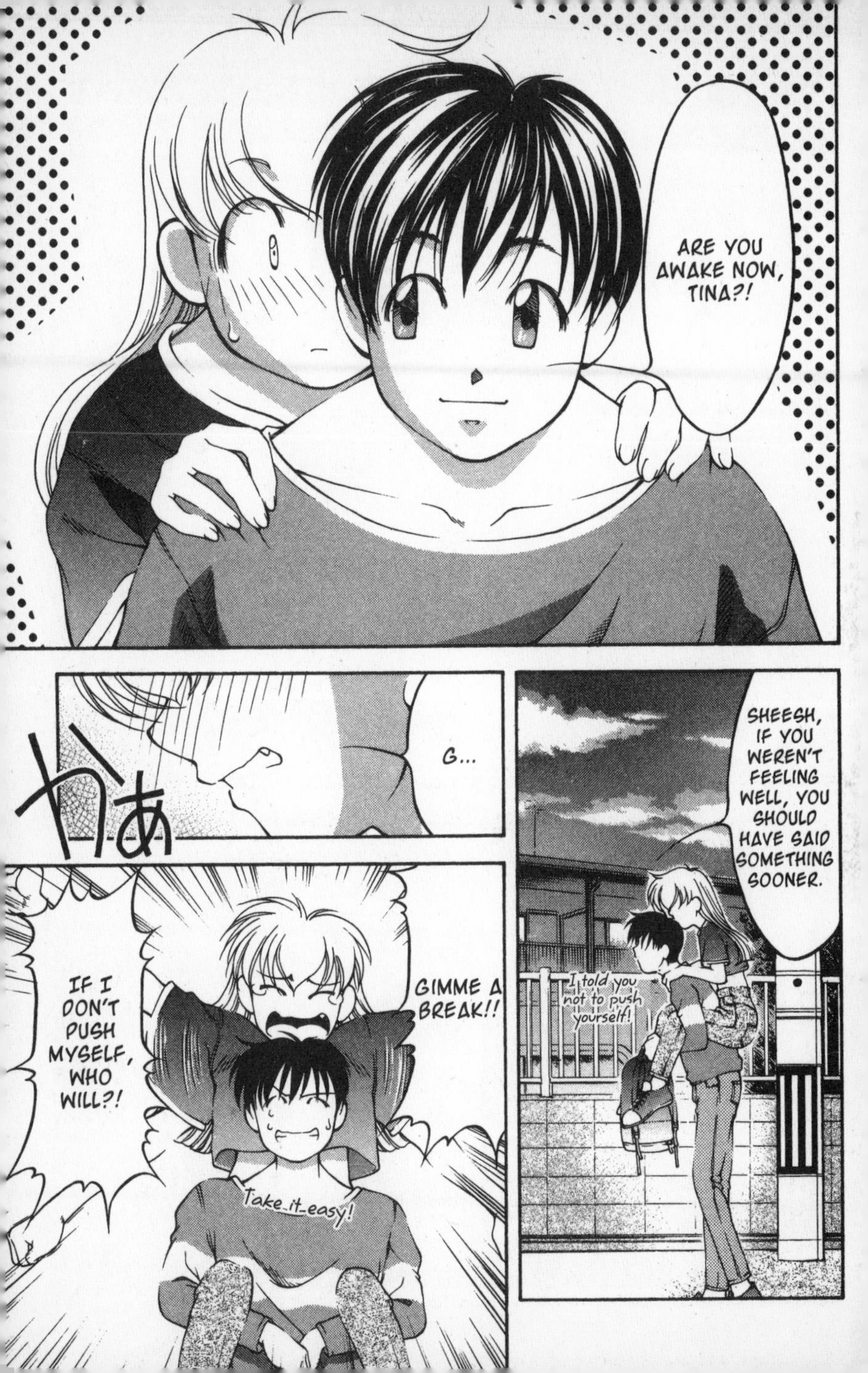
ARE YOU AWAKE NOW, TINA?!
SHEESH, IF YOU WEREN'T FEELING WELL, YOU SHOULD HAVE SAID SOMETHING SOONER.
I told you not to push yourself!
G...
かあ
GIMME A BREAK!!
IF I DON'T PUSH MYSELF, WHO WILL?!
Take it easy!

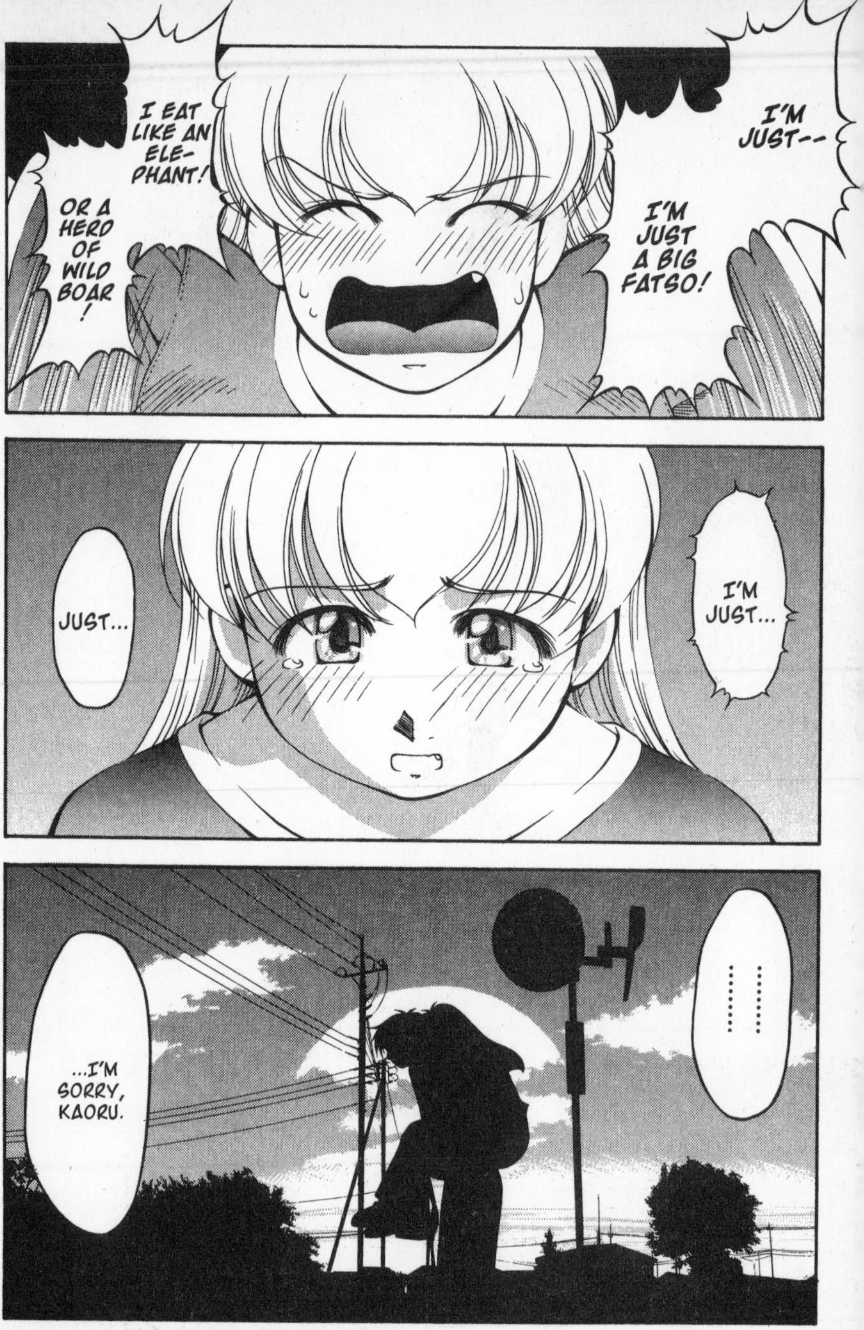
I'M JUST--
I'M JUST A BIG FATSO!
I EAT LIKE AN ELE-PHANT!
OR A HERD OF WILD BOAR!
I'M JUST...
JUST...
......
...I'M SORRY, KAORU.

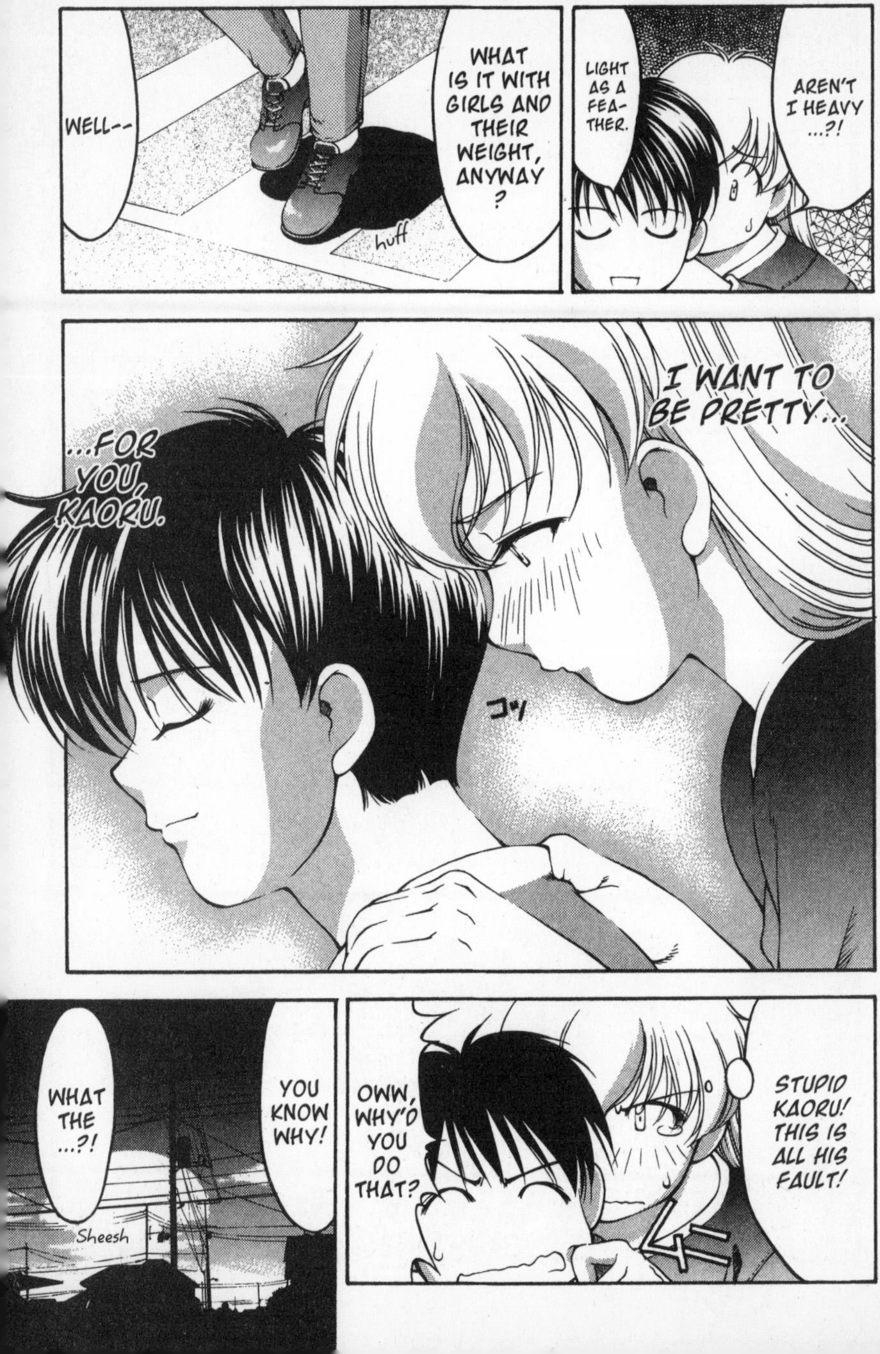
AREN'T I HEAVY ...?!
LIGHT AS A FEA-THER.
WHAT IS IT WITH GIRLS AND THEIR WEIGHT, ANYWAY?
WELL--
huff
I WANT TO BE PRETTY...
...FOR YOU, KAORU.
ゴッ
STUPID KAORU! THIS IS ALL HIS FAULT!
OWW, WHY'D YOU DO THAT?
YOU KNOW WHY!
WHAT THE ...?!
Sheesh

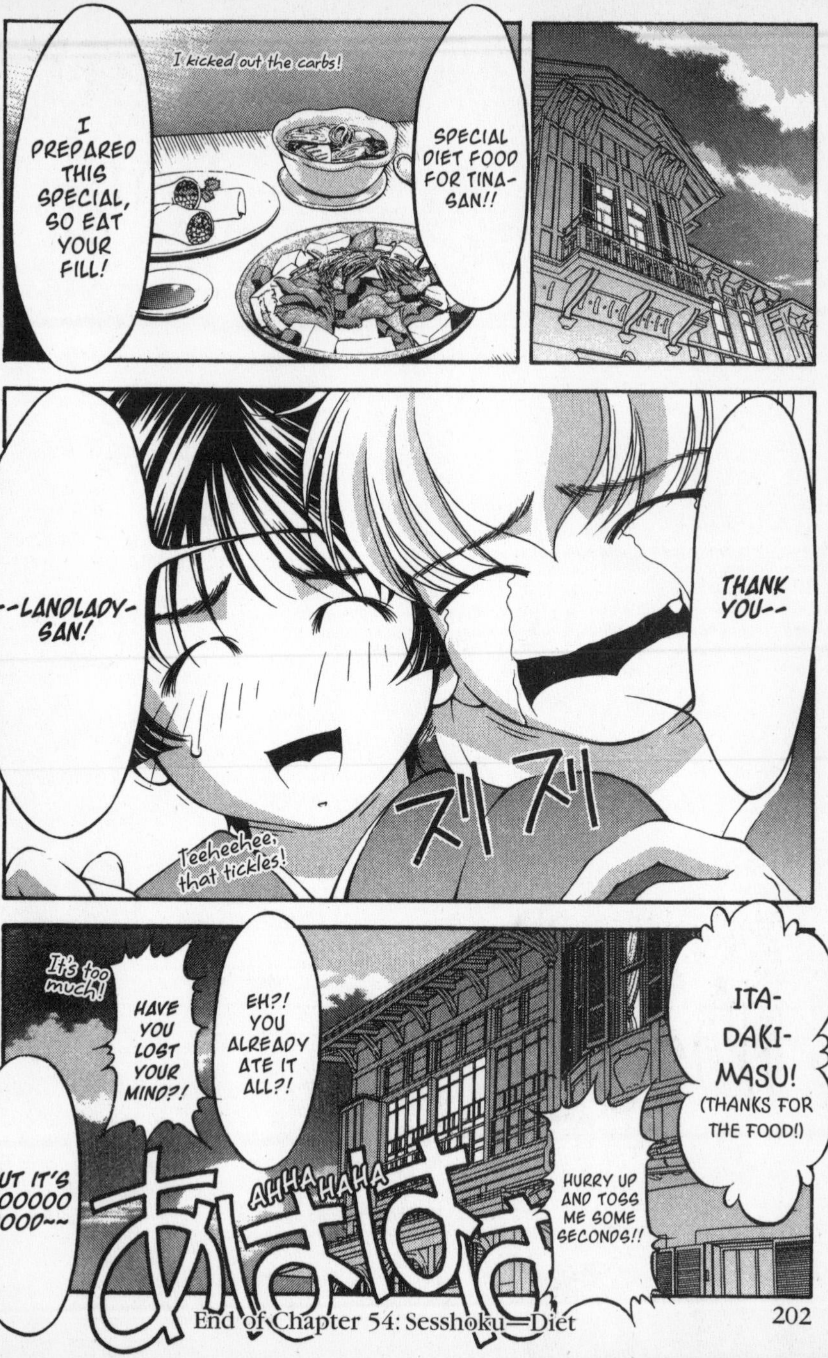
SPECIAL DIET FOOD FOR TINA-SAN!!
I kicked out the carbs!
I PREPARED THIS SPECIAL, SO EAT YOUR FILL!
THANK YOU--
--LANDLADY-SAN!
ズリズリ
Teeheehee, that tickles!
ITA-DAKI-MASU! (THANKS FOR THE FOOD!)
HURRY UP AND TOSS ME SOME SECONDS!!
EH?! YOU ALREADY ATE IT ALL?!
HAVE YOU LOST YOUR MIND?!
It's too much!
BUT IT'S SOOOOO GOOD~~
AHHAHAHA
あははは

End of Chapter 54: Sesshoku=Diet

# 藍(あい)より青(あお)し

AI YORI AOSHI

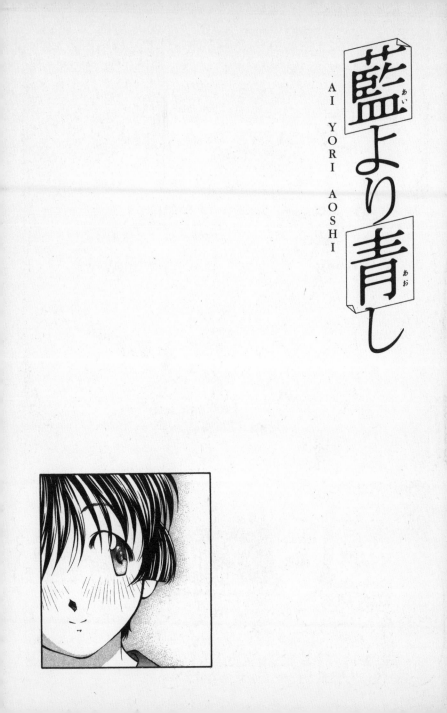

## ASSIST THANKS

Etuko Ichinohe
Hidenori Iwanaga
Hiroaki Satou
Hozumi

Mitukage Syoutengai
Miyuki
School Izumi
Tomohiro Horie

## EDITOR

Syouichi Nakazawa
<HAKUSENSHA>

## PRODUCE

Kou Fumizuki
<STUDIO LITTLE COTTON>

# 藍より青し

### AI YORI AOSHI ™

**Who's that girl?!**
When the summertime heat gets to be too much, Kaoru and the girls head for the beach. But in their search for the perfect swimsuit, the gang ends up picking up a stowaway—the spunky junior high student Chika! Can the Sakuraba estate make room for one more?

Ai Yori Aoshi Vol. 7—
Available January 2005

# TINA'S MANGA-LIB!

HOWDY! DIDJA LIKE MY BOARD GAME? IF YOU THOUGHT THAT WAS FUN,
YOU AIN'T SEEN NOTHING YET! HERE'S A LITTLE WORD GAME I CAME UP WITH.
JUST ASK A FRIEND TO GIVE YOU WORDS TO FILL IN THE BLANKS.
THEN READ THEM BACK THE FINISHED STORY.
HILARITY WILL ENSUE, I GUARANTEE IT!
IF YOU DON'T HAVE ANY FRIENDS, DON'T WORRY—
JUST FILL IT IN BY YOURSELF LIKE I DID!

_____**Tina**_____ 's Story
(your name)

Once upon a _____**Poop**_____ there was a beautiful _____**President**_____.
　　　　　　(something "abstract")　　　　　　　　　(a noun that girls can be)
She was born in the far off land of __**Your butt**__, but was razed in __**Transylvania**__.
　　　　　　　　　　　　　　　(a place)　　　　　　　　(a different place)
Peeple made fun of her becuz she was _____**A genius**_____, but really they were all a
　　　　　　　　　　　　　　　　　　　(something rad)
bunch of **Tae-chin's gyoza**, so what do they know?
　　　　　　(something gross)

One day the _____**Kick-ass**_____ girl went to **Your mom's butt** to seek her fortune.
　　　　　　(a really cool adjective)　　　　　(an institution)
When she got there she met _____**Spike**_____, the local _____**Choirboy**_____. It was
　　　　　　　　　　　(some dude's name)　　　　　　(a dumb job)
_____**Poop**_____ at first site. This boy had a pet _____**T-Rex**_____ which he used to
(an emotion)　　　　　　　　　　　　　　　　　(a critter)
_____**breed**_____ ninjas.
(exciting verb)

The boy and the girl were totally going to _____**do the nasty**_____, but
　　　　　　　　　　　　　　　　　　　　(something a boy and a girl do together)
then this evil _____**Mayu**_____ showed up with plans of his/her own. The _____**Mayu**_____
　　　　　　(something evil)　　　　　　　　　　　　　　　(repeat the evil thing)
used a poisoned _____**Beer**_____ to turn the boy into a _____**Pervert**_____. When she
　　　　　　　(type of food)　　　　　　　　　　(something lame)
saw this, the girl realized that the boy wasn't _____**Luscious**_____ at all, but was actually
　　　　　　　　　　　　　　　　　　　　(a good attribute)
_____**Kinda stinky**_____. And so she jumped on her _____**Zepplin**_____ and moved to
(a sucky attribute)　　　　　　　　　　　　　(mode of transportashun)
_____**Madagascar**_____, where she made _____**A bazillion**_____ dollars and married **Jude Law**
(someplace cool)　　　　　　　(a really big number)　　　　　(really hot actor)
and they lived happily ever _____**Kaoru's butt**_____.
　　　　　　　　　　　　(something REALLY gross)

_______________ (your name) 's Story

Once upon a _________________ (something "abstract") there was a beautiful ___________________ (a noun that girls can be).
She was born in the far off land of __________ (a place), but was razed in _______________ (a different place).
Peeple made fun of her becuz she was _____________ (something rad), but really they were all a
bunch of _____________ (something gross), so what do they know?

One day the _________________ (a really cool adjective) girl went to _____________ (an institution) to seek her fortune.
When she got there she met _______________ (some dude's name), the local _____________ (a dumb job). It was
_____________ (an emotion) at first site. This boy had a pet _____________ (a critter) which he used to
_____________ (exciting verb) ninjas.

The boy and the girl were totally going to ______________________________ (something a boy and a girl do together), but
then this evil _____________ (something evil) showed up with plans of his/her own. The __________ (repeat the evil thing)
used a poisoned _____________ (type of food) to turn the boy into a _____________ (something lame). When she
saw this, the girl realized that the boy wasn't _____________ (a good attribute) at all, but was actually
______________ (a sucky attribute). And so she jumped on her ___________________ (mode of transportashun) and moved to
_____________ (someplace cool), where she made ________________ (a really big number) dollars and married ________ (really hot actor)
and they lived happily ever _______________________ (something REALLY gross).

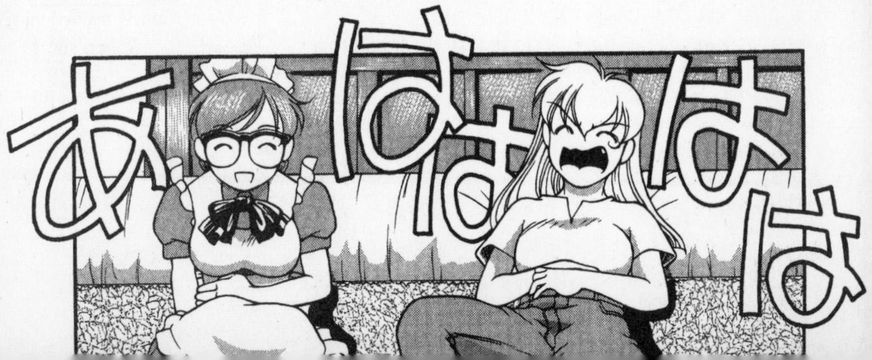

あははは

# GLOSSARY

## Ema

In Japan, visitors to Shinto shrines can purchase ema, wooden plaques, to write their wishes on. One side of the ema is blank, where the wish is written—the other side features an image representative of a god or theme that the temple or wish represents. The ema are hung up on racks for public viewing. Periodically, the ema are removed and ritually burned so that the wishes written on them can reach the gods. Some shrines specialize in certain kinds of wishes, like money, health or marriage. Shrines charge a small fee for the service, which is one of the ways they pay for operating expenses. If you should find yourself in Japan, be sure to stop by a temple and make a wish!

## Bath Trivia

Did you know…

• The symbol written on the strips of cloth in front of public baths is the character "yu," which in this case means "hot water."

• In Japan, people wash with soap before getting into the bath. The bath itself is for relaxation, not cleansing. Getting soap in the bath is a big no-no.

• Public baths are called "sento." Only baths from natural hot springs are called "onsen."

• While traditional sento are on the decline, new modern sento have been designed to include extra features like saunas, Jacuzzis, fitness clubs and even water slides!

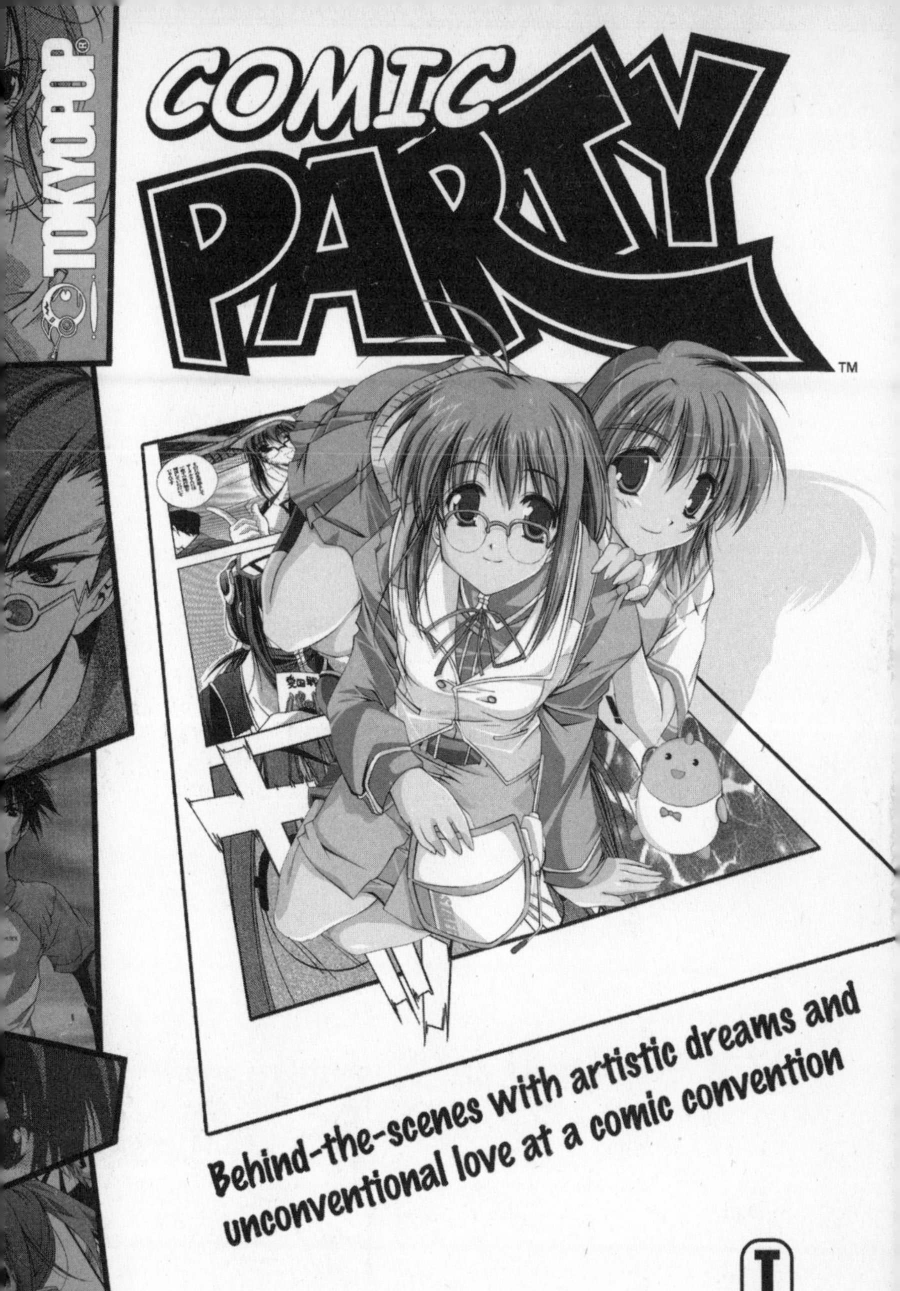
TOKYOPOP®
COMIC PARTY™
Behind-the-scenes with artistic dreams and unconventional love at a comic convention
T
TEEN
AGE 13+

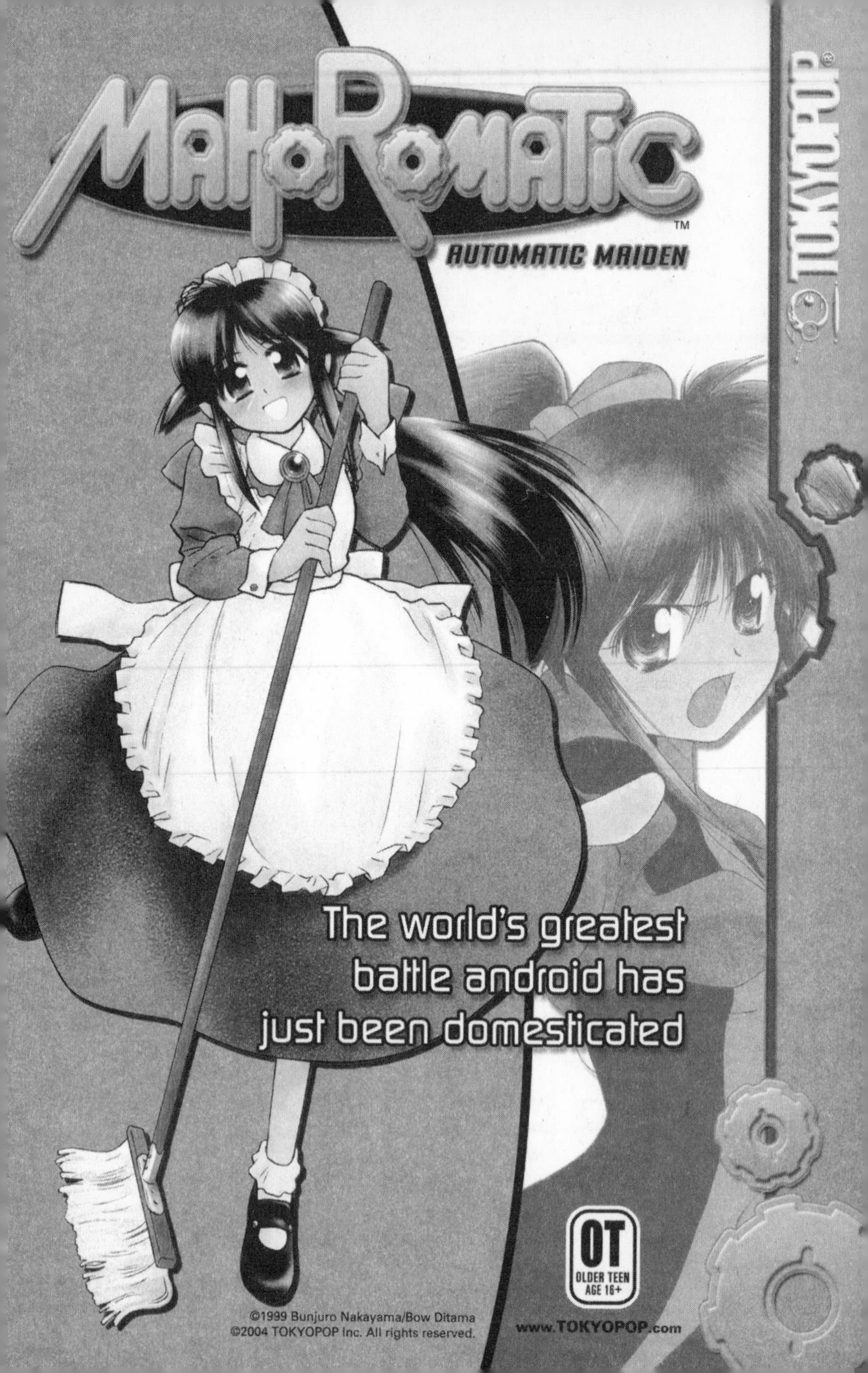

MAHOROMATIC™
AUTOMATIC MAIDEN
TOKYOPOP®
The world's greatest battle android has just been domesticated
OT
OLDER TEEN AGE 16+
©1999 Bunjuro Nakayama/Bow Ditama ©2004 TOKYOPOP Inc. All rights reserved.
www.TOKYOPOP.com

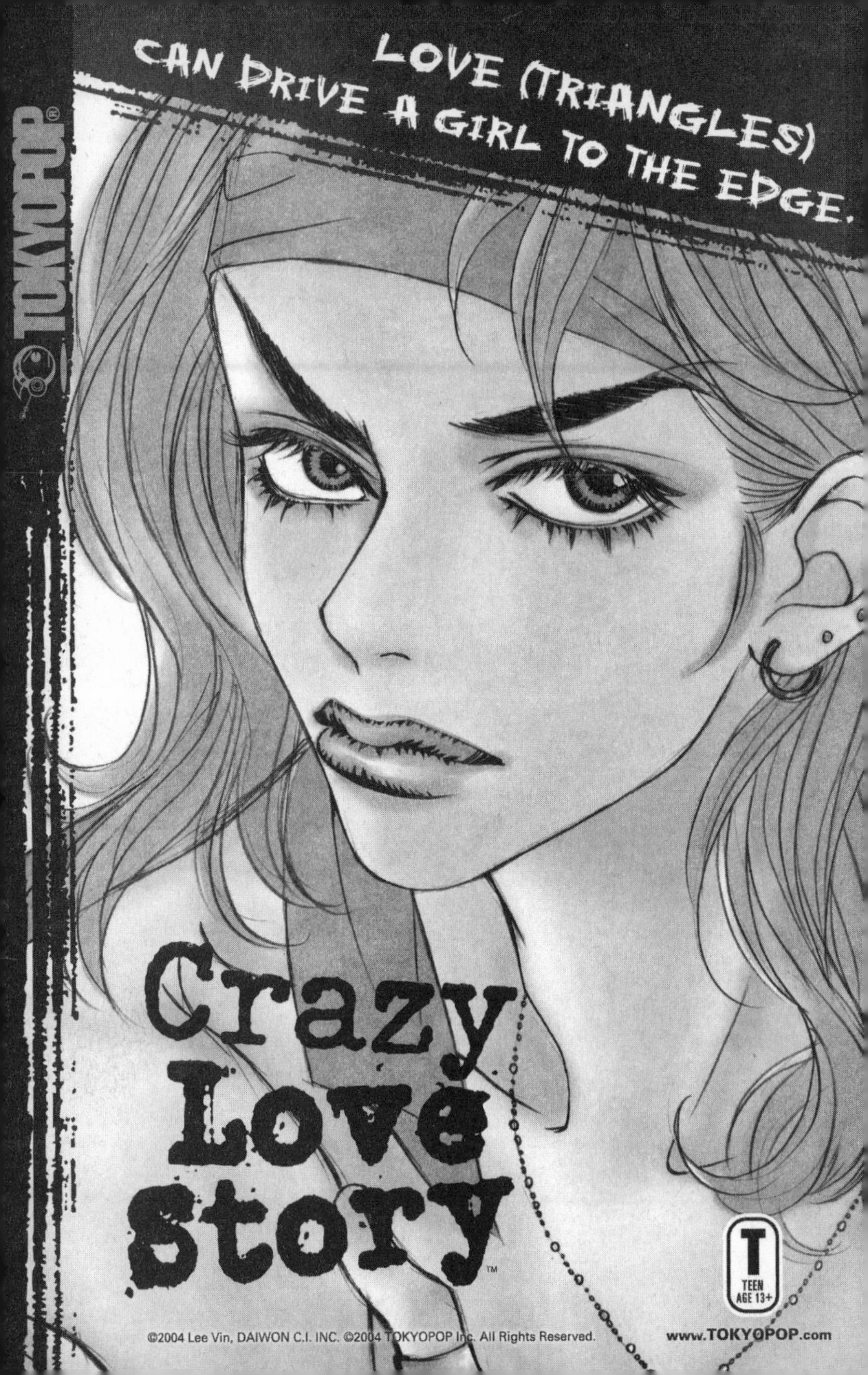
TOKYOPOP®
LOVE (TRIANGLES)
CAN DRIVE A GIRL TO THE EDGE.
Crazy Love Story™
T
TEEN
AGE 13+
©2004 Lee Vin, DAIWON C.I. INC. ©2004 TOKYOPOP Inc. All Rights Reserved.
www.TOKYOPOP.com

# ALSO AVAILABLE FROM  TOKYOPOP®

# ALSO AVAILABLE FROM ⌖TOKYOPOP®

## MANGA

.HACK//LEGEND OF THE TWILIGHT
@LARGE
ABENOBASHI: MAGICAL SHOPPING ARCADE
A.I. LOVE YOU
AI YORI AOSHI
ANGELIC LAYER
ARM OF KANNON
BABY BIRTH
BATTLE ROYALE
BATTLE VIXENS
BOYS BE...
BRAIN POWERED
BRIGADOON
B'TX
CANDIDATE FOR GODDESS, THE
CARDCAPTOR SAKURA
CARDCAPTOR SAKURA - MASTER OF THE CLOW
CHOBITS
CHRONICLES OF THE CURSED SWORD
CLAMP SCHOOL DETECTIVES
CLOVER
COMIC PARTY
CONFIDENTIAL CONFESSIONS
CORRECTOR YUI
COWBOY BEBOP
COWBOY BEBOP: SHOOTING STAR
CRAZY LOVE STORY
CRESCENT MOON
CROSS
CULDCEPT
CYBORG 009
D•N•ANGEL
DEMON DIARY
DEMON ORORON, THE
DEUS VITAE
DIABOLO
DIGIMON
DIGIMON TAMERS
DIGIMON ZERO TWO
DOLL
DRAGON HUNTER
DRAGON KNIGHTS
DRAGON VOICE
DREAM SAGA
DUKLYON: CLAMP SCHOOL DEFENDERS
EERIE QUEERIE!
ERICA SAKURAZAWA: COLLECTED WORKS
ET CETERA
ETERNITY
EVIL'S RETURN
FAERIES' LANDING
FAKE
FLCL
FLOWER OF THE DEEP SLEEP, THE
FORBIDDEN DANCE
FRUITS BASKET

G GUNDAM
GATEKEEPERS
GETBACKERS
GIRL GOT GAME
GRAVITATION
GTO
GUNDAM SEED ASTRAY
GUNDAM WING
GUNDAM WING: BATTLEFIELD OF PACIFISTS
GUNDAM WING: ENDLESS WALTZ
GUNDAM WING: THE LAST OUTPOST (G-UNIT)
HANDS OFF!
HAPPY MANIA
HARLEM BEAT
HYPER RUNE
I.N.V.U.
IMMORTAL RAIN
INITIAL D
INSTANT TEEN: JUST ADD NUTS
ISLAND
JING: KING OF BANDITS
JING: KING OF BANDITS - TWILIGHT TALES
JULINE
KARE KANO
KILL ME, KISS ME
KINDAICHI CASE FILES, THE
KING OF HELL
KODOCHA: SANA'S STAGE
LAMENT OF THE LAMB
LEGAL DRUG
LEGEND OF CHUN HYANG, THE
LES BIJOUX
LOVE HINA
LOVE OR MONEY
LUPIN III
LUPIN III: WORLD'S MOST WANTED
MAGIC KNIGHT RAYEARTH I
MAGIC KNIGHT RAYEARTH II
MAHOROMATIC: AUTOMATIC MAIDEN
MAN OF MANY FACES
MARMALADE BOY
MARS
MARS: HORSE WITH NO NAME
MINK
MIRACLE GIRLS
MIYUKI-CHAN IN WONDERLAND
MODEL
MOURYOU KIDEN: LEGEND OF THE NYMPHS
NECK AND NECK
ONE
ONE I LOVE, THE
PARADISE KISS
PARASYTE
PASSION FRUIT
PEACH GIRL
PEACH GIRL: CHANGE OF HEART
PET SHOP OF HORRORS
PITA-TEN

07.15.04T

# STOP!

Sumimasen! In your haste, you have opened to the back of the book. It would be most unfortunate if you were to start reading from this point. Perhaps you are new to TOKYOPOP's 100% authentic format? You see, in Japan, pages and panels read from right-to-left, and in respect for the manga-ka, TOKYOPOP keeps this format intact in its translated manga. At first it might feel bizarre reading like this, but we assure you that it will be second nature in no time! Please, so that you may properly enjoy this manga, turn the book over and begin reading from the other side. Arigatou gozaimasu!

100%
AUTHENTIC
MANGA

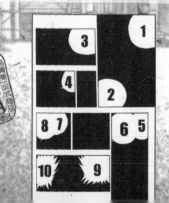